Burke Museum of Natural History and Culture Research Report No. 9

IS IT A HOUSE?

Archaeological Excavations at English Camp, San Juan Island, Washington

Edited by Amanda K. Taylor and Julie K. Stein

Burke Museum of Natural History and Culture
Research Report No. 9

Burke Museum
Seattle, Washington

Distributed by University of Washington Press, Seattle and London

Library of Congress Cataloging-in-Publication Data
Is it a house? : archaeological excavations at English Camp, San Juan Island, Washington / edited by Amanda K. Taylor and Julie K. Stein.
p. cm. — (Burke Museum of Natural History and Culture research report ; no. 9)
Includes bibliographical references.
ISBN 978-0-295-99147-4 (pbk. : alk. paper)
1. English Camp Site (Wash.) 2. San Juan Island (Wash.)—Antiquities. 3. San Juan Island National Historical Park (Wash.)—Antiquities. 4. Excavations (Archaeology)—Washington (State)—San Juan Island. I. Taylor, Amanda K. II. Stein, Julie K. III. Burke Museum of Natural History and Culture.
F897.S2I7 2011
917.97'74—dc23 2011019849

The paper used in this publication meets the minimum requirements of American National Standard for Information Sciences — Permanence of Paper for Printed Library Materials, ANSI Z39.48-1984.

Contents

Contributors

Cristie Boone
Anthropology Department
UC Santa Cruz
361 Social Sciences 1
Santa Cruz, CA 95064
cboone@ucsc.edu

Kristine Bovy
Department of Sociology and Anthropology
University of Rhode Island
507 Chafee Building
Kingston, RI 02881-0808
kbovy@uri.edu

Chin-yung Chao
Institute of History and Philology
Academia Sinica
Nankang, Taipei 11529
Taiwan
cooper@asihp.net/cooper@mail.ihp.sinica.edu.tw

Angela Close
Department of Anthropology
Box 353100
University of Washington
Seattle, WA 98195-3100
aeclose@u.washington.edu

Phoebe Daniels
University of Washington Press
PO Box 500096
Seattle, WA 98145-5096
phoebea@u.washington.edu

J. Tyler Faith
Center for the Advanced Study of Hominid Paleobiology
Department of Anthropology
The George Washington University
2110 G Street, NW
Washington DC 20052
tfaith@gwmail.gwu.edu

Debra K. Green
Metcalf Archaeological Consultants, Inc.
PO Box 2154
Bismarck, ND 58502
dgreen10@uic.edu

Robert Kopperl
NWAA/SWCA Environmental Consultants
5416 20th Avenue Northwest
Seattle, WA 98107
rkopperl@northwestarch.com

Mary Parr
Past Perfect Software
3000 N. Pottstown Pike
Suite 200
Exton, PA 19341
mary@museumsoftware

Laura Phillips
Burke Museum of Natural History and Culture
Box 353100
University of Washington
Seattle, WA 98195
lphill@u.washington.edu

Sarah Sherwood
Department of Anthropology
Dickinson College
P.O. Box 1773
Carlisle, PA 17013
sherwood@dickinson.edu

Julie Stein
Burke Museum of Natural History and Culture
Box 353100
University of Washington
Seattle, WA 98195
jkstein@u.washington.edu

Amanda Taylor
Department of Anthropology
Box 353100
University of Washington
Seattle, WA 98195-3100
aktaylor@u.washington.edu

Catherine Foster West
Department of Anthropology
National Museum of Natural History
Smithsonian Institution
PO Box 37012
Washington, DC 20013-7012
foster.west@gmail.com

Acknowledgments

The San Juan Island Archaeological Project has been supported by many people over the years between excavation and publication. This book summarizes the excavation of one area within the boundaries of San Juan Island National Historical Park – English Camp, referred to as Operation D (OpD). This area is a large shell midden preserved in a forested area near the shore of Garrison Bay, adjacent to glaciated upland, and composed of obvious geometric, topographic ridges. OpD was primarily excavated in 1988, 1990, and 1991. Material was processed over the next 10 years, and analyzed in the last 20. Most of the people studying the collections never excavated the site. They did, however, visit the location numerous times, and discussed the results in classes, retreats, and over beverages. This book is an assemblage of those people's hard work, creative minds, and considerable assistance. We thank all of our contributors for their energy and inspiration.

Our thanks begin with those who supervised the excavation and taught the students. These staff provided an engaging educational experience for students from all over the country who attended the University of Washington field school. The staff primarily responsible for supervising the OpD excavation in 1988 (a year when both OpA and OpD were excavated simultaneously) was Meg Nelson, Mary Parr, and Fran (Whittaker) Hamilton. In 1990, the staff members were Tim Canaday, Kim Kornbacher, Mary Parr, Eric Rasmussen, Patty Rasmussen, and Kris Wilhelmsen. In 1991, they were Martha Jackson, John Kendra, Kim Kornbacher, Sarah Sterling, and Kris Wilhelmsen. Thank you for your work and especially your notebooks that allowed the analyses described in this volume to be completed.

The following individuals were students who contributed their hard work to our research efforts. The 1988 students who worked on both OpA and OpD included Kari Aunan, Edward Bakewell, Deborah Blehm, Robert Bohus, Karen Carmer, Helen Cullen, Amy Eggler, Dottie Foskin, Kathryn Frost, Kirk Ghio, Dennis Gosser, Montgomery Nelson, Shannon Paulsen, Coral Rassmussen, Celeste Ray, Katherine Russell, Amy Sievers, Heidi Thorsen, Della Valdez, and Annemarie Williams. In 1990 the students were Eric Bangs, Sherstin Busby, Annell Chambers, Elizabeth Clappi, John Daly, Marie Dion, Andrew Fahlund, Connie Grafer, Tim Hunt, Erica Kaplan, Craig Magaret, Sherry McLaren, Jane Orvis, Laura Phillips, Laurie Schild, Johonna Shea, Edna Thaler, and Claudia Vergnani Vaupel. In 1991 the students were Jenny Ball, Shannon Bouton, Julie Drummond, Amy Glick, Brad Hafford, Michelle Huntley, Cyndi Johansen, Paula Johnson, Anne Lessmann, Katie Mitchell, Michele Parvey, Shannon Plank, John Ross, Chrisoula (Chris) Roumeliotis, Heather Seal, David Shapiro, Elizabeth (Beth) Simpson, Peter Smith, Brad Snowdon, and Rachel Stallings. Many of these students have continued working on shell middens and archaeology in the Northwest.

In addition to students, OpD was excavated with the help of many volunteers, especially in 1988 when Fran (Whittaker) Hamilton started the first excavations at the site with a volunteer crew. We would like to thank Debra Blehm, Tony Cagle, Stan Chernicoff, Amanda Cohn, Rinita Dalan, Jerome Hawkins, Rick Hilton, Kathy Kornbacher, Elonna Lester, Angela Linse, Mark Madsen, Tony Neimann, Pat Ryan, Teresa Schuwerd, Ann Stevenson, Barbara Terzian, Nancy Todd, Irene Warner, and George Warner.

This research was only possible because the personnel at the San Juan Island National Historical Park supported and assisted with the operations. We would like to acknowledge the Superintendents, Richard Hoffman (1990) Robert Scott (1991-1998), Cicely Muldoon (1998-2002), and Peter Dederich (2002-present), and the help with information and logistics of Chief Ranger William Gleason, Interpretation Staff Detlef Wieck, Michael Vouri (Chief Interpreter), Darlene Wahl, Joshua Boles; and Resource Managers Shirley Hoh, Bill Gleason, Chris Davis, and Jerald Weaver. Mike Vouri was especially helpful throughout the years and we would like to give him a special thank you.

At National Park Regional Headquarters we are especially appreciative of the support from Stephanie Toothman, Jim Thomson, Kent Bush, Diane Nicholson, and Kirstie Haertel. We could never have navigated the NPS systems without your help. At Marblemount collection facility we are grateful to Camille Evans, Deborah Wood, Brooke Keleman, and Kelly Cahill for help with the collections.

No one suffered our interruption more than the archaeological curation staff at the Burke Museum. We would like to thank Curator of Archaeology Peter Lape, collections managers Mary Parr, Laura Phillips, Megon Noble, collections staff Steve Denton and Kelly Meyers, and especially our NPS cataloger Walter Bartholomew.

Many students at the University of Washington worked on this project, helping us prepare this book. We would like to thank Shelby Anderson, Phoebe (Anderson) Daniels, Jacob Fisher, Stephanie Jolivette, Becky Kessler, Chris Lockwood, and Jennie Deo Shaw. We also acknowledge our gratitude to our friends and family for their help, support and patience over the course of this project, especially Stan, Matt, and David Chernicoff and Matt Saunders. They will share our joy at the completion of this project.

Lastly we would like to thank the members of the Lummi Nation for sharing their history, and for their insights and understanding.

IS IT A HOUSE?

Archaeological Excavations at English Camp, San Juan Island, Washington

1
Introduction

Amanda K. Taylor
and Julie K. Stein

This chapter provides context for archaeological investigations at OpD, English Camp, San Juan Island, Washington. As shown in the photograph above, the site is characterized by a horseshoe-shaped shell midden in a forested area approximately 20 meters northwest of the modern shoreline. The research goal of this volume is to assess whether OpD should be interpreted as a domestic structure using multiple material types and perspectives. In this introduction, we describe previous research on house sites in the Gulf of Georgia and summarize the chapters in this volume.

Houses are essential to understanding social phenomena on the Northwest Coast. Differences in house size are associated with differences in political power and social inequality; the appearance of large villages is associated with sedentism and population growth. The layout of hearths, benches, and walls provide clues about the daily activities of the people who lived in the houses (e.g., Grier 2001; Matson et al. 2003; Sobel et al. 2006). Our volume asks a more basic question about prehistoric houses in the Gulf of Georgia. In the absence of preserved wooden architectural features, how do archaeologists recognize house structures in complex shell midden deposits? Further, how do they determine what is inside and what is outside the house, and how to evaluate those distinctions? As noted by Schaepe (2003) and Moss and Erlandson (1992), inadequate critical analysis of features at Northwest Coast sites that are assumed to be houses precludes the identification of other functions associated with a structure. The chapters in this volume explore these issues for the Operation D (OpD) site at English Camp, San Juan Island, Washington (Figure 1.1).

The OpD shell midden is part of the English Camp shell midden (45SJ24) at San Juan Island National Historic Park. The National Park Service (NPS) created the park in 1966 to preserve the American and British military outposts occupied from 1859 to 1872 (Thomas and Thomson 1992; Vouri 1999). This location was originally referred to by the British as British Camp, but local residents later changed the name to English Camp. In 1985, the NPS officially changed the name back to British Camp, but in recent years the residents of the community successfully convinced the NPS to rename the park English Camp. Since the historic occupation was located in the same general area as the prehistoric occupation where a large shell midden accumulated, the prehistoric site (45SJ24) has been referred to as both English Camp and British Camp. Both names refer to the same site. The prehistoric English Camp site is an immense shell midden with variable surface expression. A portion of the site on the historic parade ground that did not show any topographic or stratigraphic evidence for house structures was called Operation A (OpA) and the details of this work have been previously reported (Stein 1992). A portion of the site with horseshoe-shaped topographic ridges is called OpD. The focus of this publication is the question of whether or not OpD represents a domestic structure.

The English Camp midden has been the focus of two research efforts. In 1950 A. E. Treganza excavated

Chapter opening photo: Students standing along the U-shaped ridge at the site.

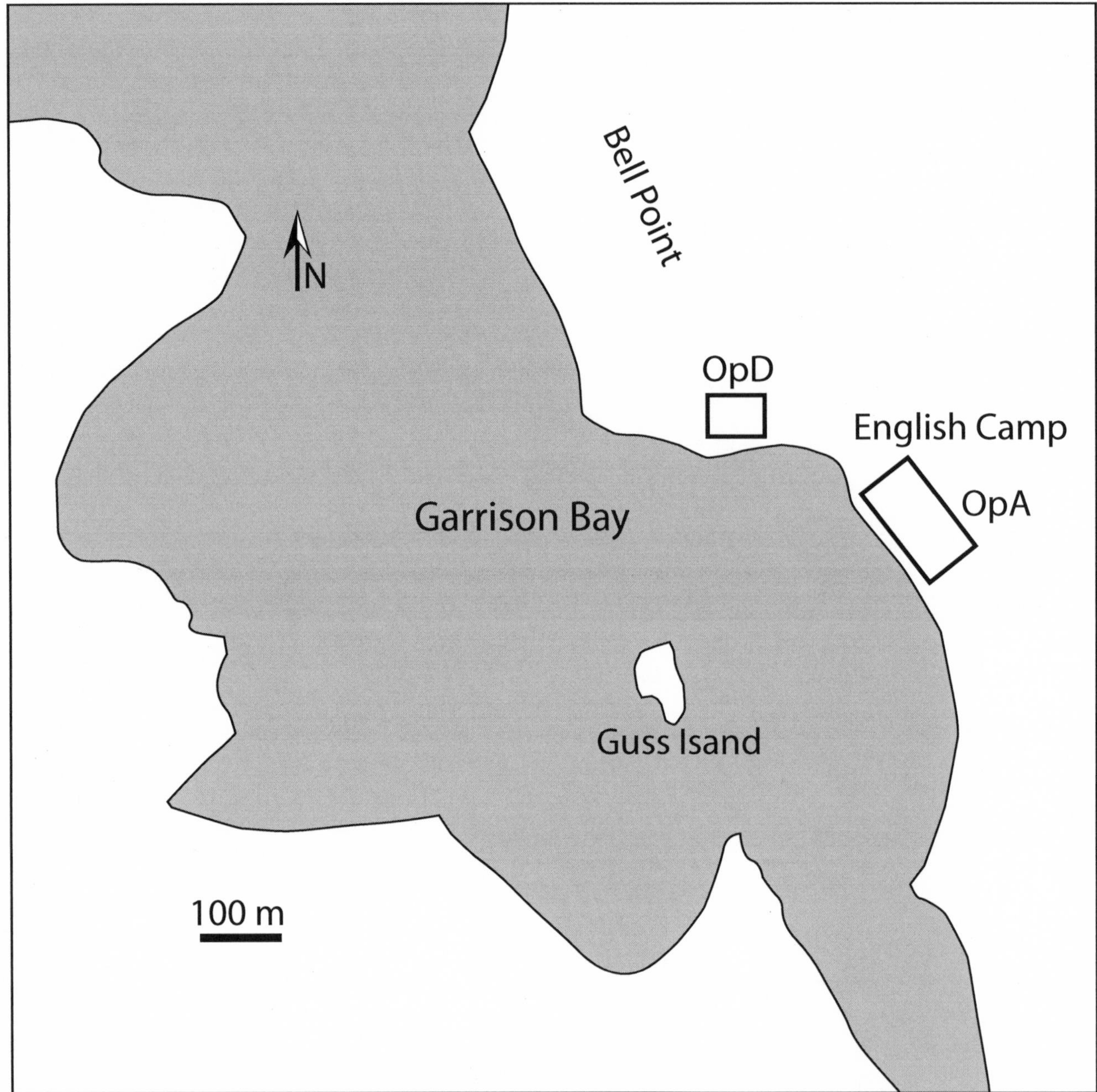

Figure 1.1 Location of English Camp OpA and OpD on Garrison Bay.

in the area of OpD (Faith, this volume Chapter 2) as a University of Washington field school. In 1985, Julie Stein directed a small group of students who were part of the excavation at OpA to explore the edge of a "barrow pit" at the request of NPS personnel. The barrow pit was believed to be the handiwork of the original settler, William Crook. The area was named OpD and students excavated a 1 x 1 meter test unit (Unit I). In 1989, OpD was augered to determine the thickness of the shell midden and the topography of the underlying landforms (Stein and Taylor, this volume). Stein directed excavations at the site in 1990 and 1991.

The surface topography at OpD is similar to other shell midden sites around the world where topographic expressions suggest that prehistoric people processing and discarding shell were purposefully sculpting the surface of their landscape. The results are often displayed as circular or elliptical mounds, linear or curved ridges, or circular rings surrounding depressions. These features are interpreted as outlines of domestic structures, defensive barriers, or unknown architectural features. The research reported in this publication focuses on a portion of the OpD shell midden that defines just such a topographic feature. This particular shell midden was piled into roughly

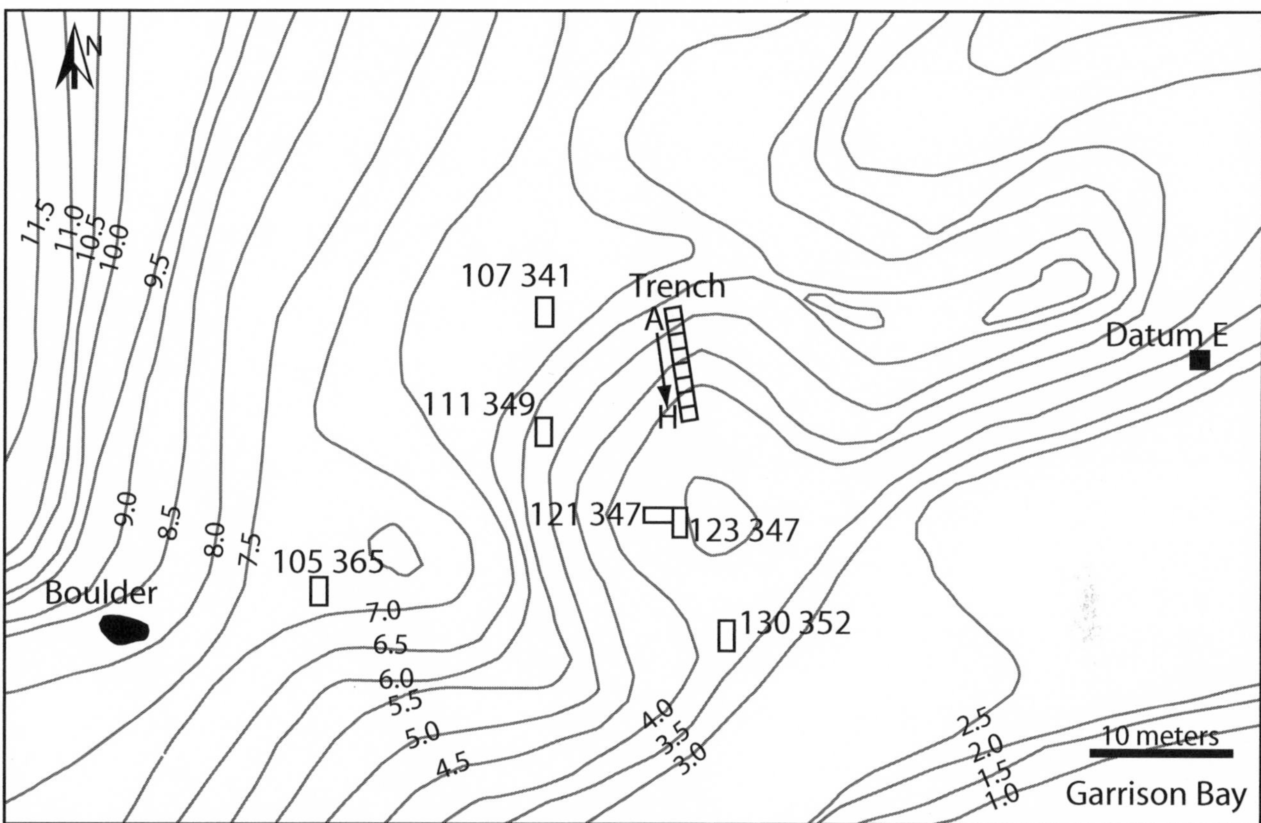

Figure 1.2 A topographic map showing the horseshoe-shaped ridge at the OpD site and placement of excavation units. Modified from a map drafted by Fran Hamilton.

three ridges, arranged in a horseshoe shape with the opening of the horseshoe facing the water. One possible interpretation of this topography is that the ridges piled around the outside walls of a domestic structure. People would have lived in the middle with the entrance facing the water. After the wooden walls collapsed, the shell midden would have slumped into the central area of the house and covered the edges of the living surface. The excavation of OpD was proposed to test that explanation and therefore excavation units were located in the ridges, in the central depression, and behind the ridges (Figure 1.2).

We note that in the Gulf of Georgia literature, excavation and lab analyses are not always designed to explore whether topographic features in shell midden represent houses. Rather, the identification of a house is based usually upon similarities to the ethnographic record and common sense. Topographic house features include shell ridges, depressions, bench features, and flat platforms. Supporting stratigraphic information focuses on floor deposits, post holes, post molds, hearths, and walls. Excluding OpD, there are nine well-documented "house sites" in the Gulf of Georgia/Puget Sound region: Beach Grove (DgRs1), Crescent Beach (DgRr1), Dionisio Point (DgRv3) False Narrows or Senewélets (DgRw4), Long Harbour (DfRu44), Pender Canal (DeRt1 and DeRt2), Shingle Point (DgRv2), Tualdad Altu (45-KI-59), and Whalen Farm (DfRs3) (Figure 1.3). There may also be evidence of a house structure at the Marpole site; however, this site is insufficiently documented to evaluate the evidence. Below we review the ways in which investigators at various Gulf of Georgia "house sites" have identified and described cultural deposits associated with houses.

At the Beach Grove site in the Fraser Delta area near Tsawwassen, Harlan Smith noted 11 circular depressions in 1921. He and his team interpreted the topographic features as plank houses where middens formed around the structures, resulting in three meter tall U-shaped ridges around the depressions. Midden was about one meter deep in the depressions, and they were identified as "house platforms" (Ham 1980; Matson et al. 1980). D.G. Smith (1964:4-5) describes the site as "a long mound of undulating contour and profile, a series of humps and hollows strung out along what appears to have been an old strand-line." One of the goals of the 1980 excavation directed by R.G. Matson was to determine if the depressions were truly used as houses. Uncertain whether their excavations cross-cut a U-shaped area, researchers found several post molds but only one the size of

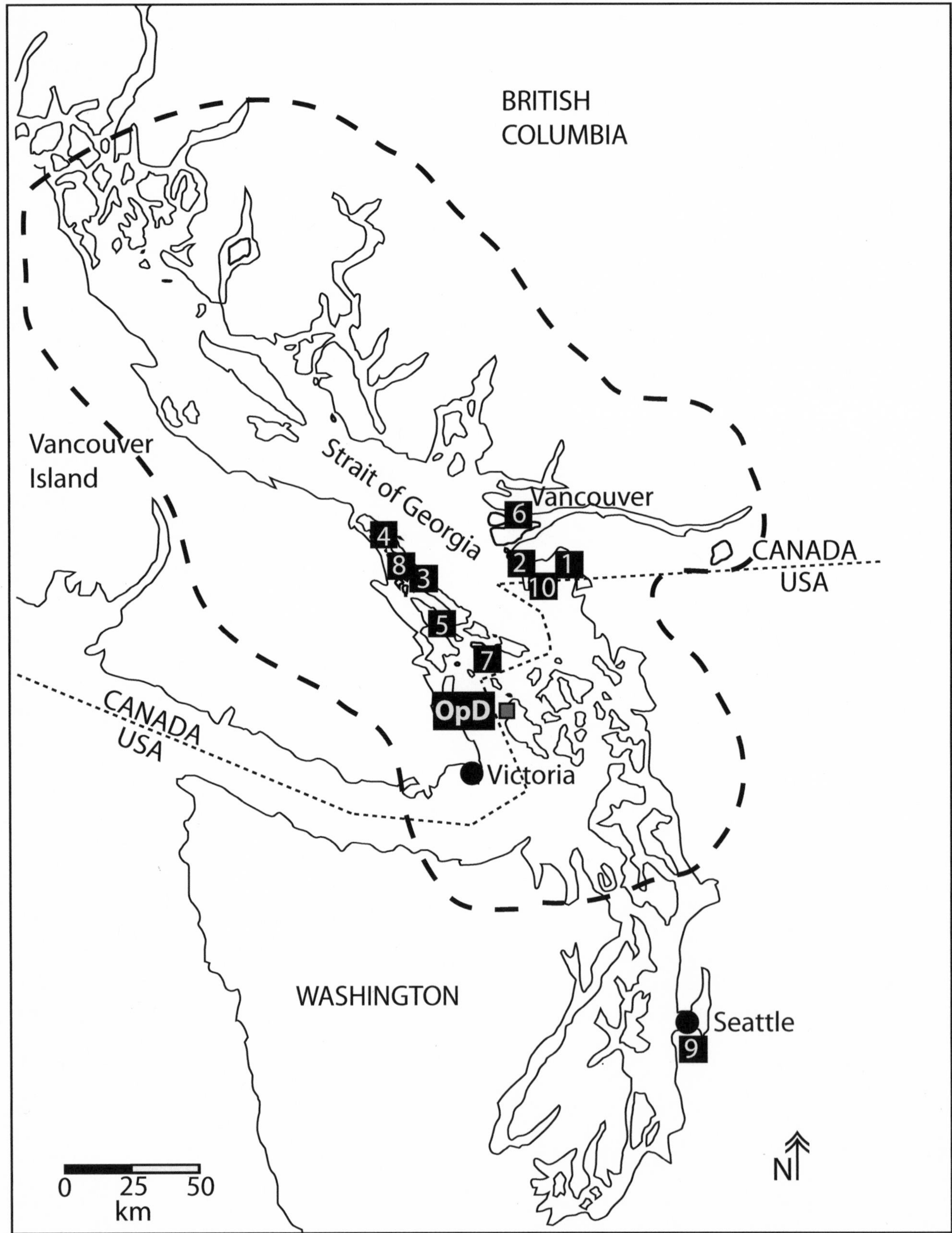

Figure 1.3 The Gulf of Georgia area defined by Mitchell (1971) modified from Grier (2001). 1-Beach Grove, 2-Crescent Beach, 3-Dionisio Point, 4-False Narrows, 5-Long Harbour, 6-Marpole, 7-Pender Canal, 8-Shingle Point, 9-Tualdad Altu, 10-Whalen Farm.

a post used for a house frame. They note, however, that it would be difficult to come up with an equally plausible explanation for the formation of the shell ridges (Matson et al. 1980).

In contrast to Beach Grove, at the Crescent Beach site near Vancouver, British Columbia, only one potential domestic area was identified by R.G. Matson's field school in 1990. "Feature 9" was identified as a house by shape and stratigraphy rather than topography. It was a large semi-circle 3.5-4.5 meters in diameter with a 35 centimeter thick layer of mussel shell with markedly denser shell than adjacent deposits. Large cobbles and fire-cracked rock were also present. That the feature might be a hearth was ruled out because of the size and because orange ashy deposits were not found throughout. Investigators also identified four potential post molds and came to a tentative conclusion that the feature was a shallow semi-subterranean house (Matson 1996; Matson et al. 1991).

Dionisio Point is located on northern Galiano Island, one of the Gulf Islands off of the coast of British Columbia. Five house depressions have been identified at this site, and as part of his dissertation work, Colin Grier (2001, 2003) conducted excavations at one house and a small portion of another. The topography here is particularly complex in that four of the depressions are located on terraces that create steps in the slope. Ridges of shell are built up around the perimeters of the depressions, and post holes, post molds, hearths, and pit features were noted during excavations. Grier (2001) also discusses the differences in stratigraphy between silty black shell-poor house deposits and the shell-rich deposits outside. The details provided about surface topography and stratigraphy support a convincing argument that the features at Dionisio point were domestic structures.

The False Narrows site on Gabriola Island off of Vancouver Island was first excavated by Donald Mitchell (1966), who observed two large platforms that he associated with house structures. Mitchell excavated several units and John Sendey of the BC Provincial Museum expanded the investigation in 1967. Along with house platform areas, investigators also excavated an area identified as a dump at the northern edge of cultural deposits. Burley (1989) notes that Mitchell did not document the house platforms in detail and that the scarcity of post molds and apparent "nonarchitectural function" of some of these features makes interpretation difficult. Current information about the topography and stratigraphy of the site by the excavators may not be sufficient to determine the nature of the structures.

At the Long Harbour site on Saltspring Island, British Columbia, David Johnstone (1991, 2003) reports four mounds. In an excavation of one of these high areas in Layer 4 of Stratum 4, his interpretation of the stratigraphy and features at the site is that midden was piled outside the walls of a house. He notes that post holes have two size ranges: small (10-12 centimeters in diameter) and large (25-30 centimeters in diameter). There are large cobbles in the walls of the post molds. The eight small post molds are arranged in an eight meter long line at the foot of an area of redeposited till that may represent the back wall of the house. The larger holes have been interpreted as posts that supported the roof. The excavation was not large enough for the beachward wall to be recovered, but hearth features are located in the probable center of the structure. Johnstone also found evidence for subsistence, including steaming pits, a refuse pit, and two areas of high concentrations of boiling stones. In non-house areas, shell was sparse and highly fractured consistent with trampling.

At the Pender Canal sites (DeRt2) located on Bedwell Harbour, Pender Island, British Columbia, Johnstone (2003) notes that five post molds 20 centimeters in diameter spaced one meter apart extend in a line over six meters. He describes a 40 centimeter thick shell midden adjacent to the line of post molds that appears to have been banked against the wall or perhaps cleared away during the construction and interprets this feature as a "curtain wall" rather than a row of roof supports. At nearby DeRt1 on Browning Harbor, Johnstone reports seven post molds defining a 5 x 6 meter rectangular area. In the corner of the structure is a box made from sandstone slabs. A hearth feature lies in the center of the structure and a steaming pit and clay lined pit are adjacent to the structure (Johnstone 2003).

An excavation of one of at least three prehistoric house depressions was directed by R.G. Matson at the Shingle Point site on Valdes Island in the Gulf Islands, British Columbia. The excavated house depression was built into the back of a beach ridge composed of shellfish remains. At 76 meters square, the excavation uncovered over half of a house. Excavators identified the structures through a floor, post holes, U-shaped bench areas along the walls of the house, and a hearth (Matson 2003). Matson emphasizes what the stratigraphy reveals about the dimensions of the house and architecture. He also notes differences in the stratigraphy inside the depression, outside the depression, and below the house floor.

The Tualdad Altu site on the Black River near Seattle, Washington is a village site with several longhouses. James Chatters (1989) describes the results of coring over 68% of the site and the discovery of two linear hearth clusters thought to be associated with longhouses. Similarities in features and artifacts between the excavated hearth clusters with those of the Sbabadid house, an historic longhouse site, are cited to support the interpretation that the hearth clusters were located in a longhouse (Chatters 1989:174). Fire-cracked rock clusters between the hearths are thought to be entryways and middens are thought to be dumps. Chatters notes that no post molds or evidence of walls were found.

At the Whalen Farm site on the eastern shore of the Point Roberts Peninsula, British Columbia, Thom (2008) reports that early investigators found two midden ridges that follow the contour of Boundary Bay. They range in size from low mounds to ridges three meters above the ground. During his investigations in 1925, Harlan Smith noted a row of large, deep pits at the site. In 1949 and 1950, Borden and his team excavated a trench across the ridge. They described hearths and molds but were unable to identify clear patterns in the architecture based on these remains. Later excavations by Dimity Hammon uncovered hearths and a storage pit (Thom 2008).

For several of the sites discussed above, lack of detail in notes provided by the original investigator and disturbance due to historic and modern development make it challenging for current investigators to understand the prehistoric topography. As a result, it may be difficult to determine whether a set of features resembles, rather than represents, a domestic structure. Distinguishing house depressions from storage pits and natural topography may be more complex than previously assumed. Shell ridges may result from the construction of defensive structures, refuse, and natural beach ridges. For example, at Whalen Farm, the description of the shell ridges suggests that they vary in size and shape across the site and may not be associated with the depressions. At several sites, such as False Narrows, post molds did not appear to be "architectural" and it was difficult to determine how excavators identified them.

In this volume, we seek to address this issue by examining cultural materials, sediment, and stratigraphy inside and outside the U-shaped depression at OpD. The general expectation underlying all of the chapters in this volume is that if the surface topography at OpD represents a house, there should be significant differences between the cultural deposits in the depression, within the shell ridges, and outside the shell ridges. This volume also serves as a descriptive text to disseminate information about the excavations at this site. All artifacts, samples, field notes, and other information relating to the University of Washington field school at OpD are housed at the Burke Museum at the University of Washington.

The chapters in this volume provide descriptions and analyses of material remains from OpD using a variety of methods at a variety of scales. The first set of chapters detail excavation methods and the geoarchaeology of the site. In Chapter 2, J. Tyler Faith reviews the original 1950 excavation of OpD by Dr. Adan Treganza and compares the results of this excavation with those of the more recent excavations directed by Julie Stein. In Chapter 3, Mary Parr, Laura Philips, and Julie Stein discuss in detail the field methods used during Stein's excavations at OpD. They provide a brief history of Stein's excavations, followed by a description of excavation procedures from the project's Standard Operating Procedure manual. In Chapter 4, Julie Stein, Amanda Taylor, and Phoebe Daniels detail mapping, augering methods, dating results and stratigraphy within each excavation unit. They use both landscape-level and site-level analyses to investigating whether OpD was a domestic structure. In Chapter 5, Julie Stein, Debra Green, and Sarah Sherwood provide an analysis of OpD sediment including loss-on-ignition, micromorphology, grain size analysis, and chemical tests.

The second set of chapters detail the artifacts found at OpD. In Chapter 6, Angela Close provides a *chaîne opératoire* analysis of chipped stone artifacts from the site. In Chapter 7, Chin-Yung Chao describes the commonly found groundstone tool types of the Northwest Coast and offers a summary of the OpD assemblage in particular. In Chapter 8, Catherine Foster West describes and analyzes the spatial distribution of bone and antler tools across the site.

The final set of chapters details the faunal remains found at OpD. In Chapter 9, Cristie Boone presents an analysis of the mammal bone found at OpD. In Chapter 10, Kristine Bovy describes in depth the bird bone assemblage from OpD, providing first a descriptive summary of the types of birds represented at the site and then presenting quantitative analyses of those remains. In Chapter 11, Phoebe Daniels analyzes the shellfish remains, and Robert Kopperl presents a similar analysis of the fish remains at OpD in Chapter 12.

Each contributing researcher described and analyzed material remains from OpD in such a way that it would be relevant to the question, "Was OpD a house?" This volume presents their work and provides a final synthesis of their findings in Chapter 13. We hope that this volume will be a valuable resource for researchers who work in the Gulf of Georgia and for archaeologists designing excavation and analysis strategies for potential domestic structures.

REFERENCES

Chatters, J. C.

1989 The antiquity of economic differentiation within households in the Puget Sound region, Northwest Coast. In *Households and Communities*, edited by S. MacEachern, D. Archer, and R. Garvin, pp. 168-178. University of Calgary Archaeological Assocation, Calgary, Alberta.

Grier, C.

2001 *The Social Economy of a Prehistoric Northwest Coast Plankhouse.* Unpublished Ph.D. dissertation, Department of Anthropology, Arizona State University, Phoenix.

2003 Dimensions of Regional Interaction in the Prehistoric Gulf of Georgia. In *Emerging from the Mist: Studies in Northwest Coast Culture History*, edited by R. G. Matson, G. Coupland, and Q. Mackie, pp. 170-187. UBC Press, Vancouver.

Ham, L.

1980 *The Beach Grove Archaeological Heritage Complex; a Concept Plan for Heritage Park and Interpretive Centre at Twawwassen, B.C.* Report to Heritage Conservation Division, Victoria, BC.

Johnstone, D.

1991 *The Function(s) of a Shell Midden Site from the Southern Strait of Georgia.* Unpublished Master's thesis, Department of Archaeology, Simon Fraser University, Burnaby, BC.

2003 Early Architecture from the Southern Georgia Strait Region. In *Archaeology of Coastal British Columbia: Essays in Honour of Professor Philip M. Hobler*, edited by R.L. Carlson, pp. 109-112. Archaeology Press, Simon Fraser University, Burnaby, BC.

Matson, R. G.

1996 Households as Economic Organization: A Comparison between Large Houses on the Northwest Coast and in the Southwest. In *People Who Lived in Big Houses: Archaeological Perspectives on Large Domestic Structures*, edited by G. Coupland and E. B. Banning, pp. 107-120. Monographs in World Archaeology No. 27, Prehistory Press, Madison, WI.

2003 The Coast Salish House: Lessons from Shingle Point, Valdes Island, British Columbia. In *Emerging from the Mist: Studies in Northwest Coast Culture History*, edited by R. G. Matson, G. Coupland, and Q. Mackie, pp.76-104. UBC Press, Vancouver.

Matson, R. G., D. Ludowicz, and W. Boyd

1980 *Excavations at Beach Grove in 1980.* Report on file, Heritage Conservation Branch, Victoria, BC.

Matson, R. G., H. Pratt, and L. Rankin

1991 *1989 and 1990 Crescent Beach Excavations, Final Report, The Origins of the Northwest Coast Ethnographic Pattern: The Place of the Locarno Beach Phase.* Report prepared for the Social Sciences and Humanities Research Council of Canada, Archaeology Branch and the Semiahmoo Band, Laboratory of Archaeology, University of British Columbia, Vancouver.

Matson, R. G., G. Coupland, and Q. Mackie (eds.)

2003 *Emerging from the Mist: Studies in Northwest Coast Culture History.* UBC Press, Vancouver.

Moss, M. L., and J. M. Erlandson

1992 Forts, Refuge Rocks, and Defensive Sites: The Antiquity of Warfare along the North Pacific Coast of North America. *Arctic Anthropology* 29(2):73-90.

Mitchell, D.

1966 *Archaeological Investigations, Summer 1966.* A.S.A.B. Report, Ms., Victoria, BC.

1971 Archaeology of the Gulf of Georgia, a natural region and its cultural types. *Syesis* 4 (Suppl.1), Victoria, BC.

Schaepe, D. M.

2003 Validating the Maurer House. In *Archaeology of Coastal British Columbia: Essays in Honour of Professor Philip M. Hobler*, edited by R. L. Carlson, pp. 113-152. Archaeology Press, Department of Archaeology, Simon Fraser University, Burnaby, BC.

Smith, D. G.

1964 *Archaeological Excavations at the Beach Grove Site, DgRs1 During the Summer of 1962.* Unpublished B.A. thesis, Department of Anthropology and Sociology, University of British Columbia, Vancou-

2

The 1950 Excavation of OpD by Adan Treganza

J. Tyler Faith

J. Tyler Faith reviews the 1950 excavation of OpD by Dr. Adan Treganza, and compares his excavation with the more recent excavations directed by Julie Stein. Faith proposes that Treganza's excavation was not conducted using modern field methods, but the artifacts he recovered are still relevant to modern archaeological analyses of OpD. He compares the faunal and lithic assemblages from Treganza's and Stein's excavations, and suggests that such a comparison allows modern archaeologists to better understand the amount and nature of data lost in early mid 20th-century excavations.

The archaeological record is a finite resource, and it is critical that we make use of available data from past excavations. In a discussion of archaeological ethics, Lynott and Wylie (1995) maintain that because excavation destroys part of the archaeological record, "it is especially difficult to justify opening new sites when enormous stores of archaeological material from sites that have already been excavated or collected lie unexamined in warehouses and museums" (Lynnot and Wylie 1995:30). Similarly, Lipe (1974:213) proposes a conservation model for archaeologists to maintain and preserve sites for future research, emphasizing the archaeological record as "a non-renewable resource".

In 1950, Dr. Adan E. Treganza of San Francisco State University led a University of Washington field school in the excavation of English Camp (45SJ24) and excavated a portion of the site. For over fifty years the Treganza collection has been curated at the Burke Museum of Natural History and Culture at the University of Washington but has gone unrecognized by archaeologists as a potential source of information. Researching the Treganza excavation represents our responsibility to salvage as much information as possible from this past investigation of Northwest Coast prehistory. This study is a continuation of recent research using museum collections (e.g., Field 1995), exemplifying the potential to gain knowledge from past excavations.

This chapter presents a summary of the Treganza excavation, his findings, and what can be learned from this archaeological investigation of English Camp. A comparison of lithic and faunal remains collected from Treganza's excavation with the more recent excavations reported in this volume provides a more complete picture of the prehistory of English Camp. It also illustrates the widespread changes in archaeological field methods over the past fifty years, and explores the value of museum collections.

THE TREGANZA FIELD SCHOOL

In 1946, Dr. Arden King led a University of Washington field school at Cattle Point on San Juan Island (King 1950). Based on his findings, a tentative four-phase culture history of the region was developed to define the past 9,000 years of human occupation. To gain a more complete understanding of Northwest Coast culture sequences, Dr. Adan E. Treganza led a cursory survey of San Juan Islands archaeology in 1947 and began a University of Washington excavation of English Camp in the summer of 1950. During the preliminary survey, Treganza's students walked along the shoreline, recording the location of archaeological oc-

Chapter opening photo: Excavation unit in progress.

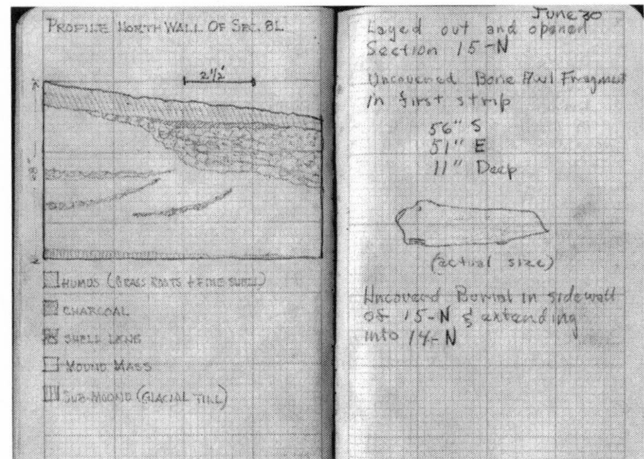

Figure 2.1 An example of the information recorded in student field journals. This entry comes from R.V. Emmons' field journal. To the left is a stratigraphic profile of the north wall of Unit 8L. Such profiles were essential for estimating the volume of sediments excavated from each unit. To the right are descriptions, drawings, and locations of the artifacts and other finds.

currences. Sites were also located through interviews with local community members on San Juan Island. Once a site was found, students recorded as much information as possible without excavating. Treganza's students recorded a total of 52 sites.

Treganza chose to excavate at English Camp in 1950 because of the high ridge of shell bordering the beach and the numerous stone cairns in the wooded uplands and nearby on Guss Island (Hoffman 1950). The following represents a summary of Treganza's excavation based on information gathered from student field journals (Figure 2.1), student papers, maps, photographs, press clippings, and personal communications with Dr. Roy Carlson, who participated in the 1950 field school. The following students excavated English Camp with Treganza: Natalie Burt, Roy Carlson, R. V. Emmons, Harry McIntyre, Arda Sprague, Derek Whitmarsh, Elizabeth Woodward and Ralph Woodward. The field school began on June 23, 1950 with a trip to English Camp and a tour around San Juan Island. Numerous archaeological sites were encountered and 21 lithic artifacts were collected from various beach sites around the island. These artifacts, labeled in the museum collection as "BEACH" finds, are currently stored in the Treganza collection although they did not come from English Camp and their provenience was not recorded. Field work at English Camp commenced with a survey of the site and the construction of a contour map (Figure 2.2). The map was constructed in one-foot contour intervals recorded every fifteen degrees

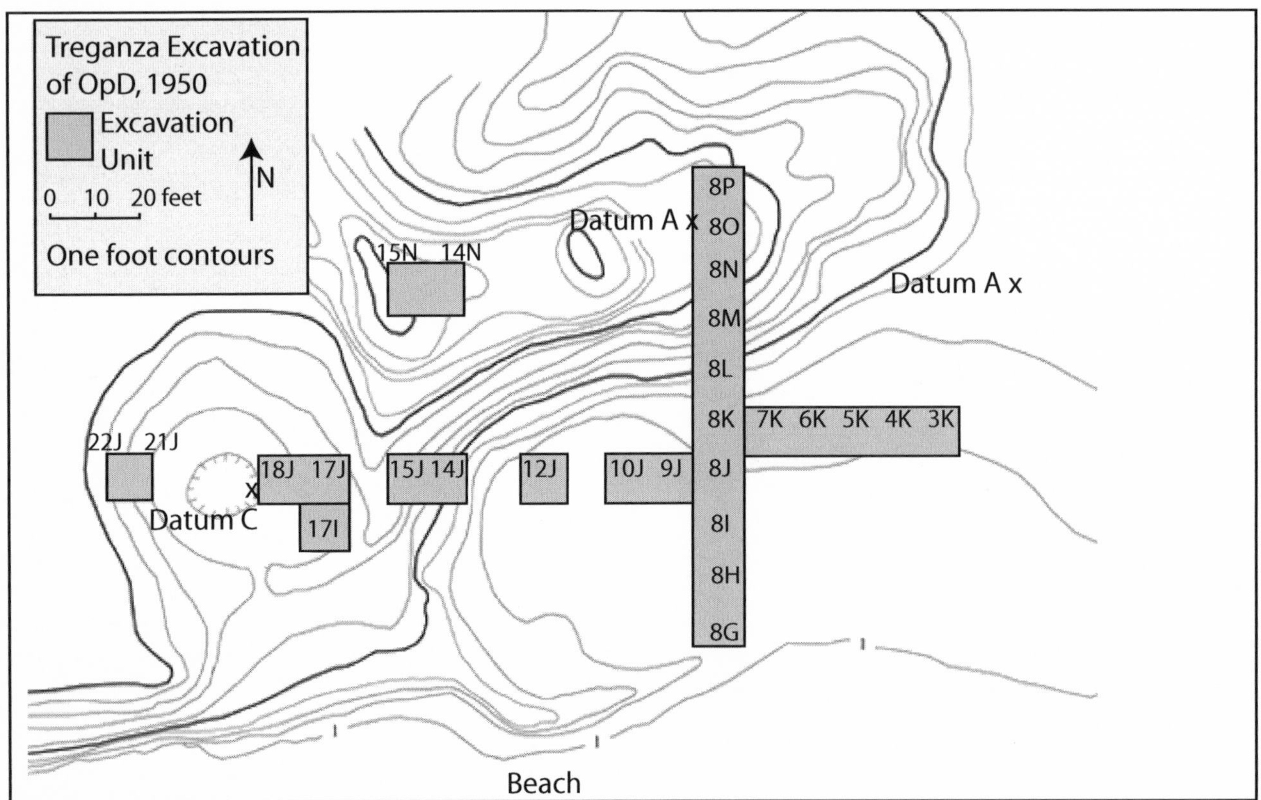

Figure 2.2 A digital copy of the original map drawn by Treganza's students in 1950. Much of the topography has been created by prehistoric shell midden deposits. Note the position of Unit 22J/21J on the left slope of the ridge. Backdirt would likely be placed near the depression.

Figure 2.3 This photograph shows Treganza's students excavating the main trench that runs from Unit 8G to Unit 8P. Large quantities of unscreened back dirt are apparent along the sides of the trench.

Figure 2.4 This photograph taken during the Treganza excavation shows units 8I through 8G. Large amounts of unscreened back dirt are piled alongside the trench. Guss Island is visible in the background.

about the compass from four separate reference points spaced throughout the site.

Excavation Methods

Treganza directed his students to excavate using relatively large 10' x 10' excavation units. Baulks were spaced between the units to aid in recording site stratigraphy (Treganza 1950). In some cases, as in Unit 14N, the students excavated 5' x 10' units. These smaller units were excavated primarily when interesting features, such as burials, intersected neighboring units. The method used to excavate was described in Elizabeth Woodward's field journal as "modified one foot stripping in ten foot sections" (SAJH 136739; Figures 2.3 and 2.4). Arbitrary one foot levels were extracted to depths ranging from four to ten feet. The back dirt was not screened. Roy Carlson (2004 pers. comm.) notes, "In 1950 Treganza was employing the 'new archaeology' of his day, at least in terms of excavation techniques. We used shovels with some trowel work and did not screen anything." Excavation units were not refilled, with consequences for later excavations of the site.

In addition to the main trench and other excavation units in the wooded area of English Camp, Treganza also excavated a unit located approximately twenty yards east of the British blockhouse. Although the unit is referred to as a test pit (Test Pit A), it was a full 10' x 10' unit that was excavated to a depth of four feet. Isolated human remains were encountered during the excavation of the unit, but no evidence of a formal burial was recorded.

Lithic and bone artifacts, faunal remains, human remains, and several historic artifacts were collected during the excavation. In accordance with the archaeological standards of the time, lithic debitage was not collected by Treganza because it was not considered as useful as formal tools for establishing culture history. Thus, the lithic assemblage includes primarily whole, flaked stone and ground stone tools with few exceptions. The provenience of each artifact was recorded in inches south and east from the northwest corner of each excavation unit. Students recorded the depth of each artifact in inches below the surface of the ground adjacent to the excavation unit. Faunal remains were not given three-point provenience, but were bagged according to the one-foot layer from which they were excavated.

Comparison with Modern Excavation Methods

Since 1950, many archaeological field methods have changed. For example, the use of screens to sift excavated deposits, which Treganza did not use, is now standard practice. There is also a tremendous difference in the volume of deposits excavated by Treganza at OpD and the volume of deposits excavated by Stein at OpD (Table 2.1). Treganza excavated roughly 420 cubic meters of shell midden, which is over 15 times the 25 cubic meters excavated by Stein. This is even more impressive considering the fact that Treganza's excavation took place over the course of one summer whereas Stein excavated over the course of several summers.

The comparatively small volume from Stein's recent excavation reflects the implementation of more care-

Table 2.1 Bifacial point density comparisons

Excavator	Points (n)	Vol. excavated (m^3)	Density (points/m^3)
Treganza	105	420	0.25
Stein	82	25	3.28

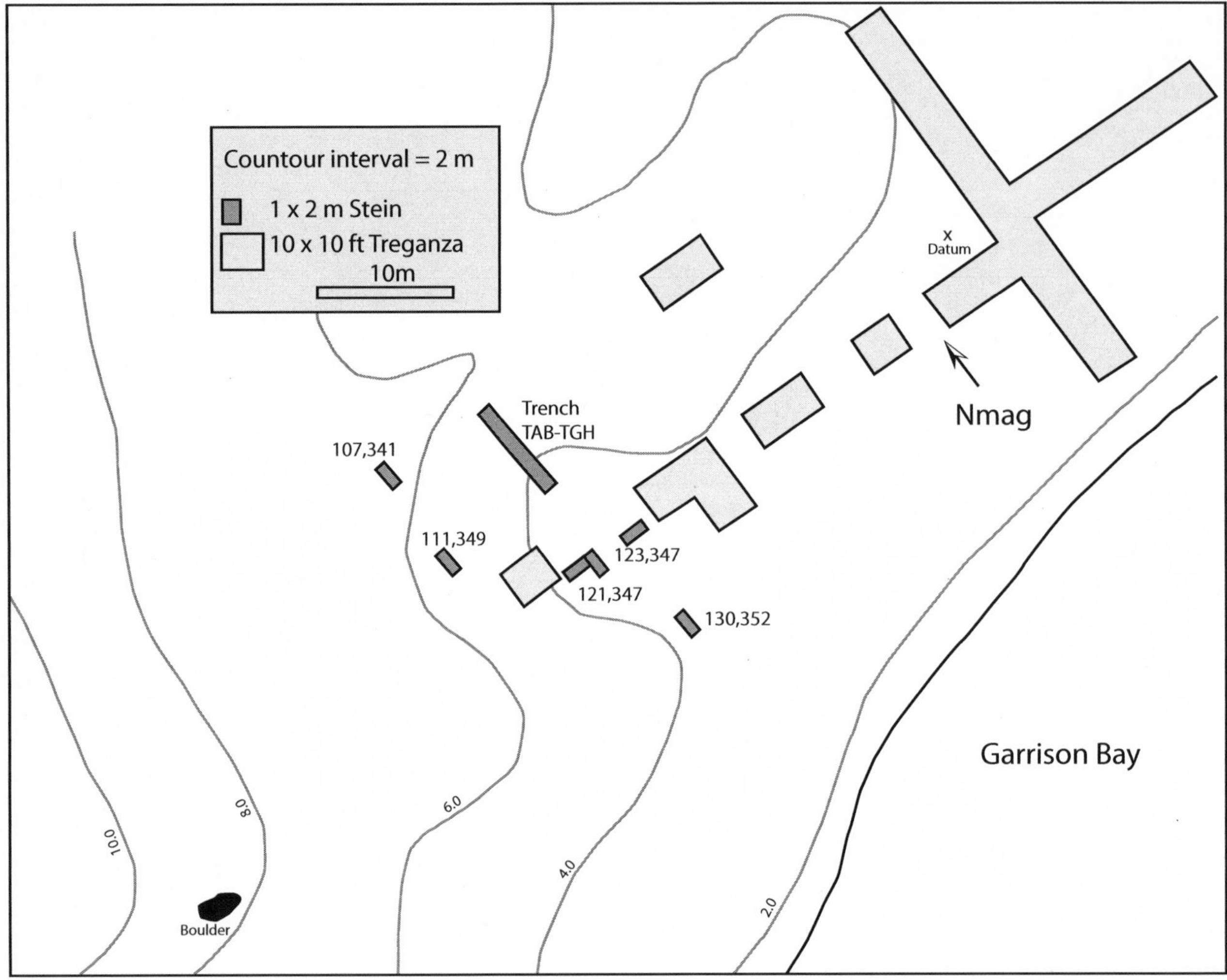

Figure 2.5 This map depicts the excavation units from the 1950 excavation superimposed over a modern map of the Stein excavation.

ful and time-consuming field methods (Figure 2.5). Such changes in excavation methods have dramatically improved artifact recovery rates. The density of projectile points per cubic meter reflects these differences (Table 2.1). For every cubic meter excavated in 1950, 0.25 projectile points were recovered during 1989-1991 excavations. During Stein's excavations, an average of 3.28 projectile points were recovered for every cubic meter excavated. A similar pattern is seen in the recovery rates of faunal remains. Over 12,000 mammal specimens were recovered in the modern excavation compared to the just over 1,300 mammal specimens found by Treganza. It is clear that in Treganza's 1950 excavation, many artifacts were inadvertently tossed into the back dirt.

As noted above, Treganza's excavation units were not back filled. The excavated sediment was left sitting adjacent to the excavation units. Given the location of unit 21/22J on the slope of a ridge, the back dirt was probably tossed downhill towards the center of the depression. This is precisely where Stein's excavation units 121 347 and 123 347 are located (Figure 2.5). Thus, the upper levels of these units may contain Treganza's backdirt, including prehistoric and historic artifacts missed during the 1950 excavation. Stein's students noticed a mixture of prehistoric and historic artifacts in Unit 121 347 through facies 1B03 (SAJH 107532). This is not the case for Unit 123 347.

Human Remains

Throughout the Treganza excavation, students frequently encountered isolated human remains including cranial fragments, parts of mandibles, and fragmentary long-bones. Numerous artifacts found near these bones are considered associated burial goods. The identification of human remains is suspect, however, as students often misidentified animal remains as human remains. In particular, the temporal bones of harbor seals (*Phoca vitulina*) were commonly identified as remains of pathologically deaf humans (see Carlson's 1950 field notes, SAJH 136734).

Table 2.2 Inventory of the Treganza collection

Item	Count	Description
Artifacts		
Lithics	182	Chipped stone: primarily bifaces with some modified flakes and other flaked stone tools
	61	Ground stone: primarily abraders, adze blades and beveled points
	8	Other: incised concretions, weights, hammerstones
Bone tools	182	Bone points, awls, pendants, wedges, and assorted modified bone artifacts
Faunal remains	1300	Samples from each 1' excavation level.
Charcoal sample	1	Bagged charcoal sample from unit 8M
Historic	2	Glass and ceramic sherds
Shells	5	Bags of shell samples consisting of a variety of whole shells
Archives		
Field journals	9	Student field journals: includes information and drawings on excavation methods, daily activities, artifacts, features, profiles, and site surveys.
Field notebook	1	Catalogue number, provenience, description, measurements, observer, find #, date, and description of lithic and bone tool artifacts
Maps	1	Topographic map: limited, does not contain all units
	1	Survey: recorded sites from Garrison bay and surrounding shorelines
	1	Stratigraphic map of main trench
Profile drawings	8	Profiles of the main trench
Forms	2	Burial forms: descriptions and measurements of recovered human remains
	5	Feature forms: hearths and caches of cooking stones
Papers	7	Student Papers: "Worked Bone and Antler," "The Stratigraphy of English Camp Site," "Flaked Stone Projectile Points," "Design," and notes from interviews with a resident "An Archaeological perspective of the Southern North Pacific Coast," A. E. Treganza "Site Survey of Garrison Bay and Adjoining Shorelines," A. E. Treganza
Press clippings	3	"Thrust of Shovel Turns Back Time 1,500 Years." Post-Intelligencer, 27 July 1950 "San Juan Island Diggings Reveal Tools Made by Man 1,500 Years Ago." Post-Intelligencer, 28 July 1950 "San Juan Pioneers Holding the Fort." Seattle Times, 23 July 1950
Photographs	1	Pictures of fieldwork, artifacts, features, and burials

Two formal burials were recovered from the 1950 excavation of English camp. One, an adult male, came from Unit 14N and Unit 15N. Two lithic artifacts were found in association with this burial. The other was an infant burial removed from unit 8G. In addition, students also removed the remains of two individuals found on Guss Island. During the analysis of the mammal remains recovered by Treganza, numerous human remains were identified in the level bags containing faunal remains. These remains were incorrectly identified as non-human during the original excavation. Procedures to repatriate human remains and funerary objects from the 1950 Treganza excavation have been undertaken by the National Park Service and the Burke Museum of Natural History and Culture in accordance with Native American Graves Protection and Repatriation Act (NAGPRA).

Historic Artifacts

In the 1950 excavation, students encountered historic artifacts manufactured within the past 200 years. According to the field journals of Whitmarsh and Woodward, remains of an historic building were located in Unit 8M and Unit 8N. The students noted the presence of an historic house floor below a collapsed roof (E. Woodward Field Journal SAJH 136739) as well as square nails (Whitmarsh Field Journal SAJH 136737). It appears that historic artifacts were not consistently recorded in student field notebooks. For example, the two recorded historic artifacts in the Treganza collection come from units 9J and 21J. There is no reference to these artifacts in any student field journal. Many historic artifacts were likely found but not recorded or collected because they were not as relevant to the research goals.

Figure 2.6 A fine-grained volcanic stemmed point from the Treganza collection.

THE TREGANZA COLLECTION

The Treganza collection, stored at the Burke Museum, consists of the artifacts collected during the 1950 field season and the accompanying archival materials (Table 2.2). The primary artifact record consists of stone artifacts, bone tools, faunal remains, shells, a charcoal sample, historic glass, and historic ceramics. The archives include student field journals, field notebooks, maps, profile drawings, excavation forms, student papers and reports, press clippings, and photographs. This archival material is central to the reconstruction of Treganza's excavation.

In this study, the recovered bifacial points and faunal remains were analyzed to gain further insight into the archaeological value of Treganza's excavation. The projectile points were chosen as a focus of analysis because the completed bifaces were among the few materials that were collected in sufficient numbers (n = 146). Of the 146 stone points, only those points with proveniences tied directly to 45SJ24 (n = 105) are included in the analysis. Mammal remains were also selected for analysis because the large sample of specimens provided an adequate sample size for comparison with the modern excavation.

Figure 2.7 A triangular projectile point from OpD.

Table 2.3 Frequencies of projectile point types and adjusted residuals for the Treganza and Stein excavations

Projectile Point Type	Excavator			
	Treganza		Stein	
	n	Adjusted Residual	n	Adjusted Residual
Stemmed	16	**2.94**	2	**-2.94**
Triangular	71	1.28	48	-1.28
Leaf	1	-0.80	2	0.80
Fragmentary	17	**-3.19**	30	**3.19**

Significant values in bold.

Bifacial Points

The bifacial points were initially classified according to Cochrane's (1994) typology:

(1) *Stemmed* points exhibit distal modification that produces a protrusion that is thinner than the great-

Table 2.4 Number of identified mammal specimens (NISP) for each excavation unit

Taxon	Provenience				
	Inside Ridge	Ridge	Outside Ridge	Test Pit A	Unknown
Odocoileus hemionus	288	159	167	13	88
Cervus elaphus	21	32	42	8	10
Cervidae	9	3	2	0	8
Canis sp.	49	25	61	11	25
Phoca vitulina	80	20	28	1	8
Eumetopias jubatus	8	4	8	1	1
Procyon lotor	4	0	1	0	0
Lontra canadensis	1	0	0	0	0
Castor canadensis	0	0	1	0	0
Cetecea	0	0	2	0	17
Delphinidae	0	0	0	0	1
Bos taurus	3	0	2	0	0
Sus scrofa	1	2	2	0	0

Note: The area outside the ridge was not excavated by Stein.

est width of the biface in plan view (Figure 2.6); (2) *Unstemmed* points exhibit no such distal modification (Figure 2.7); (3) *Fragmentary* points are broken and distal modification is unknown. Unstemmed points were further subdivided into *leaf-shaped* and *triangular* points, resulting in three distinct point types: stemmed, leaf-shaped, and triangular (Table 2.3). These three styles of points were originally noted by King (1950) in his excavation of Cattle Point.

Treganza's bifacial point assemblage is typical of the Marpole culture type (Mitchell 1971). The Marpole lithic toolkit includes "chipped-stone points in a number of forms, both stemmed and unstemmed; most of 'medium' size, but some large-leaf shapes occur; a common small basalt variety is asymmetrically triangular" (Mitchell 1971:52). Mitchell places the Marpole phase between 400 BC and AD 450. Radiocarbon dates, however, bracket the prehistoric occupation of English Camp from around AD 500 to 800 (Stein 2000; Stein et al 2003). The disagreement between Mitchell's dates for the Marpole phase and the radiocarbon dates for English Camp illustrates problems with the culture history established for the San Juan Islands.

Mammal Remains

Over 1,300 mammal specimens were recovered in Treganza's excavation. Of these, 1,217 were identified to skeletal element and taxon, including 34 specimens from Test Pit A (Table 2.4). As noted earlier, the faunal remains from the Treganza excavation were bagged according to arbitrary one-foot intervals. In many cases, however, the bags lack information concerning the unit, the stratigraphic level, or both, hindering comparisons of taxonomic abundance between stratigraphic levels and units. A total of 158 specimens come from bags lacking any information regarding their associated excavation units and consequently there are no data for excavation units 8G, 8L, 8O, 5K, 3K, 10J, 12J, or 14N. Taxonomic identifications were determined using comparative collections from the Burke Museum.

To facilitate comparisons between the Treganza mammal remains and those from the recent excavations of English Camp, identified specimens were quantified according to the Number of Identified Specimens (NISP). The mammal assemblage is dominated by mule deer (*Odocoileus hemionus*, NISP = 715), with moderate amounts of dog (*Canis* sp., NISP = 171), harbor seal (*Phoca vitulina*, NISP = 137), and elk (*Cervus elaphus*, NISP = 113). Less frequent remains of Steller sea lion (*Eumetopias jubatus*, NISP = 22), whale (*Cetecea*, NISP = 19), raccoon (*Procyon lotor*, NISP = 5), pig (*Sus scrofa*, NISP = 5), cow (*Bos taurus*, NISP = 5), river otter (*Lontra canadensis*, NISP = 1), beaver (*Castor canadensis*, NISP = 1), and dolphin (*Delphinid* NISP = 1) are also present. In addition, 22 antler fragments were identified as *Cervidae*, as it was not possible to distinguish between deer and elk.

A chi-square (χ^2) test was used to compare species abundances for excavation units within the ridge (17I, 17J, 18J), on the ridge (14J, 15J, 21/22J, 8M, 8N, 15N, 8P), and outside the ridge (8H, 8I, 8J, 9J, 14J, 4K, 6K, 7K, 8K) (Table 2.5). Adjusted residuals were calculated to illustrate how observed frequencies deviate from expected frequencies; they are to be read as standard normal deviates with absolute values greater than 1.96 representing statistically significant differences (Everitt, 1977). As illustrated in Table 2.5, large mammal abun-

Table 2.5 Spatial variation in taxonomic abundances as reflected by adjusted residuals.

Taxon	Provenience		
	Inside ridge	Ridge	Outside ridge
Odocoileus hemionus	1.29	1.83	**-3.08**
Cervus elaphus	**-4.76**	**2.35**	**2.97**
Cervidae	1.44	-0.22	-1.35
Canis sp.	**-2.25**	-1.57	**3.88**
Phoca vitulina	**4.19**	**-2.35**	**-2.35**
Eumetopias jubatus	-0.48	-0.41	0.9
Procyon lotor	1.56	-1.26	-0.53
Lontra canadensis	1.1	-0.56	-0.67
Castor canadensis	-0.91	-0.56	1.5
Cetecea	-1.29	-0.79	2.12
Bos taurus	0.66	-1.26	0.45
Sus scrofa	-1.14	0.85	0.45

Significant values in bold. $\chi 2 = 69.85, p < 0.001$

dances differ significantly across the site ($\chi^2 = 69.85$, $p < 0.001$). Significant adjusted residuals are obtained for mule deer, elk, dog, and harbor seal. Mule deer are relatively scarce outside the ridge, whereas elk are rare within the shell ridge and especially abundant on or outside the ridge. In addition, the adjusted residuals indicate that dog specimens are particularly abundant outside the shell ridge and rare within the ridge. Lastly, there is an abundance of harbor seal specimens within the ridge compared to a paucity of specimens elsewhere.

Comparison with Stein Excavation

Since the 1950 excavation of English Camp, excavation methods employed by archaeologists increasingly emphasize higher recovery rates, particularly of smaller and more fragmentary objects. A comparison of material remains from Stein's excavation with material remains from the Treganza excavation can be used to assess the degree to which museum collections from mid-20th century excavations can contribute to current analyses.

A comparison of bifacial points from the Treganza and Stein excavations indicate significant differences in lithic artifacts recovered. The bifacial points recovered from Stein's excavations of English Camp were classified according to the typology described above (Table 2.3). A chi-square test reveals significant differences between the Stein collection and the Treganza collection ($\chi^2 = 16.69$, $p = 0.001$). The adjusted residuals indicate that this difference is driven in part by variation in the frequency of fragmentary points recovered from each excavation. Fragmentary points constitute 36.6% (30 of 82 total points) of the recently excavated assemblage compared to 16.2% (17 of 105 total points) of the Treganza assemblage. In addition, the Treganza excavation yielded significantly greater frequencies of stemmed points, which comprise 15.2% (16 of 105 total points) of the 1950 assemblage compared to only 3.7% (2 of 82 total points) of the Stein assemblage.

In contrast to the bifacial points, a comparison of mammal remains from the Treganza and Stein excavations indicates that the two different excavation methods generally yielded similar results. Stein's excavation is distinguished from the Treganza excavation by differences in the number of recovered specimens and in the number of identified specimens. The sample of over 12,000 specimens recovered in the Stein excavation is an order of magnitude larger than the 1,300 specimens collected in the Treganza excavation. Interestingly, the number of identified specimens is nearly equal, with 1,220 specimens identified by Boone (Chapter 9, this volume) from Stein's excavations and 1,217 identified from Treganza's excavation. Whereas only a small fraction of remains recovered in the modern excavation were identified to taxon, the majority of those from the Treganza excavation could be identified to the species level.

A majority of the species recovered by Treganza are also present in the Stein assemblage. The Treganza assemblage confirms the presence of historic cattle at English Camp with five specimens identified as *Bos taurus*. One bovid specimen was recovered from Stein's excavation but it was not possible to identify the bone to species. The primary difference between the two excavations is that Stein recovered a substantial number of smaller taxa including mice, rats, voles, and other micromammals (Table 2.4, Table 13.1). It is apparent that the assemblage collected in the Treganza excavation is dominated by larger animals. However, for those taxa recovered in both excavations, there is general agreement in their abundances. Figure 2.8 illustrates the NISP for those taxa recovered by both Treganza and Stein (Figure 2.8). The taxonomic abundances are positively correlated with one another (Spearman's rho: $r_S = 0.830$, $p < 0.001$).

Discussion

The analysis of the bifacial points illustrates several important differences between the Treganza and Stein excavations. Given the differences in artifact density between Treganza's excavation and Stein's (Table 2.1), it is likely that many points were not recovered in the earlier excavation. The difference in relative number of fragmentary projectile points recovered by Stein's excavations can be attributed to the use of screens. Projectile point fragments are smaller and more incon-

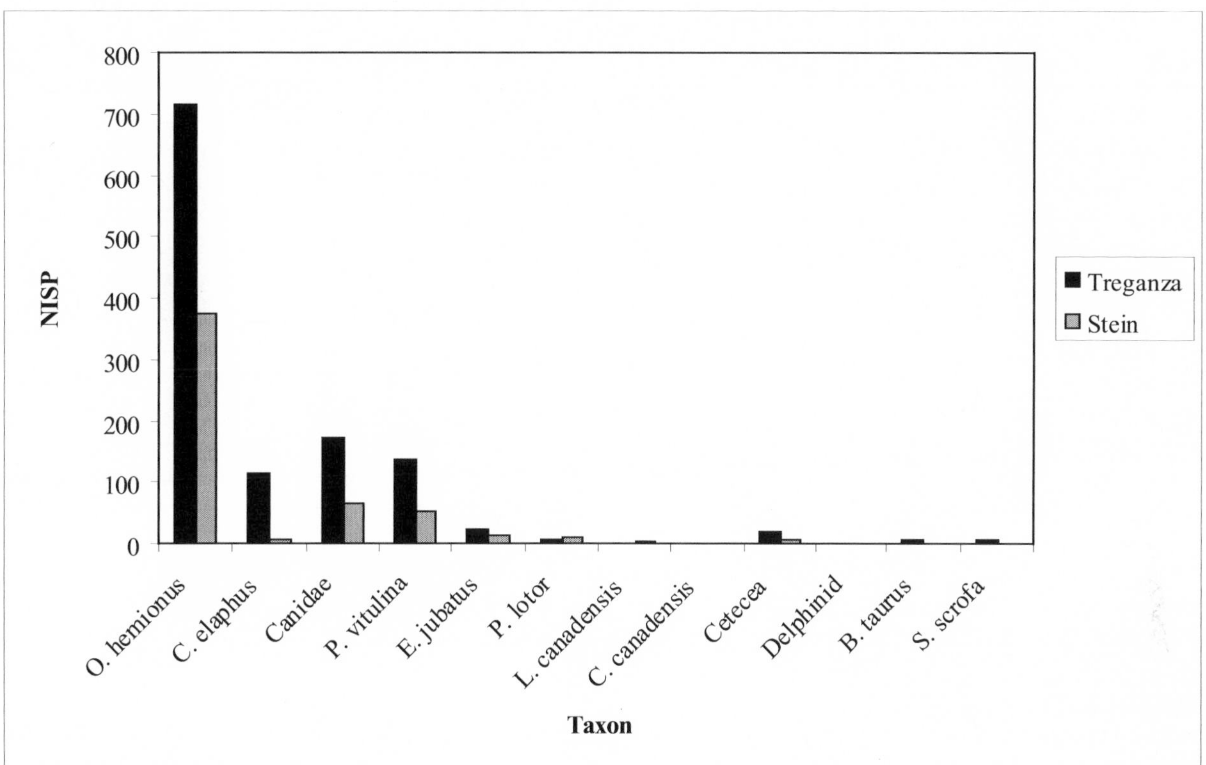

Figure 2.8 A comparison of large mammal abundances (NISP) recovered by Treganza and Stein. The abundances are significantly correlated with one another (Spearman's rho: $r_S = 0.830$, $p < 0.001$). Micromammals (e.g., rodents), however, are absent from the Treganza excavation.

spicuous than complete points. Consequently, Treganza's students were unable to recover the fragmented points while excavating with shovels and trowels. The use of ¼" and ⅛" screens, on the other hand, ensure that these smaller fragments will be found.

Although many bifacial points were surely passed over in the 1950 excavation, Treganza's collection does significantly increase the sample size of points at 45SJ24. By adding 105 projectile points to Stein's assemblage from 45SJ24, it is possible to gain a more refined picture of the types of points used by the prehistoric inhabitants of the site. The most noticeable difference between Treganza's excavation and the more recent excavations of English Camp is the high number of stemmed points recovered in 1950 (n = 16) compared to the Stein excavation (n = 2). Although stemmed points are one of the many point varieties that define a Marpole assemblage, they are also characteristic of the preceding Locarno Beach phase. All of Treganza's units containing stemmed points are located east of Stein's units. Given the different location of his units, it is possible that he encountered older deposits.

As with the bifacial points, the analysis of the mammal bones once again indicates that Treganza recovered only a fraction of the available sample. This is highlighted by the difference in the number of recovered specimens between the two excavations (over 1,300 from Treganza's excavation and over 12,000 from Stein's). Once again, it is important to emphasize that Treganza's excavation was much larger than the modern excavation and thousands of specimens were likely passed over. Despite the differences in overall sample size, however, the number of identified specimens for each excavation is nearly identical. This is likely the result of two factors. As with the bifacial points, the smaller and more fragmentary pieces of bone were not recovered by the excavators because screens were not used to sift through back dirt. In addition, the high number of identified specimens relative to the overall sample size suggests that Treganza directed his students to save only those specimens that are more easily identified (i.e., complete specimens or elements retaining the easily identified long bone epiphyses). Discarding long-bone shaft fragments was consistent with excavation methodologies at the time (Marean and Frey 1997) and is likely a major contributor to the high proportion of taxonomically identifiable specimens in the Treganza collection. Differences in taxonomic richness between the two excavations are also likely the result of recovery techniques. Many of the taxa recorded in the Stein excavation that were not found in the Treganza collection are smaller mammals. This is likely due to the use of screens during the Stein excavation.

Variation in taxonomic abundance across the site provides some insight into how the prehistoric occupants differentially processed and discarded certain species (Table 2.5). Although Treganza's techniques greatly decreased recovery rates of smaller and more fragmented artifacts and bones, it is unlikely that there would be any preferential excavation bias across different portions of the site. Furthermore, the abundances of large mammals recovered in both the Treganza and Stein excavations are positively correlated with one another, suggesting that Treganza's collection does provide a representative sample of the large mammals deposited at English Camp.

Differences in the spatial distribution of various taxa across the site may provide insights on whether OpD was a domestic structure by offering clues on site use and site formation processes. Treganza's collection is especially valuable because it provides an additional set of data from outside the shell ridge (Figure 2.5). The Treganza excavation is characterized by relatively high frequencies of harbor seal remains within the shell ridge. If the area inside the ridge does, in fact, represent a prehistoric structure, perhaps seal remains were stored or processed within the house, inflating their abundances relative to the rest of the site.

Dog remains were found in low numbers inside the ridge, moderate numbers on the ridge, and high numbers outside the ridge. Such a pattern is consistent with the burial of domestic dogs in ethnographic accounts of the Coast Salish. Suttles notes that "when dogs died, they were buried out of the way, away from the house" (1951:105). Buried dogs would not likely be incorporated into deposits inside the ridge, but rather buried away from the house and other nearby refuse. More than one probable canine burial (which included 35 specimens from at least four individuals) was excavated in Unit 6K, located outside the ridge.

Elk remains recovered by Treganza are found primarily on or outside the shell ridge, indicating that they were more frequently discarded away from the house. Conversely, mule deer are particularly scarce outside the ridge. The behavioral significance of these differences is not immediately clear, although they do suggest variation in how elk and deer remains were processed at the site.

CONCLUSIONS

Like every archaeological excavation, the 1950 excavation of English Camp permanently destroyed a portion of the archaeological record. Sitting unanalyzed in the Burke museum, the Treganza collection was an untapped source of information concerning the prehistoric inhabitants of San Juan Island. Now, over half a century since Treganza's excavation of English Camp, his finds are being put to use. The greater scope of his excavation at 45SJ24 provides a clearer picture of the archaeological material found at the site. Of equal importance, the earlier excavation provides a picture of how archaeological field methods have changed over the years. By current standards, Treganza's methods resulted in the loss of invaluable information about OpD. However, the same holds for future archaeological research: "Just as methods used by archaeologists a century ago seem primitive to us today, our current methods and techniques will seem primitive to archaeologists of the next century" (Lynnot and Wylie 1995:30). The archaeological record is a finite resource that must be preserved for future work. Collections gathered in the past are a valuable resource towards furthering our knowledge and preserving the archaeological record.

REFERENCES

Cochrane, E.

1994 *An Examination of Lithic Artifacts from the British Camp Site 45SJ24 and Discussion on the Adequacy of Culture Historical Predictions.* Senior honors thesis, Department of Anthropology and Burke Museum, University of Washington, Seattle.

Everitt, B. S.

1977 *The Analysis of Contingency Tables.* Chapman and Hall, London.

Field, J.

1995 *Finders Keepers: private collections and the prehistory of the Alderdale site (45KL5).* Senior honors thesis, Department of Anthropology and Burke Museum, University of Washington, Seattle.

Hoffman, F.

1950 "Thrust of Shovel Turns Back Time 1,500 Years." The Seattle Post-Intelligencer, 27 July.

King, A.

1950 *Cattle Point: A Stratified Site in the Southern Northwest Coast Region.* American Antiquity Memoir 7, supplement to vol. 15:1-94.

Lipe, W. D.

1974 A Conservation Model for American Archaeology. *The Kiva* 39:213-245.

Lynott, M. J. and A. Wylie

1995 *Stewardship: The Central Principle of Archaeological Ethics. Ethics in American Archaeology: Challenges for the 1990s.* Society for American Archaeology.

Marean, C. W., and C. J. Frey

1997 Animal Bones from Caves to Cities: Reverse Utility Curves as Methodological Artifacts. *Ameri-*

can Antiquity 62:698-711

Mitchell, D. H.
1971 Archaeology of the Gulf of Georgia, a natural region and its cultural types. *Syesis* 4 (Suppl.1), Victoria, BC.

Stein, J. K.
2000 *Exploring Coast Salish Prehistory: The Archaeology of San Juan Island.* University of Washington Press, Seattle.

Stein, J. K., J. N. Deo, and L. S. Phillips
2003 Big Sites-Short Time: Accumulation Rates in Archaeological Sites. *Journal of Archaeological Science* 30:297-316.

Suttles, W. P.
1951 *Economic Life of the Coast Salish of Haro and Rosario Straits.* Unpublished Ph.D. dissertation, Department of Anthropology, University of Washington, Seattle.

Treganza, A. E.
1950 *An Archaeological Perspective of the Southern North Pacific Coast.* Unpublished manuscript on file at the Burke Museum of Natural History and Culture, Seattle.

3

Field Methods

Mary Parr, Laura S. Phillips, and Julie K. Stein

The authors discuss the details of field methods used during the 1988-1991 excavations at OpD. They provide a brief history of Stein's excavations followed by a description of the project Standard Operating Procedure manual. The artifact coding and cataloging system is described, as are the procedures governing the collection of sediment and biological samples, field forms, screening procedures, sampling methods, and laboratory procedures.

The most recent excavation at Operation D (OpD) at English Camp began in 1988 as an extension of the San Juan Island Archaeological Project (SJIAP) at 45SJ24. The project had concentrated its major efforts on Operation A (OpA), a shell midden under the parade grounds near the shore of Garrison Bay. The shell midden that was located in the wooded area northwest of OpA had been identified years earlier, named Operation D (OpD), and tested (Unit I) in 1985. In 1988, OpD was revisited with the intention to excavate a test trench within the shell ridge. The test excavation was to be one meter wide and four meters long and would be placed to intersect the ridge and the floor of the U-shaped shell midden.

In 1988, University of Washington graduate student Fran Whitaker chose the location of the test excavation. The trench was to be excavated by volunteers from the community. The four 1 x 1 meter units were named OPDTRA, OPDTRB, OPDTRC, and OPDTRD. These names were used because, unlike the other excavation units, these units were not selected from the numeric site grid. Four other 1 x 2 meter units, selected from the numeric site grid, were chosen to excavate: 105 365, 107 341, 111 349, and 123 347. The entire project was scheduled to be completed by the end of the 1988 field season. In actuality, only one unit, Unit 107 341, was fully excavated in 1988.

In 1990, Julie Stein decided to continue the work at OpD. Under the direction of University of Washington graduate student Kim Kornbacher, the four original trench units were combined into two 1 x 2 meter units and renamed OPDTAB and OPDTCD. The trench was then extended by four meters and the new units were named OPDTEF and OPDTGH. Work resumed at units 105 365, 111 349, and 123 347. Two new 1 x 2 meter units were opened: 121 347, and 130 352.

Understanding the excavation strategy and the various types of samples collected from the site is necessary to understand the results of this research. Every particle in a shell midden is an artifact of human activity. Therefore, the field methods used to recover, describe, record, and catalog the excavated material required an extraordinary level of detail. This chapter presents a description of each type of sample recovered for analysis. Field and site forms used to record artifact and feature information will also be discussed. The field methods outlined here may be explored in depth by reading the *San Juan Island Archaeological Project: Standard Operating Procedure 1991* (SAJH 128829, NPS Collection on file at the Burke Museum of Natural History and Culture, University of Washington).

Chapter opening photo: A student weighing a sample from an excavation unit in the depression.

EXCAVATION PROCEDURES

Between 1988 and 1991, approximately 25 cubic meters of material was excavated and processed. Adherence to a formalized set of operating procedures was essential to ensure that the data were preserved as carefully and accurately as possible. Basic provenience information was included on all tags, bags, forms, and catalog records. This high level of redundancy allowed for multiple cross-checks along the line as the excavated material moved through the system from excavation, through screens, to the lab and eventually to the cataloging and analysis phase. A brief explanation of the tracking and recording system developed for the SJIAP follows. This information served as the project's cataloging system and was included with every excavated item and on all paperwork that accompanied the excavated material:

Site refers to the Smithsonian site number based on the state, county, and numerical order in which sites are recorded. The site number for English Camp is 45SJ24.

Operation refers to a general location within English Camp National Historic Park. OpA was the area near the Blockhouse building on the parade ground. OpD was located in the woods northwest of the parade ground.

Excavation unit refers to the coordinates of a 1 x 2 meter grid square. By convention, the coordinates of the northwest corner of the square are used to name the unit. A total of 10 1 x 2 meter units were excavated for this project between 1988 and 1991: OPDTAB, OPDTCD, OPDTEF, OPDTGH, 105 365, 107 341, 111 349, 121 347, 123 347, and 130 352.

Facies are subdivisions of the shell midden that are distinguished and delimited on the basis of lithologic characteristics. A facies represents an event over time that results from a transport agent bringing material from similar sources and depositing them in the shell midden. (Stein et al. 1992). Facies were observed and described in the field using the following attributes: particle size, composition, condition, color and abundance of each particle type. Here, facies refered by alpha-numeric designation. As facies were excavated they were assigned sequential alpha-numeric designations beginning with 1A, 1B,…, 1Z, 2A, 2B,…, 2Z, etc.

Level refers to arbitrary 10 centimeter vertical layers excavated within a facies. They were assigned two-digit sequential designations as follows: 01, 02,…,05, etc.

Bucket refers to a filled bucket of excavated material. Buckets were filled to an eight liter capacity (unless otherwise noted) during excavation and were assigned three-digit sequential designations as follows: 001, 002,…,079, etc.

SJIAP 45-SJ-24
Op ____ Unit ______
Facies _____ Level _____
FS/Bucket # [ ]
Excavated: Date _____
By _____
Bag Number:
Screened: Date _____
By _____
Sorted: Date _____
By _____
Cataloged: Date _____
By _____

BIO SED

Figure 3.1 An example of a bucket tag from OpD.

Material and *location codes* were used throughout the various stages of fieldwork whenever it was necessary to identify an artifact or sample by material type and location or screen size. The material and location codes form the final two digits of all catalog numbers.

Catalog number for each artifact or bulk sample was derived directly from the provenience for that material. For example, a fish bone (material code for bone = 2) from Unit 105 365, facies 1A, level 02, bucket 001, caught on the 1" screen (location code for material recovered on 1" screen = 1) would be given the following catalog number: 1053651A0200121.

TRACKING BY BUCKET

The excavated material from each facies was placed into eight liter buckets lined with plastic bags. The volume of each facies was then calculated by counting the number of eight liter buckets removed for that facies. As discussed above, the excavator continued excavating sequentially numbered buckets until she or he observed a marked change in the sediment to identify a new facies. If the depth of the facies exceeded 10 centimeters, the excavator would proceed by 10 centimeter levels until a new facies appeared. For each bucketful of material, the excavator placed two bucket tags in the plastic bucket bag (Figure 3.1). These tags would accompany the bucket to screens and would be placed with the ¼" and ⅛" material that was recovered during screening. By convention, the tag marked Bag Number 1 accompanied the ¼" material through the system and the tag marked Bag Number 2 accompanied the ⅛" material (Figure 3.1).

The excavator was responsible for a number of forms over the course of the excavation. The *facies description form* (Figure 3.2) provided a guide for the description of the facies. This form was completed upon the identification of a new facies. The purpose of the form was to standardize the description of facies and levels and to minimize the variation in descriptive terminology from year to year and student to student. The excavator was instructed to circle the appropriate descriptors, including items present in significant amounts. A Harris Matrix diagram was included on the form so that the excavator could include information about which facies were above and adjacent to the facies described on the form.

For each facies and/or level, two large samples were taken. These were the *sediment sample* and the *biological sample*. The sediment sample was a representative sample of each facies or level to be saved either for future analysis not envisioned at the time of the excavation or as a representative example of the midden material to be saved for posterity. This conservative approach to excavation became a hallmark of the SJIAP. Each sediment sample was approximately four liters in volume and was double bagged in 10 x 12" Ziploc bags. By convention, the sediment sample was given the field specimen number FS 2 and recorded on the field specimen form. Each sediment sample was recorded, cataloged, and labeled for permanent storage.

The biological sample, also a representative sample of each facies or level excavated, was intended to be used for mechanical, chemical, shell and botanical analyses. Each biological sample was approximately eight liters, with its location and size determined by the supervising archaeologist. The general convention for size of the sample was approximately 25 x 25 x 10 centimeters and was taken from a place considered representative of the facies as a whole. Before excavation, the horizontal dimensions of the biological sample were recorded on the biological sample form and the sample was given the field specimen number FS 1 and recorded on the field specimen record. The three-point provenience of the center point of the biological sample was recorded on the plan/profile record and the field specimen record.

The excavator was responsible for filling out the *field specimen record* as excavation progressed. A field specimen was defined as any material for which three-

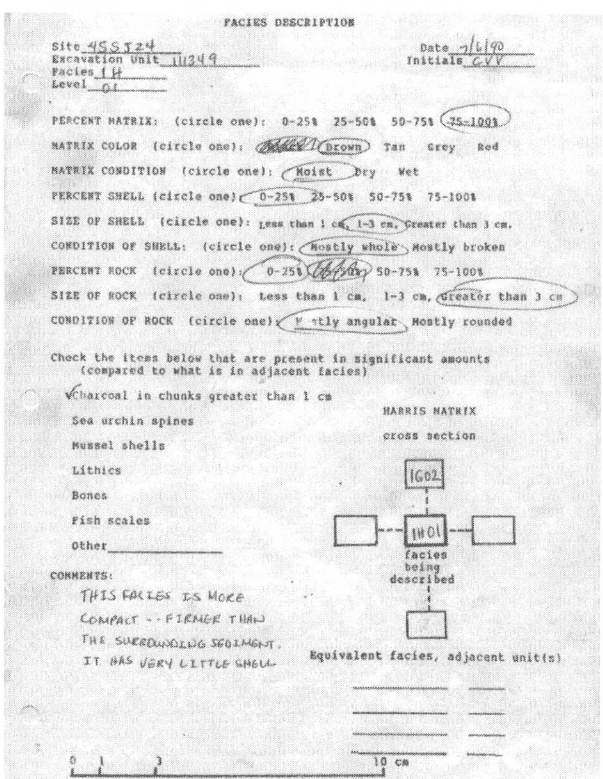

FACIES DESCRIPTION

Site 45SJ24
Excavation Unit 11349
Facies 1H
Level 01

Date 7/6/90
Initials GVV

PERCENT MATRIX: (circle one): 0-25% 25-50% 50-75% 75-100%
MATRIX COLOR (circle one): Black Brown Tan Grey Red
MATRIX CONDITION (circle one): Moist Dry Wet
PERCENT SHELL (circle one): 0-25% 25-50% 50-75% 75-100%
SIZE OF SHELL (circle one): Less than 1 cm, 1-3 cm, Greater than 3 cm.
CONDITION OF SHELL: (circle one): Mostly whole Mostly broken
PERCENT ROCK (circle one): 0-25% 25-50% 50-75% 75-100%
SIZE OF ROCK (circle one): Less than 1 cm, 1-3 cm, Greater than 3 cm
CONDITION OF ROCK (circle one): Mostly angular Mostly rounded

Check the items below that are present in significant amounts
(compared to what is in adjacent facies)

✓Charcoal in chunks greater than 1 cm
Sea urchin spines
Mussel shells
Lithics
Bones
Fish scales
Other________

HARRIS MATRIX
cross section
1G02
1H01
facies being described

COMMENTS:
THIS FACIES IS MORE COMPACT -- FIRMER THAN THE SURROUNDING SEDIMENT. IT HAS VERY LITTLE SHELL

Equivalent facies, adjacent unit(s)

0 1 3 10 cm

Figure 3.2 A facies description form from OpD.

point provenience was recorded. These materials were placed in small paper bags and checked in to the field lab at the end of each day of excavation. The following materials were collected as field specimens if identified as significant during excavation: manufactured lithic artifacts (not debitage), manufactured bone artifacts, teeth, bones that contain teeth, mammalian skulls, articulated skeletal remains, charcoal (for C-14 or botanical analysis), glass, metal, ceramic, basketry, and plant material (such as burned seeds). Each field specimen was recorded in order of discovery on the field specimen record and assigned the appropriate FS number. The field specimen record was designed in such a way that it provided an actual catalog sheet of all field specimens recovered. The excavator filled in the unit, facies, level, field specimen number, material, location code, and provenience for each find.

The excavator was also responsible for recording information on the *plan/profile form*. Field specimens were recorded on the form by placing a dot or small triangle on the map where the artifact was found along with the FS#. An additional form, the *rock/bone plan* map, was used to record the spatial distribution of bones and rocks larger than five centimeters that were not taken as field specimens. The *rock/bone plan* was the only way to preserve information about the spatial relationships of these objects before they were removed.

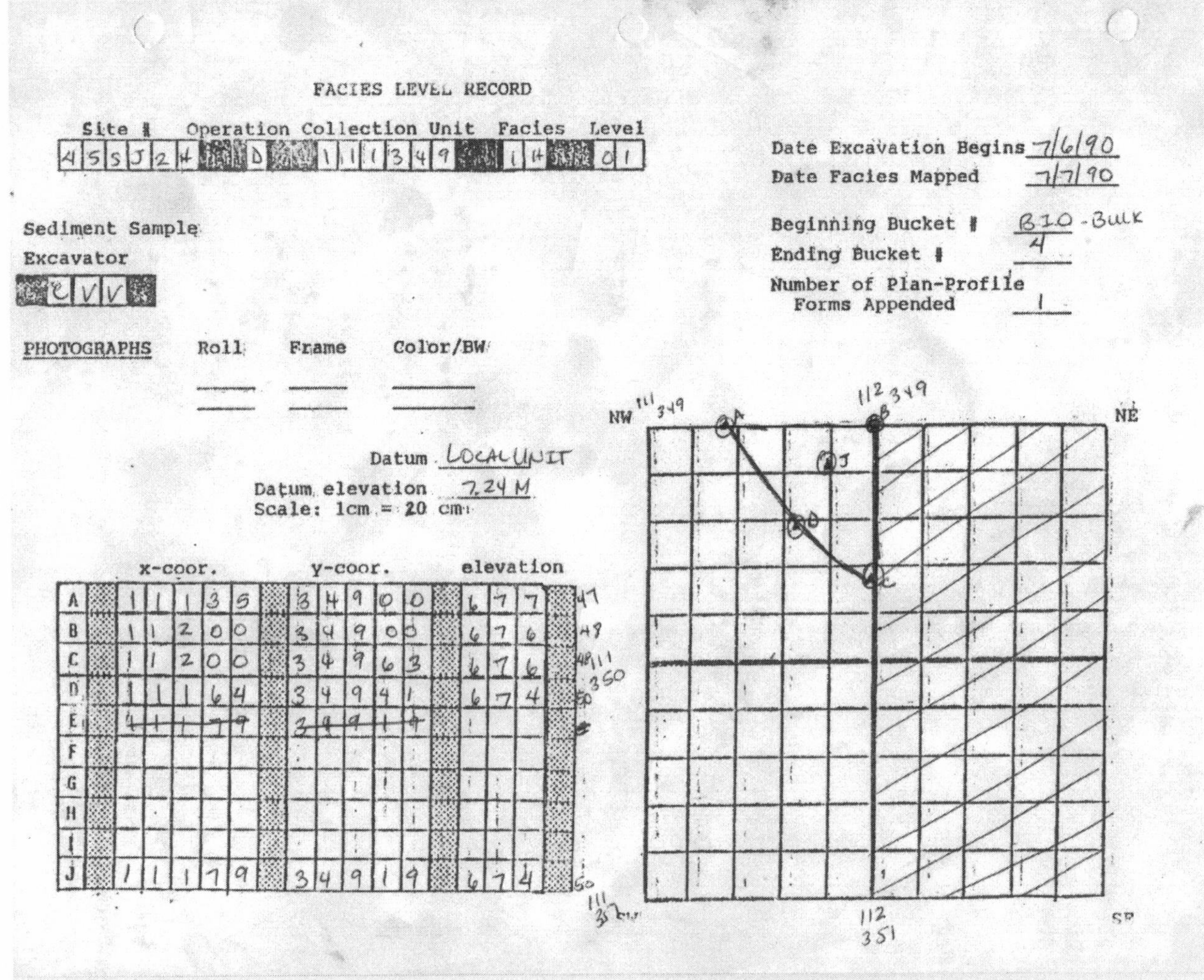

FACIES LEVEL RECORD

Site # Operation Collection Unit Facies Level

4 5 S J 2 4 D 1 1 1 3 4 9 1 4 0 1

Date Excavation Begins 7/6/90
Date Facies Mapped 7/7/90

Sediment Sample
Excavator
C V V

Beginning Bucket # B10-BULK
Ending Bucket # 4
Number of Plan-Profile Forms Appended 1

PHOTOGRAPHS Roll Frame Color/BW

Datum LOCAL UNIT
Datum elevation 7.24 M
Scale: 1cm = 20 cm

	x-coor.	y-coor.	elevation
A	11135	34900	677
B	11200	34900	676
C	11200	34963	676
D	11164	34941	674
E	~~11179~~	~~34914~~	
F			
G			
H			
I			
J	11179	34919	674

Figure 3.3 A facies level record form from OpD.

Upon completion of each facies or level, the *facies level record* (Figure 3.3) was completed by the excavator. This form was used to record the shape and the maximum horizontal extent of the facies or level and its elevation at various points. This form was completed after the facies was completely excavated and before describing and excavating the next facies. The *facies level record* contained a grid square in which the shape of the facies was drawn, and a place to record the x, y, and z coordinates for 10 locations around and within the bottom of the facies. The convention for mapping the bottom of a facies was to physically mark 10 points labeled "A" through "J" in the ground outlining the extent of the facies. Point A was always the northwesternmost point on the map and points "B" through "I" continued in a clockwise direction from "A". The tenth point, "J", was conventionally located in the center of the facies. These 10 points were defined on the ground using colored golf tees.

SCREENING PROCEDURES

All eight-liter buckets were taken to the screening area where they were organized by unit, facies, and bucket number, and then processed by screening teams. All buckets were processed first by dry screening and then wet screening for the ¼" and ⅛" fractions. To begin the screening process, the total weight of the bucket was taken using a *Detecto, Series #31S* hanging balance. Once the total weight was recorded on the *screening record*, the material was poured onto the top screen of the nested screens. Students poured the material through nested 1", ½", ¼", and ⅛" screens. They weighed, sorted, and bagged the material and recorded information on the screening forms.

The 1" screen was shaken to remove loose sediment; the remaining material was placed on the table. The material was sorted and weighed and the recorder entered the weights on the screening record. The following materials were weighed and discarded: 1" rounded rock, 1" angular rock, 1" shell. Other materials were

Figure 3.4 Screening at OpD.

sorted by material type and placed in paper screen bags. *Screen bags* were pre-stamped on the outside with the same information as the bucket tags. The dry screeners added the unique provenience data to the bag of 1" and ½" recovered material. The following materials were collected and bagged: bones, lithics, significantly modified shell, charcoal, teeth, glass, metal, ceramic, basketry, or plant material. The material from the ½" screen was sorted, weighed, and recorded in the same way. This system allowed the weight and percentage of every major compositional type of particulate to be quantified for each facies (Figure 3.4).

The ¼" and ⅛" material was wet screened to remove any remaining sediment. After the material was thoroughly washed, each fraction was bagged separately in a clean plastic bag. The bucket tag for Bag # 1 was placed in the bag with the ¼" fraction and the bucket tag for Bag #2 was placed in the bag with the ⅛" fraction. Both samples were taken to the field lab where the material was dried and then returned to the University of Washington to be sorted.

SAMPLING STRATEGY

The problem of how to sample and analyze shell from a shell midden without overwhelming the curation and storage capacity of the University and the National Park Service became a real consideration in determining what to save for analysis. The SJIAP generated tens of thousands of samples and artifacts that required permanent care and storage. Each facies and level within a facies had a *biological sample* for which each particle would be saved and analyzed. In addition, all 1" and ½" shells and fire modified rocks were counted, weighed, recorded, and then discarded. All other 1" and ½" material was saved. For the rest of the material from each facies or level within a facies, a sampling design was developed. All ¼" materials from buckets numbered 1-10 were saved. After bucket 10, only the material from buckets evenly divisible by 4 was saved. Material from the ⅛" screen was selected in the same manner, with the exception of charcoal and plant remains, which were discarded.

A screening record was used to keep a running total of the weights of different materials within the facies. Buckets were screened and recorded in consecutive order. This provided another way to cross-check the excavators' recordkeeping and to make in-field observations about the excavated material. Each form pertained to only one facies/level. Weights were recorded to the nearest 25 grams. If the weight of any material was less than 25 grams but more than zero, a "T" for trace was written in the appropriate box on the form. Because wet screening was used for the ¼" and ⅛" fractions, weights were not recorded for these fractions at the screening station. Instead, weights for these fractions were entered later at the lab after the samples were thoroughly dry. The screen bag list was a running list of all bags of ¼" (Bag #1) and ⅛" samples (Bag #2), as well as any bone, charcoal, lithics, worked shell, or historic artifacts that were collected from the 1" and ½" screens. This form was mainly used at the lab check-in station when materials were brought to the field lab at the end of the workday.

MICROARTIFACT SAMPLES

Beginning in 1990, microartifact samples were recovered during the screening process. During dry screening, sediment smaller than ⅛" was caught under the nested screens in a container. For each bucket screened, approximately one cup of this matrix was removed from the container and placed in a Ziploc bag. These samples were combined with the less-than-⅛" sample from each bucket within the same facies. This recovered matrix became the microartifact sample. The microartifact sample was, then, a combination of matrix from all buckets, and as such was considered a representative sample of the microartifacts present in a given facies. If the facies was larger than 10 buckets, the customary sampling procedure was followed by saving one cup of matrix from every fourth bucket after 10.

LABORATORY PROCEDURES

Every aspect of the SJIAP was examined, organized, and systematized to create a smooth-running operation, including the field lab. At the end of each day, all excavation forms were brought to the lab to be checked. The excavator would pick up his/her excavation forms from the lab the following morning on the way to excavation. All forms for completed facies were examined and placed in the appropriate unit notebooks. All sediment samples, biological samples, and field specimens were checked into the lab at the end of each workday. The excavators, with the assistance of the lab crew members, were responsible for making sure the materials from their unit were properly checked in.

The screeners were also responsible for bringing their forms to the lab. All screen bags were checked in using the screen bag list to make sure that all material recovered from the screens was accounted for at the end of each day. All wet screened ¼" and ⅛" materials were brought to the lab where they were dried, weighed, recorded and packed for return to the University of Washington where the material would later be sorted.

Drying and Weighing the ¼" and ⅛" Fraction

Each day, the wet ¼" and ⅛" material that had been brought up from screens the previous day was put out in the sun to dry. The material was poured onto clean sheets of butcher paper and placed on drying racks. When the material was dry, it was placed in plastic bags with the bucket tag and then put in boxes marked "To be weighed". The next step was to weigh the ¼" and ⅛" fractions and record the weights on the screening record. Once these tasks were accomplished, the material was placed in boxes labeled by unit number and marked "To be sorted". Most of this material was taken back to the University of Washington for sorting. Some sorting was also completed in the field (Figure 3.5). Sorting was conducted twice on each sample to make sure that nothing was missed. The recovered materials were placed in Ziploc bags separated by material type. The following material was saved from the ¼" size fraction: charcoal, bone, lithics, significantly modified objects, metal, glass, ceramic, and burnt seeds. The same items were saved from the ⅛" fraction, with the exception of charcoal. The charcoal from the ⅛" fraction was so fragile that even the slightest handling caused it to disintegrate.

Washing

With the exception of charcoal, plant material, and friable bones, all field specimens were washed. The procedure was to gently rinse the artifacts in water and/or gently clean them with a soft brush. The artifacts were placed in trays on top of their screen bag or field specimen bags. When they were dry they were examined by the lab supervisor to make sure that the items matched the excavators' or screeners' identification. The materials were then cataloged and organized for transportation to the University of Washington.

Cataloging

Because 45SJ24 falls within a National Historical Park and recovered material belongs to the National Park Service, each specimen or sample was assigned a SJIAP catalog number as well as a National Park Service Number. The SJIAP number was derived from the actual provenience of the material as described above. A label with the project name and site number stamped on it was placed in each sample bag. Using the provenience information, the catalog number was also written on the bag. The FS# is 3 digits and replaces the bucket number in the catalog number. The catalog number and a brief description of the items in the bag were then entered in the *general catalog record*. The excavator's initials and excavation date, the screener's initials and screening date, and the cataloger's initials and catalog date were also recorded for each item or sample. An NPS number was assigned once the collections were brought to the University of Washington. An NPS curator provided a sequence of numbers for each year of excavation, each one beginning with the park acronym SAJH.

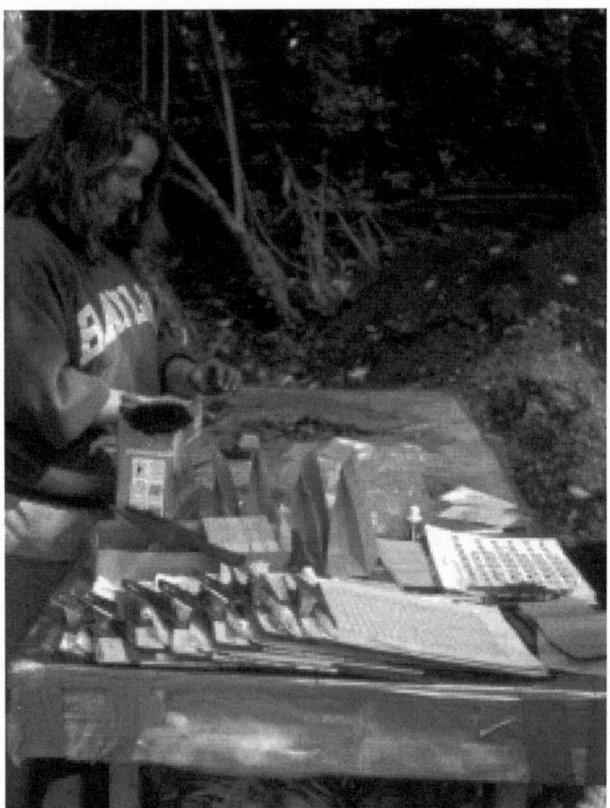

Figure 3.5 A field school student bagging at OpD.

Processing the Biological Samples

The biological samples were processed differently than the other samples before analysis. Using a process called *Bio Splitting*, sample was divided into a number of different samples that were then analyzed by different archaeologists. The material was first divided into two portions: material greater than 1/16" and material less than 1/16" (which was called the matrix). Half of the matrix was reserved for sedimentological analysis, the other half was poured back into the original bag and formed part of the sample used for flotation. After flotation, the remaining heavy fraction was used for faunal analysis.

In Bio Splitting, the total weight of the sample was recorded on the *bio sample form* along with the initials of the people involved in the procedure. The biological sample was poured through a set of nested screens with the purpose of separating out all of the material that was less than 1/16". The matrix was passed through a Jones Splitter to create two portions of equal size. Each portion was weighed and recorded on the *bio sample form*. One half of the matrix was placed in a Ziploc bag, weighed, cataloged, and labeled for later sedimentological research. The other half of the matrix was returned to the original bag along all material larger than 1/16" and the two original 3" x 5" tags created when the biological sample was excavated. One tag was marked "Heavy Fraction" and the other tag marked "Light Fraction". These tags followed their respective materials through the system to insure that records were accurately maintained.

Flotation

Flotation is the process of recovering small particles of organic material by immersing sediment samples in water or other fluids. Particles that float on the surface (the "light fraction), such as carbon samples and microfloral and microfaunal remains, are then skimmed off the surface and saved for further analysis.

Teams of two students, supervised by the lab assistant, were responsible for floating biological samples. This process was completed in the screening area when water was available. The light fraction was recovered on cheesecloth placed between two nested geological screens and secured in place with rubber bands. These were placed in a bucket hung on the float tank overflow pipe. As the tank filled and water began to flow gently out of the tank through the overflow pipe, botanical remains and charcoal were caught on the cheesecloth (Figure 3.6). The recovered botanical sample was rubber banded inside the cheesecloth with the light fraction tag secured to it. The remaining heavy fraction was caught inside the float tank using a 1/16" mesh. This material was returned to the original bag and labeled with the heavy fraction tag. Both samples were dried and placed in bags with catalog labels and transported to the University of Washington for analyses. As a quality control method, one hundred poppy seeds were added to about twenty percent of the float samples. The poppy seeds enabled researchers to determine the percent-recovery error for the flotation process.

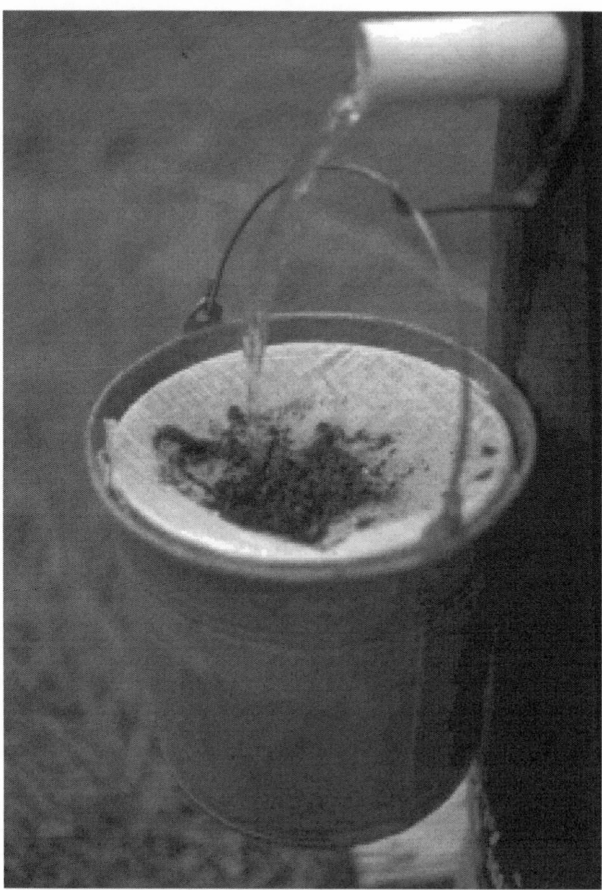

Figure 3.6 Light fraction material collected during flotation.

THE 1991 FIELD SEASON

During the 1991 field season, several changes were made to the standard operating procedure by field directors Kris Wilhelmsen and Kim Kornbacher, both University of Washington graduate students (*SJIAP Standard Operating Procedure 1991, Protocol Change #1.* SAJH 128829, NPS Collection on file at the Burke Museum of Natural History and Culture, University of Washington). Wilhelmsen and Kornbacher were concerned that in the final year of the excavation, the units would not be completed. Rather than excavating in facies, they excavated in arbitrary levels. Consequently, the following changes were made to the excavation and processing protocol:

(1) All bags and tags were labeled Facies 000 and the words "Arbitrary Level" were written on the bottom of all bags, tags, and labels.

(2) Facies Description Forms were no longer used.

(3) Sediment Samples were no longer taken.

(4) A biological sample was taken for each arbitrary level. Auxiliary biological samples were taken at the discretion of the teaching assistant.

(5) Two maps were made for each level, one at the top and one at the bottom. The maps were made

using the Facies Level Record and Rock/Bone Plan Map.

(6) Screening procedures, including sorting and weighing angular and rounded rock and shell, remained the same but the pace was accelerated to accommodate additional material.

As it became clear that reaching the sterile glacial marine drift was not possible in the time remaining, certain excavation units were prioritized. Wilhelmsen and Kornbacher concentrated on the trenches so that selected profiles could be drawn before closing the units. This new methodology was instituted on August 15, 1991 and dubbed "Fast Excavation Protocol" (*SJLAP Standard Operating Procedure 1991, Protocol Change #2, Document 1*. SAJH 128829, NPS Collection on file at the Burke Museum of Natural History and Culture, University of Washington). The following protocol was initiated:

(1) Units were excavated in 10 centimeter arbitrary levels using shovels until close to the GMD at which point trowels were used to expose the GMD surface.

(2) Level contents were shoveled directly into a ¼" screen. No bucket tags or bags were created.

(3) The material found in the ¼" screen would be given the location code 3 or "No provenience".

(4) Three-point provenience would still be taken on artifacts when found in situ.

(5) No sediment or biological samples were to be taken. A column sample would be taken after excavation was completed.

(6) Screening was to continue on material excavated before the "Fast Excavation Protocol" was put into effect. However, there was no sorting or weighing of material screened through the ¼" screen.

When the field school returned to the University of Washington after the 1991 field season they brought back a total of 155 boxes of material that were unprocessed or partially processed. In addition, 135 boxes of ¼" and ⅛" material that was ready to sort were also brought back to the University. The research presented in this publication focuses on the material recovered prior to the 1991 field season.

4

Paleotopography and Stratigraphy

Julie K. Stein, Amanda K. Taylor, and Phoebe S. Daniels

To understand the landforms at OpD, we focused on reconstructing the paleotopography of the prehistoric landscape and the stratigraphy of the site. This chapter describes mapping and augering methods, dating results, and stratigraphy within each excavation unit. Both the landscape-level and site-level analyses are directed towards investigating whether OpD was a domestic structure.

To investigate the origin and nature of the horseshoe-shaped topographic ridges at OpD, we designed our mapping and augering methods to reveal the paleotopography of the prehistoric landscape. We centered our sampling strategy and dating work on understanding the stratigraphy within the ridges. To understand how the ridges formed, we investigated the deposits of shell midden that create the complex layering. For each deposit, depth, inclination, size, and constituent parts were measured and analyzed to address whether they were once part of a prehistoric house.

MAPPING AND AUGERING

We mapped OpD in 1989 using a transit and stadia rod in a controlling point survey. All readings were tied to the grid system and datum established in 1985 at OpA (Whittaker and Stein 1992:26-27). At OpA, the grid system was oriented parallel to the wave-cut bank located between the historic block house and commissary (Whittaker and Stein 1992:Figure 1). Extending this orientation to OpD resulted in a grid that was not aligned with the ridge; however, adhering to one consistent grid system for the entire English Camp site outweighed this inconvenience.

As described in Chapter 1 of this volume, the topography of OpD is dominated by ridges of shell midden in a horseshoe shape with the open end facing the water to the south. The shell ridge abuts a hill that slopes gently southward. The ridge extends to the west only as far as the intersection with the slope of the hill, but to the east the ridge extends approximately 50 m where it ends adjacent to a wetland. (F. H. Whittaker OpD 1988 Field Notebook; Figure 4.1). The topography and integrity of the eastern extent of the shell ridge has been significantly altered by activities since the British occupation. Shell midden was excavated by the British to use as foundation fill for the officers' houses, and it was spread to create a flat walking area along the entire shore. The first homesteader, Crook, used the shell midden as feed for his chickens, to fill the wetland for his orchard, and to pave the road now used by visitors to the park (the shell midden in the road was visible in 1983 when this project was first started). There were indications that another horseshoe shaped depression existed in this eastern section but that only the back of the structure still exists. Also, a trench excavated by Treganza seems to have been placed adjacent to the quarry created by Crook.

The OpD depression in the middle of the horseshoe is not topographically lower than the area in front of or beside the ridges. It is at the same elevation as the area in front and extending to the shore. The ef-

Chapter opening photo: A student drawing a stratigraphic profile in the trench.

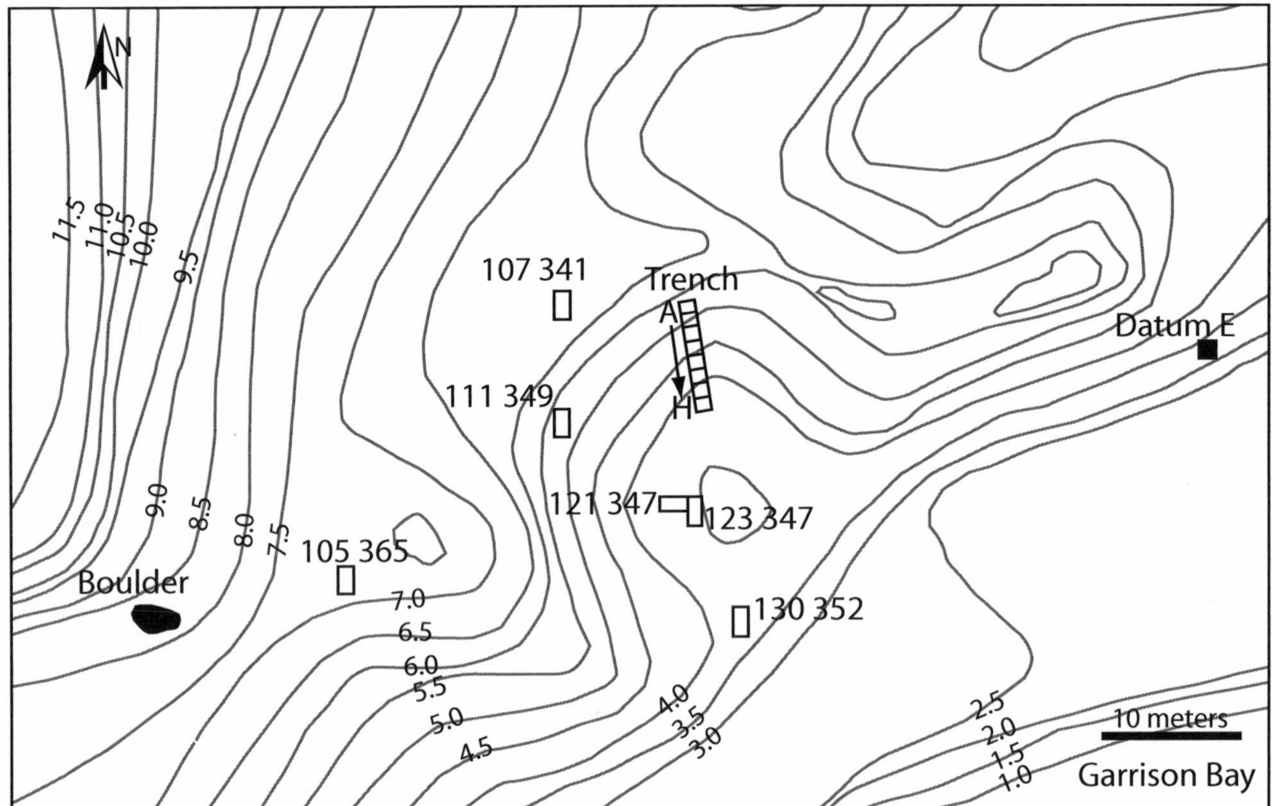

Figure 4.1 Modern topography in the vicinity of OpD showing the location of excavation units modified from a map drafted by Fran Hamilton.

fect of a depression is produced by the proximity to the elevated ridges and by vegetation that has grown in front of the depression that creates the appearance of a sheltered enclosure. Historic artifacts have been found on the surface of the site and in the uppermost levels, which suggests that the depression was used as a camping spot since the time of British settlement on the islands.

The augering method used at OpD was similar to that used at OpA (Whittaker and Stein 1992). We began the process at each auger location by raking forest litter from the surface and removing roots and moss from a roughly 10 cm diameter circular area. A 4-inch diameter bucket auger was used that in one motion cut through the shell midden and pushed sediment, shell, and rocks upwards into the bucket (Stein 1986, 1991) (Figure 4.2, 4.3).

The 4-inch diameter bucket was required to maneuver the fire-cracked rocks up into the bucket. One problem we encountered was that the bucket failed to hold small or fragmented shell if the sediment was dry and no large rocks or shells were present. As the auger was pulled to the surface, the contents of the bucket would spill back into the hole. In these cases we attempted a second auger extraction nearby. Each time we extracted the auger from the hole, we made note of the depth to assess whether we were continuing to progress below the surface. If the auger caught on a rock and began to slice sideways or if the hole began to collapse, we would attempt to correct the problem or begin a new hole.

In the field, we used two augers, one that was attached to a 1 m long rod with a handle, and another that was attached to a 2 m long rod (two 1 m long extension rods) with a handle. Switching between augers was more time efficient than adding and removing extension rods in the field. We twisted the bucket into the ground to a depth of approximately 20 cm, the height of the auger bucket. After each "punch" we extracted the auger from the hole and removed its contents. We then replaced the auger in the hole and twisted it 20 cm farther into the ground. As each auger "punch" was removed from the hole, the contents were examined and systematically described. Attributes recorded included the overall proportion of shell (greater or less than 50%), the proportion of rock larger than 2 cm, whether the edges of the rocks were rounded or angular, and the color of the matrix (gray, tan, or brown). We also noted the percentage of shell that was burned. These data were compared across the site for an overall stratigraphic landscape overview.

Figure 4.2 Augering at OD in 1983.

The termination of each auger hole occurred when the sediment in the bucket changed from black or dark brown shell midden deposits to tan glacial deposits. The entire area upon which the English Camp archaeological site is deposited is composed of glacial drift left by the melting of Pleistocene glaciers (Easterbrook 1969, 1986; Porter and Swanson 1998). Although the texture and color of these glacial sediments vary, they are predominantly tan and homogenous sandy silts, a marked contrast with the black cobble-rich midden sands. We recorded the depth of the boundary between midden and glacial drift by lowering a folding ruler into the hole and comparing that depth to the length of the auger. The boundary was usually discovered within the bucket so the exact depth of the top of the glacial deposits was determined by subtracting the location of the boundary apparent in the bucket from the total depth of the hole.

PALEOTOPOGRAPHY

We reconstructed the paleotopography of the shell midden by combining the topographic information and the augering data. At every auger location, the depth of the boundary between the glacial drift and the shell midden was subtracted from the elevation of the modern surface (Stein 1986). These new elevation points were used to create a paleotopographic map representing the configuration of the landscape before any shell midden was deposited (Figure 4.4).

The paleotopographic map reveals that prior to human occupation, the slope behind OpD gently sloped from the north to the south, toward the water, until it flattened out to a bench perpendicular to the shoreline. The original geomorphic process that cut this bench was most likely wave action at a time of higher sea

Figure 4.3 A bucket auger.

level, most likely dating to Early Holocene eustatic and isostatic adjustments. We know that sea level was lower than it is today at least by 2000 years ago based on geological research on southwestern British Columbia and the San Juan Islands (Beale 1990; Clague 1989; Clague and Bobrowsky 1990; Mathews et al. 1970). Corroborating evidence exists at OpA where augering and paleotopographic investigation led to the discovery that sea level remained 1 m lower than it is today approximately 1000 BP (Whittaker and Stein 1992). By the time people began living at OpD about 2000 years ago, the bench had been there for thousands of years and provided an attractive flat surface adjacent to the shoreline.

One question of this research concerns why OpD is located adjacent to a steep slope over 100 m away from the open flat area at OpA. The wind comes predominantly from the southwest and would blow directly into the structure, but since Garrison Bay is small and protected from the full force of the wind, the southwesterly winds may not have been strong. In fact, the winds may have helped move the smoke from the structure and therefore were not a concern to the prehistoric inhabitants of OpD in their choice of settlement location. Also, an advantage of a southwestern aspect is increased sun exposure and may outweigh the effects of strong storms or smoke management.

SAMPLING THROUGH EXCAVATION

We chose a stratified random sample to ensure that our excavation of a small portion of the site would be representative of the whole (approximately 30 m x 50 m), and would also be appropriate to our research goal to determine if OpD was a house. Rather than excavating one large unit in the middle of the feature, we chose to excavate six 2 x 1 m units from the four geomorphic areas of the site: behind the ridge, on the ridge, inside the ridge (in the depression), and in front of the ridge (the area in front of the ridge and depression). The

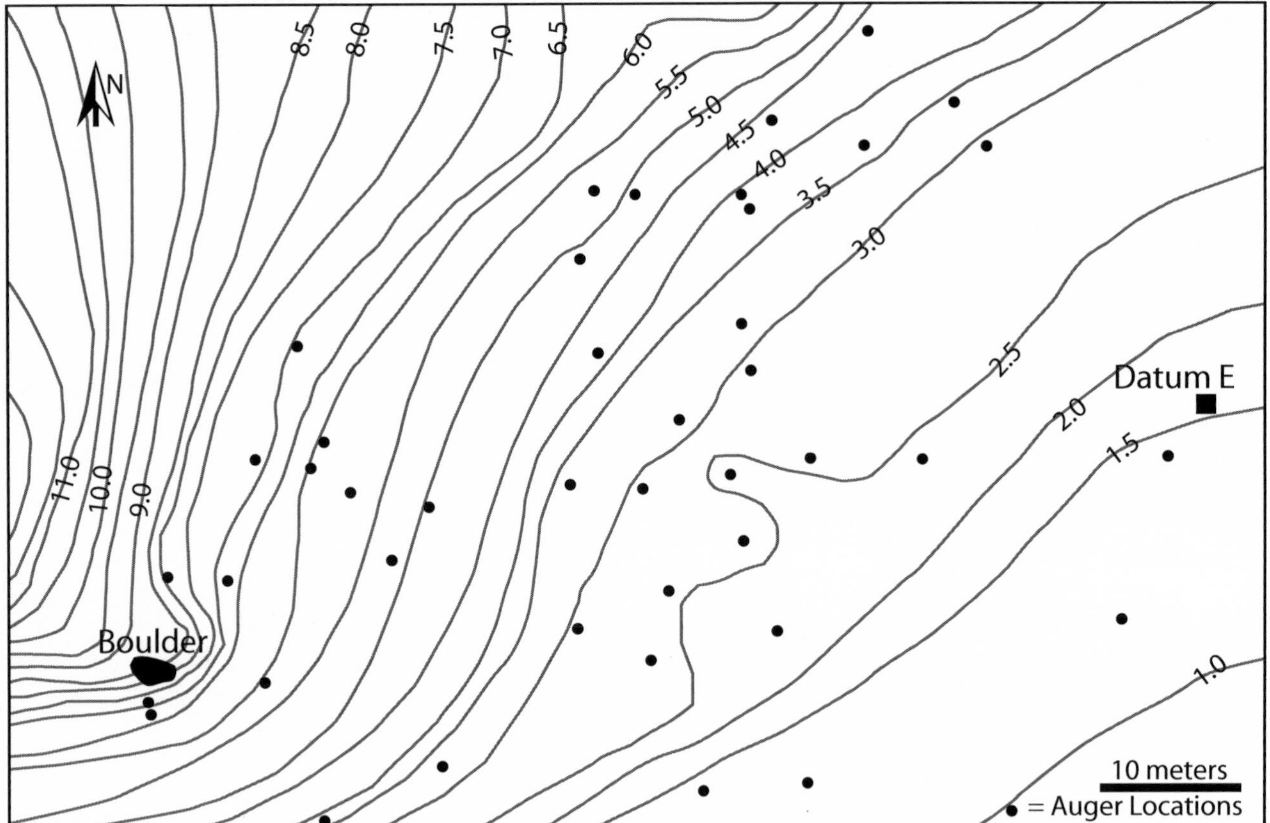

Figure 4.4 A paleotopographic reconstruction of OpD modified from map in Figure 4.1.

grid points for each of these four areas were grouped together and one grid point was selected for each of the four areas using a random number table. That grid point became the northwest corner of a 2 x 1 m unit (Figure 4.1). Four additional 2 x 1 m units were excavated as a trench from the highest point of the ridge to the lowest point of the depression to reveal a continuous stratigraphic profile transecting the ridge. This trench was not oriented to the grid, but it was divided into 2 x 1 m units to offer comparable volumes to the other units. The trench units were labeled using alpha designations to stress the fact that they were not located on the grid. The excavation strategy used at OpD described in Chapter 3 of this volume similar to the methods developed for OpA, especially in the definition and description of a facies (Stein et al. 1992:97-103).

DATING AND ACCUMULATION RATES

Extensive dating work at OpD was conducted during an accumulation rate study by Stein et al. (2003) and a dissertation on shellfish and paleoclimate in the San Juan Islands by Daniels (2009). All dates were obtained using charcoal samples and are reported as 2-sigma calibrated results (Table 4.1). Dates and accumulation rates were used to help interpret stratigraphic sequences.

STRATIGRAPHY OF THE DEPOSITS

During excavation, the shell midden was divided into natural layers called "facies." Each facies was defined by the excavators based on particle size, composition, condition, color and the amount of each particle type (Parr et al., this volume). As excavation progressed, a new facies was defined when one or more of these attributes changed significantly. The ability to see attribute changes is impacted by the size of the excavation unit. In a 2 x 1 m unit, excavators who had worked in OpA had more difficulty in delimiting small changes in percentages of rock, shell, or matrix. They remarked that the overall sizes of facies in the 2 x 1 m units of OpD were larger than most facies in OpA, which were all contiguous 2 x 2 m units.

The facies defined are all arranged in stratigraphic order using a revised form of the Harris Matrix, originated by Edward Harris in 1974 (Harris 1979). During excavation, only the extent of the bottom of the facies was mapped. The top of each facies was later defined by the bottom of the facies above it. By superimposing these maps, a stratigraphic series was constructed. Each facies was represented by a box and drawn above and below the facies nearest to it. Some facies did not extend over the entire 2 x 1 m exposure of the excavation. In this case a box was placed adjacent to the box

Table 4.1 Dates and accumulation rates for OpD calculated from previously published dates

Unit	Sample ID	Material	Facies	Avg. Depth Below Surface	2-sigma calibrated results (BP)	Pairwise Accum. Rate	Accum. Description*	Reference
105 365	105B7	charcoal	1B07	60	1180-1560			Stein et al. 2003
105 365	OS-66976	charcoal	1K02	97.5	1170-1390	-0.41	Rapid	Daniels 2009
105 365	105O1	charcoal	1O01	118	1420-1820	0.06	Medium	Stein et al. 2003
105 365	105T1C	charcoal	1T01	137	1090-1520	-0.06	Rapid	Stein et al. 2003
105 365	OS-66815	charcoal	1U02	151.5	1300-1530	0.14	Rapid	Daniels 2009
111 349	111P1	charcoal	1P01	70.5	1450-1880			Stein et al. 2003
111 349	111W1	charcoal	1W01	74.5	1280-1520	-0.02	Rapid	Stein et al. 2003
111 349	111EE2	charcoal	2E02	107.5	1610-2290	0.06	Medium	Stein et al. 2003
123 347	123A5	charcoal	1A05	56	660-930			Stein et al. 2003
123 347	OS-67018	charcoal	1G01	67	660-710	-0.10	Rapid	Daniels 2009
123 347	123I1	charcoal	1I01	92	1080-1410	0.04	Medium	Stein et al. 2003
130 352	130C1	charcoal	1C01	34	960-1260			Stein et al. 2003
130 352	130H1	charcoal	1H01	82.5	1000-1210	-5.39	Rapid	Stein et al. 2003
130 352	130K1	charcoal	1K01	105	1090-1300	0.25	Medium	Stein et al. 2003
TAB	TABC1	charcoal	1C01	16.5	1270-1540			Stein et al. 2003
TAB	TABD2	charcoal	1D02	68	1190-1520	-0.91	Rapid	Stein et al. 2003
TAB	TAB003	charcoal	003	126.5	1350-1690	0.35	Medium	Stein et al. 2003
TAB	TAB004	charcoal	004	136	1290-1510	-0.08	Rapid	Stein et al. 2003
TAB	TAB007	charcoal	007	165	1540-1860	0.10	Medium	Stein et al. 2003
TCD	TCD002	charcoal	002	55.5	1270-1520	N/A		Stein et al. 2003
TEF	TEF0073	charcoal	002	73	1010-1350			Stein et al. 2003
TEF	TEF0077	charcoal	003	77	1290-1510	-0.02	Rapid	Stein et al. 2003
TGH	TGHB3	charcoal	1B03	32	1560-1880			Stein et al. 2003
TGH	TGH008	charcoal	008	99.5	960-1260	-0.11	Disturbed	Stein et al. 2003
TGH	TGH009	charcoal	009	107	1180-1520	0.03	Medium	Stein et al. 2003

** - Descriptive terms for accumulation rates "rapid" and "medium" are based on categories defined in Stein et al. (2003) for relative rates of San Juan Islands shell midden accumulation.*

representing other facies of the same depth. This is the standard method of building a Harris Matrix.

A convention of the standard Harris Matrix method is to use boxes of the same size to represent layers of unequal thickness or extent. The revision to the Harris Matrix method employed at OpD was to use box size to represent elevational thickness of each facies and its depth below surface. The top of the box for each facies represents the depth at which the facies was first observed. The bottom of each box represents the depth at which the facies was last observed. To construct this revised Harris Matrix, we (Stein and Daniels) examined the stratigraphic profiles, facies maps, and facies descriptions and determined the first and last depth for each facies. In the descriptions below each excavation unit is discussed by including one profile drawing and the revised Harris Matrix.

Unit 107 341

Unit 107 341 was located behind the ridge. Excavators observed a simple stratigraphic sequence characterized by a small pocket of shell and other cultural materials underlain by glacial marine drift (GMD) (Figure 4.5, 4.6). The upper facies 1A01 extended across the whole unit and was approximately 5 cm thick. The second facies 1A02 was also 5 cm thick and extended across the unit, but it contained more large (greater than 3 cm^2) angular rocks. This facies also contained some animal bone and shell. Percentage of shell increased in 1A03 to a depth of about 12 cm below the surface. Facies 1B01 and 1B02 were found in only a 20 cm^2 area in the southeast corner of the unit. They contained shell, charcoal and burned bone. Outside the southeast corner of the unit, the upper facies (1A01 and 1A02) lie directly above facies 1C01, 1C02, and

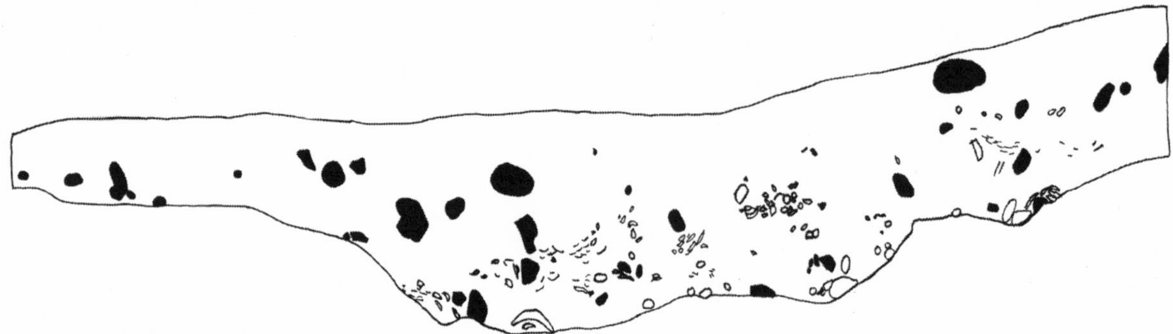

Figure 4.5 Profile drawing of Unit 107 341, east wall. Black objects represent rocks, and individual shells are drawn as seen in profile - accurate in size and orientation. Top line represents the forest surface. Lower line is the base of the excavation. Profile is 2 meters wide. Depth is approximately 40 cm.

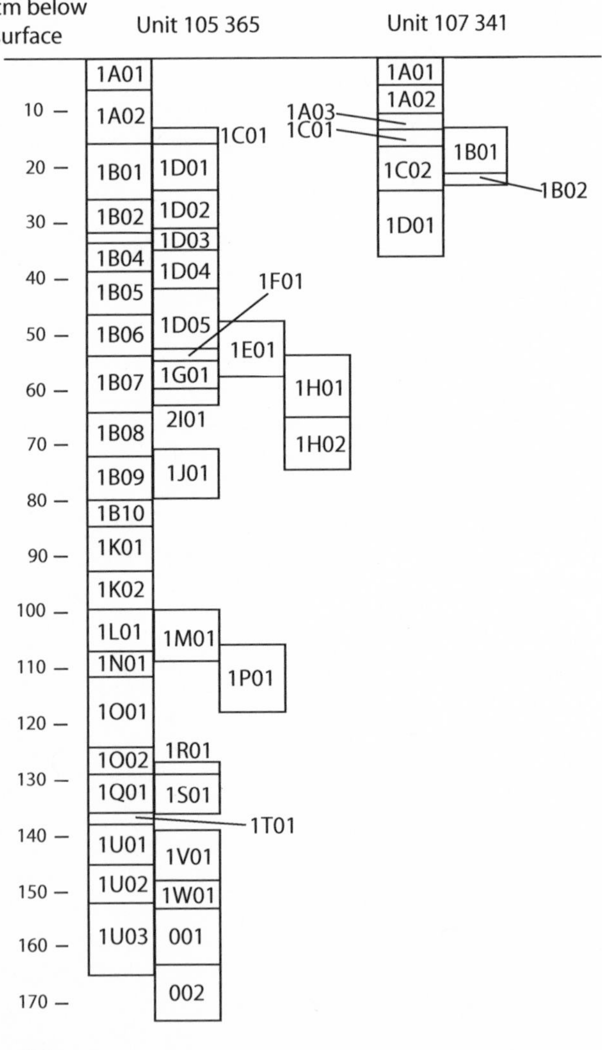

Figure 4.6 Harris matrix for Unit 105 365 and 107 341. These units are not located near each other but are displayed together here to demonstrate the extreme difference in the thickness of the shell midden from location to location. The elevation of the surface can be determined from topographic map. Depths are recorded only from surface, even if those surfaces have vastly different elevations.

Figure 4.7 Excavation at Unit 105 365. Sheets of plywood were needed to keep walls from collapsing. Note person standing up in bottom of the unit indicating a depth of 180 cm below the surface.

1C03, brown facies that did not contain cultural material. The lowest layer in the unit was interpreted as GMD with some areas of pedogenesis.

Unit 105 365

Unit 105 365, located on the top of the ridge in a thick shell midden deposit, had more complex stratigraphy than Unit 107 341 (Figure 4.6, 4.7, 4.8). Most facies in unit 105 365 contained 50-75% shell, most of which was greater than 3 cm^2. Charcoal and burned shell layers were also abundant, and the matrix was black. The complexity of the various shell layers are obvious in the Harris Matrix (Figure 4.8) with the southern part of the unit identified by series 1B01 to 1B10, and the northern part of the unit labeled 1C01 to 1D05 due to darker sediment and less broken shell. At 55 cm below the surface, excavators encountered four different facies at the same depth. They varied in color from black to brown, in amount of shell from 0-50%, and in amount of angular rock. At 80 cm below the surface, the four facies

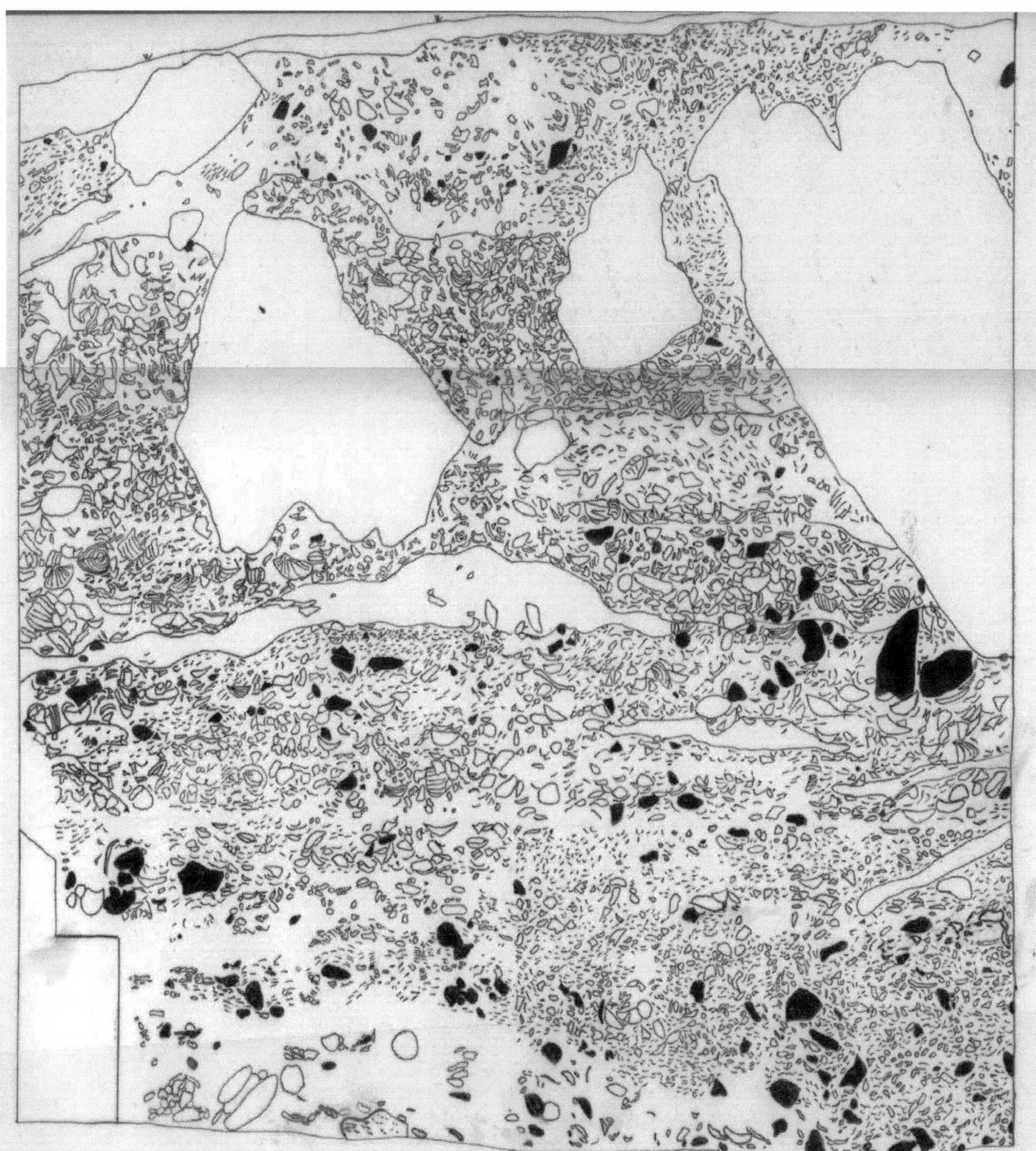

Figure 4.8 Profile drawing of Unit 105 365, west wall. Large areas of white are tree roots. Black areas are large rocks. Shells are drawn as seen in walls with accurate orientations and size. Lines represent boundaries observed in the wall after excavation was complete and most often correlate to facies boundaries.

became more similar to one another, characterized by angular rock and by both large and small barnacles and mussels. Bird bones and deer bones were also present. In the lowest meter of the unit, the stratigraphy was divided into two series of facies. One was represented by 1L01 to 1U03, characterized by black matrix and abundant shell. The other was represented by 1R01 to 0002, characterized by black matrix with much less shell. Variability in shell abundance may be attributable to disturbance caused by a large tree roots (white areas in Figure 4.8) each one appearing from the side of the unit and growing down through the middle of the unit. Excavators noted that these roots were partially decomposed and made excavation difficult.

Dates from Unit 105 365 from the surface to 1.5 m below the surface overlap at approximately 1100-1500 BP suggesting rapid deposition. A slightly older date in facies 1O01 in the middle of the stratigraphic sequence at 1418-1816 BP may be the result of tree root disturbance (Table 4.1).

Figure 4.9 Excavation at Unit 111 349. Note the steeply dipping surface caused by excavation unit's placement on the slope of the shell ridge. Also, the profile behind the excavator seemed to show a break in the layering of shell (on left in this photograph) to a sequence of less layered shell in a darker matrix (on the right).

Unit 111 349

Unit 111 349 was located on the slope of the ridge facing the central depression (Figure 4.9, 4.10, 4.11). The angle of the facies do not follow the angle of the surface. Slumping of ridge deposits in recent years may have accentuated the slope in this area. This unit displayed a wide variety of facies types, some with relatively small total volumes. In most cases, the excavators defined different facies in the northern and southern half of the unit, with a pit feature discovered in the middle of the unit at about 50 cm below the surface. At various times, excavators noted disturbances they tentatively interpreted as pits, edges of house walls, tree roots, and slumping. The unit showed many signs of disturbance either during or after occupation. The nature of the disturbance was difficult to pinpoint because the unit of observation was only a 1 x 2 m window into a larger occupation area.

The facies defining the pit fill in the center of the unit was characterized by 40% shell, much of which was randomly oriented. The color of matrix was brown and contained only 10% angular rock. The excavator found charcoal and organic material described as "burned bark." This facies was called "pit fill" and interpreted as fill in a small depression caused by a tree tip up.

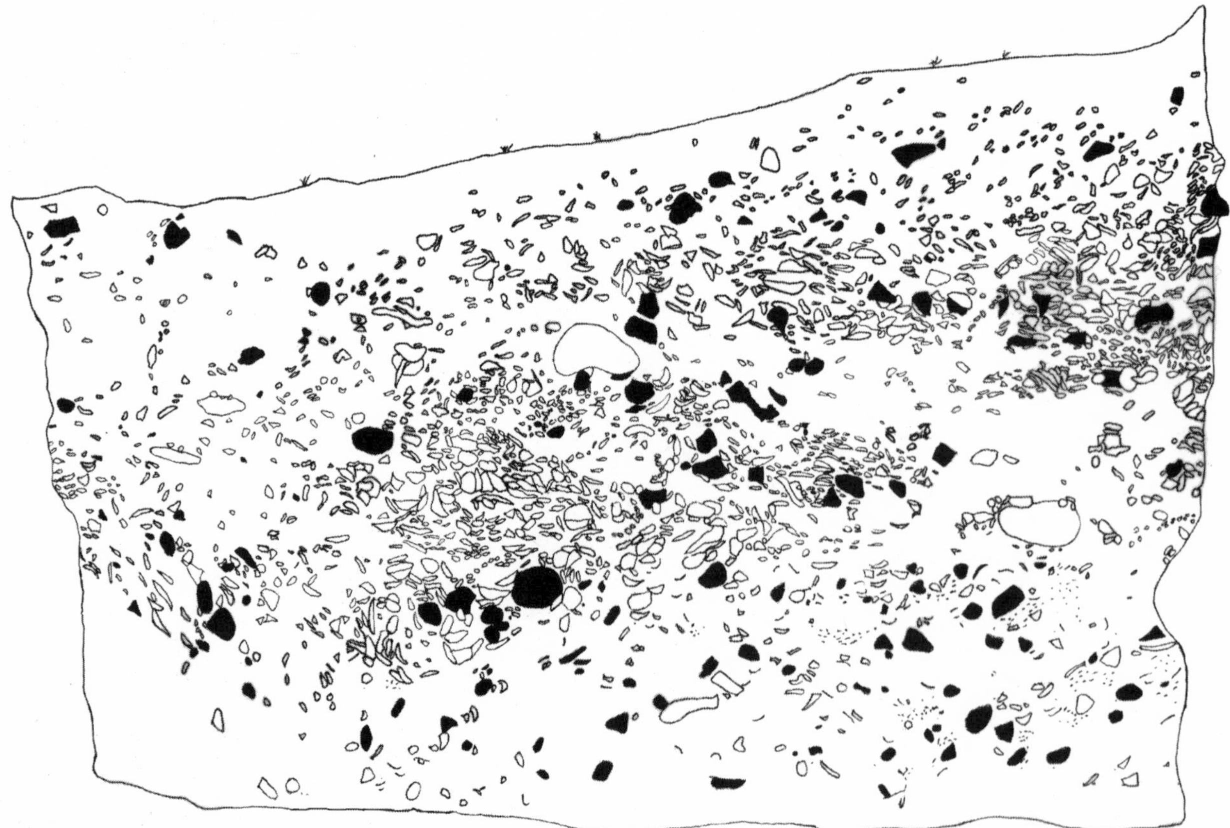

Figure 4.10 Profile drawing of Unit 111 349 east wall.

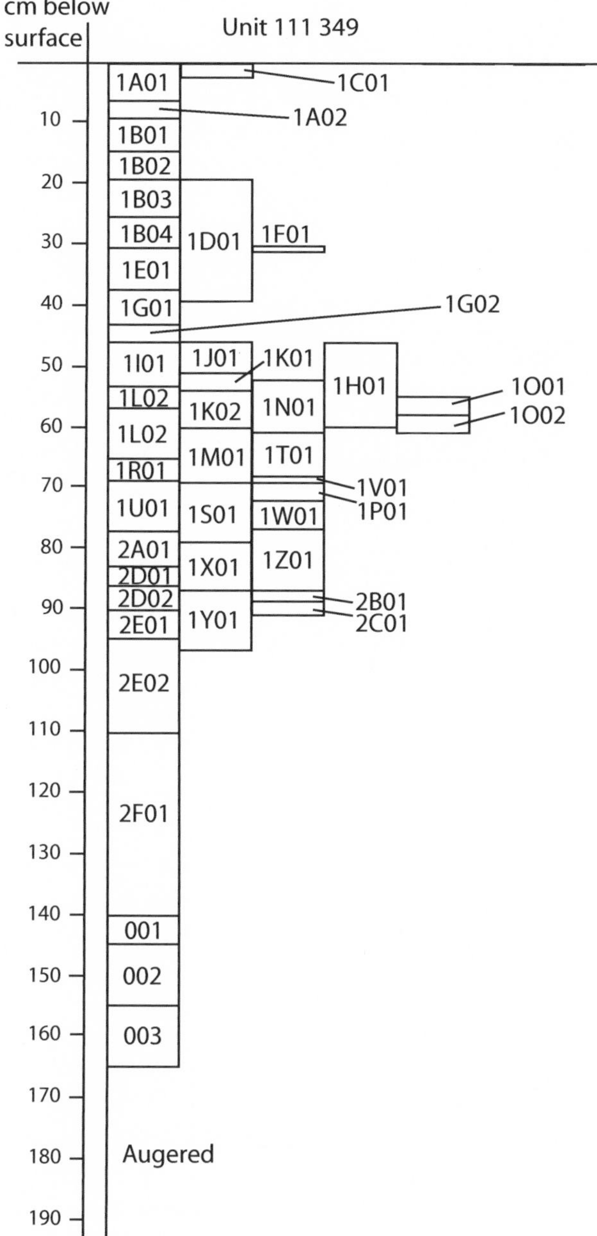

Figure 4.11 Harris matrix for Unit 111 349.

To the north of the pit, excavators found only a few midden facies, including a light colored (tan) facies with 90% shell that was horizontally oriented, abundant burned shell, ash, and almost no angular rock. Below this was a facies of similar midden composition but with brown matrix and minimal evidence of burning. To the south of the pit, excavators observed many facies that were differentiated based on changing abundance of shell and rock, and color of matrix. The facies slanted toward the depression, and shell was also oriented in this direction.

Since Unit 111 349 was at the corner of the depression, excavators expected that they might encounter a house wall where facies representing deposits inside the house would be smaller and more variable, and layers on the outside the house created by dumping of refuse or construction material would be larger and show less variation. Rather than finding evidence of a house wall, excavators found a "pit" in the center of the unit, likely created by a tree growing and later dying and decomposing. The depression left behind may have been filled with midden. This pit obscured the boundary between the two stratigraphic sequences and made it difficult to reconcile facies identified on the north and south side of the unit. Extensions of this pit and the proximity of the tree are clearly visible in Figure 4.9.

Figure 4.12 Excavation at Units 121 347 and 123 347. Note pedestal in center of unit 121 347 created during excavation to protect the wooden stake. Also note the orientation of unit 121 347 with 123 347.

Dates for Unit 111 349 are consistent with a slightly older occupation than surrounding units ranging from approximately 1200-2200 BP. That facies 1W01 (1280-1520 Cal. BP) is slightly younger than overlying facies 1P01 (1448-1879 BP) may indicate either simultaneous deposition or slumping of midden materials from upslope (Table 4.1).

Unit 121 347

Unit 123 347 was selected to investigate the central area of the depression (Figure 4.12, 4.13, 4.14). Within the upper 50 cm, excavators encountered shell midden with black matrix that contained abundant roots, fire-cracked rock and shell. Several historic artifacts were noted. Excavators reached facies 1F in 1990 and found large angular rocks in the northern

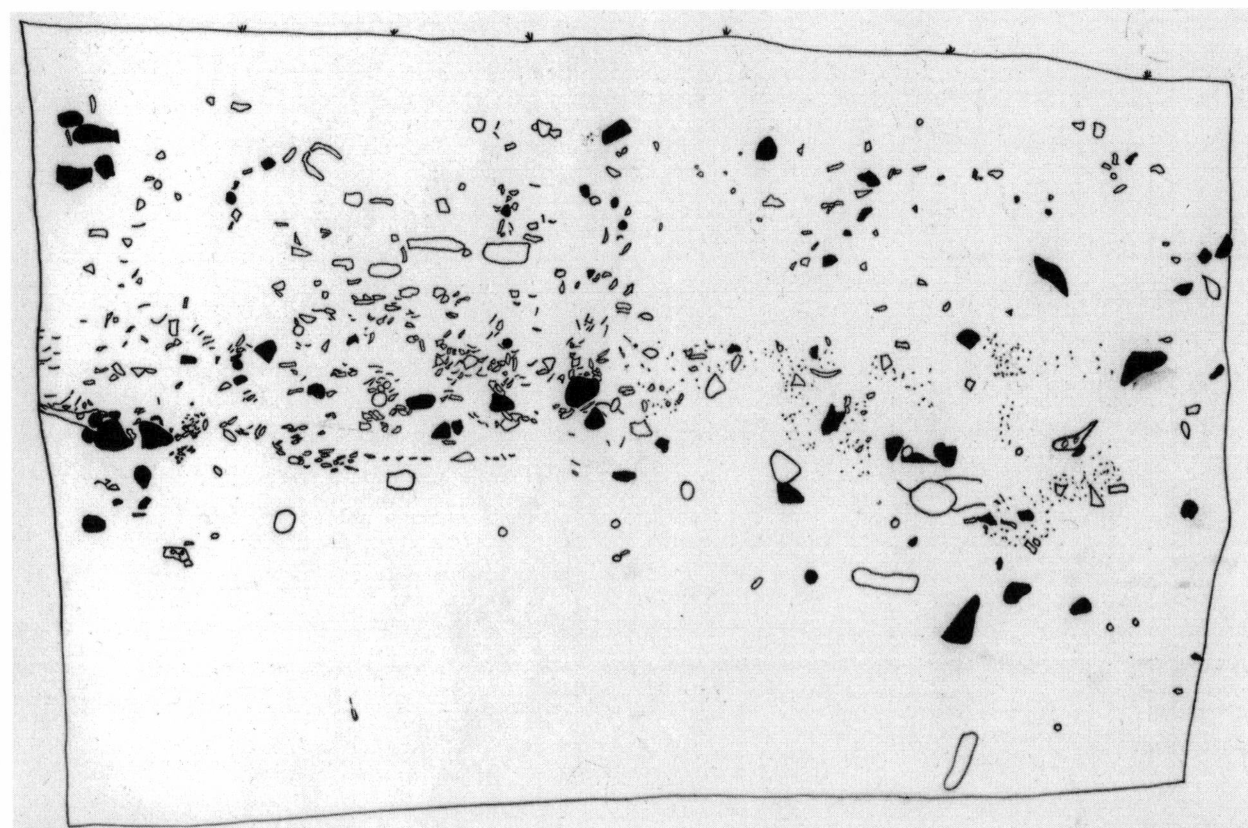

Figure 4.13 Profile drawing of Unit 123 347 east wall.

portion of the unit. As the rocks were removed, charcoal concentrations appeared and were excavated as facies 1G. Below 1G, an additional layer of angular rock marked the outline of a pit containing dark matrix and shell midden materials. Pre-occupation glacial marine drift appeared at approximately 65 cm below the surface in all but the northwest corner of the unit where it appeared at 110 cm below the surface. The midden in the pit facies in the northwest corner was designated 1I01 and 1I02. It was filled with clams, mussels, barnacles, and sea mammal bone. Both the color and contents of this pit differed from other pits at OpD.

Dates for Unit 123 347 are younger than other units at OpD within the upper 70 cm at approximately 650-900 BP. Facies 1I01 at 92 cmbs dates to 1078-1412 BP, consistent with either a medium rate of deposition by a small group of people, or a possible break in occupation over a few hundred years followed by a re-occupation after 1000 BP (Table 4.1).

Unit 121 347

Unit 121 347 was not part of the stratified random sample of units originally selected in 1988. Beginning in the 1990 field season, this unit was excavated for the sole purpose of exposing the rest of the pit discovered in the northwest corner of Unit 123 347 (Figure 4.12, 4.14, 4.15). Excavators encountered in situ historic artifacts in the upper layers of Unit 121 347. In layers 1A and 1B, a rotted wooden post was discovered in a vertical position. Historic occupants of OpD—perhaps British soldiers or a member of the Crook household—had dug a hole and inserted a roughly 10 x 10 cm wooden post approximately 50 cm into the shell midden. The shell midden deposits surrounding the post contained many historic artifacts including a bone knife handle with two nails (Figure 4.16).

In the northern section of the unit, excavators encountered pit deposits continuous with the pit uncovered in Unit 123 347. In facies 1H about 60 cm below the surface, abundant fish vertebrae were found, including six that were fully articulated. These vertebrae were within midden deposits that contained only a few shell fragments and were surrounded by abundant fire modified rock. Similar finds were noted at the Keatley Creek site (Speller et al. 2005). Facies 1H01 of Unit 121 347 is at equivalent depth to facies 1G01 in unit 123 347. No samples from Unit 121 347 were submitted for dating.

Unit 130 352

Unit 130 352 was selected to sample materials deposited in front of the U-shaped depression and activities that took place outside the structure (Figure 4.17, 4.18,

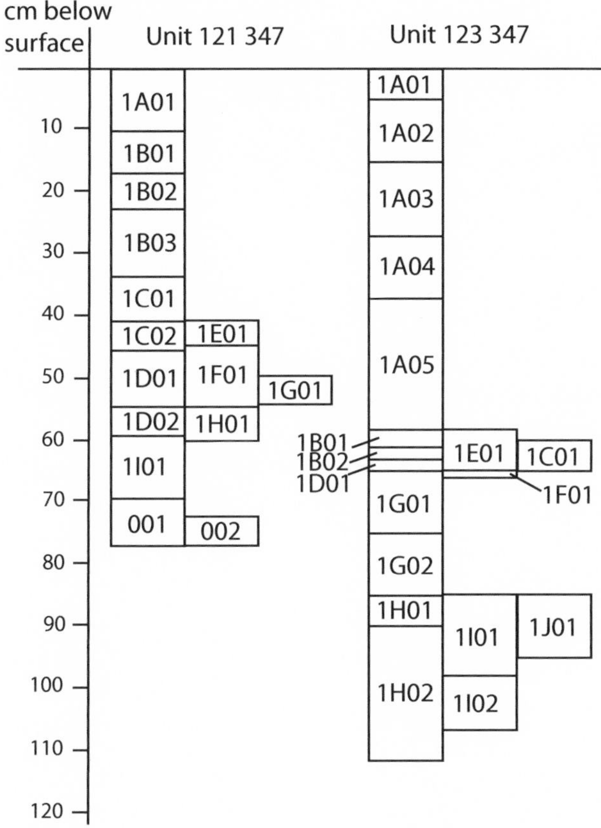

Figure 4.14 Harris matrix for Units 121 347 and 123 347.

4.19). Excavators noted that the matrix in this unit was darker and finer than in units inside the depression, and that shell size was more variable. Historic artifacts were scarce in contrast to the units investigated from the center of the depression. Lower facies in Unit 130 352 were dominated by large, whole shells, especially in lower facies 1H01, 1J01, and 1K01. In the upper 70 cm, shell (primarily broken) was more densely distributed than found in other excavation units. Roots, charcoal, dark matrix, and angular rocks were also more abundant than in other excavation units. Excavators noted large concentrations of whole shells and flaked stone artifacts and cores in situ. Within this unit was a facies with ashy tan matrix containing burned shell.

Dates for Unit 130 352 indicate rapid deposition with overlapping dates at approximately 950-1300 BP taken from samples ranging from 34 to 105 cm below the surface.

The Trench

A trench was excavated from the middle of the ridge to the center of the depressions to expose a continuous profile bisecting the landform (Figure 4.20, 4.21, 4.22). As shown in Figure 4.1, it consists of 4 consecutive units that are each 2 x 1 m (AB, CD, EF, and GH). The trench was excavated in facies defined for each 2 x 1 m unit until the summer of 1991 when excavation

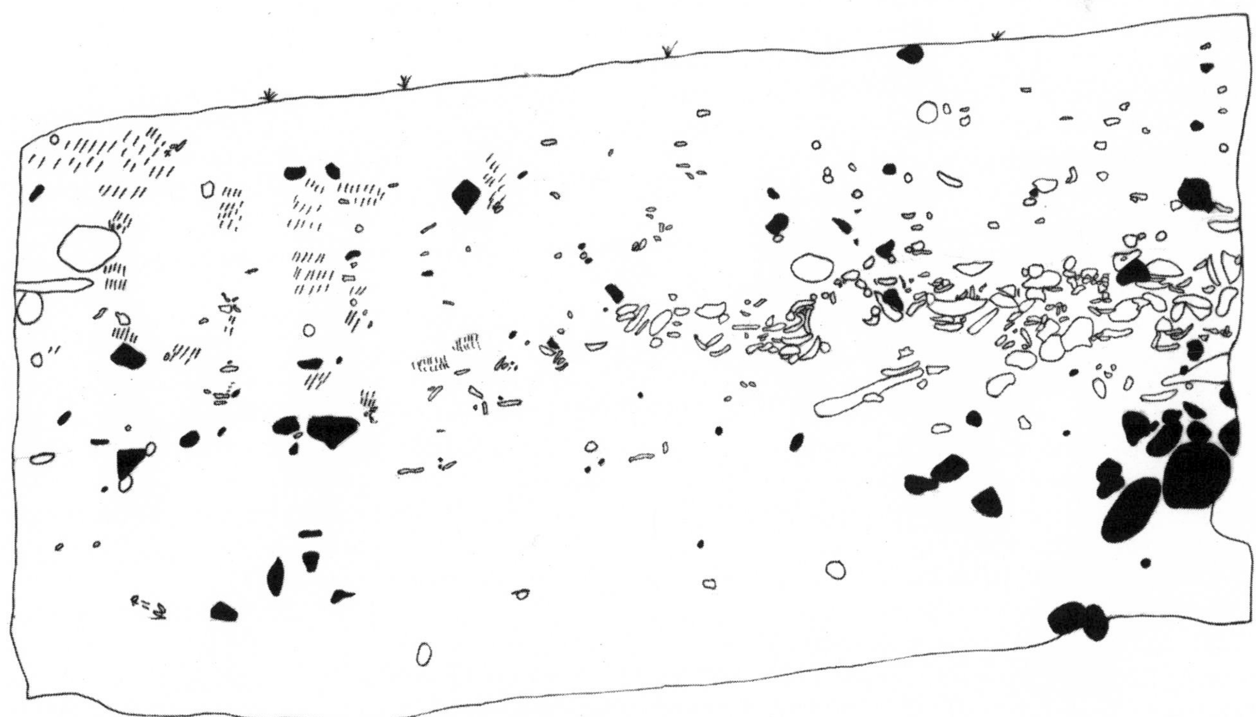

Figure 4.15 Profile drawing of Unit 121 347 south wall.

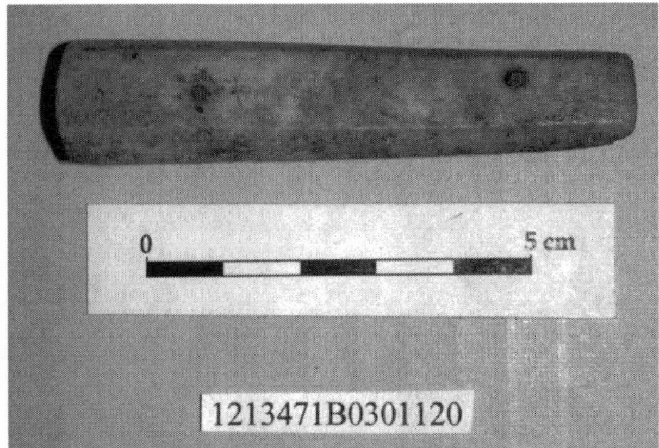

Figure 4.16 Bone knife handle from Unit 121 347.

Figure 4.17 During excavation at Unit 130 352.

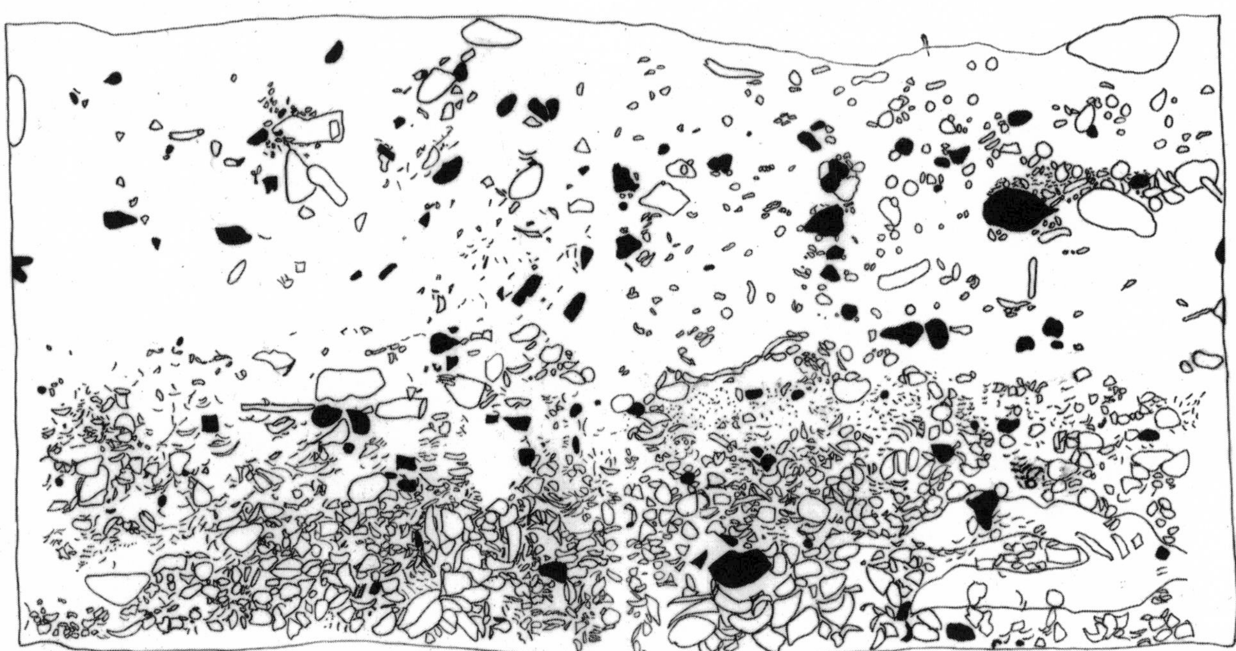

Figure 4.18 Profile drawing of Unit 130 352, west wall.

strategy was shifted to arbitrary levels and screened through quarter-inch screens. Excavators also collected bulk samples.

The stratigraphy observed in the trench was similar to that observed in randomly located 2 x 1 m units. More shell was observed in the ridge than in the center of depression. No post holes or hearths were noted, and pits were the only features observed at the base of the midden facies (Figure 4.23). The pits were filled with midden that had no visible stratigraphic layering, and no artifacts were found concentrated at the base of the pits or within the pit fill. The formation and function of these pits is therefore difficult to identify.

Dates for Trench AB indicate medium to rapid deposition at approximately 1100-1700 BP at 16-136 cm below the surface. An older date at 165 cm below the surface at 1543-1857 BP provides evidence of a slightly older occupation, but the same date of 1558-1878 BP is found in facies 1B03 at 32 cmbs downslope in Trench GH. This date is likely the result of slumping. Dates for Trench EF and lower dates for Trench GH cluster within the 1000-1500 BP range.

CONCLUSIONS

Overall, OpD units accumulated at a medium to rapid rate with most dates clustering at approximately 1200-1500 BP. Inside the depression, dates from the upper levels of 123 347 indicate two occupations later than the 1200 to 1500 primary one. A slightly later occupation occurred at approximately 600-900 BP, as

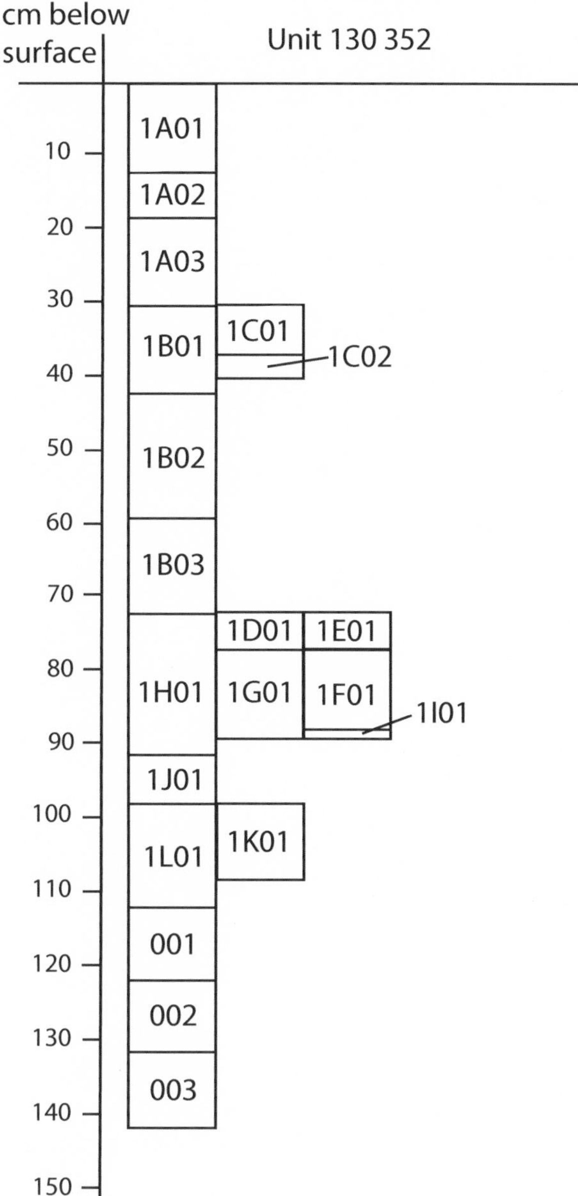

Figure 4.19 Harris matrix for Unit 130 352.

defined by two samples located only approximately 10 cm apart in depth. These two dates result in an accumulation rate of -0.101, suggesting that the shell midden between these two facies accumulated over a short time period, which further suggests either an intensive year-round occupation or a short-term shellfishing activity by a large group of people. One can envision that the obvious topographic shell ridges acted as a beacon for a later group looking for shelter. This group then added deposits of shell, rock, and sediment to the bulk of the ridges and depression, which had been laid down over 600 years earlier. The second occupation is defined by the presence of historic artifacts at and near the surface of the central depression. This suggests that contempo-

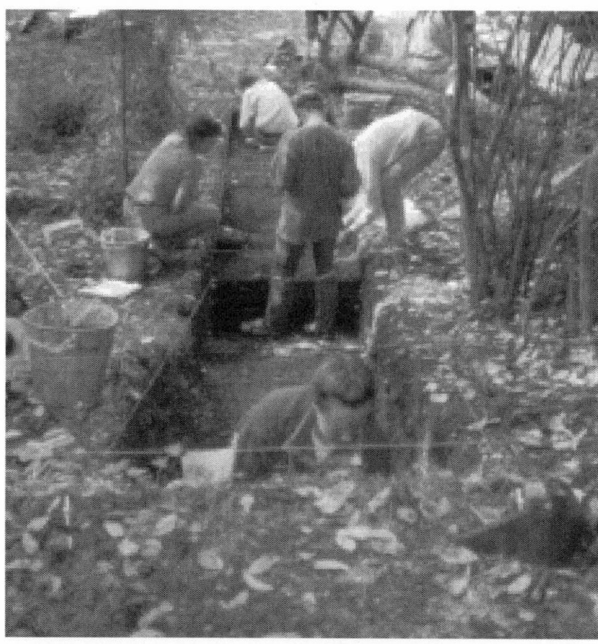

Figure 4.20 Excavations at the trench. Photo taken from top of the shell ridge looking south toward the water. Shell midden was approximately 2 meters thick at the ridge and less than a meter at the center of the depression.

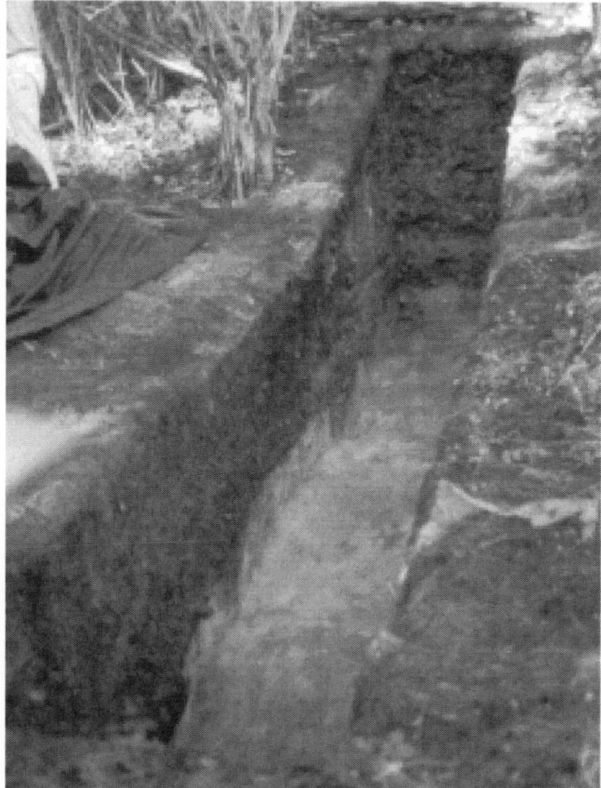

Figure 4.21 Trench stratigraphy as seen at the end of all excavation. Pits intruded into the glacial marine drift are seen in the profile, but in this photo the base of the trench was leveled, eliminating the pit outlines found in the center of the units (see Figure 4.23).

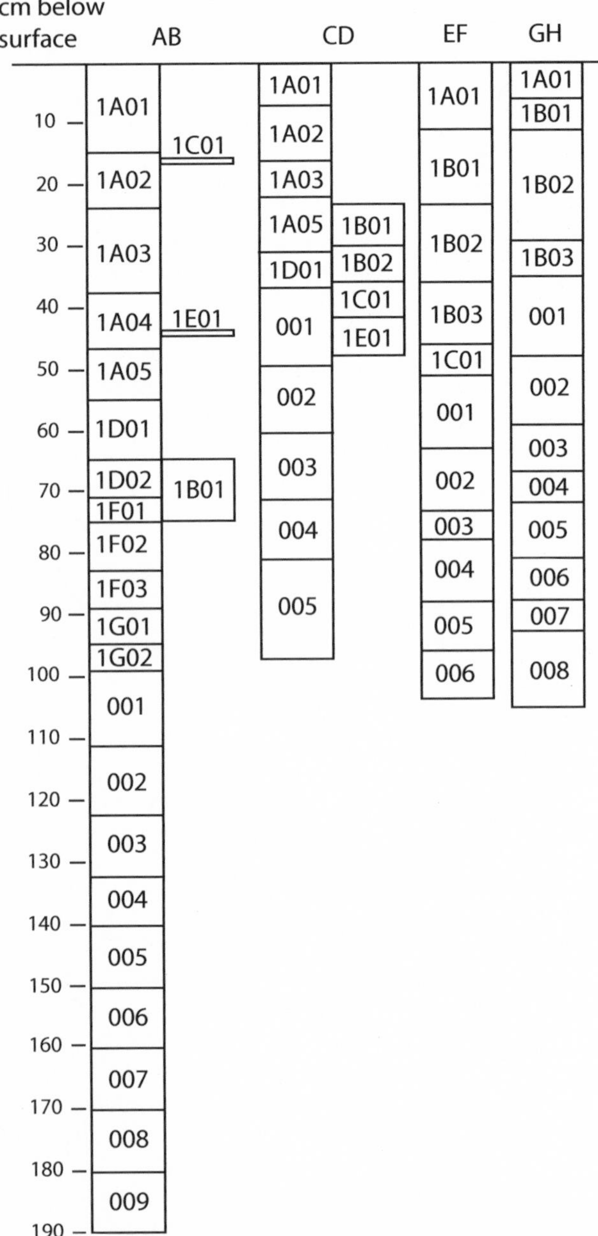

Figure 4.22 Harris matrices for the trench at OpD. Each meter of the trench was given a letter designation, but the units were excavated in 2 x 1 meter units, and therefore referred to as AB, CD, EF, and GH.

rary with or immediately following the British occupation, native peoples were again drawn to the protection offered by the topographic shell ridges.

Dates in lower levels of units 111 349, 105 365, and Trench GH indicate the earliest occupation of the ridge occurred at approximately 1800-2300 BP (Table 4.1). In units 111 349 and 105 365, the earlier dates are from charcoal samples taken at approximately 100 cm below the surface. Accumulation rates for the bottoms of these units are slow relative to accumulation rates for the 1200-1500 occupation. The paucity of dates

Figure 4.23 Pits at the bottom of the trench.

at 1800-2300 BP suggests that a brief occupation by a small number of people occurred at the site. In Trench GH, the earlier date is from 32 cm below the surface and overlying much younger strata, indicating post-depositional disturbance, likely slumping from upslope.

Paleotopographic investigations at OpD demonstrate that prehistoric people modified the landscape to create a horseshoe-shaped ridge on what had previously been a gentle slope. Stratigraphic investigations demonstrate differences in deposits inside and outside the ridge but do not support unequivocally the hypothesis that OpD was a house. The stratigraphy of the midden differs in concentration of shell and color of matrix in various parts of the U-shaped ridge. Behind the ridge almost no shell was found in most deposits. Within the ridge Unit 105 365 contained abundant shell and dark organic-rich matrix, interfingered with thin lenses of tan matrix that contained burned shell. The midden exposed in the center of the ridge contained less shell than within the ridge. Most of the shell was heavily fragmented. In the front of the ridge Unit 130 352 was similar to the ridge in density of shell but differed in color with lighter brown and tan matrix, and an abundance of whole shells. Excavators also noted more lithics and larger stone artifacts in the front of the site.

Features that excavators designated "pits" were found in several units. In Unit 111 349, the feature is likely attributable to post-depositional disturbance caused by tree roots. In Units 123 347 and in the trench, pits at the contact between midden strata and sterile GMD may be the result of human activities; however, the contents of these pits did not differ substantially from overlying midden deposits. The formation processes that created these pits remain uncertain, but mostly is the result of people's activities. No clear evidence of either floor surfaces or post holes were encountered during the excavation of OpD. If the ridge defined the outside of a dwelling, then evidence of compacted surfaces on which people cooked food, walked, and laid down mats should have been found. Other archaeologists in the region have noted floors and posts in shell midden sites (Greir 2001). Given features and stratigraphy described for plank house structures at other other Gulf of Georgia sites, evidence from OpD is not consistent with the construction and maintenance of a house. The contrast between ridge and non-ridge deposits in abundance and fragmentation of shell does, however, indicate intentional construction of an inhabited structure. That structure does not features and stratigraphy observed in plank houses at other Gulf of Georgia shell midden sites.

REFERENCES

Beale, H.

1990 *Relative rise in sea level during the past 5000 years at six salt marshes in northern Puget Sound, Washington.* Report prepared for Washington Department of Ecology, Shorelands and Coastal Zone Management Program, Olympia, WA.

Clague, J. J.

1989 Late Quaternary sea level change and crustal deformation, southwestern British Columbia. *Geological Survey of Canada.* Paper 89-1E: 233-236.

Clague, J. J., and P. T. Bobrowsky

1990 Holocene sea level change and crustal deformation, southwestern British Columbia. *Geological Survey of Canada.* Paper 90-1E: 245-250.

Clague, J. J., and T. S. James

2002 History and isostatic effects of the last ice sheet in southern British Columbia. *Quaternary Science Reviews* 21:71-87.

Clague, J. J., J. R. Jarper, R. J. Hebda, and D. E. Howes

1982 Late Quaternary sea level and crustal movements, coastal British Columbia. *Canadian Journal of Earth Science* 19:597-618.

Daniels, P. S.

2009 *A Gendered Model of Prehistoric Resource Depression: A Case Study on the Northwest Coast of North America.* Unpublished Ph.D. dissertation, Department of Anthropology, University of Washington, Seattle, WA.

Easterbrook, D. J.

1986 Stratigraphy and chronology of Quaternary deposits of the Puget Lowland and Olympic Mountains of Washington and the Cascade Mountains of Washington and Oregon. *Quaternary Science Reviews* 5:145–159.

1969 Pleistocene Chronology of the Puget Lowland and San Juan Islands, Washington. *Geological Society of America Bulletin* 80:2273-2286.

Grier, C.

2001 *The Social Economy of a Prehistoric Northwest Coast Plankhouse.* Unpublished Ph.D. dissertation, Department of Anthropology, Arizona State University, Phoenix.

Harris, E. C.

1979 The Laws of Archaeological Stratigraphy. *World Archaeology* 11:111-117.

Mathews, W. H., J. G. Fyles, and H. W. Nasmith.

1970 Postglacial crustal movements in southwestern British Columbia and adjacent Washington state. *Canadian Journal of Earth Sciences* 7:690-702.

Porter, S. C., and T. W. Swanson

1998 Radiocarbon Age Constraints on Rates of Advance and Retreat of the Puget Lobe of the Cordilleran Ice Sheet during the Last Glaciation. *Quaternary Research* 50:205-213.

Speller, C. F., D. Y. Yang, and B. Hayden

2005 Ancient DNA investigations of prehistoric salmon resource utilization at Keatley Creek, British Columbia, *Canada. Journal of Archaeological Science* 32(9):1378-1389.

Stein, J. K.

1986 Coring Archaeological Sites. *American Antiquity* 51:507-527.

1991 Coring in CRM and Archaeology: A Reminder. *American Antiquity* 56:138-142.

Stein, J. K., K. D. Kornbacher, and J. L. Tyler

1992 British Camp Shell Midden Stratigraphy. In *Deciphering a Shell Midden*, edited by J. K. Stein, pp. 95-134. Academic Press, San Diego.

Stein, J. K., J. N. Deo, and L. S. Phillips

2003 Big Sites—Short Time: Accumulation Rates in Archaeological Sites. *Journal of Archaeological Science* 30:297-316.

Whittaker, F. H., and J. K. Stein

1992 Shell Midden Boundaries in Relation to Past and Present Shorelines. In *Deciphering a Shell Midden*, edited by J. K. Stein, pp. 25-42. Academic Press, San Diego.

5

Sediment Analysis

Julie K. Stein, Debra K.Green,
and Sarah Sherwood

In this chapter, Stein, Green, and Sherwood describe the results of sediment analyses designed to interpret the origin of the shell ridge at OpD. They use grain size analysis, chemical analysis, microartifact analysis, and micromorphology to investigate whether differences in sediment inside and outside the ridge are consistent with differences in activities that take place inside and outside of a house. Their results indicate marked differences on the ridge, in the depression, and in front of the depression.

The primary question explored at OpD revolves around the origin of the shell ridge and the suggestion that the horseshoe-shaped topographic feature was an architectural structure surrounding a house. This chapter presents sediment analyses that assess whether differences in deposits on the ridge, in the depression, and in front of the depression are consistent with differences in activities that take place inside and outside a house. Sediment analyzed includes mineral and organic grains less than 2 mm including substances dissolved in solutions. These sediments were sampled in three ways: 1) as bulk sediment samples taken as 10 x 10 meter blocks from each facies, 2) as subsamples of all material passed through the set of screens (the smallest of which had ⅛" mesh) and 3) as oriented blocks impregnated with resin and cut into thin sections. The bulk samples were used for grain-size and chemical analyses. Subsamples of the entire facies were used for microartifact analysis, and thin sections were used for micromorphology.

GRAIN SIZE AND CHEMICAL METHODS

For grain-size and chemical analyses, bulk samples were chosen from each facies of excavation units located behind the ridge (Unit 107 341), on the ridge (Unit 105 365 and Unit 111 349), in the depression (Unit 123 347), in front of the ridge (Unit 130 352), and from Trench Units TAB (on the ridge) and TGH (in the depression), which resulted in a total of 73 facies sampled.

Grain sizes were measured following the pipette and screening method (Folk 1980). Timed pipette withdrawals determine the grain-size distribution for silt and clay, and nested dry screens for sand. The percentage of organic matter (OM) and carbonate (most likely CaCO3 derived from shell) was measured using the Loss-on-Ignition (LOI) technique (Dean1974; Stein 1984). Samples were burned in a muffle furnace with weight loss measured after one hour at 550°C and again after one hour at 1000°C. The pH was measured in sediment/water slurry using a pH electrode and meter with a digital display.

GRAIN-SIZE RESULTS

Figure 5.1 provides data on the average percentage of sand, silt, and clay for each excavation unit. Sand is the dominant material type found in all of the facies at OpD, ranging from 60-75% in each of the samples. Silt percentages hover around 20% and clay percentages range between 5 and 10%. The source of the sand, silt, and clay is most likely the glacial marine drift underlying the entire landscape of Garrison Bay. This

Chapter opening photo: Wall profile in Unit 105 365.

Table 5.1 Grain size results for each excavation unit

Unit Facies	Grain Size												
	-1 Φ	0 Φ	1 Φ	2 Φ	3 Φ	4 Φ	5 Φ	6 Φ	7 Φ	8 Φ	9 Φ	10 Φ	11 Φ
Behind Ridge													
1073411A01	0.032	0.108	0.14	0.137	0.155	0.102	0.071	0.031	0.036	0.067	0.03	0.014	0.065
1073411B01	0.032	0.122	0.152	0.143	0.147	0.101	0.08	0.053	0.053	0.036	0.049	0.017	0.015
1073411B02	0.05	0.084	0.098	0.116	0.17	0.08	0.102	0.076	0.049	0.036	0.041	0.043	0.054
1073411C01	0.004	0.026	0.149	0.255	0.194	0.106	0.061	0.072	0.046	0.036	0.022	0.018	0.013
1073411D01	0.012	0.057	0.100	0.135	0.236	0.116	0.088	0.062	0.058	0.058	0.036	0.021	0.028
Ridge													
1053651A02	0.000	0.082	0.273	0.211	0.147	0.100	0.087	0.020	0.030	0.021	0.016	0.005	0.008
1053651B09	0.003	0.045	0.212	0.196	0.154	0.083	0.024	0.026	0.075	0.066	0.061	0.041	0.014
1053651D01	0.000	0.040	0.171	0.191	0.102	0.209	0.092	0.094	0.015	0.082	0.020	0.009	0.017
1053651D04	0.003	0.107	0.265	0.209	0.129	0.045	0.024	0.041	0.049	0.041	0.036	0.030	0.020
1053651H01	0.020	0.080	0.097	0.167	0.196	0.134	0.047	0.096	0.048	0.053	0.034	0.018	0.009
1053651J01	0.066	0.153	0.171	0.160	0.175	0.064	0.052	0.032	0.051	0.047	0.013	0.007	0.009
1053651K01	0.076	0.246	0.098	0.108	0.114	0.084	0.021	0.022	0.052	0.066	0.053	0.042	0.017
1053651L01	0.062	0.159	0.123	0.113	0.119	0.073	0.055	0.035	0.066	0.065	0.048	0.080	0.003
1053651O01	0.048	0.159	0.120	0.009	0.201	0.073	0.021	0.030	0.079	0.130	0.045	0.062	0.022
1053651S01	0.038	0.140	0.162	0.146	0.129	0.055	0.095	0.050	0.055	0.056	0.041	0.031	0.004
1053651T01	0.026	0.173	0.176	0.143	0.126	0.090	0.051	0.004	0.063	0.012	0.095	0.025	0.017
1053651U02	0.064	0.257	0.168	0.116	0.093	0.078	0.047	0.041	0.025	0.031	0.028	0.051	0.003
1053651001	0.049	0.161	0.121	0.009	0.204	0.074	0.132	0.061	0.050	0.021	0.046	0.063	0.007
Ridge													
1113491A01	0.003	0.077	0.289	0.188	0.184	0.118	0.031	0.042	0.030	0.014	0.007	0.003	0.012
1113491B02	0.000	0.092	0.239	0.252	0.098	0.058	0.064	0.058	0.034	0.074	0.009	0.018	0.005
1113491B03	0.000	0.087	0.242	0.296	0.155	0.034	0.062	0.025	0.027	0.035	0.027	0.009	0.000
1113491B04	0.000	0.014	0.195	0.176	0.186	0.189	0.087	0.056	0.043	0.022	0.022	0.008	0.003
1113491E01	0.000	0.040	0.171	0.191	0.102	0.209	0.092	0.094	0.015	0.082	0.020	0.009	0.017
1113491G01	0.077	0.228	0.143	0.103	0.089	0.062	0.048	0.033	0.050	0.076	0.046	0.038	0.014
1113491J01	0.060	0.199	0.223	0.283	0.094	0.018	0.001	0.026	0.039	0.023	0.024	0.009	0.002
1113491M01	0.037	0.143	0.145	0.130	0.132	0.102	0.044	0.073	0.060	0.056	0.040	0.022	0.017
1113491W01	0.058	0.177	0.136	0.099	0.069	0.052	0.119	0.077	0.059	0.063	0.042	0.034	0.014
1113492A01	0.050	0.137	0.111	0.140	0.238	0.209	0.050	0.014	0.020	0.006	0.001	0.008	0.016
1113492E01	0.019	0.039	0.062	0.113	0.217	0.260	0.100	0.049	0.053	0.037	0.022	0.017	0.011
1113490002	0.018	0.051	0.069	0.130	0.235	0.205	0.143	0.014	0.038	0.035	0.063	0.014	0.017
Inside Ridge													
1233471A01	0.000	0.087	0.203	0.186	0.171	0.107	0.084	0.027	0.042	0.041	0.026	0.018	0.009
1233471A03	0.003	0.078	0.211	0.165	0.142	0.160	0.044	0.087	0.045	0.033	0.017	0.013	0.003
1233471G01	0.040	0.095	0.111	0.115	0.201	0.242	0.071	0.048	0.033	0.019	0.016	0.001	0.006
1233471H01	0.002	0.017	0.061	0.123	0.221	0.243	0.098	0.075	0.055	0.044	0.026	0.021	0.015
1233471I01	0.018	0.058	0.057	0.077	0.288	0.268	0.116	0.049	0.033	0.005	0.030	0.000	0.000

Table 5.1 Grain size results for each excavation unit (continued)

Unit Facies	Grain Size												
	-1 Φ	0 Φ	1 Φ	2 Φ	3 Φ	4 Φ	5 Φ	6 Φ	7 Φ	8 Φ	9 Φ	10 Φ	11 Φ
Inside Ridge													
1303521A03	0.000	0.041	0.275	0.253	0.187	0.109	0.048	0.031	0.009	0.010	0.003	0.016	0.017
1303521B02	0.000	0.060	0.215	0.239	0.135	0.053	0.025	0.029	0.068	0.074	0.055	0.038	0.009
1303521C01	0.053	0.190	0.194	0.171	0.118	0.090	0.072	0.026	0.041	0.026	0.012	0.005	0.002
1303521G01	0.030	0.162	0.224	0.233	0.170	0.055	0.023	0.032	0.031	0.011	0.006	0.009	0.015
1303521J01	0.000	0.032	0.253	0.216	0.182	0.118	0.007	0.035	0.031	0.054	0.037	0.025	0.011
1303521K01	0.019	0.158	0.171	0.141	0.099	0.058	0.027	0.025	0.040	0.025	0.086	0.025	0.127
1303520001	0.001	0.054	0.198	0.161	0.119	0.071	0.008	0.080	0.080	0.091	0.090	0.005	0.043
1303520002	0.047	0.248	0.243	0.132	0.066	0.031	0.047	0.031	0.040	0.029	0.037	0.029	0.029
Trench-Ridge													
TAB1A01	0.030	0.206	0.119	0.146	0.172	0.125	0.069	0.071	0.025	0.018	0.008	0.008	0.002
TAB1A02	0.047	0.146	0.102	0.123	0.128	0.108	0.065	0.089	0.070	0.069	0.019	0.023	0.012
TAB1A03	0.036	0.122	0.084	0.125	0.198	0.192	0.048	0.068	0.052	0.033	0.015	0.012	0.015
TAB1A04	0.051	0.109	0.099	0.129	0.133	0.201	0.800	0.072	0.050	0.370	0.019	0.011	0.011
TAB1A05	0.037	0.132	0.074	0.102	0.138	0.139	0.105	0.060	0.048	0.067	0.050	0.030	0.018
TAB1B01	0.041	0.175	0.119	0.119	0.122	0.107	0.096	0.035	0.104	0.018	0.038	0.017	0.010
TAB1C01	0.000	0.032	0.130	0.164	0.236	0.189	0.013	0.096	0.028	0.073	0.023	0.014	0.001
TAB1D01	0.035	0.110	0.090	0.133	0.163	0.162	0.106	0.067	0.047	0.045	0.020	0.014	0.008
TAB1D02	0.025	0.122	0.082	0.118	0.157	0.152	0.066	0.099	0.055	0.054	0.036	0.024	0.010
TAB1E01	0.052	0.171	0.119	0.129	0.137	0.111	0.051	0.059	0.075	0.051	0.022	0.017	0.006
TAB1F01	0.040	0.158	0.104	0.131	0.164	0.141	0.048	0.061	0.046	0.047	0.030	0.020	0.009
TAB1F02	0.031	0.140	0.111	0.137	0.147	0.123	0.085	0.055	0.038	0.052	0.044	0.023	0.013
TAB1F03	0.011	0.113	0.063	0.150	0.170	0.158	0.101	0.042	0.076	0.057	0.036	0.017	0.006
TAB1G01	0.029	0.140	0.108	0.119	0.132	0.128	0.068	0.037	0.088	0.060	0.034	0.044	0.012
TAB1G02	0.037	0.126	0.113	0.137	0.168	0.108	0.043	0.115	0.048	0.050	0.031	0.017	0.007
TAB001													
TAB002													
TAB003	0.037	0.165	0.130	0.137	0.142	0.130	0.065	0.042	0.047	0.037	0.042	0.027	0.010
TAB004													
TAB005	0.001	0.074	0.383	0.226	0.059	0.031	0.049	0.045	0.054	0.036	0.021	0.013	0.007
TAB006	0.000	0.027	0.080	0.110	0.189	0.285	0.040	0.103	0.066	0.051	0.020	0.014	0.015
TAB007	0.000	0.044	0.116	0.115	0.178	0.188	0.132	0.074	0.076	0.043	0.012	0.015	0.008
TAB008	0.000	0.019	0.089	0.120	0.171	0.187	0.110	0.072	0.047	0.070	0.050	0.039	0.027
TAB009													
Trench-Inside Ridge													
TGH1B01	0.083	0.186	0.154	0.140	0.146	0.069	0.046	0.037	0.011	0.052	0.041	0.016	0.020
TGH1B02	0.057	0.174	0.142	0.285	0.099	0.061	0.047	0.050	0.038	0.026	0.012	0.007	0.003
TGH1B03	0.023	0.065	0.081	0.064	0.226	0.075	0.029	0.230	0.095	0.077	0.046	0.032	0.016
TGH001	0.035	0.124	0.071	0.098	0.146	0.150	0.090	0.088	0.052	0.063	0.035	0.027	0.022
TGH002	0.018	0.069	0.079	0.134	0.171	0.184	0.121	0.064	0.064	0.048	0.027	0.015	0.007

Table 5.1 Grain size results for each excavation unit (continued)

Unit Facies	Grain Size												
	-1 Φ	0 Φ	1 Φ	2 Φ	3 Φ	4 Φ	5 Φ	6 Φ	7 Φ	8 Φ	9 Φ	10 Φ	11 Φ
Trench-Inside Ridge													
TGH003	0.035	0.167	0.121	0.153	0.199	0.224	0.029	0.031	0.023	0.011	0.004	0.002	0.001
TGH004	0.036	0.091	0.079	0.117	0.151	0.166	0.076	0.090	0.066	0.058	0.037	0.021	0.012
TGH005	0.000	0.029	0.105	0.146	0.241	0.225	0.050	0.066	0.064	0.036	0.018	0.013	0.007
TGH006	0.000	0.310	0.890	0.135	0.182	0.248	0.060	0.127	0.047	0.036	0.026	0.012	0.008
TGH007	0.000	0.047	0.130	0.158	0.208	0.283	0.024	0.090	0.030	0.018	0.003	0.007	0.002
TGH008	0.002	0.017	0.069	0.116	0.189	0.293	0.122	0.081	0.046	0.030	0.018	0.013	0.007
TGH009	0.000	0.031	0.098	0.118	0.173	0.207	0.125	0.036	0.088	0.066	0.024	0.017	0.016

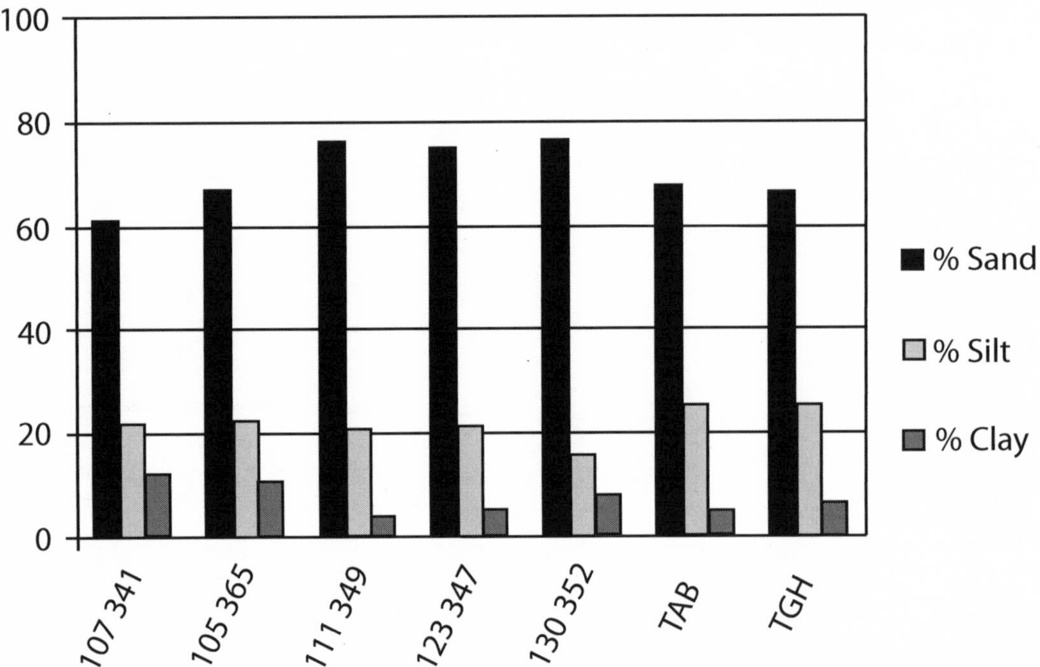

Figure 5.1 Grain size analysis results for each excavation unit at OpD.

material is currently eroding into the bay and is mixed by biological agents in the near-shore intertidal zone. The sediment in the midden most likely was derived from the intertidal area and the underlying substrate.

Data on grain size distributions of all the samples from each excavation unit are provided in Table 5.1. A few general observations of these distributions can be made.

The first observation is that in almost every excavation unit, the location of the modal grain size shifts from coarse sand to fine sand as the depth of the midden increases. Coarse sand (0-1Φ) is the modal size class in samples collected closest to the surface. Fine sand (3-4 Φ) is the modal size class in the deeper facies. This is only a slight shift but it supports an observation seen in the micromorphology that small grains are transported through the porous midden and draped over the larger sized shells and rocks. The same translocation occurs within the small-sized grains, with fine sand, silt and clays moved to the base of the midden.

The second general observation of the grain size distributions is that the samples from the deepest facies have a distribution more closely resembling a bell-shaped curve (although with bimodal peaks). A primary mode is at 4Φ and a secondary mode is in the fine-silt/coarse-clay size (7-8 Φ). This distribution matches that of samples taken from a control profile and reported in Stein (1992b:142). The control samples were taken from a wave cut bank where glacial marine drift was exposed and no shell midden was present. The sam-

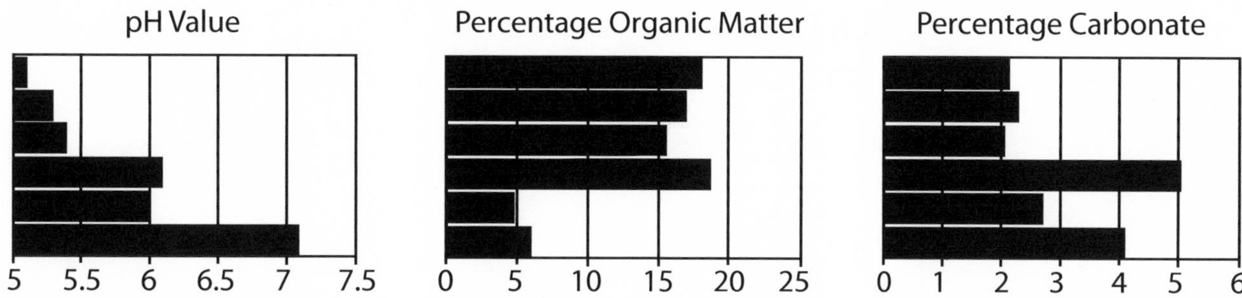

Figure 5.2 Chemical analysis results for Unit 107 341.

ples had the same primary and secondary modes as the samples taken from the deepest facies in OpD. This is likely due to the fact that the deepest facies rest on glacial marine drift, the same drift exposed in the control profile. When people first occupied English Camp, the drift was more likely to be incorporated into the midden.

The source of the fine-grained fraction not only could be derived from the glacial marine drift, but it could also come from the substrate in the intertidal zone. The waters of Garrison Bay do not sort this intertidal substrate because the bay is protected from wind and waves and little reworking of the substrate occurs. The sediment is incorporated into the ridge and depression when people transport it, along with other marine resources particularly shellfish, to the adjacent habitation site. But this intertidal mud is, in turn, derived from the glacial marine drift eroding at the shores. The grain-size distributions are therefore similar, and cannot be used to determine the exact source – other than to say that the fine-grained fraction seems to come from very close by.

A third observation is that most samples have very-poorly-sorted grain-size distributions. Some samples have three or four modes with distributions that are almost flat. The most extreme examples are found in the samples from the shell ridges where porous, whole, shell facies are common. The samples taken from these ridges had very small amounts of sand, silt and clay, often composed of crushed shell, rock fragments, in addition to the mineral fine-fraction. The poorly sorted samples likely results from a combination of the poorly-sorted sediment at the source (as measured in the control profile) and a mechanical weathering of the shell and fire-cracked rock in the midden. The shell ridge has been forested since occupation and roots are found penetrating deeply within the porous midden.

CHEMICAL RESULTS

Three excavation units were sampled for their pH, organic matter, and carbonate. Unit 107 341 (behind the ridge) is significantly different from the other two (Figure 5.2). The pH is acidic, ranging from 5.1 at the surface to 7.1 at the base. The organic matter is highest at the surface at 18% and lowest at the base at 6%. The carbonates are all below 5%, a level not significant given the accuracy of the method. These parameters reflect a naturally occurring forest soil with leaf litter accumulating at the top and acidification of the sediment.

The other two units (Unit 105 365 and 130 352) display values expected of shell middens (Figure 5.3 and 5.4). Both units have alkaline pH, highly variable organic matter percentages, and carbonate values above 30%. In Unit 105 365 the variability is greater than in the other unit. This is a unit from the ridge, which is characterized by more whole shells, vastly different sizes of shell (mostly broken but some containing large numbers of whole shells). The variability of the chemistry in such a midden is expected. One sample from this unit was not measured and is recorded as having zero organic matter and carbonate.

In Unit 130 352 (Figure 5.4) the consistency of the pH, organic matter, and carbonate values is surprising. As stated above, Northwest Coast shell middens chemical values are usually variable (see Stein 1992a for data from OpA). The consistency may relate to the location of this unit in front of the ridge where exposure to rain beyond a forest canopy might have smoothed over variations in the midden. Percolating water with consistent sizes of shell and amounts of matrix would produce such a chemical profile.

Unlike OpA, where the values of carbonates in this fine-grained fraction decreased significantly with depth because of groundwater effects (Stein 1992a), OpD does not seem to be affected by this phenomenon. Because the OpD shell midden is on a landscape higher than the water table, it does not exhibit the light and dark coloring apparent at OpA. In torrential rains water must flow down the hill behind the midden and through the midden on its path to the shoreline, but the effects are not visible in the stratigraphy. Perhaps there was not enough rainfall in one period to saturate the forest litter, the hill, and produce runoff sufficient to flow beneath the midden.

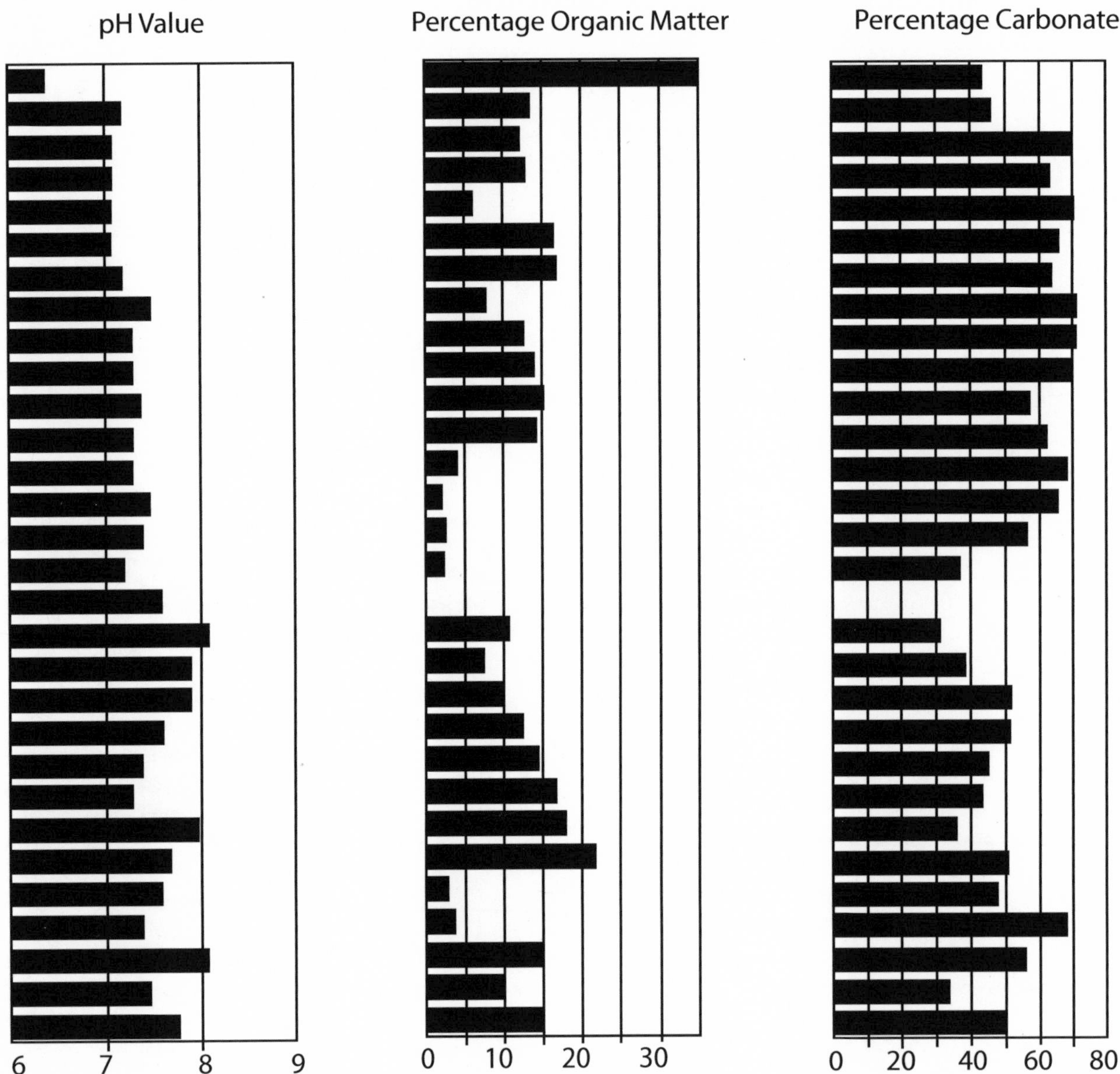

Figure 5.3 Chemical analysis results for Unit 105 365.

MICROARTIFACT METHODS & RESULTS

Microartifact analysis focuses on sand-sized particles recovered from archaeological sediments to determine patterns of behavior across a site or feature (Fladmark 1982; Hull 1987; Metcalf and Heath 1990; McKellar 1983; Rosen 1989, 1991, 1993; Simms and Heath 1990; Sherwood et al. 1995; Stein and Teltser 1989). Because the size distribution of sediments reflect the ways in which they enter the archaeological record (Stein and Teltser 1989), it is possible to understand the nature of prehistoric activities by examining the tiny artifacts (microartifacts) in those sediments.

Microartifacts are defined as artifacts less than 2 mm in size. Due to the nature of their size, micro-artifacts are less likely to be removed by post-depositional processes than their larger counterparts. Thus processes such as cleaning, sweeping, or reuse will systemically remove macroartifacts, while leaving the microartifacts in the original depositional or primary refuse context (Schiffer 1987; McKellar 1983). Microartifacts are, however, susceptible to water and wind transport, therefore their value in archaeological analyses has been in areas that afford protection from these types of geological processes.

Dunnell and Stein (1989) stress the importance of comparing different size classes of artifacts. They argue that microartifact data provides different information from macroartifact data. Microartifacts "are

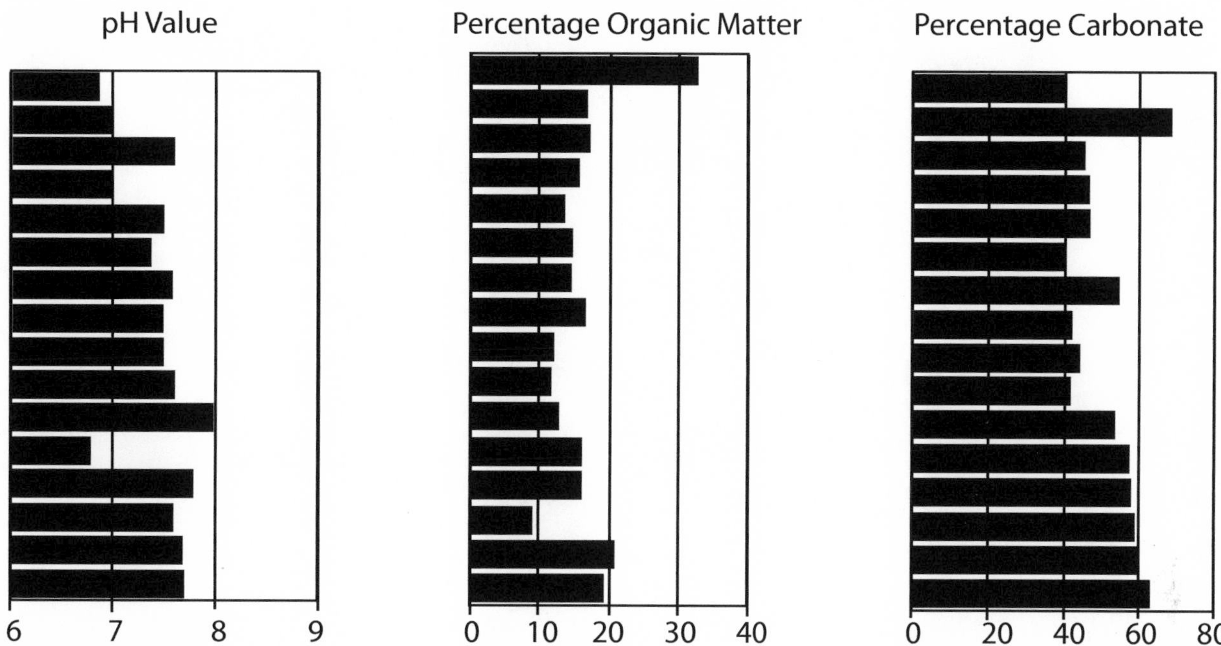

Figure 5.4 Chemical analysis results for Unit 130 352.

transported differently, by different agents of different competencies" (1989:37). Furthermore, when interpreting cultural site formation processes, micro- and macroartifact distributions should be examined together. This does not imply, however, that microartifact data should be supplementary data to the information obtained from macroartifacts. Microartifacts provide a different set of archaeological data, only the microartifacts are discussed in this chapter.

Microartifacts are counted and quantified as a percentage of the sand fraction caught on a geological screen. Phi sizes (1Φ intervals) –1Φ to 4Φ were selected for microartifact analysis based on the boundaries set by Dunnell and Stein (1989). Microartifacts were quantified for each sand-size fraction using the point-counting method discussed by Stein and Teltser (1992). In this analysis, five compositional types were identified and consist of shell, charcoal, bone, lithic, and "other". The arbitrary category of "other" represents the remaining material (e.g., unmodified rock, plant, etc.) found at the site. For the microartifact analysis five facies were sampled from Units 107 341 and 123 347, eight from Unit 130 352, twelve facies from Units 105 365, 111 349 and Trench GH and twenty facies from Trench AB.

Unit 107 341 (Behind Ridge)

Facies 1A01, 1B01, 1B02, 1C01, 1D01 have similar distributions. Each facies contains low percentages of bone, lithic, and shell material for all phi fractions. There is more charcoal in the smallest sand fractions (2Φ – 4Φ) compared to the other compositional types, with the exception of unmodified "other" category. This is not surprising, since charcoal is easily crushed and thus is more susceptible to post-depostional processes. "Other" constituted the highest percentage of any material and is unmodified rock, with quartz comprising most of the rock material (Figure 5.5).

Unit 105 365 (Ridge)

In Unit 105 365 shell is the most abundant material type. The percentage of shell is highest in the larger sand fraction and decreases in abundance in fine sand. Shell is more difficult to crush than bone and charcoal, and the presence of significant whole shell nearby provides ample material as sources for the smaller sand-sized shell. Bone and lithic materials constitute the lowest percentages of material in this excavation unit.

Facies 1A02, 1D04, and 1U02 have the lowest percentages of charcoal in the ridge, with Facies 1U02 having the highest abundance of charcoal at the 4 Φ interval. In the other facies charcoal abundance varies significantly All of the facies have a similar pattern, with the amount of charcoal increasing to the 2Φ fraction and gradually declining to the 4Φ interval. These differences are most likely separate depositional events representing people dumping material with more or less charcoal (Figure 5.6).

Unit 111 349 (Ridge)

For most facies in Unit 111 349, shell and "other" represent the highest proportion of material types in all fractions. Similar to Unit 105 365, shell is most abundant between –1Φ to 1Φ, but decreases in abundance from 2Φ to 4Φ, while unmodified rock comprises the

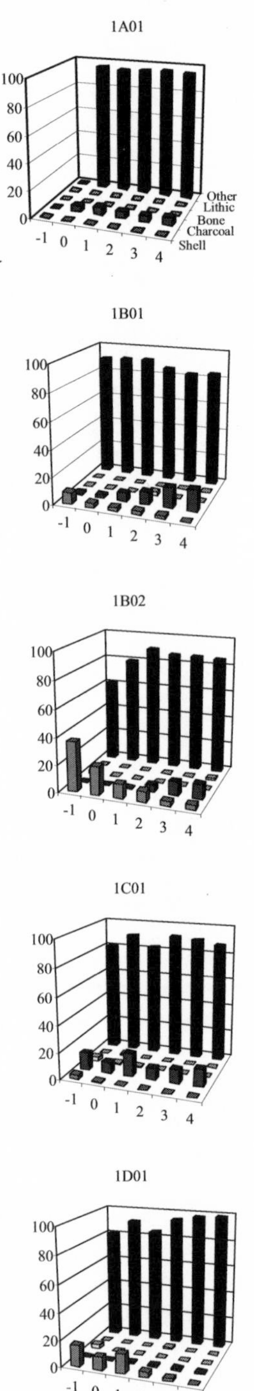

Figure 5.5 Microartifact Distributions for Unit 107 341 Behind Ridge. The facies are in stratigraphic order, starting with the top left corner. Facies 1A01 is the topmost facies, while Facies 1D01 is the bottommost in the unit. The vertical axis represents the percentage of compositional types for each size fraction. The horizontal axis indicates phi classes.

highest in the 2Φ to 4Φ fractions. Charcoal represents the third most abundant artifact type and dominates the 1Φ to 3Φ intervals. Unit 111 349 also contained low densities of both bone and lithics microartifacts. An odd exception is Facies 1A01, 1B01, and 1B04, which contain the highest percentage of lithics in the ridge (Figure 5.7).

Unit 123 347 (Inside Depression)

Overall, there are fewer microartifacts inside the depression (as seen in Unit 123 347) than in the ridge. Shell is less abundant in the depression, while charcoal, bone, lithics, and unmodified rock are greater in abundance, particularly at the smallest phi fraction. Unmodified rock, mainly quartz dominates the facies from inside the depression. In Facies 1G01 and 1H01, charcoal dominates at the 3Φ and 4Φ fractions and exhibits a continuous grain size distribution. Bone consists of up to 8% inside the depression, in contrast to less than 5% in the ridge.

One explanation for this distribution of microartifacts is that the area inside the depression was a loci for subsistence activities and was periodically cleared of the larger materials, leaving behind micro-refuse. Greater percentages of charcoal, bone, and lithics (compared to shell) in the smaller phi fractions inside the depression suggest such removal of large sized objects relative to microartifacts (Figure 5.8).

Unit 130 352 (Front of ridge)

The pattern of shell in Unit 130 352 is similar to the ridge deposits, but different from inside the ridge. There is a higher percentage of shell in the -1 to 1Φ fractions, but shell represents less of the total percentage among the compositional types. Charcoal is more abundant in the 3Φ and 4Φ fractions compared to the charcoal distributions from the depression. Bone constitutes nearly 9% of the material in the phi fractions and has a distribution similar to those from inside the ridge. Lithics comprise a very small percentage of the overall material from in front of the ridge, but Facies 1J01 contains the highest percentage of lithics at the 2Φ interval.

Because of the location of Unit 130 352 in front of the depression and closest to the shoreline, one might expect it to have the most differences in the amounts of various sized microartifacts. But like the grain-size analysis, the microartifacts types are distributed in a very similar way from facies to facies. The excavation unit was placed at a point in the midden where the facies are similar from top to bottom and different from the unit in the depression where there is less shell and lithics, and more charcoal and bone. This obviously suggests that the activities that occurred there included a lack of sweeping as compared to the area inside the depression (Figure 5.9).

Trench AB

The microartifact data for Trench AB represents a

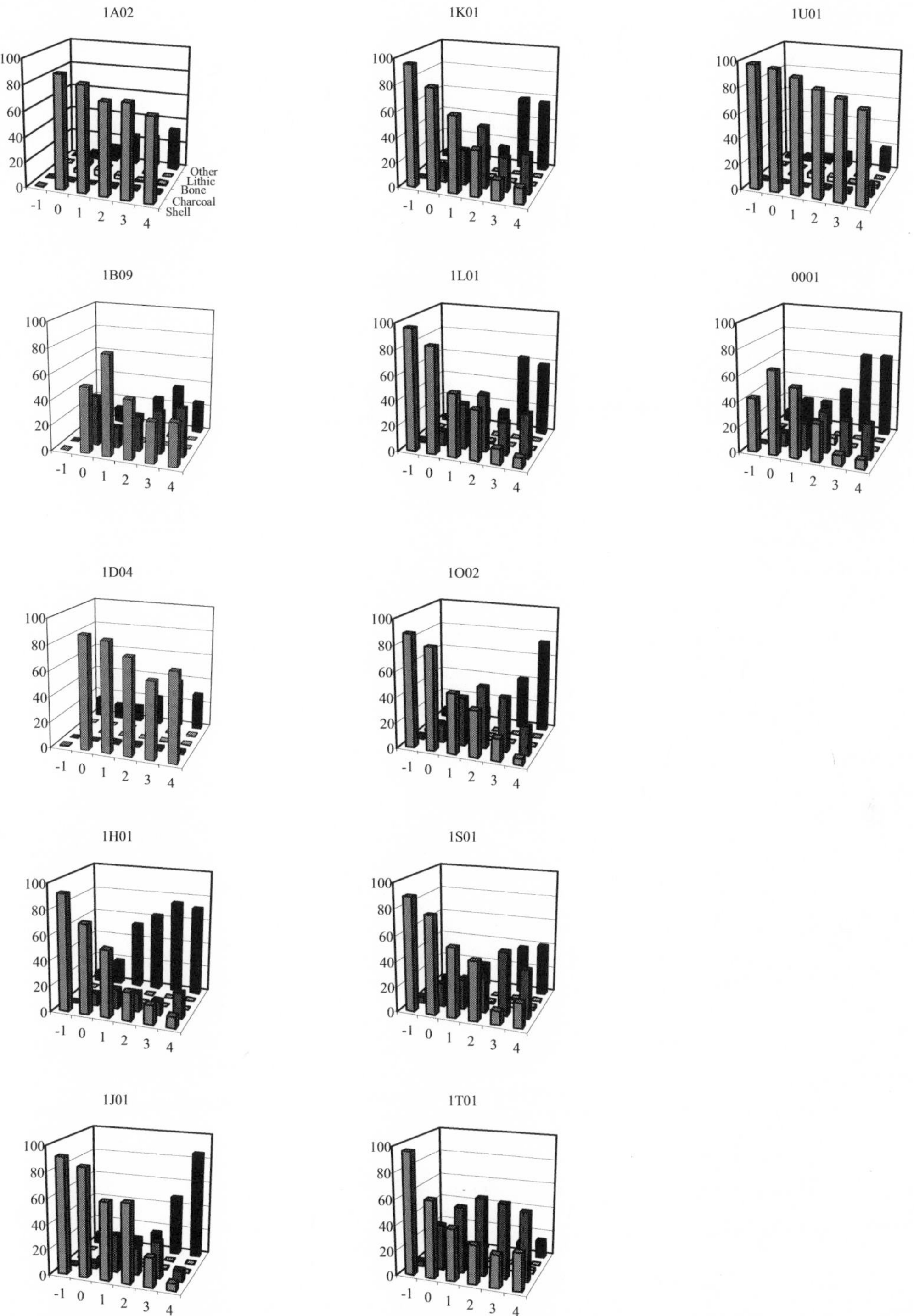

Figure 5.6 Microartifact Distributions for Unit 105 365 Ridge. The facies are in stratigraphic order, starting with the top left corner. Facies 1A02 is the topmost facies, while Facies 0001 is the bottommost in the unit. See Figure 5.5 for further explanation.

unit excavated into the ridge. There is a higher percentage of shell at 0Φ and 1Φ. Charcoal dominates the finer sand fractions, with a bimodal distribution created by the increase at both 1Φ and 3Φ intervals. Lithics reach some of their lowest levels for the whole site in Trench AB, with the exception of Facies 0004 containing an unusually high percentage of lithic material in the smallest sand fractions (most likely caused by human error). Unlike the lithics, there is more bone in this portion of the ridge compared to the other areas in ridge.

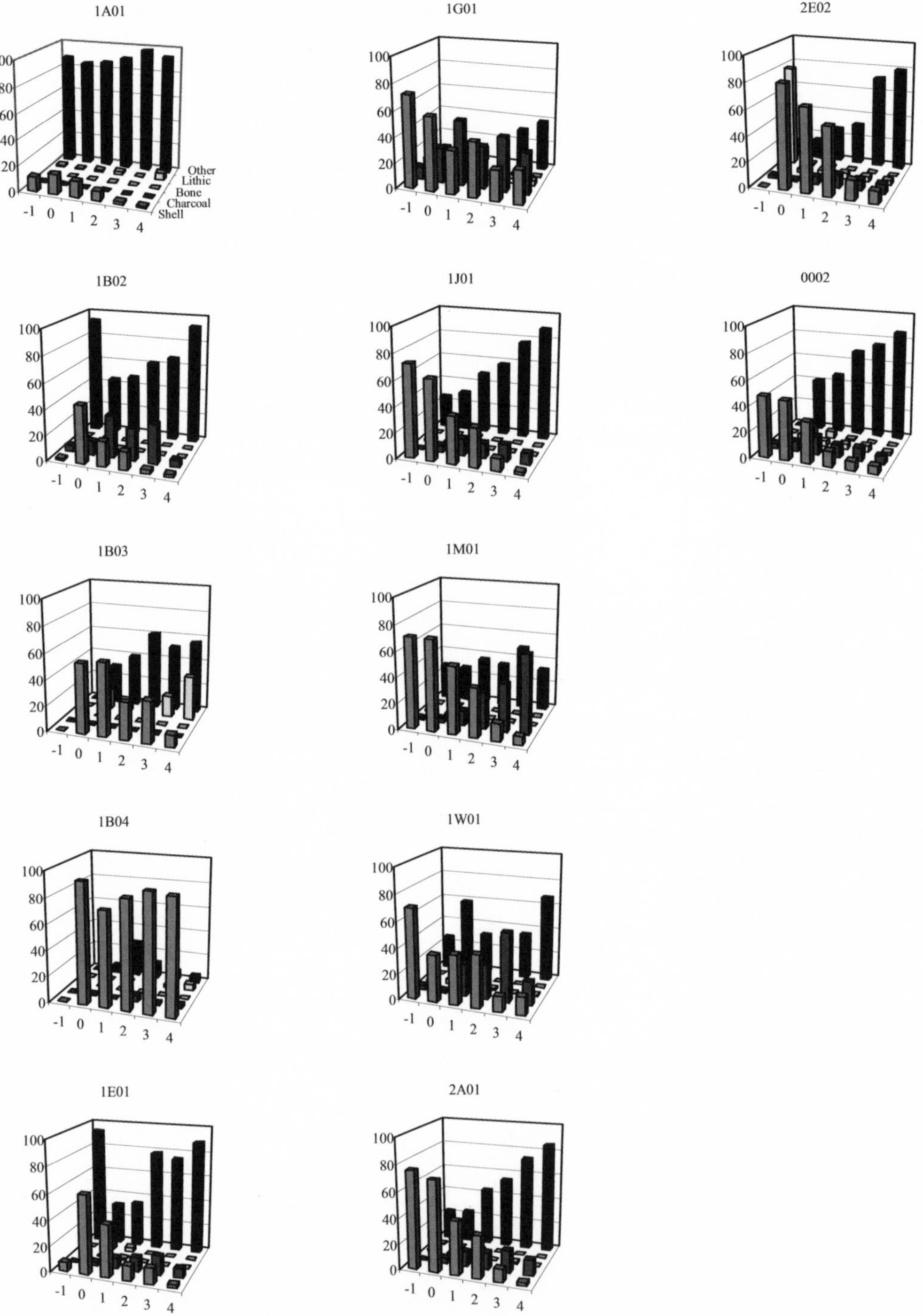

Figure 5.7 Microartifact Distributions for Unit 111 349 Ridge. The facies are in stratigraphic order, starting with the top left corner. Facies 1A01 is the topmost facies, while Facies 0002 is the bottommost in the unit. See Figure 5.5 for further explanation.

The charcoal and charred shell suggests that the northeastern side of the ridge may have been the place where old hearth refuse was discarded (Figure 5.10).

Trench GH

Despite the fact that both Trench GH and Unit 123 347 were located inside the depression, their microartifact assemblages were strikingly different. Trench GH microartifacts were more similar to the microartifacts from Unit 130 352 (Front of the ridge). The shell is characteristic of shell grain-size distributions of the whole site, with the highest percentage in the 0Φ to 1Φ intervals. In contrast to Unit 123 347, Trench GH has more shell and discontinuous distributions of charcoal, and it has the highest percentage of bone at the

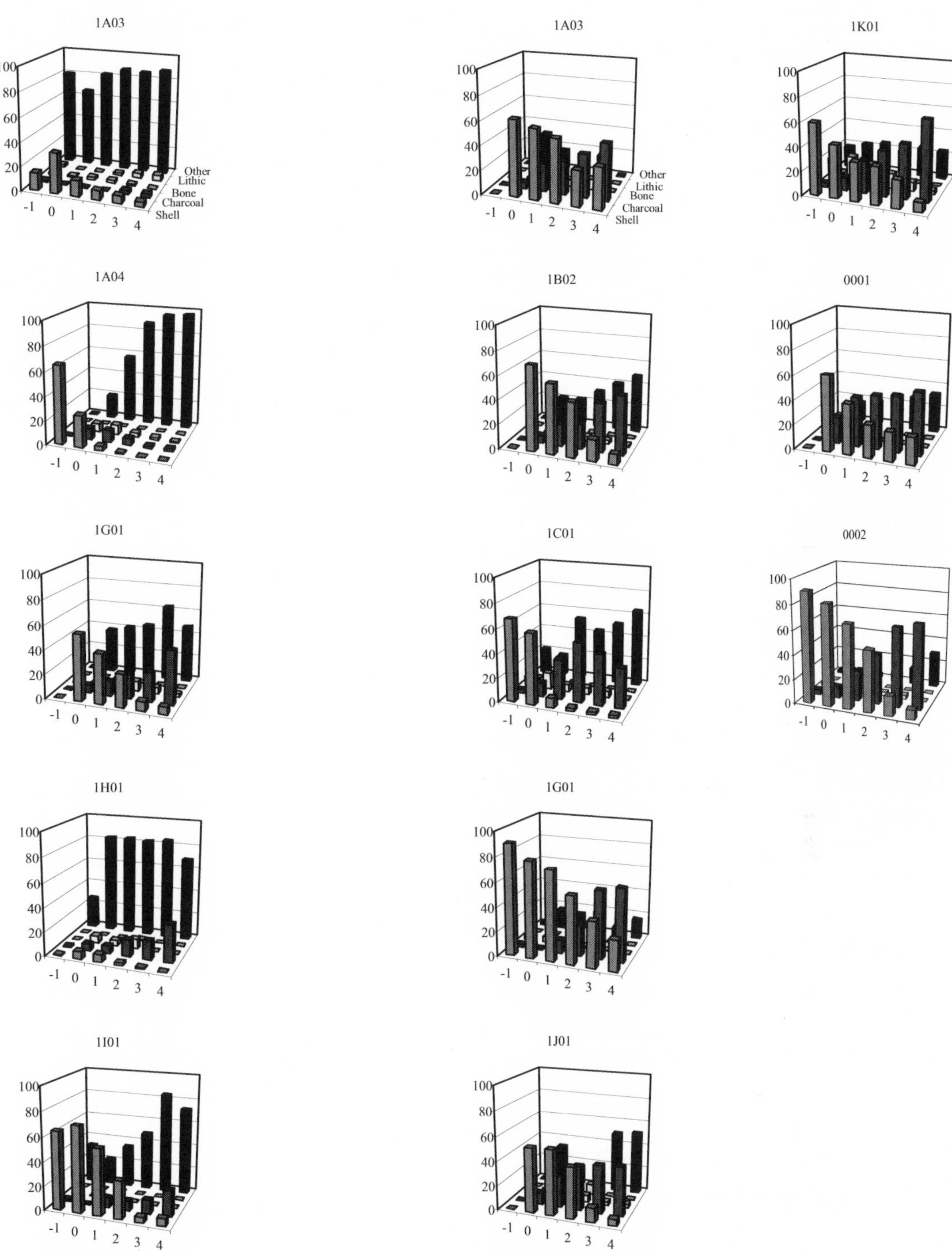

Figure 5.8 Microartifact Distributions for Unit 123 347 Ridge. The facies are in stratigraphic order, starting with the top left corner. Facies 1A03 is the topmost facies, while Facies 1I01 is the bottommost in the unit. See Figure 5.5 for further explanation.

Figure 5.9 Microartifact Distributions for Unit 130 352 Front of Ridge. The facies are in stratigraphic order, starting with the top left corner. Facies 1A03 is the topmost facies, while Facies 0002 is the bottommost in the unit. See Figure 5.5 for further explanation.

entire site. Bone in Facies 0001 comprises 23% of the material in the 2Φ fraction, while constituting 16.2% in the 3Φ fraction.

Trench GH also contains significant amounts of charcoal and the shell from many of the facies appeared to be burned. Taken with the data from Trench AB this may indicate an area of hearth use and cleaning (Figure 5.11).

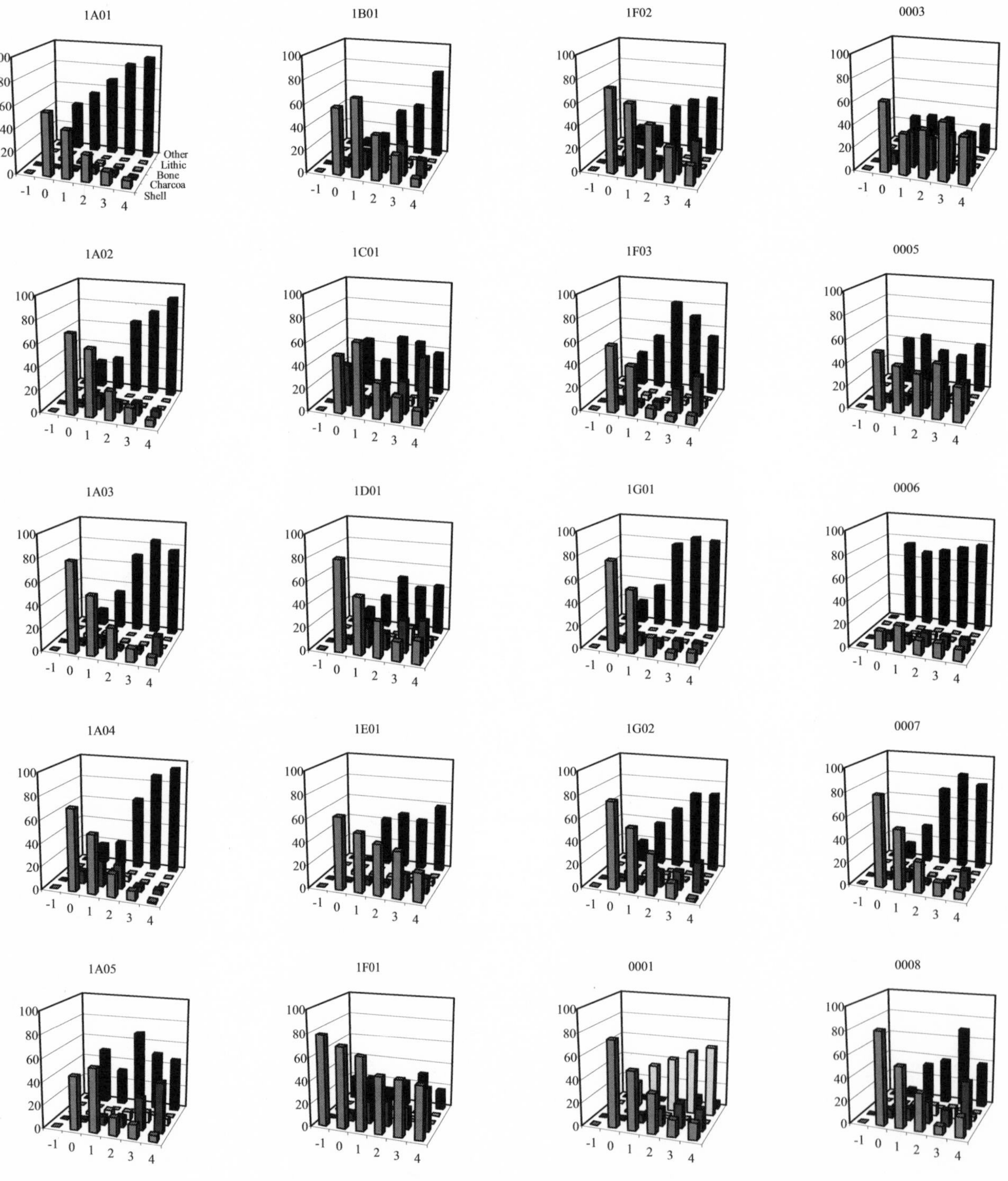

Figure 5.10 Microartifact Distributions for Unit 130 352 Front of Ridge. The facies are in stratigraphic order, starting with the top left corner. Facies 1A03 is the topmost facies, while Facies 0002 is the bottommost in the unit. See Figure 5.5 for further explanation.

MICROMORPHOLOGY METHODS & RESULTS

Micromorphology involves the petrographic analysis of in situ sediments that have been impregnated with resin, mounted onto a glass slide, and then-ground into thin sections (Fitzpatrick 1993; Bullock et al. 1985) This technique was used at OpD to identity microstratigraphy and to search for any mi-

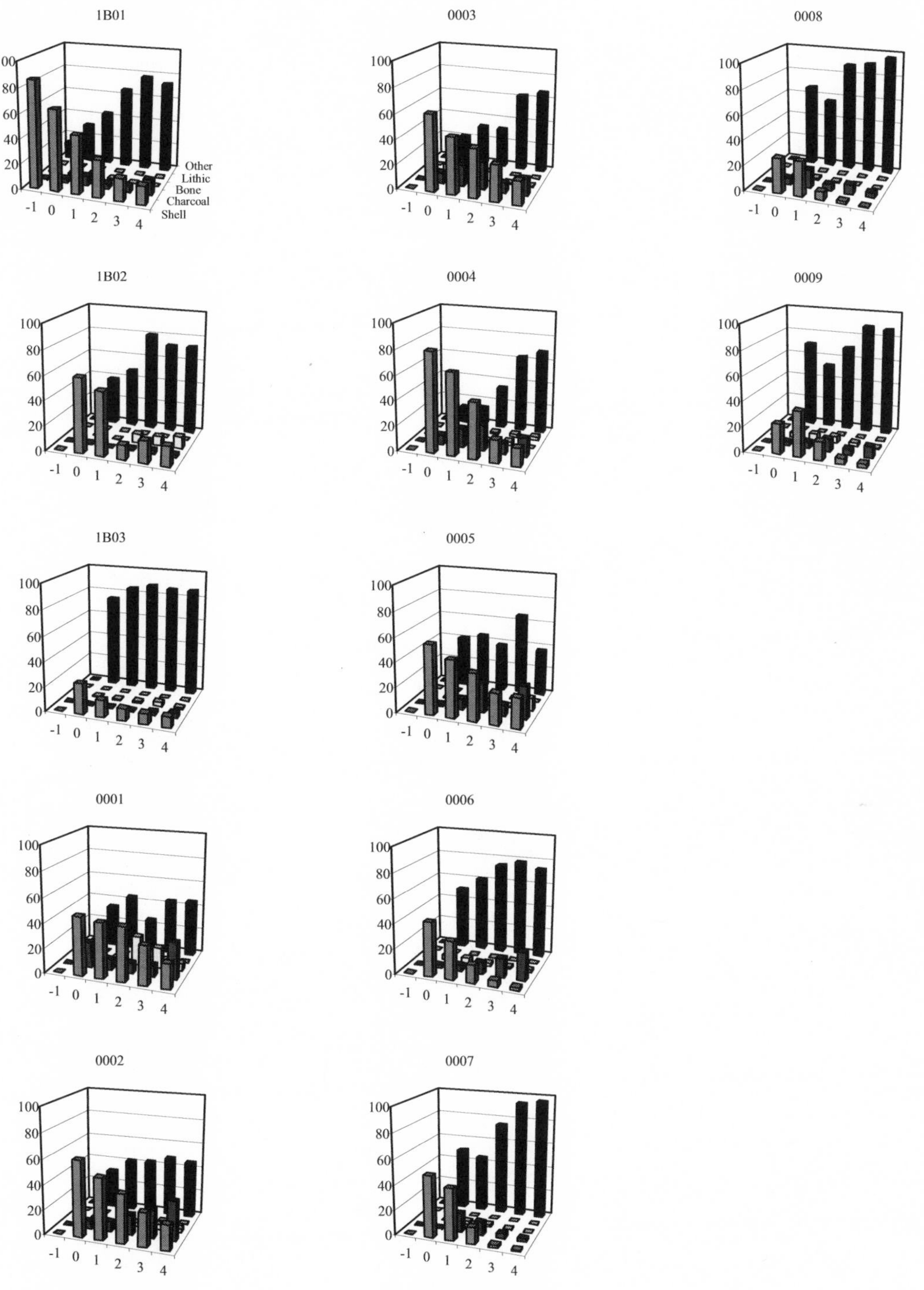

Figure 5.11 Microartifact Distributions for Trench GH. The facies are in stratigraphic order, starting with the top left corner. Facies 1B01 is the topmost facies, while Facies 0009 is the bottommost in the unit. The vertical axis represents the percentage of compositional types for each size fraction. The horizontal axis indicates phi classes.

croscopic features or structures that might differentiate the ridge from the depression. Micromorphology samples were collected from the Trench AB and Trench GH representing the ridge and depression respectively.

Micromorphological analyses indicated that the ridge contained more coarse material and a different microstructure or fabric than the sections from the

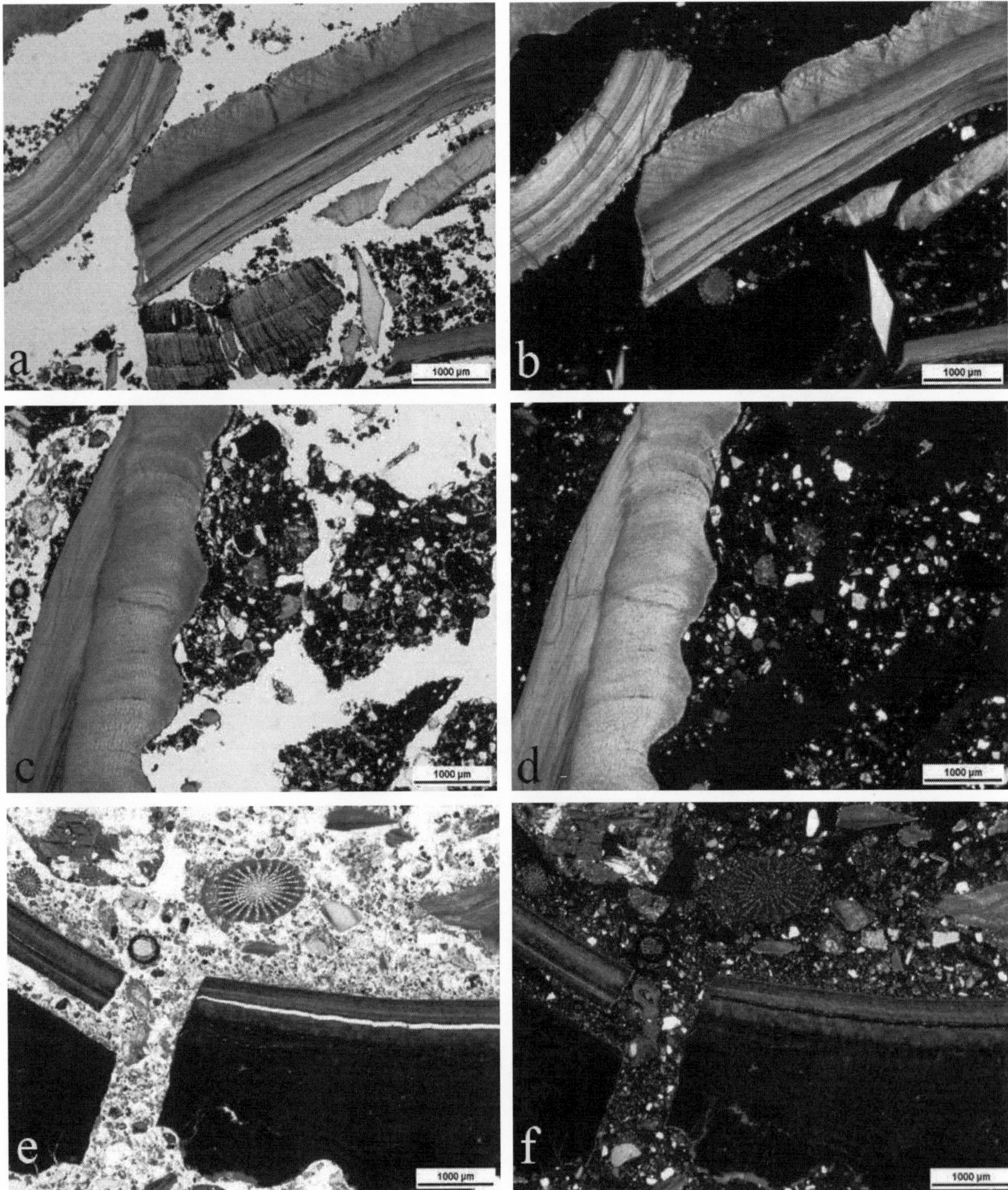

Figure 5.12 a,b) Photomicrograph showing sample 93SJ12 coarse fraction in the ridge (a ppl, b xpl); c,d) Photomicrograph of the fine fraction next to a large shell clast sample 93SJ12. The fine fraction is composed of fine sand and silt size amorphous organic matter, charcoal, shell, and various rocks, (c ppl, d xpl); e,f) Photomicrograph of the fine fraction capping and filling gaps between the the larger clasts (in this case lenticular shell fragments) in sample 93SJ12, (e ppl, f xpl).

depression. Samples from the depression display two different patterns. Those from the upper facies of the depression are nearly identical to those of the ridge but those from the base of the depression are unique with less coarse material and variable microstructures.

The coarse fraction is distinguished, for the micro-

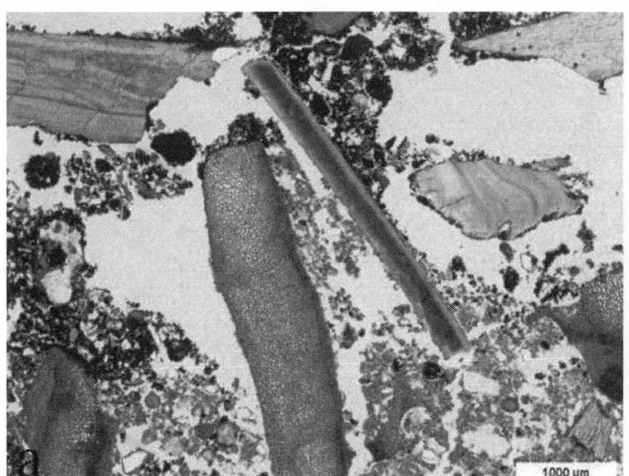

Figure 5.13 a,b) Photomicrograph illustrating two contiguous fine fractions in sample 93SJ5; in the upper left hand corner is the typical black, charcoal rich, non calcareous (absence of ash) and in the lower right hand corner is a brown calcareous fine matrix (a ppl, b xpl).

morphological observation, as the particles greater than 0.25 mm. The coarse fraction in the ridge is primarily composed of shell, both whole and fragmented, but also rock, charcoal and bone (Figure 5.12 a, b). The fine fraction is composed of clay and silt-sized aggregates partially filling the inter-granular spaces, supporting the coarse fraction (Figure 5.12 c, d).

In the ridge, the fine fraction is often observed capping the top of the larger clasts (Figure 5.12 e, f). This feature suggests that the fine material is being transported downward. In addition, the charcoal and the burned shell in the ridge are rarely observed in association with finer particles of ash. The disassociation, specifically between the coarse charcoal and fine ash (particles that were most likely deposited together) indicate the differential downward movement of fine materials. This downward movement probably occurred through post-depositional translocation and dissolution. The result is an absence of microstratigraphy or preservation of variable fine fractions. The processes, however, do not appear to significantly affect the large size constituents of the ridge, because macroscopic differences in stratigraphy remains visible. Only in one area of the thin section was it possible to observe a different fine fraction (Figure 5.13). In this case a relatively unique fine fraction of brown calcareous material is visible below a charcoal-rich non-calcareous fine matrix.

The micromorphology of the depression suggests a different depositional history. Here the midden is fine grained with the coarse fraction composed primarily of materials less than 1 cm (Figure 5.14 a,b). These materials are typically well-sorted and include bone, charcoal, burned and unburned shell, lithics, and unburned wood (Figure 5.14 c, d). The fine fraction includes silt- and clay-size organic matter and diagenetic calcium carbonate in the form of micritic coatings and aggregates (Figure 5.14 e, f). The appearance of micrite at the base of the midden (Figure 5.15) is probably due to the dissolution of calcium carbonate from shell and specifically wood ash high in the profile that precipitated in the lower reaches of the midden.

SUMMARY OF EACH AREA

The goal of this chapter was to see if the various areas of this horseshoe shaped topographic expression could be differentiated on the bases of sedimentological data. The various areas are discussed in turn, summarizing all the data presented above.

Behind the Ridge

Unit 107 341 has facies with distributions that trend from poorly sorted to well sorted. The upper facies have sand fraction that are evenly distribution from coarse to fine, seemingly with little or no sorting. The lower level, however, is represented by a single modal peak at 3Φ similar to the control profile mentioned above. This trend must be related to the presence of shells in the upper two facies (Figure 5.1, Table 5.1).

The chemical data strongly indicate that this area of the site is an undisturbed forest soil with acidic A Horizon, with high levels of organic matter. The chemistry of the unit indicates that soil forming processes have produced a typical weathering profile that contains almost no carbonates. These properties compare nicely with the control profile as reported in Stein (1992b:155 and 160) (Figure 5.2).

Ridge

The Ridge (Unit 105 365, Unit 111 349, and Trench AB) contains different grain-size distributions compared to the area behind the ridge, with modal peaks in the coarse sand sizes (between 0Φ to 2Φ), and second-

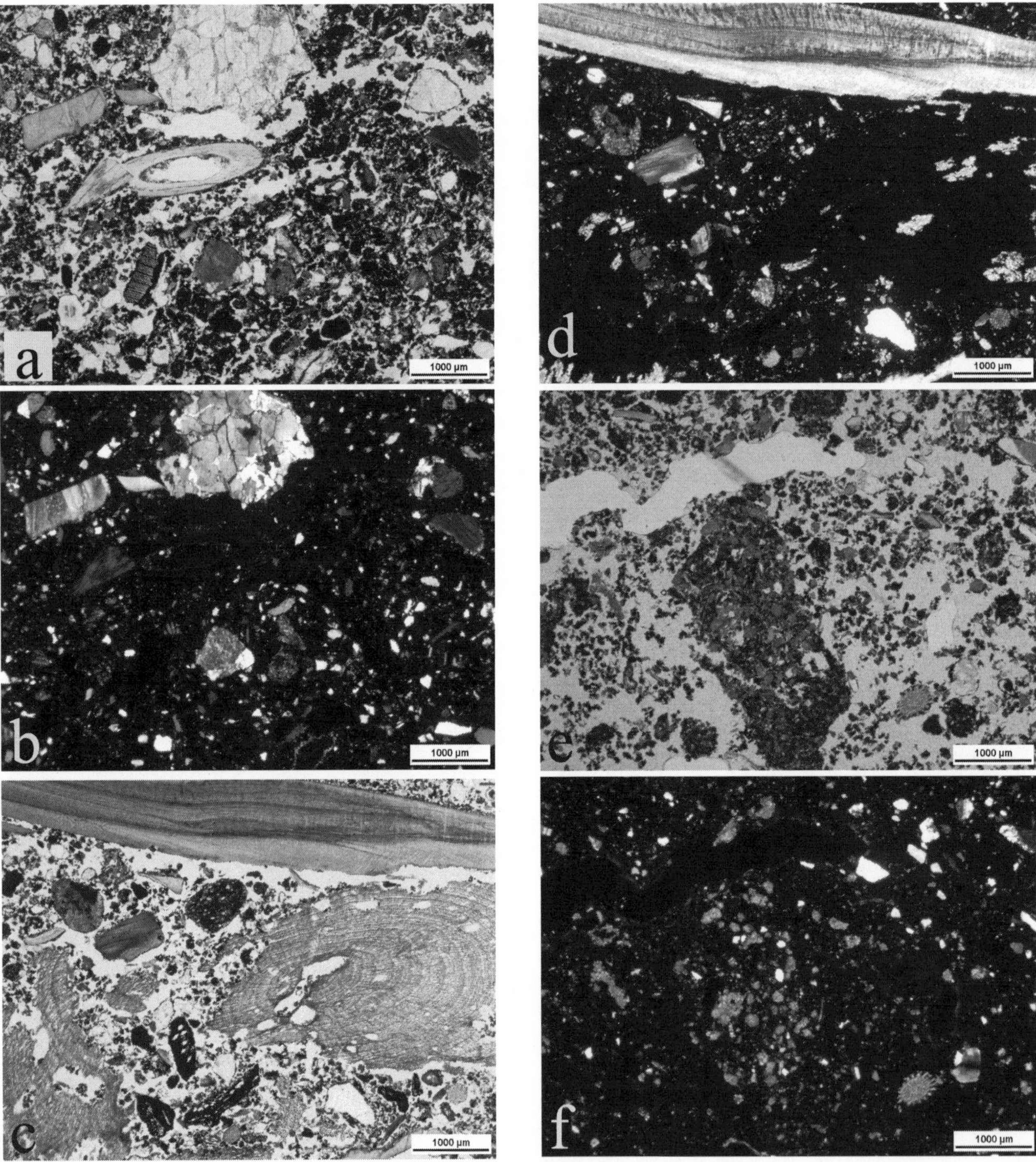

Figure 5.14 a,b) Photomicrograph of sample 93SJ2, the reduced coarse matrix in the depression. Note the bone broken in situ (a ppl, b xpl); c, d) Photomicrograph of sample 93SJ2, a possible unburned wood fragment among the coarse fraction (c ppl, d xpl); e,f) Photomicrograph of sample 93SJ4a showing a large aggregate primarily composed of amorphous organic matter and carbonate (e ppl, f xpl).

ary modes in the clay range (8-9, and 10Φ sizes) (Figure 5.1; Table 5.1). The explanation for the differences between facies is that each reflects a slightly different sources and activities. If the shell ridges were purposefully built through dumping of load after load of shell and other debris associated with fires and subsistence activities, then each facies would contain different types of artifacts in both the large and small (sand, silt and clay) sizes. Based on the radiocarbon dates, these individual dumping events appear to have occurred

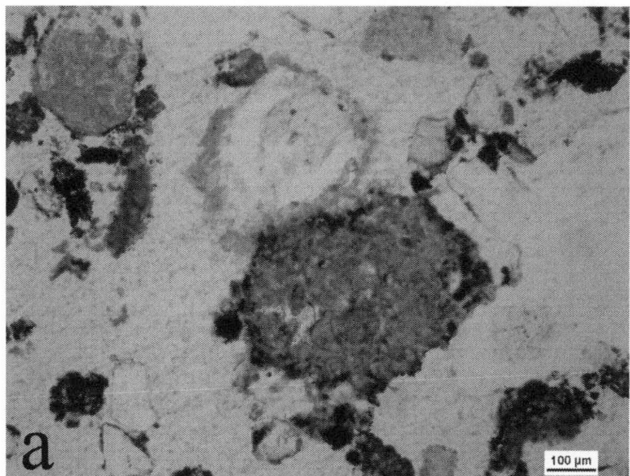

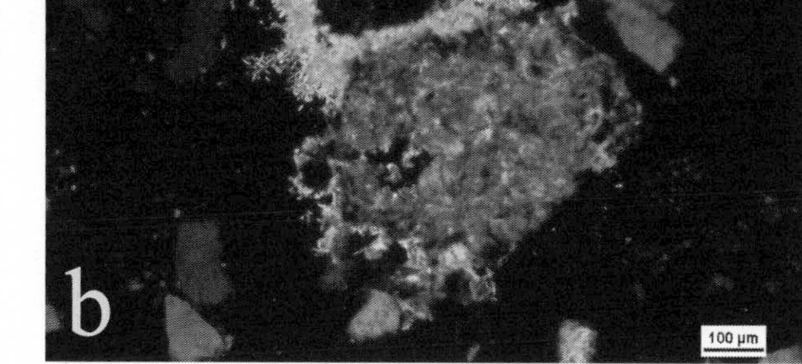

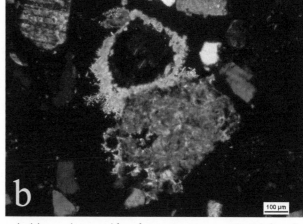

Figure 5.15 a,b) Photomicrograph of sample 93SJ2 illustrating micritic coating a void and coarse aggregate (a ppl, b xpl).

rapidly. Excavators note the abundance of shells in the ridges and these grain-size distributions indicate that the smaller sizes are also highly variable. The importance for this study is that these small-sized grains do not reflect evidence of systematic post-depositional soil horizonation, nor the subsurface alteration at the base (similar to the effects of groundwater at Op A).

In Trench AB one sample (facies 0005) is better sorted than almost any other sample in the study. This facies was dominated by coarse sand and may represent a place where sand was dumped from an excavation of subsurface pits. The base of the trench was riddled with pits that were dug by the prehistoric inhabitants. The sediment from the underlying glacial drift was obviously heaped in nearby midden. This one facies may represent a particularly sandy portion of the drift (Figure 5.1; Table 5.1).

The chemical data from the ridge indicates that the fine fraction is almost 40% carbonates with high levels of organic matter. The pH is alkaline, as one would expect with that much shell. The variability of the chemistry is expected, swinging from high to low and indicates that the material being dumped in the ridge came from multiple sources with varying amounts of organic material (Figure 5.3).

The microartifact data indicated that the ridge is made up of more shell and charcoal than the depression. The ridge also contains larger sand size microartifacts, while the depression is made up of smaller sand size materials (Figure 5.6, 5.7, 5.10). This is perhaps due to the systematic downward translocation of the fine fraction through the porous midden of the ridges. The high percentage of shell in the ridge suggests deliberate discard and placement of shell around the central depression perhaps as construction material for habitation sites. Some authors have suggested that shell was used to insulate or support the cedar plank walls of houses on the Northwest Coast of North America (Ames et al. 1992; Onat Blukis 1985).

The micromorphological sections indicate that fine fraction is moving through the coarser shells and rocks (Figure 5.12). The coatings on the larger clasts are clear evidence of this translocation. The coarser objects are not moving. Their edges are touching, and this holds them in place. However, one can imagine that over a thousand years the small sized mineral and organic fraction has been transported downward and changed significantly the distribution of fine sand, silt, and clay that comprise the ridges of the midden.

Depression

In contrast to the ridge, the depression (Unit 123 347 and Trench GH) contains better sorted distributions and finer grain-sizes (Figure 5.1; Table 5.1). At the very top of each unit there seems to be midden with sediments more similar in their size distribution to the ridge, than they are to what lies below. The most likely explanation for these facies is that they represent slumped portions of the ridge that fell down into the depression. We know that Treganza's crew excavated a unit close to the location of 123 347. Perhaps these archaeologists spread their backdirt around the area of 123 347, and thus created the difference from the upper to the lower facies of the units. The grain-size pattern in Facies 1G01 from inside the depression separates the slump facies from the "in situ" facies.

These microartifact data, however, do not provide strong evidence for specific floor feature. They prove that deposits from the depression contain smaller-sized charcoal fractions than those in the ridge, suggesting that the depression may represent an occupation area where charcoal was crushed into smaller bits. A continuous distribution of charcoal is considered a defining feature of floor deposits (Rosen 1989). The grain size distribution of charcoal in the depression clearly shows a continuous pattern but there is no stratigraphic indication of a floor, nor any feature originating from a surface that could be a floor - no trampled layer or hearth. All that can be said is that this pattern of higher percentage of charcoal with decreasing grain size suggests that the depression was once an occupation area. The bone and lithic data do not support occupation in the depression, as their values are very low, and one would expect them to be high if processing and eating were taking place there. The highest bone concentrations were found in the ridge (Trench AB), so perhaps the supposition is incorrect (Figure 5.8, 5.11).

One possible interpretation for the high percentage of "other" (mainly unmodified sand grains) in the depression is that the floor of the house at OpD was made of (or reinforced by) textiles, wood, or hard-packed earthen materials. If the floor was covered with mats, wooden planks, or textiles, then mineral sand grains are likely to have been tracked in and sifted through to the midden below.

The micromorphological sections indicate that significantly larger amounts of fine fraction exist in the depression (Fgiure 5.14). The gravel-sized material is all smaller than those in the ridge and the few gravel-sized clasts that are present are surrounded by significant amounts of fine-grained material. Clumps of different colored fine fraction indicate that clods of dirt have been mixed with the midden in the depression. There are numerous pits found intruding into the subsurface glacial drift. Perhaps these clods are from digging those pits, which suggests that the sediments in the midden were being moved laterally around and perhaps not all dumped on the ridges above.

In Front of the Depression

The facies from the unit located in front of the ridge (Unit 130 352) have modal peaks between 0Φ and 1Φ, similar to the grain-size pattern of samples from the ridge (Figure 5.1, Table 5.1). Unlike the facies from the depression, especially those in the lower portions of units (with modes of 3Φ and 4Φ), these facies seem to have lots of whole shell and fine-grained sediments that have been moved through the porous shell and fire-cracked rock layers. In two facies (1K01, and 0001) there are significant amounts of clay in secondary and tertiary modes not found in other facies. This clay may be related to post-depositional processes, representing the translocation of fines from higher in the profile to the base of the shell midden where they became trapped. This unit is closest to the water and may have been out from under a forest canopy. Or people may have conducted activities different from those inside the house that brought water to the area, which percolated through the midden.

The chemical data for the area in front of the depression were remarkably consistent. The carbonate values hovered at 40% and organiç matter at 20%. It is remarkable that more variation was not detected and is consistent with the microartifact data, which may indicate that people were doing something very consistently at this location (Figure 5.4).

The microartifact data from in front of the depression show differences in the amount of shell, charcoal, and bone from other areas, suggesting a different depositional history than the ridge and depression (Figure 5.9). These data indicate that food processing activities may have taken place in front of the depression at OpD. The higher percentage of charcoal in the smaller sand fractions for in front of the ridge and depression are evidence for trampling. Given these charcoal data, the depression and area in front of the depression were areas of high foot traffic. Ethnographic accounts indicate that some domestic activities were conducted in front of plank houses. Thus, it is possible that at OpD, activities related to food processing took place in front of the depression. This would account for the higher percentages of charcoal and bone from in front of the depression compared to the percentages from the ridge and in the depression. Interestingly, the distribution of charcoal from in front of the ridge shows a similar continuous pattern that is apparent in the depression. These data may imply post-depositional processes associated with trampling and sweeping. Within trampled areas, the smallest microartifacts will remain in their place of origin (Nielson 1991). Consequently, the charcoal distributions from the depression and in front of the ridge are consistent with traffic zone areas.

REFERENCES

Ames, K. M., D. F. Raetz, S. Hamilton, and C. McAfee

1992 Household Archaeology of a Southern Northwest Coast Plank House. *Journal of Field Archaeology* 19:275-289.

Bullock, P., N. Fedoroff, A. Jongerius, G. J. Stoops, and T. Tursina

1985 *Handbook for Soil Thin Section Description.* Waine Research Publishers, Wolverhampton, England.

Dunnell, R. C., and J. K. Stein

1989 Theoretical Issues in the Interpretation of Microartifacts. *Geoarchaeology* 4:31-42.

FitzPatrick, E. A.

1993 *Soil Microscopy and Micromorphology.* John Wiley and Sons, Chichester, England.

Fladmark, K. R.

1982 Microdebitage Analysis: Initial Considerations. *Journal of Archaeological Science* 9:205-220.

Folk, R. L.
1980 *Petrology of Sedimentary Rocks.* Hemphill, Austin, TX.

Ham, L.
1982 *Seasonality, Shell Midden Layers, and Coast Salish Subsistence Activities at the Crescent Beach Site.* Ph.D. Dissertation, Department of Anthropology and Sociology, University of British Columbia, Vancouver, BC.

Hull, K. L.
1987 Identification of Cultural Site Formation Processes through Microdebitage Analysis. *American Antiquity* 52(4):772-783.

Hunt, T.
1990 *An Investigation of Macroartifact Grain-Size Distribution at British Camp (45SJ24).* Unpublished manuscript, on file at the Archaeology Division, Burke Museum, University of Washington, Seattle, WA.

Madsen, M. E.
1992 Lithic Manufacturing at British Camp: Evidence from Size Distributions and Microartifacts. In *Deciphering a Shell Midden*, edited by J.K. Stein, pp. 193-210. Academic Press, San Diego, CA.

Mauger, J. E.
1991 Shed-Roof Houses at Ozette and in Regional Perspective. In *Ozette Archaeological Project Research Report, Volume 1, House Structure and Floor Midden*, edited by S. R. Samuels, pp. 29-174. Reports of Investigations 63. Department of Anthropology, Washington State University, Pullman, WA.

Matson, R. G., D. Lubowicz, and W. Boyd
1980 *Excavations at Beach Grove (DgRs1) in 1980.* Unpublished manuscript, Laboratory of Archaeology, University of British Columbia, Vancover, BC.

McKellar, J. A.
1983 *Correlates and the Explanation of Distributions.* Atlatl 4. Department of Anthropology, University of Arizona, Tucson, AZ.

Metcalfe, D., and K. M. Heath
1990 Microrefuse and Site Structure: The Hearths and Floors of the Heartbreak Hotel. *American Antiquity* 55(4):781-796.

Mitchell, D. H.
1968 Excavations at Two Trench Embankments in the Gulf of Georgia Region. *Syesis* 1:29-46.

Onat, Astrida R. Blukis
1985 The Multifunctional Use of Shellfish Remains: From Garbage to Community Engineering. *Northwest Anthropological Research Notes* 19(2):201-207.

Rosen, A. M.
1989 Ancient Town and City Sites: A View from the Microscope. *American Antiquity* 54(3):564-578.
1991 Microartifacts and the Study of Ancient Societies. *Biblical Archaeologist* 54(2):97-103.
1993 Microartifacts as a Reflection of Cultural Factors in Site Formation. In *Formation Processes in Archaeological Context*, edited by P. Goldberg, D.T. Nash and M.D. Petraglia, pp. 141-148. Monographs in World Archaeology, Volume 17, Prehistory Press, Madison, WI.

Samuels, S. R. (editor)
1991 Shed-Roof Houses at Ozette and in Regional Perspective. In *Ozette Archaeological Project Research Report, Volume 1, House Structure and Floor Midden*, edited by S. R. Samuels, pp. 29-174. Reports of Investigations 63. Department of Anthropology, Washington State University, Pullman, WA.

Schiffer, M. B.
1987 *Formation Processes of the Archaeological Record.* University of New Mexico Press, Albuquerque, NM.

Sherwood, S., J.F . Simek, and R. R. Polhemus
1995 Artifact Size and Spatial Process: Macro- and Microartifacts in a Mississippian House. *Geoarchaeology* 4:1-30.

Simms, S. R., and K. M. Heath
1990 Site Structure of the Orbit Inn: An Application of Ethnoarchaeology. *American Antiquity* 55(4):797-813.

Stein, J. K.
1992a *Deciphering a Shell Midden.* Academic Press, San Diego, CA.
1992bSediment Analysis of the British Camp Shell Midden. In *Deciphering a Shell Midden*, edited by J. K Stein, pp. 135-162. Academic Press, San Diego, CA.
1987 Deposits for Archaeologists. In *Advances in Archaeological Method and Theory, Vol 11*, edited by M.B. Schiffer, pp 337-393. Academic Press, Orlando, FL.

Stein, J. K., and P. S. Teltser
1989 Size Distributions of Artifact Classes: Combining Macro- and Micro-Fractions. *Geoarchaeology* 4(1):1-30.

Vance, E. D.
1989 *The Role of Microartifact in Spatial Analysis.* Unpublished Ph.D. dissertation, University of Washington, Seattle, WA.
1986 Microdebitage Analysis in Activity Analysis: An Application. *Northwest Anthropological Research Notes* 20(2):179-189.

6

A *Chaîne Opératoire* Analysis of the Flaking of Stone

Angela E. Close

Close describes a chaîne opératoire *approach to chipped stone artifacts from OpD. The primary toolstone used for flaked stone tool technology at the site was crystalline volcanic rock, also referred to by Northwest Coast archaeologists as dacite or fine-grained volcanic rock. In this chapter, Close reconstructs the prehistoric activities that resulted in the OpD lithic assemblage. She discusses commonly found tool types at OpD and examines the spatial distribution of two of those types, triangles and scaled pieces.*

THE *CHAÎNE OPÉRATOIRE* CONCEPT

Almost all of the flaked stone from OpD is crystalline volcanic rock, dark gray to black in color and usually quite coarse grained. Other raw materials, including chert, quartz, sandstone, and granite, occur in vanishingly small numbers and are described elsewhere (Close 2006).

The analytical approach to the assemblage of crystalline volcanic rock (CVR) from OpD is that of the *chaîne opératoire* ("sequence of actions", although most of the anglophone world uses the French term). *Chaîne-opératoire* analysis, as now practised, attempts to trace the life histories (the biological metaphor is apt) of all the artifacts in the assemblage of interest from birth (raw material procurement) to death (final discard and entry into the archaeological record), and to link them to each other and to the other sub systems in society.

Chaîne-opératoire is a cognitive approach to the study of flaked stone, in that it explicitly deals with people – often individuals – who are engaged in making decisions about what to do next, and are making those decisions at different levels of consciousness. For Leroi Gourhan, operating sequences (*chaînes opératoires*) are followed in all aspects of life at different levels of consciousness. He saw three levels: automatic or unconscious (which is irrelevant to flaking stone); mechanical or somewhat conscious; and lucid or fully conscious (1993:230 232). Mechanical *chaînes opératoires* are culturally determined ways of doing recurrent, everyday things, that are learned early in life and are performed with only partial attention. For example, one travels to work in the morning while thinking of other things. An individual's integration into society depends on the smooth performance of these elementary sequences in normal life. When something unexpected happens, lucidity or full consciousness intervenes, in order "to rectify the operational process by adjusting the appropriate links of the chain" (Leroi Gourhan 1993:233) – as, for example, when the morning commuter rediscovers gridlock.

Similarly, Perlès (1992) makes a distinction between lithic "strategies" – recurrent choices – and lithic "tactics" – "variants… which can be explained purely in circumstantial terms" (Perlès 1992:225). Knappers of stone learn early in their training that there are certain ways of achieving the purposes of knapping which are approved by the social group. They also learn to make entirely situational adjustments to the links in the *chaîne opératoire* if there is divergence from approved ways. Together, these are the "'syntax' that imparts both fixity and flexibility" (Leroi Gourhan 1993:114).

Chapter opening photo: Fine-grained volcanic toolstone from the San Juan Islands.

Following Perlès, I divide the *chaîne opératoire* for the CVR from OpD into three stages. (The number of stages is quite arbitrary and the divisions between them are artificial, since each affects the others.) The first stage is raw material procurement, which is constrained by a variety of factors arising from what sources of stone are known, what sort of stone is needed or preferred, what is available near and/or far, and how much of the group's limited (limited both by practical and purely social constraints) resources can be devoted to procurement.

The second stage is tool production. The knapper has known from the very beginning what sorts of tools will be required (so this had already been a consideration in the procurement stage), and will, therefore, create a core and strike flakes from it in order to meet those requirements (not in order to reduce the core). If the need is simply for many fresh cutting edges, this may be achieved with very little technological sophistication (for example, Close 1996, 1997). If tool requirements are more stringent, then considerable effort may be expended in producing ideal blanks (as in Levallois and some blade technologies), or blanks may be produced which are less than ideal but can be modified later. The creation of blanks encompasses most of the core and flake technology (and is, of course, constrained by the raw materials that had previously been procured). Individual flakes are then selected for use as tools. It is very unlikely that all flakes could be selected, since the process of flaking will require a number of tactical adjustments to the sequence, directly proportional to the level of standardization attempted in that process. Such adjustments result in flakes which are not, themselves, intended to be tools and so may be unsuitable. The selected blanks may be used immediately, or may require additional shaping by retouch, depending (*inter alia*) upon the nature of the flake and the nature of the desired tool. (Some forms, such as barbed and tanged points, can only be produced by retouch.)

Perlès's third stage is tool kit management. This includes tool use, determined by what needs to done, and tool maintenance. Some tools can be resharpened or reworked, such as tools on the ends of blades; others cannot, including those on which the working edge is a sharp, unretouched edge and hafted stone tools in which one stone component is replaced by another one. Finally, the tool enters the archaeological record, by processes such as being discarded, or lost, or cached, or deliberately buried.

This study is based upon analyses and descriptions (the primary data) of the flaked stone from OpD, which are available elsewhere (Close 2006).

RAW MATERIAL PROCUREMENT

Raw material was brought in the form of pebbles of consistent and small size. The lengths of the cores cluster quite markedly in the 35 45 mm range. If one looks at all CVR pebbles in the collection – whether cores, tools, or unworked – the mean length is still only 43.0 mm, and there are no unretouched flakes in the collection longer than 67 mm. Cores were small and there are no indications that larger pieces were sought, or found. Almost all of the pebbles brought to the site were large enough to be used, so there was probably some selection for size at the source(s). The pebbles were not tested or worked at all before coming to OpD; the only thing done at the source(s) was to collect the pebbles.

On the basis of remaining cortex, there are two clear varieties of pebbles: one variety has a smooth, evenly convex exterior surface, while the other is less smooth and is uneven, sometimes lumpy. This makes it likely that the pebbles were brought in from (at least) two different sources. The exact locations of the sources are not known, but knowledge of their locations is not essential. Wherever the sources, the pebbles of CVR must have been transported to the site by boat. By A.D. 600, substantial canoes were part of the technological repertoire of the coastal peoples. It is thus likely that the largest parts of the cost of actually transporting the pebbles, once they had been acquired, were throwing them into the canoe at the source and then throwing them out again at English Camp. That is, transportation costs were very low. Acquisition costs will be addressed below.

TOOL PRODUCTION

Creation of Blanks

The pebbles were brought in with (very little or) no preparation, and all phases of the creation of blanks took place at English Camp. At English Camp, there were also preferred orientations of the pebble cores: the evenly convex pebbles tended to be oriented so that flaking would occur in the direction of the maximal dimension, and the uneven pebbles were oriented to that one of the flatter faces served as either the platform or the flaking surface (or one flatter face for each, if possible).

A first flake (with a cortical platform and completely cortical dorsal face) was then removed from the pebble. On the evenly smooth pebbles, this was usually a quite thick, decapitation flake, removing one end of the pebble (perpendicular to the maximal dimension) and thus creating the platform. On the uneven pebbles, the first flake was a thinner flake that removed one side of the pebble; that side then be-

Table 6.1 Frequencies of types of CVR débitage (excluding tools and cores)

	Provenience												
	Unit I	107341	105365	111349	121347	123347	130352	TrAB	TrCD	TrEF	TrGH	n	%
Simple first flake	1	1	4	1	2	-	7	-	8	10	7	41	0.8
Simple flake from unidirectional core	14	8	30	13	17	14	60	30	52	121	41	400	8.0
Simple flake from multidirectional core	16	2	26	5	10	7	17	25	20	60	30	218	4.3
Other simple flake	70	18	205	59	84	60	179	162	153	335	207	1532	30.5
Simple core-/platform-rejuvation flake	-	-	1	2	1	1	1	-	4	6	6	22	0.4
Simple chip	105	35	675	100	81	46	268	270	207	153	261	2201	43.8
Bipolar first flake	-	-	-	-	-	-	1	-	1	1	-	3	0.1
Flake from bipolar core	-	-	8	3	3	5	9	2	15	40	19	104	2.1
Bâtonnet	-	1	1	-	-	-	2	2	2	15	4	27	0.5
Bipolar-related chip	-	-	1	-	-	-	1	-	-	-	1	3	0.1
Biface-thinning flake	37	-	35	3	3	2	8	10	5	12	26	141	2.8
Biface-thinning chip	22	1	50	3	5	5	3	11	2	10	28	140	2.8
Chunk (angular)	4	1	16	10	16	6	31	20	23	22	24	173	3.4
Pebble	3	1	-	3	-	1	5	4	-	-	1	18	0.4
Total	272	68	1052	202	222	147	592	536	492	785	655	5023	

came the flaking surface, adjacent to a cortical striking platform.

Table 6.1 gives the absolute and relative frequencies by type of all the CVR débitage that was not modified by use as a core, or by shaping or use as a tool. In the assemblage as a whole and in addition to the unavoidable first flake, there is approximately one (small) primary or secondary flake per core. Since it is probable that the assemblage represents the output of more cores than were found (see below), the average number of "core preparation flakes" per core is probably less than two. Thus, there was only minimal preparation of the pebbles before entering into the main phase of flake production. This accords with the lack of evidence for preparation on the cores themselves. Main phase exploitation of the cores (*en plein débitage*) thus began almost immediately.

The frequencies of types of cores found in each unit of OpD are given in Table 6.2. Flakes were removed primarily from single platform, opposed platform and wedge shaped cores (Figures 6.1-6.3). A large majority of the débitage was produced by simple flaking (normal, direct percussion technology), and most of those pieces are chips (<10 mm in maximal dimension). Débitage produced by a bipolar technique is much less common, and the paucity of bipolar chips is remarkable, particularly when compared with the frequency of simple chips. However, it is likely that the latter includes many of the former, since chip size pieces are unlikely to survive the rigors of the bipolar technique in identifiable form.

Only 141 flakes were identified as biface thinning flakes (Table 6.1). The number of flakes produced in the thinning of bifaces was undoubtedly much higher, but many (probably most) could not be positively identified as such. The flakes classified as "biface thinning" show most of the characteristics expected of this type: small absolute size; fragility; few cortical platforms; more dihedral and faceted platforms, more lipped platforms; rare dorsal cortex. Thus, their functional classification is probably correct.

Throughout the life of each core, there was a strong preference for cortical platforms (Figure 6.1: a c). This meant that core platforms were very rarely rejuvenated (a difficult process anyway on small cores). Such platform rejuvenation as occurred involved no more than the trimming of an edge of the platform: the assemblage does not include core tablets. However, when a core platform became unusable for any reason, the knapper was more likely to rotate the core and begin again with a fresh, cortical platform than to attempt rejuvenation.

In the assemblage as a whole (including tools), there are about forty CVR flakes per core (plus chips). Given the small initial size of the cores and the obdurate nature of the stone, this figure is improbably high.

Table 6.2 Frequencies of types of CVR cores

	Provenience												
	Unit I	107341	105365	111349	121347	123347	130352	TrAB	TrCD	TrEF	TrGH	n	%
Unidirectional core	1	1	-	1	2	1	3	2	5	5	4	25	38.5
Opposed-platform core	-	-	-	-	1	1	-	-	3	5	-	10	15.4
Ninety-degree core	-	1	-	-	1	-	-	-	-	1	-	3	4.6
Patterned multiple-platform core	-	1	-	-	-	-	2	-	-	-	-	3	4.6
Bipolar core	-	-	-	-	-	-	2	-	1	3	-	6	9.2
Globular core	-	-	1	-	-	-	-	-	-	-	1	2	3.1
Disc core	-	-	-	-	1	-	-	-	-	-	-	1	1.5
Initially tested core	-	-	-	1	-	-	1	-	1	-	-	3	4.6
Unidentifiable core	-	-	1	-	1	-	1	1	-	3	1	12	18.5
Total	1	3	2	2	6	2	9	3	10	17	6	65	
Unworked pebbles	3	1	-	3	-	1	5	4	4	-	1	18	

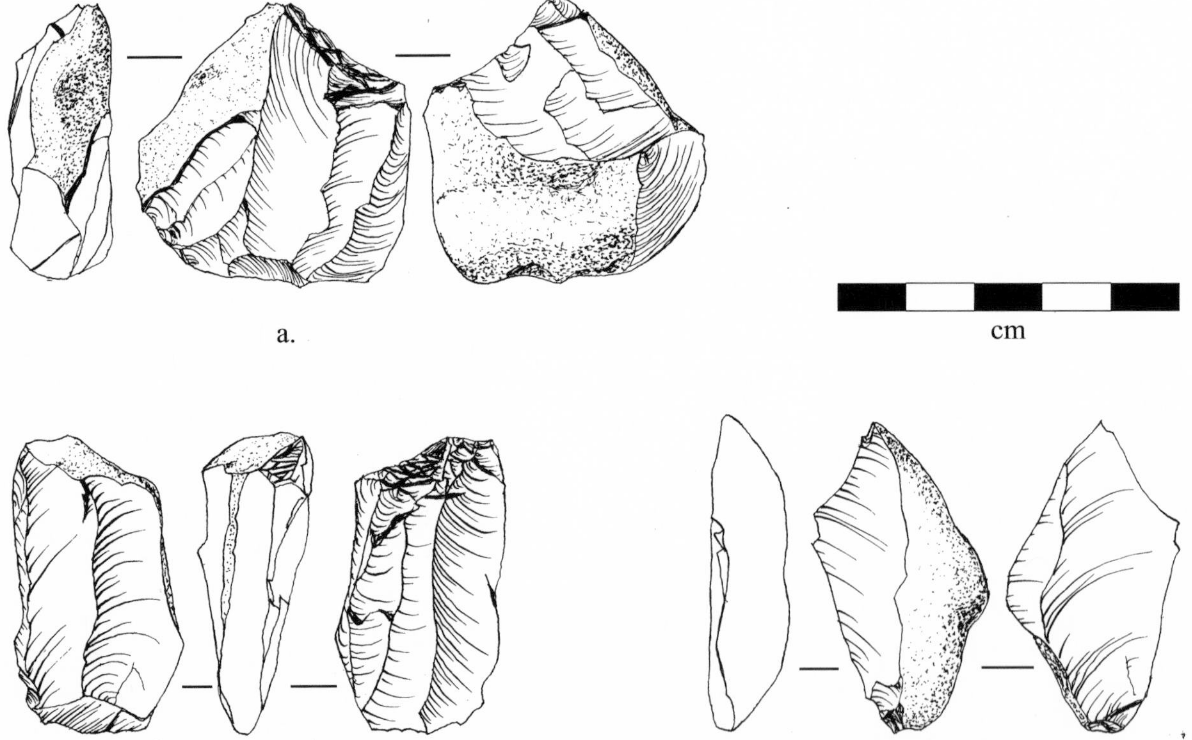

Figure 6.1 Unidirectional cores: (a) wedge shaped core; (b) and (c) single platform cores for the production of flakes (sensu lato) with cortical backs. Note that the platform on (c) is at the base of the drawing. [Provenance: (a) 1213471B0101230; (b) 1303521B03430; (c) TCD1A0500730.]

Therefore, either some CVR was brought in the form of flakes, or some of the cores used at the site are missing, or both.

When stone is imported into a site in the form of flakes, it is because the stone comes from a great distance (thus incurring significant transportation costs), or because the flakes have some property (such as large size, or particularities of the stone itself) not to be found in more local raw materials. None of these is true of the CVR flakes at OpD: as stone, they are indistinguishable from the cores, and none is too large to have been struck from the cores present in the site.

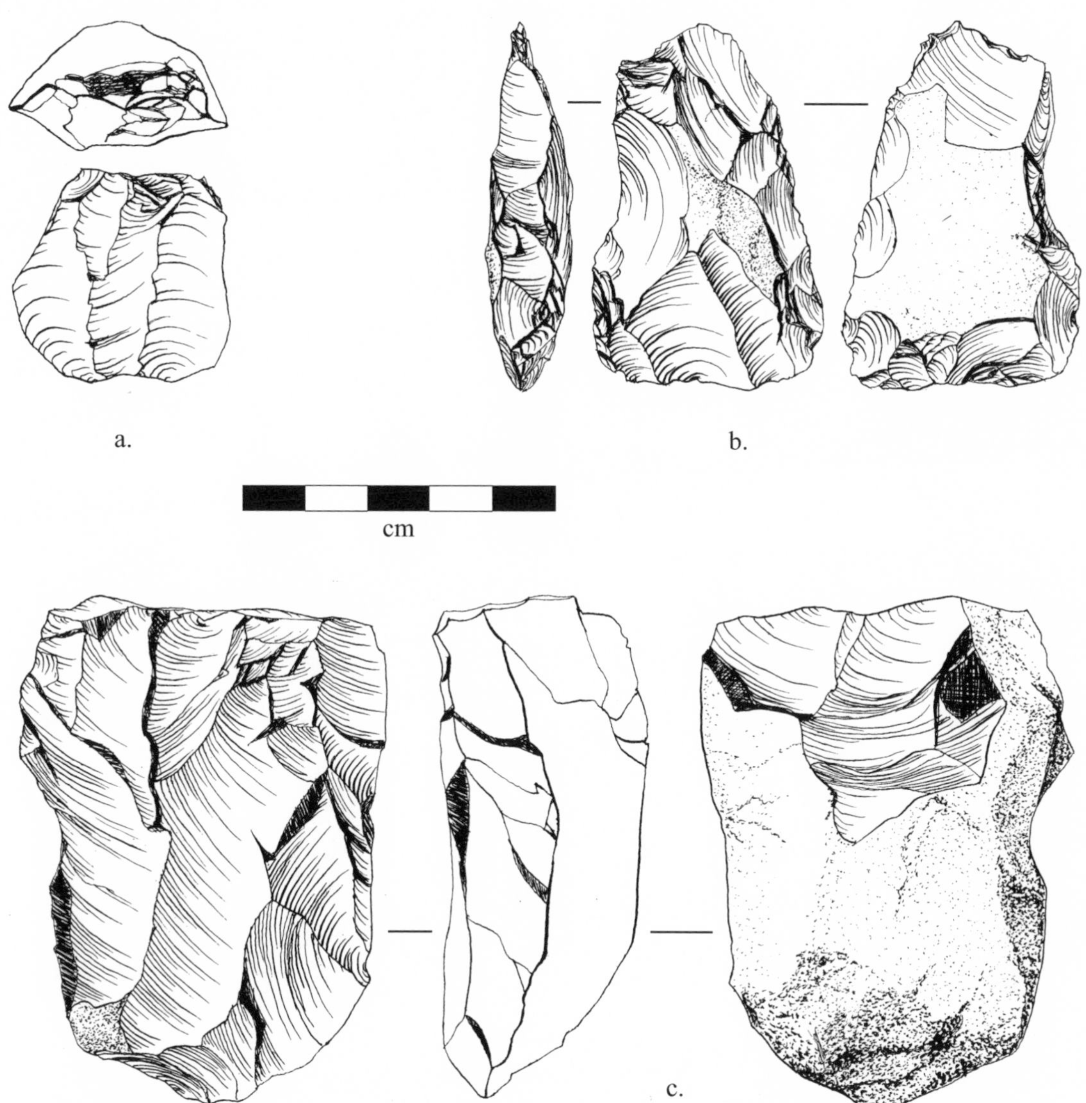

Figure 6.2 Multidirectional cores: (a) opposed platform core; (b) multiple platform core; (c) ninety degree core. [Provenance: (a) TCD0003033; (b) 1073411C0100731; (c) 1073411C0202131.]

Therefore, some of the cores used at the site are missing.

Removal of partially exploited cores from the site for use elsewhere is always a possibility and would inflate the number of flakes per core remaining. However, systematic removal of large numbers of such cores (given their small initial size and the obdurate nature of the stone) is very unlikely. It is much more probable that when a core reached the end of the main phase of production and, for whatever reason, acceptable flakes could not longer be obtained, some cores (but not all) were simply smashed in the hope that something usable might result. This is an economizing action, when raw material is limited in supply or consists of very small pebbles (especially quartz), and, as in other lithic assemblages (Andrefsky 1998:147 149; Kuhn 1995:97 99; Merrick and Merrick 1976:579 580; Perlès 1992:241 242), this is probably where the bipolar technique really came into its own. However, artifacts subjected to this technique tend not to remain recognizable. This is probably why there are so few "bipolar flakes" in the assemblage and why I identified so few "bipolar cores" (Figure 6.3: b, d). Even those examples so classified might equally well be seen as regular cores which were reused as scaled or splintered pieces (Figure 6.3: a).

Selection of Blanks

The blanks that were selected for additional shaping by retouch can be identified because they are retouched. It is also possible to identify blanks selected for use without retouch when that use was so heavy as to be unmistakable (scaled pieces). Consideration of these two groups indicates that selected blanks tended

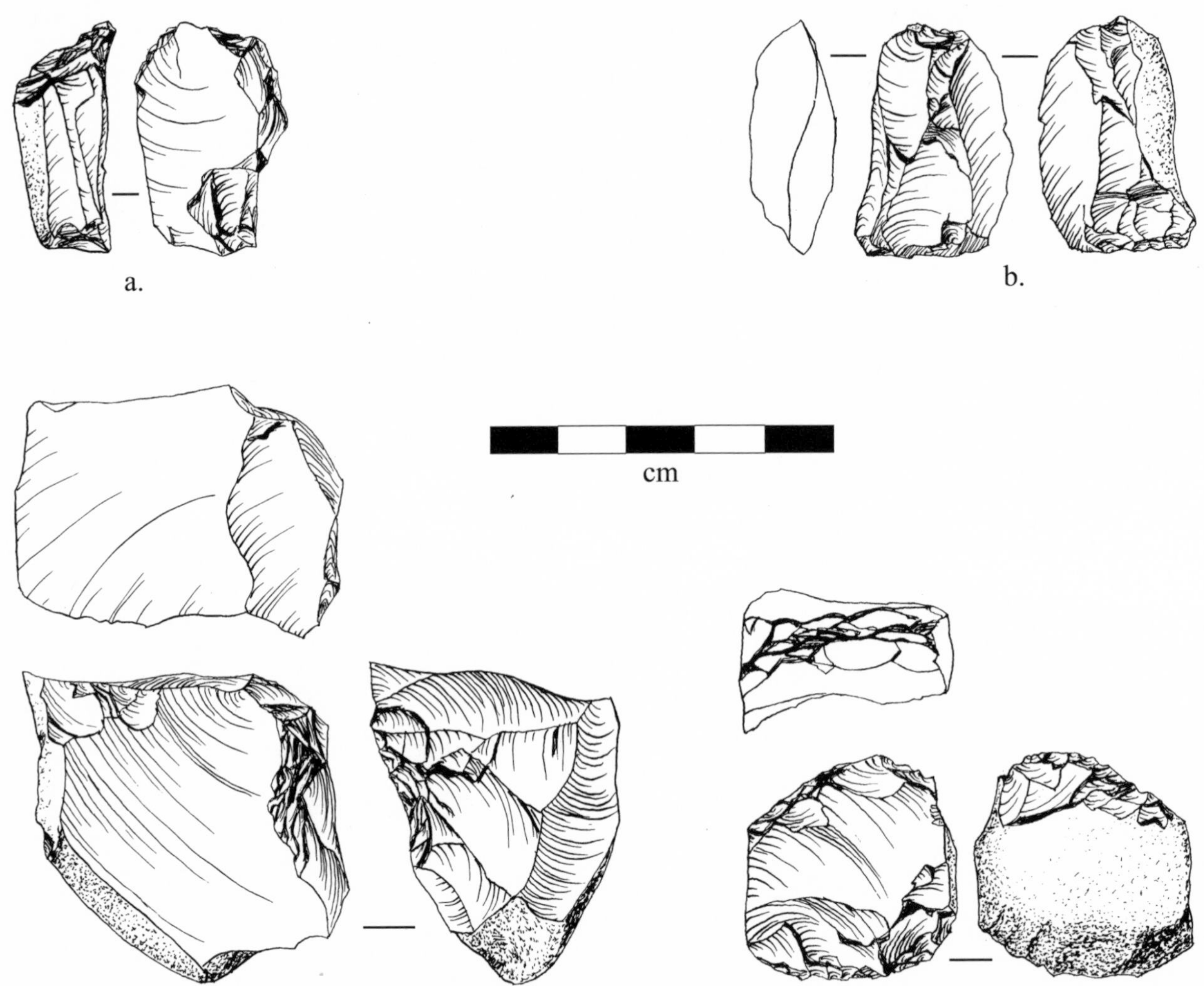

Figure 6.3 Multidirectional cores: (a) bipolar core reused as an opposed platform core; (b) and (d) bipolar cores (b is a reused opposed platform core); (c) ninety degree core. [Provenance: (a) TCD1D010732; (b) TCD0004033; (c) 1213471D0100430; (d) 1303521B0200530.]

to be regular in shape, to retain some cortex – in particular, to have cortical platforms – and to be rather large. In this context, "rather large" means at least 25 mm long (or wide), although, of course, some selected blanks were smaller.

Otherwise, it is difficult to identify blanks likely to have been selected for use, except for one group – that of "naturally backed" flakes. Some 20 30% of all flakes have cortex along one or more edges (lateral, proximal, or distal), the cortex usually being at such a high angle to the dorsal and ventral faces as to form a blunt "back". Naturally backed flakes were an actively desired end product. Compared with other flakes, they are more standardised in size, they have much less dorsal cortex (the natural back is an edge, rather than a face), and many more (>90%) have cortical platforms; all of these attributes were sought after by the makers of the assemblage. Their production was independent of flaking technique, but some cores were deliberately set up to produce flakes with natural backs. The core shown as Figure 6.1: b was flaked around the entire perimeter of its cortical platform, until only a very small line of cortex remained on one edge of the core; flaking then ceased. Similarly, the core shown as Figure 6.1: c (in which the platform is at the base of the drawing) was flaked until the first and last flake scars intersected, and the core itself resembles a naturally backed flake.

Overall, natural backs occur on flakes of a wide of shapes and sizes. The smallest are perfect, tiny bladelets (Figure 6.4: g) with unilateral cortex. Most are slightly larger blades with full or partial, unilateral cortex. The blade in Figure 6.4: a has only a partial natural back, but the backed edge is very straight and there is some damage to the distal end. Figure 6.4: h shows a complete cortical back on a classic bladelet from an opposed platform core, while the example in Figure 6.4: d has complete backing of one edge and partial

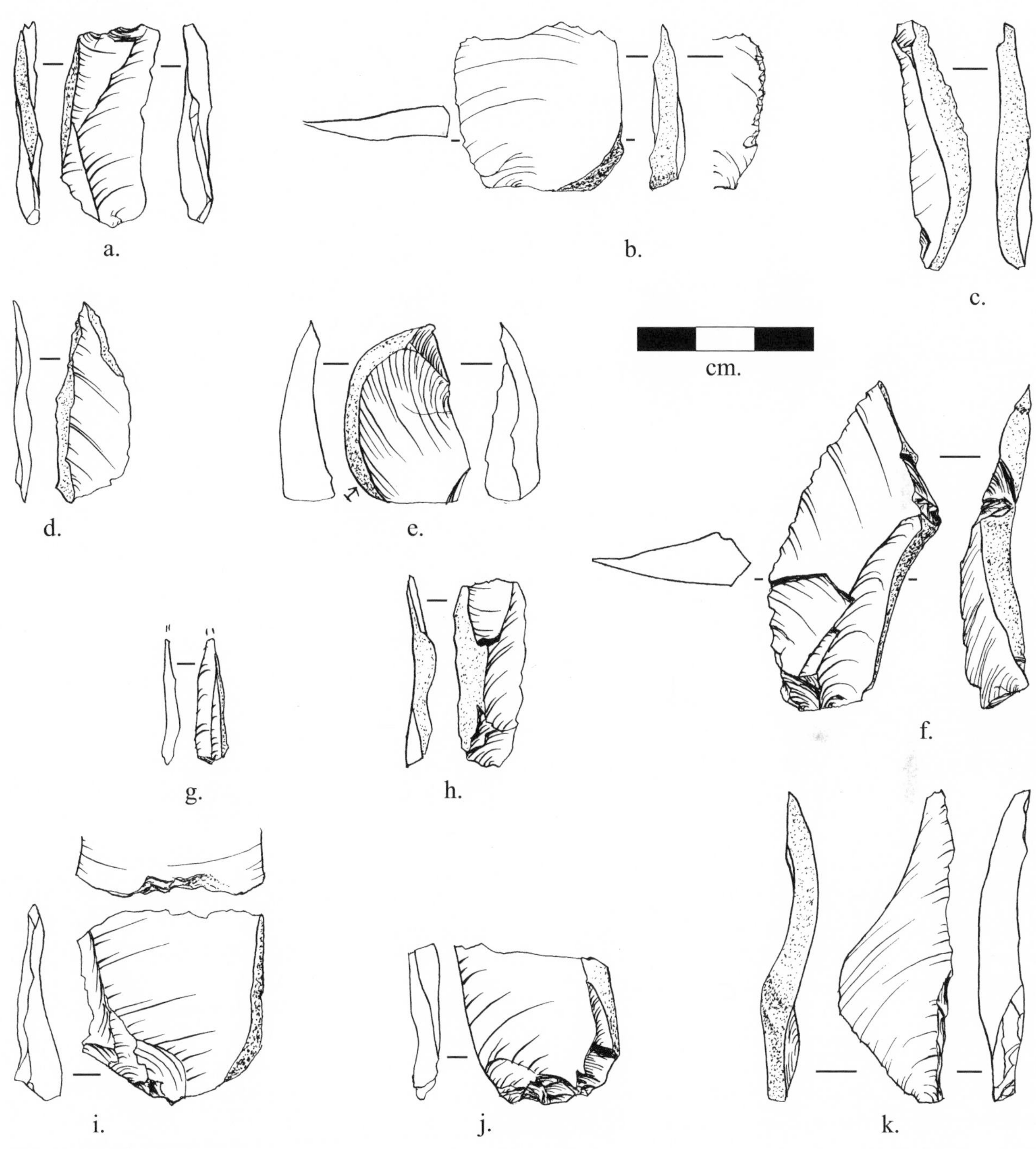

Figure 6.4 Unretouched flakes with one or more natural (cortical) backs. [Provenance: (a) TEF00021732; (b) 1113491J0100932; (c) 1213471B021432; (d) TEF1B03332; (e) TGH1B024032; (f) TAB1A0302331; (g) and (i) TDC0003033; (h) 1233471A058632; (j) TEF0001032; (k) TCD1A0500530.]

backing of the other, the two backed edges converging towards a point.

A sub group are quite classic orange segments. Figure 6.4: c is an elongated segment, on which the cortical platform is continuous with the lateral back; it is triangular in cross section. The flake in Figure 6.4: e is of the more common, relatively short type of segment. It has an unbroken cortical back running from the platform to the distal end.

Most of the cortical backs occur on rather wide flakes, with the opposed edge being thin and sharp. The flake in Figure 6.4: j is a proximal fragment of such

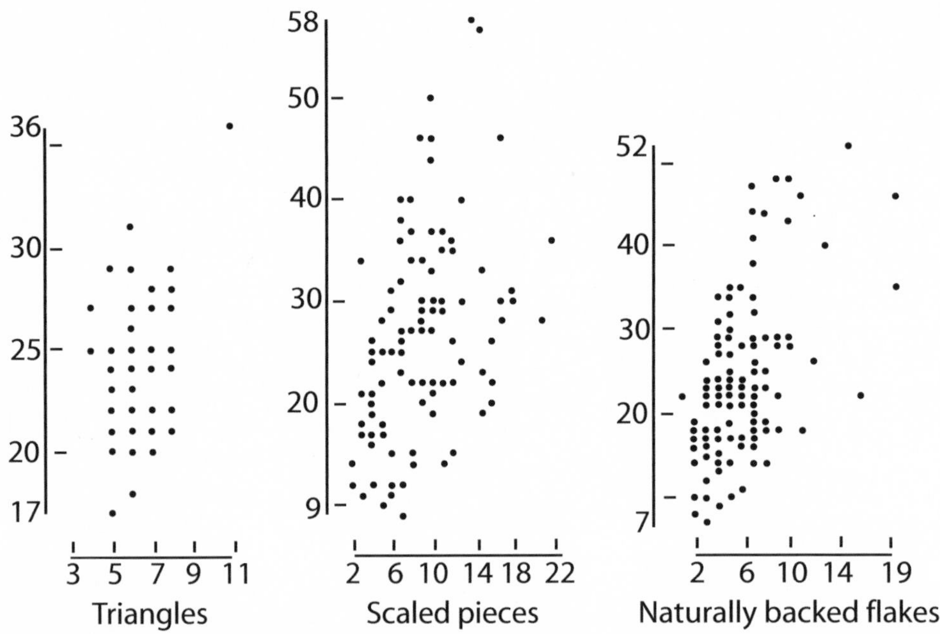

Figure 6.5 Distributions of widths (vertical axis) and thicknesses (horizontal axis) (in mm) of triangles, scaled pieces, and naturally backed flakes. Axes are range-bars. Note that the scales vary.

a piece. Figure 6.4: i shows a complete flake, on which the lateral back and the cortical platform merge; there is some damage at the distal end. A classic example of a naturally backed flake is Figure 6.4: b. The lateral back and cortical platform create a smooth curve; the flake is triangular in cross section and there is extensive and heavy damage to the opposite lateral edge.

None of the naturally backed pieces under consideration has secondary retouch, hence their inclusion in the débitage. Some (few) have edge damage which might or might not result from use. Unfortunately, CVR is a poor candidate for high power microscopic detection of use wear. Whatever these pieces were used for, it did not result in massive and unmistakable damage like that observed on the scaled pieces, and they have not, therefore, been included among the "used tools". I note, however, that naturally backed pieces do occur as blanks among both the used and the retouched tools.

The size range of the tools is rather tightly constrained. This surely results from the limited size range of the original pebbles, which, in turn, results from deliberate selection during the procurement of raw material. However, the tools include three important, cohesive and very different groups – the triangles as opposed to the scaled pieces and naturally backed flakes – and their sizes are distributed very differently from each other. Figure 6.5 plots width against thickness for triangles, scaled pieces, and naturally backed flakes (omitting the heterogeneous "other tools"). Within each group, there is a positive correlation ($p<0.001$ in each case) between the two dimensions, but this becomes insignificant for the triangles ($p>0.05$) with the removal of the outlier (unfinished and under produced) that is 36 mm wide and 11 mm thick. What Figure 6.5 shows above all is that the ranges of widths and thicknesses permitted for triangles were very limited.

Figure 6.6 plots lengths against widths for the three groups of tools. Both the scaled pieces and the naturally backed flakes have strong ($p<0.001$) positive correlations between length and width, indicating a desire for consistency in shape. For the triangles, there is no correlation ($p>0.05$) between length and width. Instead, lengths fall almost at random within the tightly constrained range of widths.

Thus, the criteria governing selection of blanks for additional shaping into triangles and those of blanks for (immediate) use as scaled pieces (or as naturally backed flakes) were very different: the *chaîne opératoire* has divided.

Shaping of Blanks (Secondary Retouch)

Table 6.3 gives the frequencies of all retouched or used tools from the various excavation units at OpD.. This section describes the blanks that received additional shaping: the "retouched tools". The used tools – the scaled pieces – are described in a later section.

Most of the retouched tools are triangles, but the assemblage does include some mundane classes of flake tools, including endscrapers (Figure 6.7: f); perforators (Figure 6.7: c, d); burins (Figure 6.7: a, b, e); backed pieces; notched and denticulated pieces; truncated pieces (Figure 6.7: g); and miscellaneous retouched

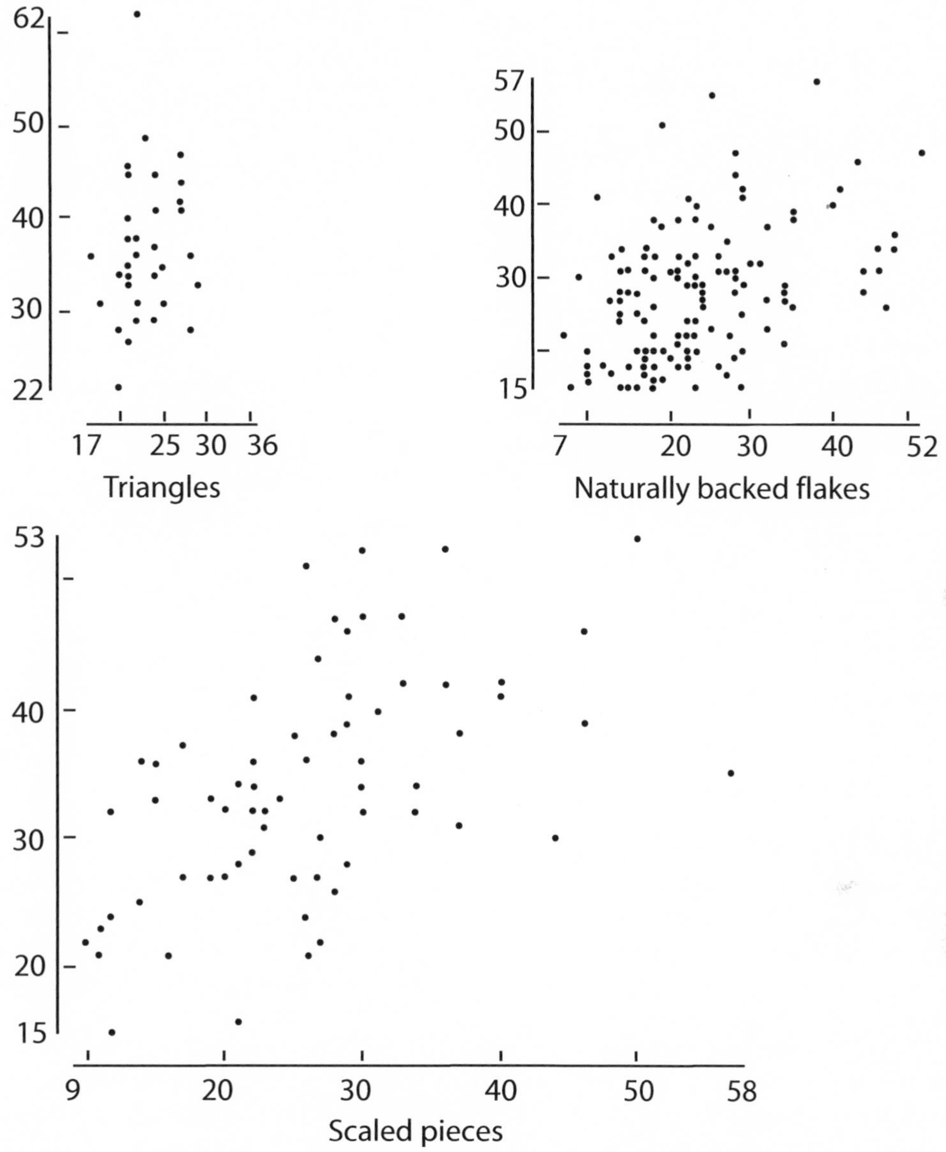

Figure 6.6 Distributions of lengths (vertical axis) and widths (horizontal axis) (in mm) of triangles, scaled pieces, and naturally backed flakes. Axes are range-bars. The scales vary (The triangle 36 mm wide is broken.)

pieces, some of them bifacially retouched and others not. The latter include two naturally backed bladelets with retouched bases (Figure 6.8: a, b), a trapezium (sensu Procli) (Figure 6.8: d) with three more or less straight, unretouched edges, and a very oblique (left), convex, proximal truncation; a tongued piece (Figure 6.8: b) which is in no way related to triangles; and a flake on which the left edge is a smooth curve from the left proximal corner to the right distal corner, shaped by discontinuous retouch (Figure 6.8: c), while the proximal end has strong retouch defining a straight and markedly denticulated edge. This might be seen as a triangle with the tip in the left proximal corner, but the attention paid to the proximal end suggests that this was the more important part of the tool.

Triangles

Most of the pieces in this class are clearly triangular, having three distinct sides in plan – even the broken specimens. However, since these are stone artifacts, rather than abstract shapes, there is considerable leeway in the definition of edges and, more particularly, of corners. In accordance with convention (Addington 1986:43 48), the triangles in Figure 6.9 are oriented as if they were triangular points, with the "point" at the top (although many are decidedly unpointed). I have also indicated the direction in which the blank itself was struck, even when it is in the default direction of vertically upward. Triangles without indication of blank orientation are those for which I was unable to determine such orientation. The flaking orientation of

Table 6.3 Frequencies of retouched or used tools

	Provenience											
	Unit I	107341	105365	111349	121347	123347	130352	TrAB	TrCD	TrEF	TrGH	n
Endscraper on flake	-	1	2	1	-	-	1	-	-	1	-	6
Endscraper on retouched flake	-	-	1	-	-	-	-	-	-	2	-	3
Simple perforator	-	-	3	1	-	-	1	-	-	-	-	5
Dihedral burin	-	-	-	-	-	-	-	-	-	1	-	1
Burin on a break	-	-	-	-	-	-	-	-	-	3	-	3
Backed flake	-	-	-	-	-	1	-	-	-	-	-	1
Arch-backed bladelet	-	-	-	-	-	-	1	-	-	-	-	1
Shouldered bladelet	-	-	-	-	-	-	-	-	-	3	-	3
Notched flake	-	-	1	1	-	-	1	-	-	-	1	4
Denticulated flake	1	-	-	-	-	-	-	-	-	-	-	1
Notched blade	-	-	-	-	-	-	-	-	-	-	1	1
Truncation	-	-	-	-	-	-	-	-	-	6	-	6
Triangle	10	1	15	5	3	2	3	12	6	9	8	74
Other bifacial piece	-	-	-	1	1	-	-	-	1	1	-	4
Other retouched piece	2	-	1	2	-	3	1	5	1	2	2	19
Unidentifiable/fragment	2	-	3	3	2	3	3	-	3	1	2	22
Scaled piece	1	-	7	4	8	4	25	10	19	53	14	145
Total	15	2	33	18	14	13	36	27	30	82	28	299

the blank usually does not coincide with the orientation of the "point". References below to "tips", "bases", and "left" and "right" sides are based upon orientation of the triangles as points. A few of the more curious triangles are formally illustrated in Figure 6.9).

Blanks were selected for the manufacture of triangles primarily on the basis of size, especially width and thickness. A majority of the blanks were flakes, and it is mostly likely that all of them were flakes. Flakes without cortex were preferred, but at least one triangle is made on a primary flake (Figure 6.9: a). There was also some deliberate selection of flakes with feathered distal terminations, since, on some triangles, the thinning of such terminations provides most of the "basal thinning" of the triangle. All of the blanks selected were within the size range of other OpD flakes; there is no reason to suppose that they were not struck there.

Shaping was generally minimal: only nine of the 63 triangles for which this could be recorded are fully bifacial, but this cannot account for the low frequency of identified biface thinning pieces in the débitage (Table 6.1). Triangles (and other bifacial tools) are most numerous in Area 105 365, Unit I and the uppermost part of the Trench (AB; this is also the part of the Trench where the best made triangles were found). These areas are also where most of the biface related débitage occurs. This makes it highly likely that the triangles were shaped at OpD, although not necessarily in any of those specific areas. (They might be dumping areas.) However, the triangles themselves show that most of the shaping involved very short removals, or slightly longer but extremely thin removals. Such pieces, or fragments thereof, would be recovered only on the 1/8" screen or in the micro débitage, which I did not study. (Tiny fragments of CVR are, curiously, almost absent from the "microartifacts" in Area 105 365 (Chapter 5, this volume).

Almost all of the retouch on the lateral edges of the triangles is scaled, the removals frequently terminating in hinges. It is most often semi abrupt, and the bulbar scars are pronounced, in some cases so much so as to resemble serrations. Most removals are short, affecting the edges of the triangle rather than the faces. Thus, most of the shaping of the triangles was by direct percussion (and probably with a hard hammer). There is no indisputable evidence for pressure flaking.

Lateral retouch is usually less pronounced near the base of the triangle (the thin distal end of the flake blank), becoming stronger towards the (thicker) tip. It is normally either semi abrupt on both faces, or plano convex, with semi abrupt obverse and semi flat inverse removals. It is not always bifacial. In most cases, only sufficient lateral shaping was done to produce an approximately isosceles triangle with straight to slightly

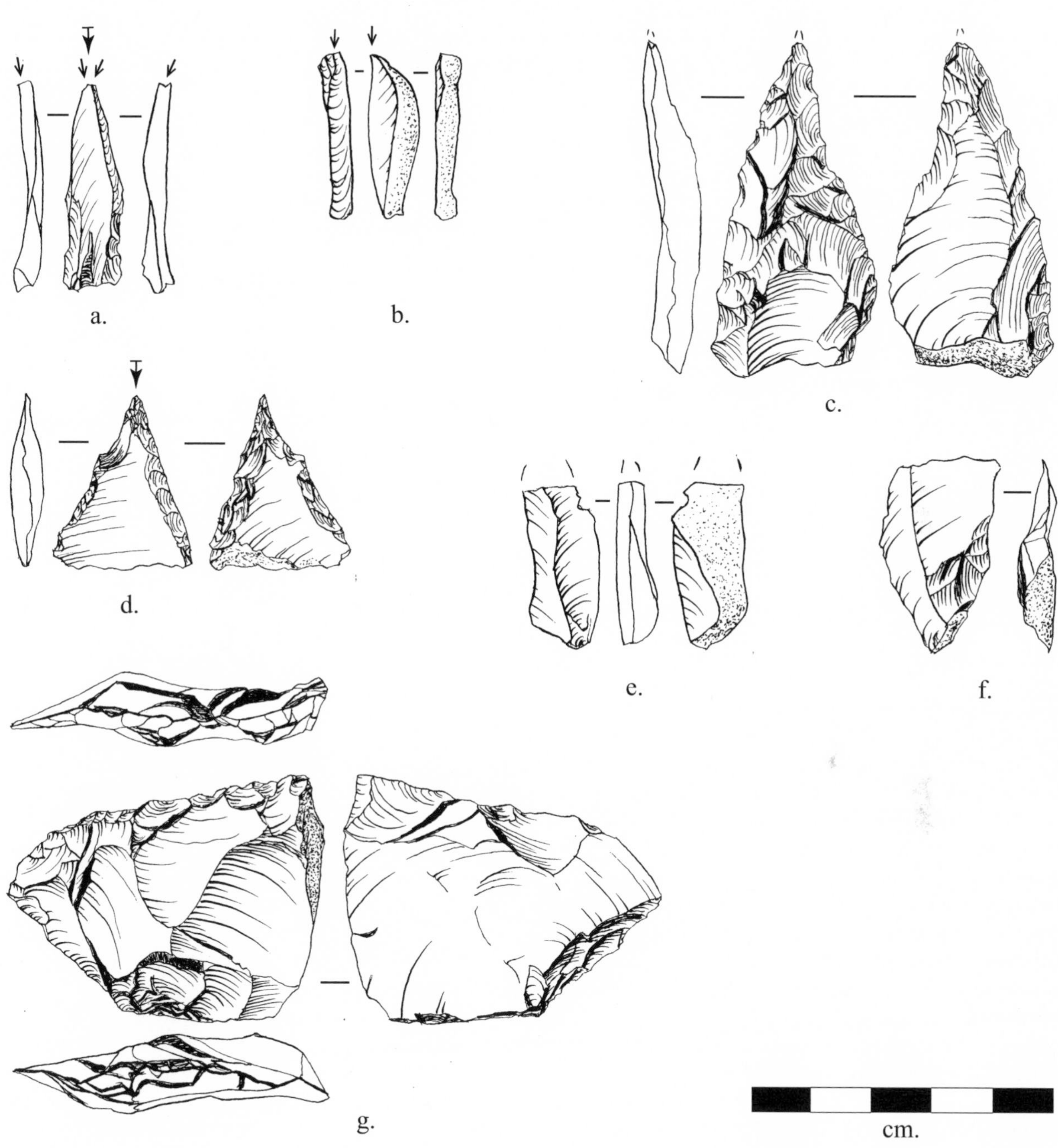

Figure 6.7 Retouched tools: (a) and (b) burins; (c) and (d) perforators (d is made on a triangle); (e) burin-spall struck from primary flake; (f) endscraper made on a scaled piece; (g) truncated piece. [Provenance: (a) TEF1B0311932; (b) TEF0001830; (c) 1113491S0100330; (d) 105 3651H02; (e) TEF0001032; (f) 1113491G0100330; (g) TEF00011832.]

convex sides.

In most cases, the "point" of the triangle, or the most important corner, was shaped at the proximal end of the flake. This frequently necessitated considerable thinning, which was not always successful. Several triangles have lumps on the (ventral) face very close to the tip, against which cascades of hinge fractures testify to the knapper's inability to remove the lump.

The tip was shaped after the lateral edges, again by direct percussion. Some tips are sharply pointed; others are not and there is no reason to think that they ever were. Many of the tips broke off during shap-

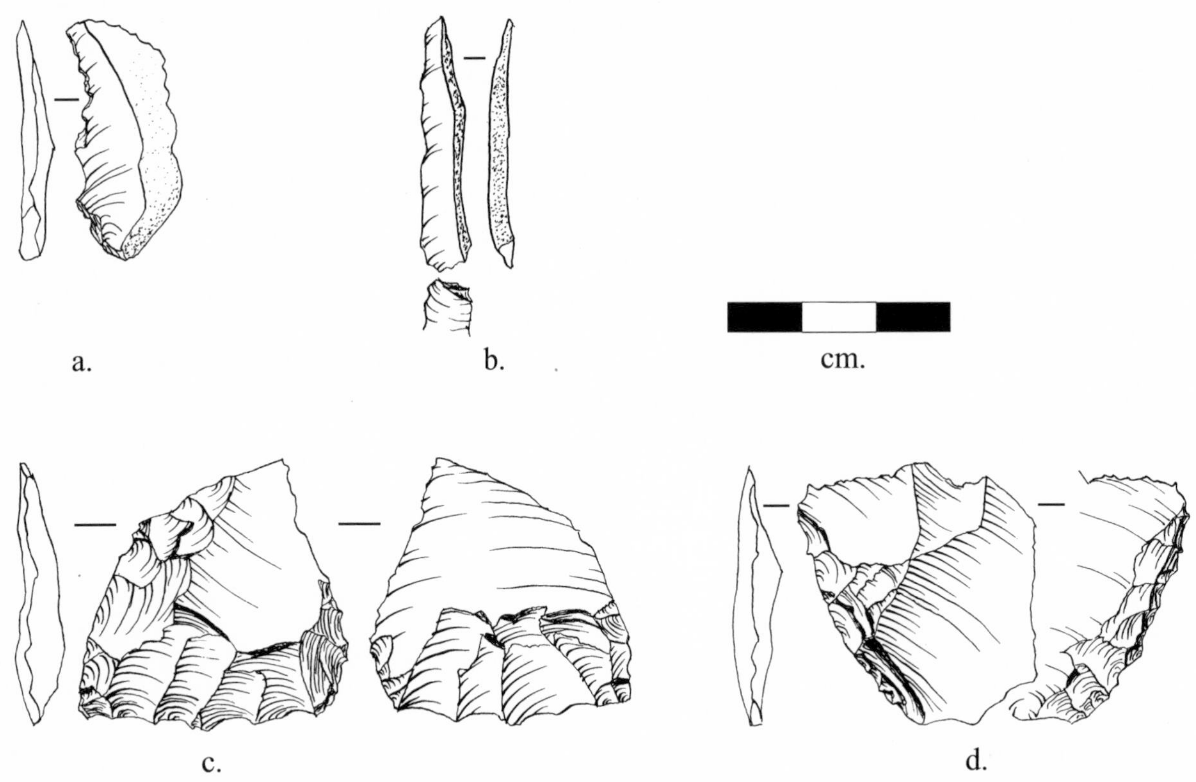

Figure 6.8 Other retouched tools. [Provenance: (a) 1233471A0100632; (b) 1233471G020632; (c) TAB1A0500430; (d) TAB1F0300730.]

ing, some of them falling victim to the unusual and hazardous technique of thinning the tip by striking it axially. After such breakage, there were often attempts to remake the tip, or even remake the entire triangle, with mixed success.

Bases are generally thin (being the feathered distal ends of flakes) and very variable in plan. The basal corners may or may not be sharp (and some are not even retouched) and the base itself may be convex, straight, or concave. Only concave bases are consistently – almost inevitably – shaped by retouch. Straight and convex bases may be lightly or partially retouched; not retouched at all, or even snapped to shape. Most bases are symmetrical about the axis of the triangle, or close to it, and the more asymmetrical ones appear to be the end of a continuum of decreasing symmetry, rather than a separate type.

TOOL KIT MANAGEMENT

Tool Use

It is axiomatic that some of the flaked stone artifacts were used for something. However, crystalline volcanic rock is a poor candidate for high power, microscopic, use wear analysis, so the actual uses remain, in general, mysterious.

Triangles

Some effort was expended upon the manufacture of triangles, so, presumably, they were intended for a purpose. The usual scenario would have triangles become damaged in some way during use, then new triangles would be made to replace the damaged ones in some kind of haft. The recovered triangles would thus be those used, broken, and replaced. However, Ahler's (1992) refitting of broken points warns us of the difficulty of recognizing breaks resulting from use, and the damage to these triangles seems more likely to have occurred during shaping. Some of the triangles are clearly unfinished and were abandoned during manufacture (Figure 6.9: b d). This is particularly true of the specimens with unremovable lumps on their faces, whether or not attempts to remove the lump led to breakage (Figure 6.9: e). Breakage of one basal corner is frequent. Tips are often broken, but only very slightly and during manufacture, since there may be subsequent efforts to remake a tip. In short, abandonment during manufacture is probably how at least most of the triangles entered the archaeological record.

If some of the triangles were ever used, the usual scenario, again, would have them serve as projectile points and, even more specifically, as arrow heads, to be used in hunting (and warfare?). The form of some of the triangles appears unsuitable for such use (for example,

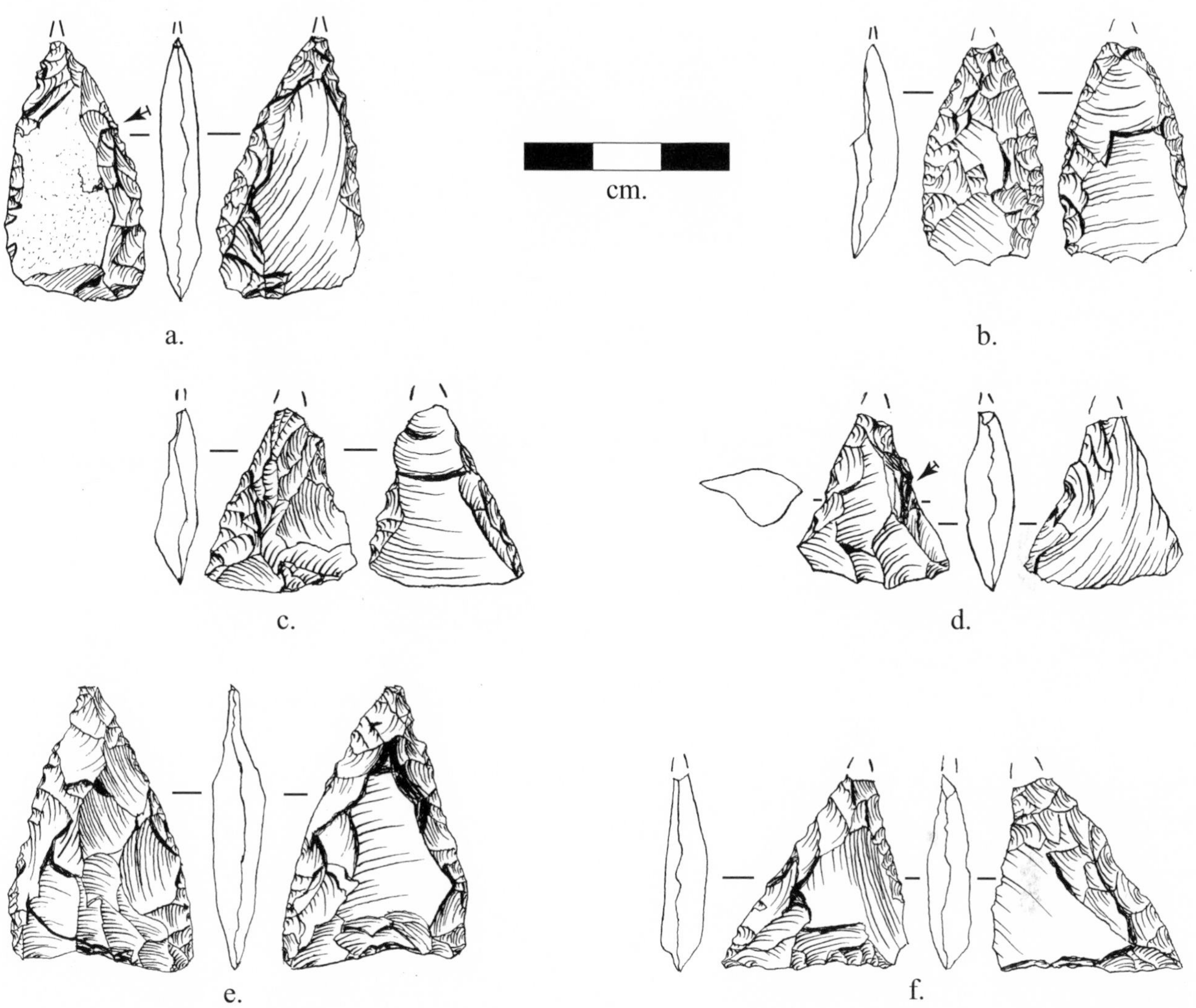

Figure 6.9 Triangles from various units. [Provenance: (a) 105 3651W0100232; (b) 1113492E0200732; (c) TEF000100032; (d) 105 3651K0200332; (e) 105 365000100230; (f) 105 3651L0100732.]

Figure 6.9: d), but this could result from their being abandoned during manufacture. On the other hand, some of the triangles are consistent with use as projectile points: the frequent thinness of the basal parts accords with that being the part that was hafted; the thickness of the pointed end (when actually pointed) would serve to make the point stronger. In this case, the arrows would be manufactured and assembled at OpD, the place of residence. The hunter(s) went out hunting and, from time to time, broke the stone arrow head, perhaps by killing something, or perhaps by dropping the arrow on a rock. If the shaft(s) and fletching were still serviceable, the damaged arrow was brought back to OpD, where a new stone arrow head was made and installed in the shaft. Thus, the artifacts found at OpD include the arrow head that was (used and) damaged elsewhere and returned to OpD for discard, plus the débitage resulting from the manufacture of the replacement point.

Norton (1985:Table 5.1) reports that, in the historical and ethnographic accounts of the Indians of the Northwest Coast, the only procurement of resources that was done solely by men was of (large) marine and terrestrial mammals. (Even so, women sometimes took part in hunting seals.) Thus, use of the arrows would be an exclusively male activity, making it likely that the manufacture of arrows was also an exclusively male activity. For example, among the Makah of Neah Bay, where whales have been pursued exclusively by men, women are not permitted even to touch whaling equipment (including those in the museum collections recovered from Ozette). Stein (2000:93), based

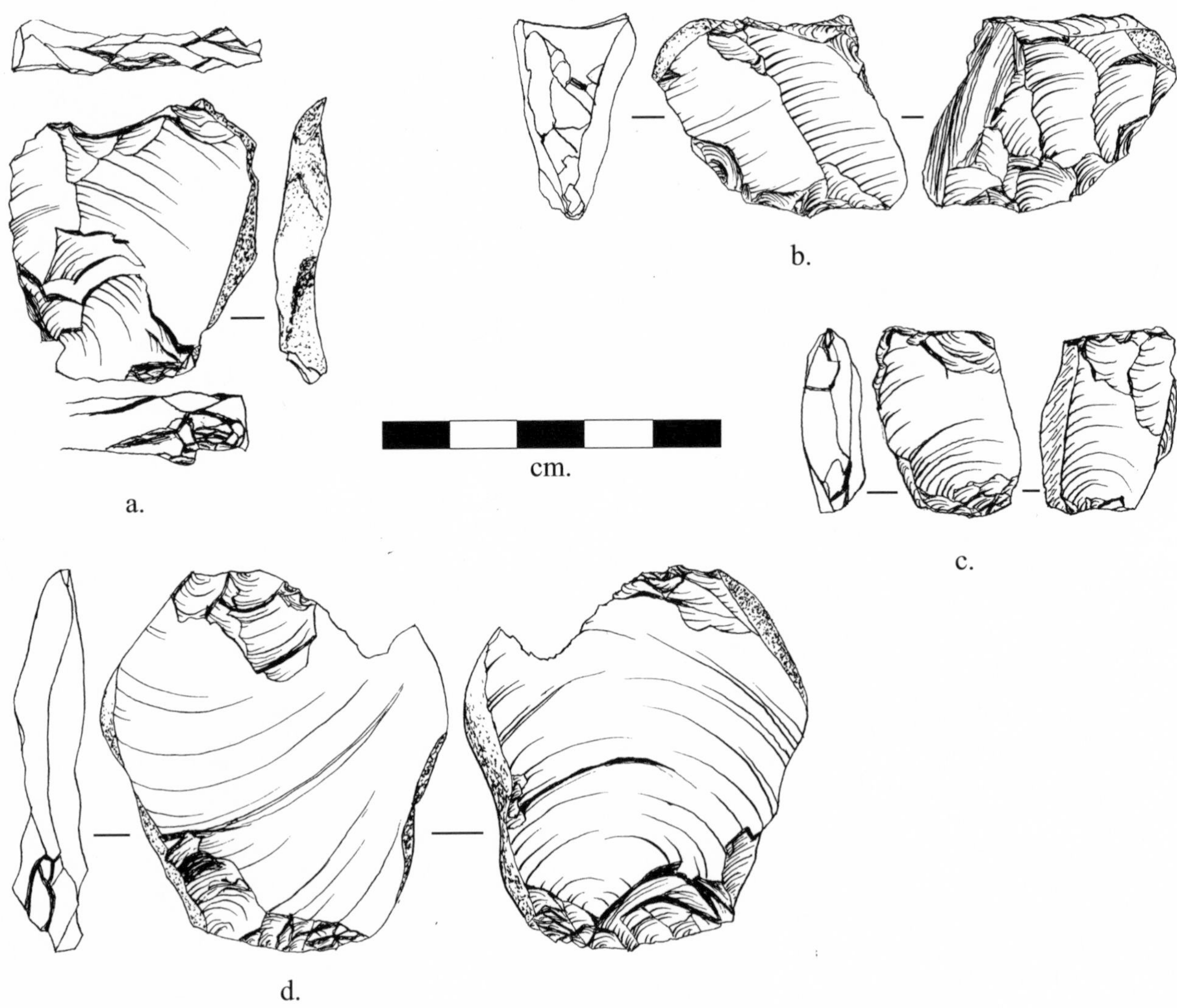

Figure 6.10 Scaled pieces. [Provenance: (a) 1213471B030033; (b) TGH1B0302531; (c) 1233471A0406432; (d) TGH1B0301731.]

on an unnamed source, reports that men left the house to make their tools privately, for ritual reasons. This could be why, at OpD, triangles and their manufacturing debris are relatively more common in the remoter parts of the site, to which men retired to make men's tools, away from the ritual impurity (in this context) of women. If so, then it becomes most likely that the triangles were made at the places where we find them. It is not parsimonious to suppose that men went far away and brought back all their debris and rejects for dumping at OpD.

However, it is not certain that the triangles were intended for use as projectile points. Swan (1870:48) described the arrow heads in use at Cape Flattery as pieces of iron wire (obviously a post Contact phenomenon), "bones with jagged edges like barbs", and other varieties made of wood or bone; there is no mention of stone. Stein (2000: 92, 99) cites historical reports of ground slate arrow heads, and ethnographic reports of bone arrow heads and of a hunting or war arrow with a point made, apparently interchangeably, of stone or mussel shell. This last is much more likely to have been a ground stone point – mussel shell also being shaped by grinding, rather than flaking. Globally, small flaked artifacts have been seen as projectile points (Ambrose 2002:16 17; Belfer Cohen and Goring Morris 2002; Elston and Brantingham 2002:104)), although, when use wear studies can be carried out, the results can indicate that this was not so (for example, Finlayson and Mithen 1997). Further, when there are ethnohistoric

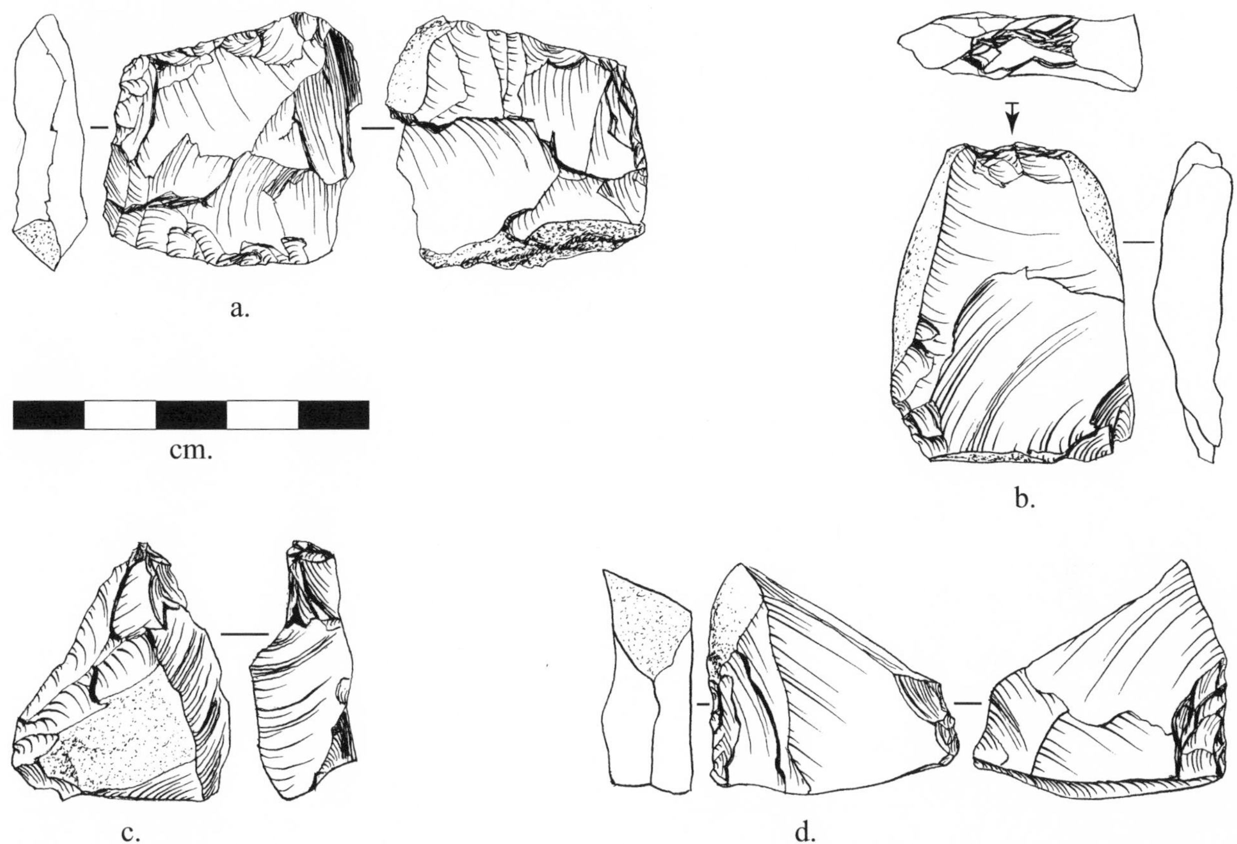

Figure 6.11 Scaled pieces. [Provenance: (a) 1303521A0200931; (b) 1303521C0100431; (c) 1303521A0201432; (d) 1303521A0201631.]

reports of projectiles, as in the Northwest, their tips are often not of stone (for example, Ellis 1997; Close and Sampson 1998).

In sum, it is not clear that the triangles recovered from OpD were ever used at all. If some of them were used, we do not know how. Emphasis in their manufacture was upon a thick and sturdy point, so they were probably piercing tools. However, the "points" are not always pointed (with apologies to Bordes 1961:21) and might have served better to pierce something tougher and less actively resistant than a living animal. Whatever their use, the manufacture of triangles had an important social aspect: either they were made away from the main area of the site, or, wherever they were made, the by products were collected and deliberately discarded away from the main area of the site.

Most of the triangles were shaped with some economy of effort: little more was done than was necessary to achieve the desired shapes in plan and profile. There are two remarkable exceptions to this, which were so carefully retouched as to be over manufactured and have shapes unique in the site. They are a very elongated triangle from Unit 121 347 and a concave sided triangle from Area 123 347. The first is exceptional in length and elongation; the second is exceptional in having concave sides, which are otherwise unknown at the site. Both come from areas depauperate in triangles.

I suggest that in these triangles – exquisitely made and spatially isolated from almost all other triangles – we have artifacts whose primary significance lay in the realm of social relations. Both of them are broken and there were no attempts made to reshape or rework them, despite the investment of skill and time already made in them. If their social roles involved simply being and being seen to be perfect, then repair would have been out of the question – they were already s(p)oiled.

Scaled Pieces

One of the most interesting groups of tools at OpD is that of scaled pieces (Figures 6.10-6.12). The type is well known through most of the Old World, particularly Africa and western Eurasia. This does not mean that it is equally well understood; it is not. In anglophone North America (where, perversely, scaled pieces are often referred to as *pièces esquillées*), however, the very existence of scaled pieces as tools has been called into question, and some have seen them simply as yet more bipolar cores. A thoughtful summary of this debate is that by Hayden (1980), who recounts most of

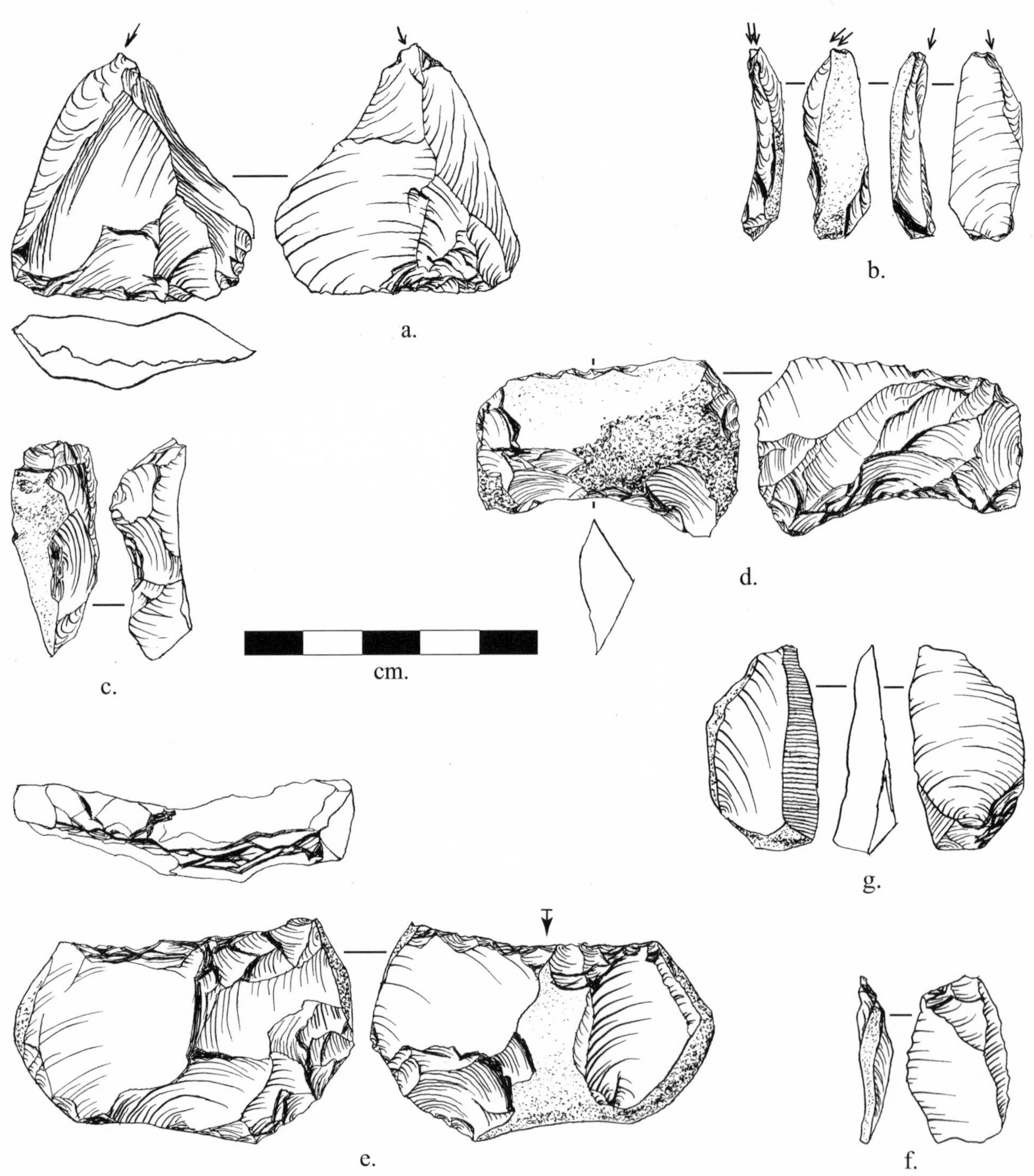

Figure 6.12 Scaled pieces. [Provenance: (a) TCD00030033; (b) TEF1B0301132; (c) TCD000202532; (d) TRC1A0201932; (e) TEF000100332; (f) TEF1B0200930; (g) TEF000200732.]

the history of scaled pieces in the literature up to 1980, except for Tixier's (1963:146 149) magisterial contribution. Some of the more recent publications concerning scaled pieces have become rather testy (Shott 1989, 1999; LeBlanc 1992). However, in the complete absence of drawings of the artifacts in question, the discussion seems rarefied.

I will, however, place myself firmly in the pro scaled pieces ranks. The purpose of "core reduction" is to produce flakes which may be used as tools. Thus, the flakes removed from "cores" should be no smaller than the minimal useful or usable. Detailed analysis of the débitage (Close 2006) suggests that the OpD flakers felt that the lower limit of usefulness fell at about 15 mm. The scaled pieces from the site have scars resulting from the application of some kind of (usually) bipolar force. However, the great majority of those removals were of pieces too small (considerably less than 15 mm) to have been desired as tools, so the scaled pieces should not be seen as cores.

Quo dicto, there is some overlap between scaled pieces and bipolar cores, and some (but not many) of the OpD pieces have been reclassified more than once. However, to classify any stone from which even the tiniest of flakes has been removed as a "core" because of that removal seems to me to be, at best, simplistic and, at worst, mindless.

Blanks were selected for use as scaled pieces primarily on the bases of size (especially thickness) and of the presence of naturally backed edges, usually on the distal ends of flakes or on one or both lateral edges. The amount of dorsal cortex was not a factor in the selection of flakes for use as scaled pieces. As with the triangles, it is almost certain that the selected blanks were made at OpD.

There is no evidence that the selected blanks received any modification before use. It was the process of being used which transformed them into "scaled pieces", and the variability in the nature and degree of scaling suggests comparable variability in the nature and degree of use.

About a third of the scaled pieces were used similarly on two opposite edges (whether sides or ends). These tend not to have natural backs, or to have natural backs only on the unscaled edges, where they would have facilitated grasping during tool use. The same relationship between scaled and cortical edges was also observed on some of the most fragmentary pieces.

Most scaled pieces show no such symmetry of use: they are (much) more heavily scaled on one edge than on the opposite edge, and the heavily scaled edge on flakes is usually the proximal end – the thickest part of the flake. Asymmetrically scaled pieces may have natural backs perpendicular to the scaled edge, which would, again, facilitate grasping. More often, however, they have a cortical back on the edge opposite the scaling, and it is likely that it was to these cortical backs that (often considerable) force was applied. Some of the opposed cortical backs are visibly battered; some show an origination of light scaling (usually unifacial) from the cortex, and some saw the origination of *bâtonnets* and pseudo burins. These features correspond closely to the development of damage identified on scaled pieces from North Africa by Tixier (1963:Figure 56), and the similar development Keeley (1980:40) described for experimentally used pieces. The most heavily scaled areas, and those with the widest edge angles (up to 78°) tend to have opposed cortical backs.

The materials on which the scaled pieces were used remain unknown. Williamson and others (2004, cited by Villa *et al.* in press) have begun residue analysis of the scaled pieces from Sibudu (South Africa), and have found a variety of organic and mineral residues, indicating, one presumes, a variety of materials.

The ways in which they were used also remain unknown. They were originally interpreted as the punches used in indirect percussion, a task for which they are eminently unsuitable (Tixier 1963:146 149). In Europe, their use as chisels (or "wedges") for splitting bone or ivory is widely regarded as apocryphal (with rare exceptions, such as Demars and Laurent [1989]), and most scholars are now non-committal about possible uses,

In the New World, the interpretation as wedges for working bone or wood was initially accepted (MacDonald 1968). More recent literature seems to have polarized into arguments about whether they are wedges or bipolar cores (LeBlanc 1992; Shott 1989, 1999) with little consideration that there are other possibilities. Kimball (1994), working on material from the Main Site (Kentucky) and elsewhere, found polish on most of the scaled pieces that was consistent with working bone or antler.

Other possibilities – other than wedges or bipolar cores – do exist. There are two major patterns among the scaled pieces from OpD. The preference for cortical backs perpendicular to the scaled edge suggests that they were hand held. The alternative preference for a cortical back opposite the scaled edge – and, indeed, the final overall condition of the artifacts themselves – suggest that some of the work was very heavy duty and did not require great precision. The scaled pieces are not large and so were probably not used to process large pieces of material. Their use as wedges or chisels to split cedar thus seems unlikely, given the ease with which cedar can be split (Flenniken 1981:73 74). Cutting is a possibility. The lightly scaled pieces could have performed light duty cutting – or, equally probable – were only in the first stages of the road to destruction by use. The heavily scaled pieces – especially those hammered at the opposite end – were used in a different way. If cutting was still involved (rather than pounding or bashing), one might think of cutting wood across the grain, or decapitating large fish.

The matter of who may have been using the scaled pieces is considered below, together with the naturally backed flakes.

Naturally Backed Flakes

Naturally backed flakes (flakes with cortical backs) without secondary retouch were an actively desired, deliberately and carefully manufactured product. Their selection for use (predetermined by the very fact of their manufacture) was based upon the presence of the cortical back. One supposes that they are a "functional" type, intended for some specific purpose(s). Bordes would not have hesitated to call them "naturally backed knives", and he might have been right. An abrupt cortical edge is at least as blunt as one backed by retouch, and more reliably produced in tough stone like CVR. Some (few) have edge damage which might or might not result from use. However, whatever these pieces were used for, it did not result in massive and unmistakable damage like that observed on the scaled pieces, and they were not, therefore, included among the definitely "used tools".

The naturally backed flakes often have the cortical edge opposed to a sharp (unretouched) edge, no matter which is the edge with the cortical back. Some of the most knife like examples are large blades with a cortical back on two contiguous edges, opposed to a straight or convex edge that is thin and sharp. However, given the variety of their forms (Figure 6.4), it is difficult to imagine them being consistently used as anything except a hand held knife. In that case, the forefinger would rest along the cortical back and the working edge of the tool was the sharp edge opposed to the back. The virtual absence of macroscopic damage along the sharp edges suggests light and precise cutting, relying on the sharpness of the edge rather than on the force behind it (in contrast to the scaled pieces).

The scaled pieces and naturally backed knives were made and used at OpD to process a variety of raw materials in a variety of ways – as, doubtless, were any other pieces of flaked stone that were serviceable. Careful reading of written records reveals that, at the time of Contact, native women of the Northwest Coast performed many tasks. (This section is based primarily upon Norton's [1985] careful reading of written records.) Women did almost everything (harvesting, processing, production, maintenance) that involved plant materials. Since many different plant and parts of plants were used in various ways, women would have needed a range of tools, including stone tools. (Men did weave their own reef nets – out of twine made by women.) Only men did the hunting of large marine and terrestrial mammals, but women took part in the procurement of all other organic resources (including birds and fish), sometimes exclusively (plants and shellfish). Men, primarily, processed large sea mammals, but all other food processing was done by women. Women carved small (reportedly, exquisite) wooden items (Norton 1985:17, 76), which would have required sharp, precision cutting tools that, before Contact, could only have been stone. Women made a variety of woven goods (such as mats, blankets and clothing), both for household use and for trade. Swan (1870:45) noted that mats were one of the main things women made in winter; Stein (2000:11) suggests OpD may have been a winter camp. That is, the flaked stone artifacts being used at OpD to process various non stone materials were certainly used by women. Further, it is highly likely that almost all of them were used exclusively by women.

TOOL MAINTENANCE

Tool maintenance may not have been an entirely alien concept to the knappers of OpD, but neither did it play a noticeable role in tool kit management.

Triangles

If triangles were indeed hafted, then replacement in the haft of a failed triangle with another would constitute maintenance of the composite tool. The triangles found at OpD would then be the failed components that were replaced. However, it remains unclear that any of the triangles did actually see use, and the breakages appear to have occurred during manufacture of the triangles themselves.

There are triangles (but very few) which appear to have been reworked after an initial manufacturing failure. On both b and c of Figure 6.9, a major inverse blow to thin the tip (the proximal end of the blank) left a hinge fracture about a third of the way down. One of these (Figure 6.9: c) was then abandoned, but, on the other, an attempt was made to reshape the tip (Figure 6.9: b). Since the tip broke yet again, this attempt may be regarded as a failure. On the triangle shown as Figure 6.9: f, a tip of the triangle was carefully pointed (the left basal angle in the main view), but the triangle was then reoriented and another point was made on a second angle; the second point broke. Examples such as these do involve the remaking of triangles; however, since they probably never got into actual use, this is not, strictly, "maintenance" of tools.

Scaled Pieces

It is logically not possible to maintain a tool if the working edge is not shaped by retouch. The working edge may be reshaped by retouch, but doing so transforms it into another type of tool. Thus, neither the scaled pieces nor the naturally backed flakes could be "maintained".

In the case of the scaled pieces, a few (Fig. 6.15: c, g) were very lightly used, but these are the exceptional pieces. Most were more heavily used, and many so heavily as to lead to their destruction, as evidenced by the spalling of *bâtonnets*, the pseudo burins and the cleavage planes. After some use, a minority of the scaled pieces were abandoned. More commonly, they were rotated to bring another edge, or pair of edges, into use (Figure 6.12: d), or continued to be battered until they fell apart (Figure 6.12: a) or until there was no longer a serviceable edge (this is probably the case for Figure 6.12: f). Even after a scaled piece had shattered, fragments deemed sufficiently large might continue in use (Figure 6.11: c).

Naturally Backed Flakes

The very acute, unretouched edge of a flake is sharper than a retouched edge and, if made on so tough a material as CVR, can be expected to retain its sharpness well, particularly if used, as suggested above, for light and precise cutting. Naturally backed knives would thus be serviceable for some time. However, the edge would eventually begin to be blunted, and an edge that is sharp by virtue of being unretouched cannot be resharpened by retouch, so there could be no maintenance of the naturally backed knives. Instead, a blunted knife would be discarded and, presumably, if the task were not completed, replaced by a fresh and sharp one.

DISCARD

There are perhaps two patterns of discard. The first is that the triangles tend to occur in the same areas as does the biface related debitage. This indicates either that these areas are where triangles were shaped, or that triangles (particularly manufacturing failures) and their associated by products were dumped in these areas. The second pattern is that scaled pieces and naturally backed knives are concentrated in areas where the triangles are not.

Scaled pieces occur with varied degrees of damage – some were scarcely used while others were reused beyond a state one would have thought usable. The blanks used as scaled pieces were almost certainly created at OpD. It is thus highly likely that the use and reuse phases of the *chaîne* also occurred at OpD as well, and that the scaled pieces were ultimately discarded where they had been used.

Similarly, since knives were discarded in the same place as they had been manufactured, it is most likely that this was also the place where they were used.

The trenches in the main area of OpD (excluding Unit I) can be grouped according to their relationship to the horse shoe shaped ridge (Stein, pers. comm.). Table 6.4 gives the relative frequencies of triangles, scaled pieces, and naturally backed flakes inside the ridge and on the ridge (Unit 107 341 had only three tools); they are significantly different ($\chi^2 = 26.448$; 2 d.f.; $p<0.001$). The difference lies in the paucity of triangles (primarily) and the higher frequencies of scaled pieces and naturally backed flakes inside the ridge compared to the ridge itself. (For the sake of completeness, in Unit I, which is far beyond the ridge, the frequencies are: triangles – 52.6%; scaled pieces – 5.3%; naturally backed flakes – 42.1% [n = 19]. Again, triangles are very frequent.)

Table 6.4 Frequencies of the major groups of tools in relation to the ridge

Location	Percentage per Location			Number of Cases
	Triangles	Scaled pieces	Naturally backed flakes	
Inside the ridge	10.4	43.3	46.3	240
Ridge	32.5	34.2	33.3	117

The triangles, scaled pieces and naturally backed knives appear to have shared the same *chaîne opératoire* through raw material procurement and the creation of blanks. Thereafter, however, the triangles are different, and spatially segregated, from the scaled pieces and naturally backed flakes in shaping, in use, and even in discard. This strongly suggests that they were the tools of two groups of people who were socially defined as different from each other. The early written records (see above) support the idea that the scaled pieces and naturally backed flakes were the tools of women, while the triangles were the tools of men. Thus, the differences in spatial distribution indicate the area where women worked (inside the ridge) as opposed to the area where men worked (on top of the ridge).

The stone artifacts (with the possible exception of the triangles) were used and discarded at OpD, in the places where they had also been produced. Given the manufacturing and productive capabilities of Northwest Coast women, it is perverse to suppose that they would not also have made their own stone tools with which to process all those other materials. The flaking of stone, as practised here, required skill, rather than brute force. It would have been women who made the tools to be used in women's work; to imagine them made by men is discordant with what is known about divisions of labor in the Pacific Northwest.

The CVR at OpD was brought into the site in the form of small pebbles from unknown sources (probably more than one). It is possible that the people were able simply to go to a source and gather up and take away as much as they wished, without interference. However, the local coasts were densely settled, and valuable resources would all have "owners", or people with rights in them. The pebbles of CVR were very intensively used at OpD, and almost all fall within a very narrow size range. There are very few that were apparently too small to use, and there is no evidence for anything larger than about 10 cm in maximal dimension (and not really for anything larger than about 8 cm). This implies that there were constraints in access: CVR pebbles were not free for the taking, but had to be obtained through other groups of people, who may have permitted access to sources (in exchange for something), or actually have traded pebbles (again, in exchange for something).

At the time of Contact, there was considerable trade of the unevenly distributed resources throughout the Northwest Coast. "The mainstay of the inter areal trade consisted of surplus food and material goods produced by women" (Norton 1985:204) – produced by women and owned by women. Stein (2000:94) cites an elder of the Lummi Nation recalling that they used to trade preserved food to people on the Columbia River for stone (in this case, probably nephrite). That is, women produced the goods (preserved food, woven objects, perhaps even the small carvings) that would, by some mechanism, "pay for" the raw pebbles out of which the women would later make their own stone tools at OpD.

At Contact, women were also important traders. European men of the eighteenth and nineteenth centuries traded with native men because they (the Europeans) could not conceive of doing otherwise (Norton 1985: 40 41, 204 206), but some of them also recorded that women made the decisions. "If the wife disapproves of the husband's bargain, he does not sell till he gains her consent… what she likes, he is obliged to approve of or afraid to disapprove of" (Sturgis [1799], cited by Norton [1985:40 41]; emphasis added). Thus, in at least some cases, native men were simply the front men for native women traders. Native women did much of the trading until the Europeans taught them not to (Norton 1985:205).

In light of this, and that goods produced by women "paid for" the raw material for women's stone tools, it becomes extremely likely that it was the women who did the actual trading to obtain the stone.

SYNTHESIS

For a rather brief period about 1400 years ago, the area of English Camp called OpD was used by Native Americans. Stein suggests that the distinctive horseshoe shaped ridge of shell midden surrounded three sides of a house that was occupied during the winter(s). "House" and "winter" are both hypotheses but they are in accord with the inferred *chaîne opératoire* of the flaked stone.

Whatever the specific ways in which OpD was used, the people there did not exist in isolation but were part of a web of social relations binding together many groups of people living in and around the Gulf of Georgia. This web also is reflected in the flaked stone. The annual round of the people at OpD was well established and had probably changed little within remembered time. Any starting point within that round is therefore arbitrary, but a *chaîne opératoire* conventionally begins with raw material procurement. One must remember that, while the *chaîne opératoire* itself goes from raw material procurement to final discard, this took place within a social environment of much longer duration, so that each part of the *chaîne opératoire* responded not only to the immediate situation, but also to what the people confidently anticipated would be done in the future.

One of the most important factors shaping the *chaîne opératoire* is that the people strongly believed that the stone locally available on San Juan Island was not acceptable raw material for the flaked stone tools that they would need. If one considers Stone Age practices throughout the world, it seems that all types of stone have been flaked by someone, somewhere, no matter how dismally unsuitable. A local example is the vein quartz used at the Hoko River site. Nonetheless, because it was their way, the people at OpD were comparatively exacting in their requirements, and so had to obtain all the stone they would need for flaking from elsewhere and transport it to OpD.

Actual transport of the stone was not expensive, but obtaining it in the first place apparently was. The stone of choice was what I have referred to as CVR: crystalline volcanic rock. This was obtained in the form of small pebbles, probably from two different sources. The preferred type was a rather irregular pebble, on which corners and angles had been blunted, but were far from obliterated. These irregular pebbles were easier to set up as cores than the less preferred and much less common type: pebbles with a very smoothly and evenly rounded outer surface.

The people did not have free access to the sources. Either they had to trade for access, or they had to trade for the pebbles themselves. From the people's side, this trade was conducted primarily by women. They may have traded salmon that they had dried and smoked in the summer and autumn, or less perishable things which they had made during the "slow" months of the previous winter – clothing, blankets, mats, small wooden carvings – or, indeed, both. In any case, the price was as high as the sellers could drive it, knowing that the people going to OpD simply had to have this type of stone. Because of this, the women were very selective in the pebbles they accepted. They knew they would not need large flaked stone tools, and so did not bargain for anything larger than about 8 cm at most (perhaps 10 cm if the trading went particularly well). They were also almost always successful in avoiding pebbles that were too small – not absolutely always, but a novice trader has to start somewhere. If the price became too high, they reluctantly settled for smoothly rounded pebbles. The women also knew with some accuracy how many pebbles they would need to get through the coming months, and did not waste their resources on extras. Before agreement was reached, the women may have tested the quality of the pebbles by striking a flake, but this was done very rarely. Their trading partners may have been like the plum seller who offers a free plum to a prospective buyer to indicate the quality of all plums.

Today, we do not know where the people obtained their CVR, but this was not a critical matter. The rolled and water worn condition of the pebbles suggests that the sources were close to water, and the pebbles certainly had to be taken to San Juan Island by boat. If all transport was by boat, then actual transportation costs were minimal. At the time of European Contact, local peoples made boats capable of moving entire households (including the house walls and roofs) around the Gulf, and boats of comparable size were probably being made by A.D. 600 Thus, as much stone as the women could bargain for would easily have been carried on one trip.

When the CVR pebbles and other necessary materials had been collected, the people loaded their boats and paddled to OpD, where they may have (re)constructed a house to occupy in the coming (winter?) months. Whatever the living arrangements at the site, the CVR pebbles now began to come into use for the production of stone tools.

Almost all of the tool production was done by the women. They created blanks for tools by using the pebbles as cores from which to strike flakes, keeping core preparation to an absolute minimum. Flaking was predominantly (or entirely) by direct percussion with a hard hammer, and cortical platforms were preferred. In most cases, the knappers were able to maintain the initial platform throughout the use of the core, and this, combined with the lack of rejuvenation, meant that the later flakes tended not to be any shorter than the earlier flakes. It was considered that 15 mm was about the lower limit for useful flakes.

One of the most distinctive aspects of the women's flaking is that they deliberately set up and flaked their cores so as to produce flakes with cortex along one or more edges. Overall, about a third of the serviceable flakes have one of more cortical edges. It made them easy (and safe) to hold and, for the smaller pieces, facilitated cutting with very precise control.

Most of the flakes probably saw some use, except for those that did not meet the 15 mm criterion. However, women generally preferred to use the larger flakes, that were consistent in proportions, and that had a cortical back. These were the foundation of their tool kits. Some were used directly – to cut, to slice, to section, to carve, to scrape – and others were used to shape the wooden tools (rarely bone) that women's work required. Some, like the naturally backed knives, were delicate precision instruments. Others, especially the larger flakes with cortical backs, were used to transmit so much force that eventually the stone itself would fail – the scaled pieces. Equipped with stone tools and the wooden tools made with stone tools, the women of OpD were able to accomplish all the many things they expected of themselves: all of the food processing, preservation, and –preparation (except for some of the seal butchery); and almost everything that was concerned with plants and parts of plants. The latter involved plants that were eaten – roots, tubers, fruits, nuts, berries – but also plant parts that were transformed into boxes, carvings, and all manner of woven things – blankets, clothing, mats, baskets. The women made these for their own (and the men's) household use, but also as trade goods for those of life's necessities which could not be obtained in any other way, such as pebbles of CVR.

Some of the flaking of stone at OpD was done by the men and was quite different from what women did. The raw material was the same, small pebbles of CVR, and flakes were produced in the same way, by direct percussion with a hard hammer. Everything else was different. Whereas women tended to work inside the ridge, the men were more often on top of the ridge. The men tried to strike fairly large flakes, but preferred them without cortex (this was not an inviolable rule), and did not make flakes with the cortical backs that women preferred. They selected flakes that were narrower than those used by women and, above all, thinner: always less than 10 mm thick. They also selected flakes with the greatest thickness at the proximal end and the greatest width at the distal end. It was very important that the distal end should have a feathered termination. Having created or selected flakes that were, in almost every respect, different from those favored by women, the men then proceeded to shape their flakes by retouch into the tools which I have called "triangles".

The retouching was adequate (it resulted in a recognizable and repeated form), but usually no more than that. It is, after all, difficult to retouch such tough stone as CVR; this is probably why the women preferred to back their tools on the core, rather than try to retouch them later. The triangles have the form of piercing tools, with a sturdy point (I use the term loosely) at one end, and are conventionally regarded as "projectile points". At OpD, however, at least most of the triangles appear to be manufacturing failures and not to have been used. Yet, they were being made, if not terribly well made, and this was being done away from the area where women were concentrated. Perhaps it was during the slow months of winter that men took the opportunity to teach boys about men's work (a boy has to start somewhere), including making their own equipment for the male tasks of hunting large mammals.

Elsewhere in the site, there were a few triangles similar in form to those behind the ridge, but very well made. These could have seen use and would have been effective weapon heads.

The group also had two extraordinary triangles, clearly different from all the other triangles and exquisitely made. Their functions must have been in the realm of ideology or social relations, andmay have extended beyond the occupants of OpD. They fulfilled their roles simply by existing and being perfect. However, both are slightly broken (no longer perfect) and they occurred inside the ridge, rather than in the men's area. The imperfection may have reduced them from potent symbols to utilitarian objects.

The tools that women made and used – unretouched flakes, some with cortical backs, and scaled pieces – were not (and could not be) resharpened or recycled into other forms. They were made and discarded at OpD and so we suppose that that is also where they were used. However, it is equally likely that women would take cutting tools with them when going out, for example, to collect roots, or bark.

The men's tools, the triangles, were shaped by retouch and so could be resharpened or reshaped by the same means, but most, formed by as little retouching as necessary, clearly have not been, and their small, initial size would militate against their being reworked into functional triangles. The triangles were apparently made and discarded in the same place, so the arguments about women's tools apply equally to the men's tools and the conclusions are the same: it is likely that some triangles were taken for use elsewhere, and may or may not have come back to OpD, but it is really hard to tell. If, as I have suggested above, these often ineptly made tools reflect the teaching of triangle manufacture, then the triangles were made, used and discarded in the same place.

The women had traded for as much CVR as they would need during their stay at OpD and no more than that. At the end of their sojourn at OpD, the group travelled on to the next stage of their annual round, probably taking with them the products of the women's labor at OpD. They probably took little, if any, of the CVR but had the wherewithal to trade for more stone.

The *chaînes opératoires* of the flaked stone artifacts were followed within the overall context of the people's life at OpD. The artifacts partially shaped that context and were, in turn, shaped by it. Many individual artifacts passed through their own sequences simultaneously, so that setting up cores and discarding used tools – and everything in between – were always going on. The people knew how to perform these actions – in the ways in which they had always been performed – and probably rarely thought about it beyond the immediate context. The *chaînes opératoires* described here are an archaeologist's construct of what the people had always known.

REFERENCES

Addington, L. R.

1986 *Lithic Illustration: Drawing Flaked Stone Artifacts for Publication.* University of Chicago Press, Chicago.

Ahler, S. A.

1992 Use-phase classification and manufacturing technology in Plains Village arrowpoints. In *Piecing Together the Past: Applications of Refitting Studies in Archaeology*, edited by J. L. Hofman and J. G. Enloe, pp. 36-62. BAR International Series 587. Tempus Reparatum, Oxford.

Ambrose, S. H.

2002 Small things remembered: origins of early microlithic industries in Sub-Saharan Africa. In *Thinking Small: Global Perspectives on Microlithization*, edited by R. G. Elston and S. L. Kuhn, pp. 9-29. Archeological Papers of the American Anthropological Association 12. American Anthropological Assocation, Arlington, Virginia.

Andrefsky, Jr., W.

1998 *Lithics: Macroscopic Approaches to Analysis.* Cambridge University Press, Cambridge.

Belfer-Cohen, A., and N. Goring-Morris

2002 Why microliths? Microlithization in the Levant. In *Thinking Small: Global Perspectives on Microlithization*, edited by R. G. Elston and S. L. Kuhn, pp. 57-68. Archeological Papers of the American Anthropological Association 12. American Anthropological Assocation, Arlington, Virginia.

Bordes, F.

1961 *Typologie du Paléolithique Ancien et Moyen.* Mémoire de l'Institut Préhistorique de l'Université de Bordeaux I. Delmas, Bordeaux.

Close, A. E.

1996 Carry that weight: the use and transportation of stone tools. *Current Anthropology* 37:545-553.

1997 Lithic economy in the absence of stone. *Journal of Middle Atlantic Archaeology* 13:27-56.

2006 *Finding the People who Flaked the Stone at English Camp (San Juan Island).* The University of Utah Press, Salt Lake City

Close, A. E., and C. G. Sampson
1998 Backed microlith clusters in Late Holocene rock shelters of the Upper Karoo. *South African Archaeological Bulletin* 53:63-72.

Demars, P. Y., and P. Laurent
1989 *Types d'Outils Lithiques du Paléolithique Supérieur en Europe*. Editions du CNRS, Paris.

Ellis, C. J.
1997 Factors influencing the use of stone projectile tips: an ethnographic perspective. In *Projectile Technology,* edited by H. Knecht, pp. 37-74. Plenum Press, New York.

Elston, R. G., and P. J. Brantingham
2002 Microlithic technology in northern Asia: a risk-minimizing strategy of the Late Paleolithic and Early Holocene. In *Thinking Small: Global Perspectives on Microlithization*, edited by R. G. Elston and S. L. Kuhn, pp. 103-116. Archeological Papers of the American Anthropological Association 12. American Anthropological Assocation, Arlington, Virginia.

Finlayson. B., and S. Mithen
1997 The microwear and morphology of microliths from Gleann Mor. In P*rojectile Technology,* edited by H. Knecht, pp. 107-129. Plenum Press, New York

Flenniken, J. J.
1981 *Replicative Systems Analysis: A Model Applied to the Vein Quartz Artifacts from the Hoko River Site.* Laboratory of Anthropology Reports of Investigations 59. Washington State University, Pullman.

Hayden, B.
1980 Confusion in the bipolar world: bashed pebbles and splintered pieces. *Lithic Technology* 9:2-7.

Keeley, L. H.
1980 *Experimental Determination of Stone Tool Uses: A Microwear Analysis*. University of Chicago Press, Chicago.

Kimball, L. R.
1994 Microwear analysis of Archaic and Early Woodland tools from the Main Site (15BL35), Kentucky. In *Upper Cumberland Archaic and Woodland Period Archaeology at the Main Site (15BL35), Bell County, Kentucky*, edited by S. Creasman, Contract Publication Series 94-56, pp. F-1-F-109. Cultural Resource Analysts, Lexington, Kentucky.

Kuhn, S. L.
1995 *Mousterian Lithic Technology: an Ecological Perspective*. Princeton University Press, Princeton.

LeBlanc, R.
1992 Wedges, *pièces esquillées*, bipolar cores, and other things: an alternative to Shott's view of bipolar industries. *North American Archaeologist* 13(1):1-14.

Leroi-Gourhan, A.
1993 *Gesture and Speech*. Translated by A. Berger. Reissued. MIT Press, Cambridge. Originally published 1964 Le Geste et la Parole. Albin Michel, Paris.

MacDonald, G.
1968 *Debert: A Palaeoindian Site in Central Nova Scotia.* National Museum of Canada Anthropology Papers 16. National Museum of Canada, Ottawa.

Merrick, H. V., and J. P. S. Merrick
1976 Archaeological occurrences of earlier Pleistocene age from the Shungura formation. In *Earliest Man and Environments in the Lake Rudolf Basin: Stratigraphy, Paleoecology, and Evolution,* edited by Y. Coppens, F. C. Howell, G. Ll. Isaac, and R. E. F. Leakey, pp. 574-584. University of Chicago Press, Chicago.

Norton, H. H.
1985 *Women and Resources of the Northwest Coast: Documentation from the 18th and Early 19th Centuries.* Unpublished Ph.D. dissertation, University of Washington, Seattle.

Perlès, C.
1992 In search of lithic strategies: a cognitive approach to prehistoric chipped stone assemblages. In *Representations in Archaeology*, edited by J.-C. Gardin and C. S. Peebles, pp. 223-247. Indiana University Press, Bloomington.

Shott, M. J.
1989 Bipolar industries: ethnographic evidencef and archeological implications. *North American Archeologist* 10(1):1-24.
1999 On bipolar reduction and splintered pieces. *North American Archeologist* 20(3): 217-238.

Stein, J. K.
2000 *Exploring Coast Salish Prehistory: The Archaeology of San Juan Island.* Burke Museum Monographs 8. University of Washington, Seattle.

Swan, J. G.
1870 *The Indians of Cape Flattery, at the Entrance to the Strait of Fuca, Washington Territory*. Smithsonian Institution, Washington, DC.

Tixier, J.
1963 *Typologie de l'Epipaléolithique du Maghreb*. Mémoires du Centre de Recherches Anthropologiques, Préhistoriques et Ethnographiques, Alger, 2. Arts et Métiers Graphiques, Paris.

Villa, P., A. Delagnes, and L. Wadley
2005 A late Middle Stone Age artifact assemblage from Sibudu (KwaZulu-Natal): comparisons with the European Middle Paleolithic. *Journal of Archaeological Science* 32:399-422.

7

Ground Stone Artifacts

Chin-yung Chao

In this chapter, Chin-yung Chao provides background information on ground stone manufacture and use at OpD. He describes the commonly found ground stone tool types of the Northwest Coast and offers a summary of the OpD assemblage. Chao notes that the majority of the ground stone tools at OpD are abraders and are highly fragmented. Ground stone is found exclusively within and inside the ridge and at three distinct depths. Chao proposes some interpretations about what this may mean for prehistoric habitation at the site.

Ground stone tools were an important part of sophisticated technologies used by Coast Salish people to exploit rich and varied marine and terrestrial resources on the landscape. Ground slate spear points and knives were critical for catching and processing fish, as were weights and anchors for positioning and securing fishing nets. Sandstone abraders acted as ready-made sandpaper for shaping wood, bone, antler, and other stone artifacts. All stages of woodworking, from hewing and splitting to carving and smoothing, depended on adzes or celts, chisels, and mauls manufactured from tough stones like nephrite or jadeite. These tools enabled people to create the wooden objects and structures – bentwood boxes, canoes, and even plank houses – that were hallmarks of culture in the Gulf of Georgia. Beyond subsistence and technology, ground stone was used to create highly polished stone beads and other decorative items. This chapter summarizes methods and results of analysis of 42 ground stone artifacts from excavations at OpD and discusses implications of the spatial distribution of these objects in understanding human activities and the nature of the shell ridge and depression at the site.

BACKGROUND

Changes in frequencies and types of ground stone tools at Gulf of Georgia archaeological sites have aided in the definition of cultural phases for this region. Along with bone and antler tools, ground stone artifacts are more abundant in San Juan phase tool assemblages than in tool assemblages from the earlier Marpole phase (Ames and Maschner 1999; Carlson 1960; Matson and Coupland 1995). The relative increase in bone and antler technology may indicate increased reliance on marine resources (Carlson 1960), which would be a potential explanation for an increase in certain types of ground stone tools, such as slate spear points and net weights used in fishing. However, this does not fully account for similar increases in ground stone tools used for woodworking, such as adzes and chisels. Some aspects of woodworking, such as building canoes and manufacturing fish spears and herring rakes, also relate to marine subsistence, but more varied and sophisticated use of wood during the San Juan phase likely initiated the increase in ground stone tools.

METHODS

Stone artifacts from OpD were identified as ground stone if they possessed one or more surface exhibiting clear evidence of grinding visible to the naked eye. It is often difficult to distinguish marks made by natural weathering processes from those made by intentional grinding on stone surfaces smaller than ½" without

Chapter opening photo: A ground slate tool from Trench AB.

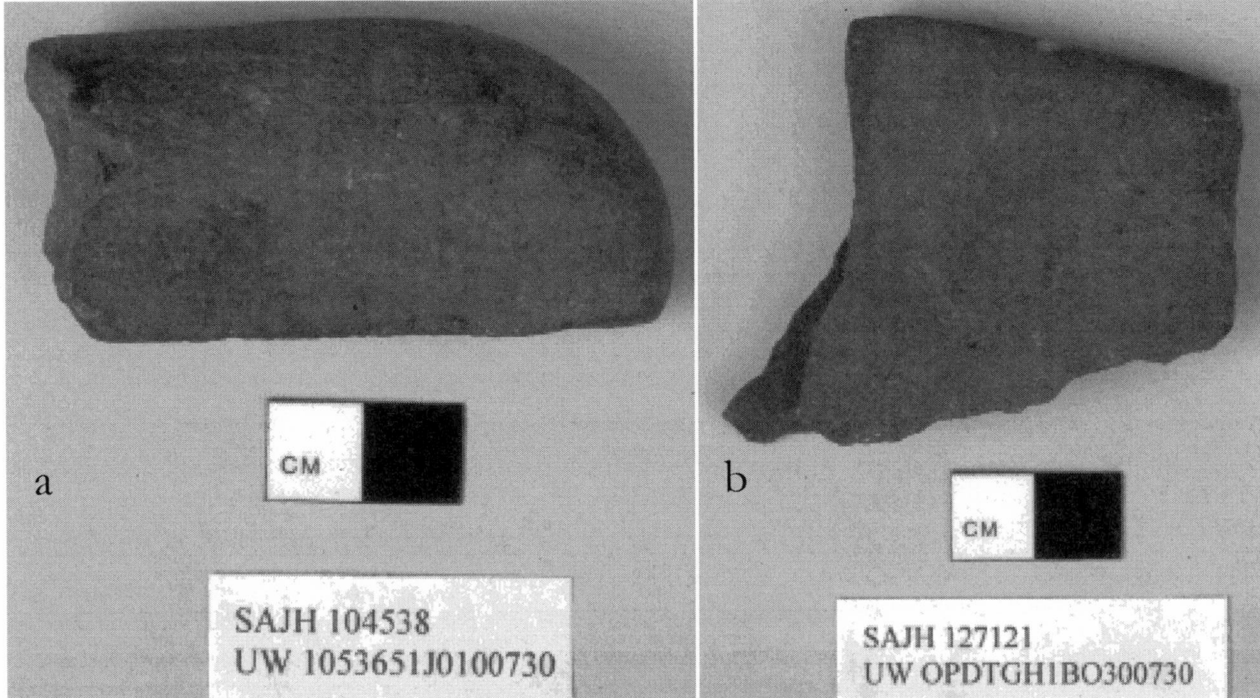

Figure 7.1 Examples of abraders from OpD (a - SAHJ 104358; b - SAJH 127121).

the aid of a hand lens, but most potential ground stone artifacts from OpD were substantially larger than ½". Artifacts smaller than ½" were identified as ground stone if they possessed clearly-defined parallel striations, which are evidence of systematic, intentional grinding action. Identification of raw material type was completed by visual inspection and comparison to published examples (Chen 1997).

CLASSIFICATION

The classification system used in this analysis is modified from one employed by Cochrane (1994) in his analysis of ground stone from OpA. Because Cochrane's system was adapted from Mitchell (1971) and Burley (1980), results reported here are generally compatible with those from other Gulf of Georgia archaeological sites. However, Cochrane's class of miscellaneous tools has been altered, and beads, mauls, and unidentified artifacts are placed in their own classes in this study.

Abraders

Abraders are ground artifacts that do not possess a blade edge but have at least one surface that has been modified by grinding. Abraders differ from other ground stone tools because they are used to grind and polish other materials, such as stone, bone, antler, and wood. Grinding and polishing observed on abraders are byproducts of the abrader's function. Coast Salish people preferred coarse-grained, sedimentary stone for these tools. Many abraders in the Gulf of Georgia are relatively unmodified tablets of sandstone (e.g., Lewarch and Bangs 1995), and are distinguished from naturally-occurring stone only by the presence of grinding and the context in which they are found. Some abraders, however, such as "shaft straighteners" for smoothing and contouring spear shafts, may be highly modified and may possess deep, well-worn grooves from repetitive use (Figure 7.1).

Bifaces

Bifaces are ground on both sides with two symmetrically worked long edges converging to a point at the distal end. These artifacts are commonly referred to as projectile points or knives, and functioned in a variety of capacities related to marine subsistence. Bifaces hafted onto long shafts were used as spears, while bifaces set into shorter handles were used as knives to process fish and other food items (Figure 7.2).

Adzes/Celts

Adzes or celts are bifacially-ground artifacts that possess at least one beveled edge that is perpendicular to the long axis. Adzes were manufactured most often from nephrite or jadeite in a multiple-step process that involved both grinding and chipping. Creation of an adze began by removing a piece of nephrite from a large boulder or shaping a smaller stone. Blades were then roughed out by chipping; shaping, smoothing, and sharpening of an edge was completed by grinding the blade against an abrader (Stewart 1973:48).

Many adzes found on the Northwest Coast are broken or exhibit substantial impact damage along the beveled edge. Occasionally, their width exceeds their

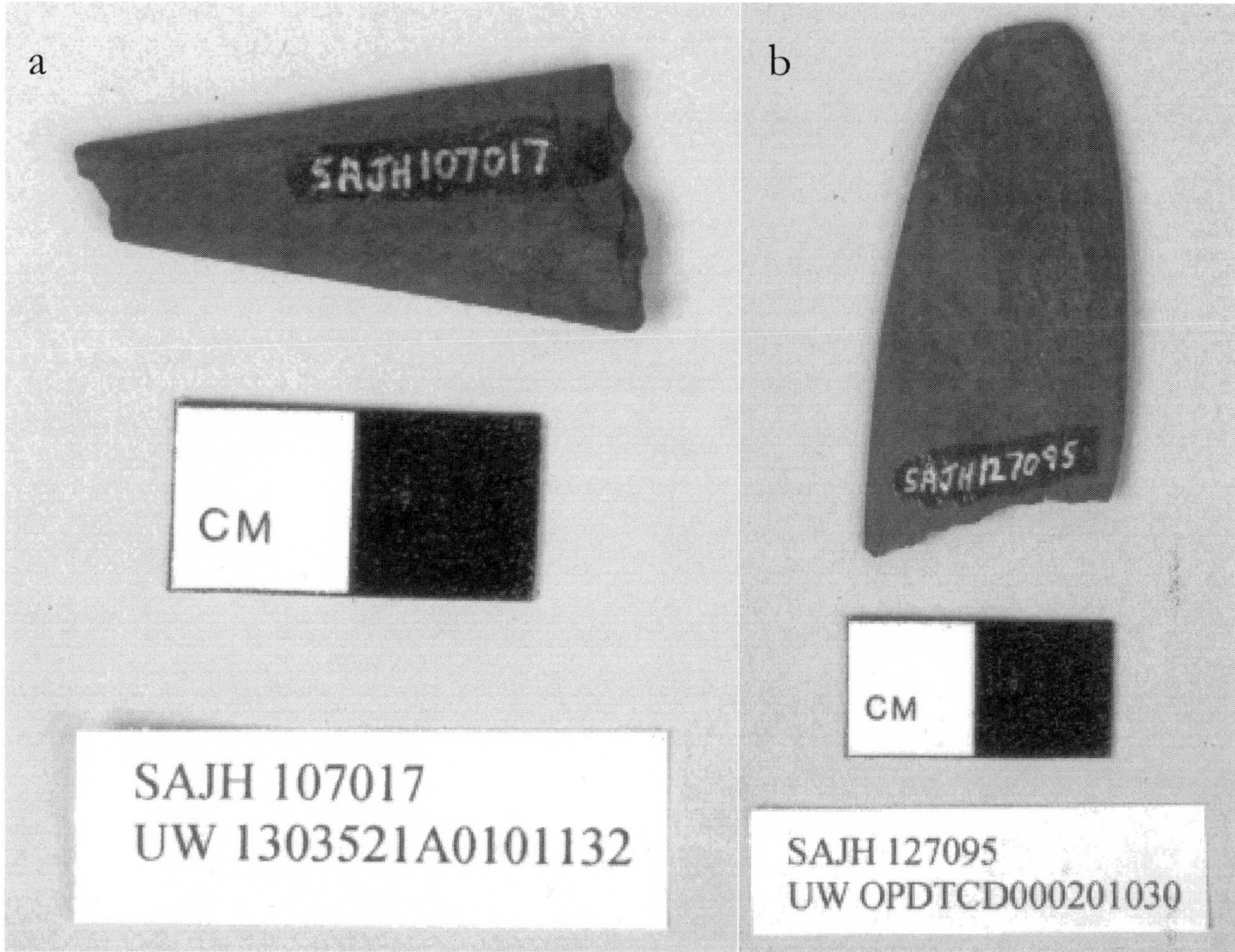

Figure 7.2 Examples of ground stone bifaces from OpD (a - SAJH 107017; b - SAJH 127095).

length, indicating repeated edge rejuvenation of a highly prized implement. Other than size, there is little morphological difference between adzes used to hew logs and chisels used to carve and plane wood, and it is likely that many chisels were manufactured from broken or exhausted adzes (Figure 7.3).

Mauls

A maul is a thick ground cylinder with a relatively flat distal end used as a striking surface in activities involving hammering or pounding. The proximal ends of mauls may be flat, or they may possess a conical or nipple shape. Mauls were either held in the hand or hafted to a shaft. Mauls are commonly associated with woodworking and were used along with bone and antler wedges to split logs (Stewart 1973). Mauls may also have been used to pound fish or process other foods (Figure 7.4).

Beads

Beads are small, highly-polished, round, oval, or disc-shaped objects that were used as jewelry or to decorate clothing or other items. The Coast Salish manufactured beads out of a variety of materials, including stone and bone. Glass and ceramic beads found at many Gulf of Georgia sites are temporal markers for the historic period. Once perforated, beads may have been strung together in necklaces and bracelets, or worn individually as pendants or on clothing. Unperforated beads likely represent artifacts that were lost or discarded before they were finished (Figure 7.5).

Unidentified

Artifacts exhibiting clear evidence of grinding but have no identifiable form have been labeled as "unidentified" in this analysis. Many of these artifacts are fragments of other tool types (Figure 7.6).

RESULTS

Compared to the larger chipped stone artifact assemblage (Chapter 6, this volume), ground stone artifacts are underrepresented at OpD. The most abundant ground stone artifacts are abraders, which account for 59.5% of the 42 artifacts analyzed (Table 1). Unidentified artifacts are the second most abundant type of ground stone artifact, comprising 16.7% of the assemblage, and are followed closely by bifaces,

Figure 7.3 An adze (SAJH 127126).

Figure 7.4 A maul from Unit 130 352 (SAJH 107019).

Figure 7.5 A bead from Trench EF (SAJH 127107).

Figure 7.6 Object with evidence of grinding but no identifiable form (SAJH 104574).

which represent 14.3% of the assemblage. Other artifact types, including adzes, mauls, and beads, occur in low frequencies.

To provide more specific details on the tools, one biface preform and proximal (base) fragment of stemmed biface demonstrate a complex manufacturing process with initial flaking followed by grinding. The single, stone bead found at OpD is a small disc, measuring only 15 mm in diameter and 5 mm in thickness (Figure 7.5). This artifact is not perforated, and there is no evidence that perforation was attempted. The only maul specimen in the assemblage is a fragment from a nipple-top type.

Table 7.1 Groundstone tools

UW Number	SAJH Number	Tool Type
42928	1053651A0100330	Unmodified
42949	1053651A0200330	Unknown
104538	1053651J0100730	Abrader
104574	1053651K0100930	Unidentifiable
104612	1053651L0100731	Unidentifiable
125884	1053651U0300131	Unidentifiable
125887	1053651U0300332	Abrader
104845	1113492A0100430	Abrader
104863	1213471A0100530	Abrader
43244	1233471C0100131	Abrader
126263	OPDTAB1G0100730	Abrader
126372	OPDTAB0O0500230	Abrader
126746	OPDTEF0O0700930	Unmodified
126805	OPDTGH1B0203432	Abrader
127105	OPDTEF1B0200630	Abrader
127107	OPDTEF1B0301432	Bead (?)
127121	OPDTGH1B0300730	Abrader
127127	OPD000000000030	Abrader
127126	OPD000000000030	Celt
127122	OPDTGH1B0302434	Celt
127090	OPDTCD1E0100430	Abrader
43386	1113491B0200330	Abrader
127055	1113492E0201431	Abrader
127057	111349000100330 (A)	Abrader
127082	OPDTAB000000033	Unknown
127058	1113490O0100430	Abrader
31733	OPD0I01V0101231	Biface
107017	1303521A0101132	Biface
31730	OPD0I01V0100130	Abrader
31612	OPDIC1	Abrader
127081	OPDTAB000500330	Abrader
127064	1303521G0100330	Abrader
127068	1303520O0200430	Abrader
107019	1303521A0300731	Maul
127080	OPDTAB0O0400430	Abrader
107032	OPDTAB1D0200530	Abrader
127070	OPDTAB1F0200430	Abrader
127078	OPDTAB1G0100432	Unknown
127077	OPDTAB1G0101030	Abrader
107023	OPDTAB1A0100330	Abrader

The most notable characteristic of the ground stone assemblage from OpD is its highly fragmentary condition. With the exception of two abraders, one bead, one adze, and one artifact that may have been used to grind ocher, all of the ground stone tools are broken along at least one axis, and many along multiple axes. All six of the adzes recovered at Op D are broken along the longitudinal (length) axis. Beveling on five of the fragmentary adzes is unfinished and the edges are incompletely ground. This pattern suggests that they may only be half finished and were broken during the manufacturing process. Only one adze is complete and unbroken, and this specimen possesses multiple sets of use-wear striations from woodworking.

DISCUSSION

The distribution of ground stone artifacts outside, within, and inside the ridge at OpD shows interesting spatial patterning. No ground stone artifacts were found outside the ridge (Unit 107 341), but 22 specimens were recovered within the ridge (Units 105 365, 111 349, OPD TAB, OPD TCD), and 15 specimens were recovered from inside the ridge (Units 121 347, 123 347, 130 352, OPDTEF, OPDTGH). These data suggest that ground stone artifacts are nearly 50% more abundant within the ridge than inside the ridge. Such comparisons, however, are valid only when controlling for differences in volume material excavated. When artifact counts are divided by excavation volume, the difference in ground stone frequencies within and inside the ridge are substantially reduced. There are 1.73 artifacts/m3 within the ridge, and 1.42 artifacts/m3 inside the ridge – a difference of approximately 20%. Given this difference between what was "inside" and "outside" the potential house, these results tentatively support the hypothesis that OpD was used as a domestic structure. The small sample size limits interpretation based on ground stone tools at the site.

REFERENCES

Ames, K. M., and H. D. G. Maschner

1999 *Peoples of the Northwest Coast: Their Archaeology and Prehistory.* Thames and Hudson, London.

Burley, D. V.

1980 *Marpole: Anthropological Reconstruction of a Prehistoric Northwest Coast Culture Type.* Simon Fraser University, Department of Archaeology, Publication No. 8. Burnaby, BC.

Carlson, R. L.

1960 Chronology and culturel change in the San Juan Islands. *American Antiquity* 25:562-586.

Chen, W. S.

1997 *Introduction to Rocks.* Observer Press, Taipei.

Cochrane, E.
1994 *An Examination of Lithic Artifacts from the British Camp Site (45SJ24): Discussion of the Adequacy of Culture Historical Predictions.* Unpublished B.A. Honors Thesis, Department of Anthropology, University of Washington, Seattle.

Lewarch, D. E., and E. W. Bangs
1995 Lithic Artifacts. In *The Archaeology of West Point, Seattle, Washington, 4,000 Yeas of Hunter-Fisher-Gatherer Land Use in Southern Puget Sound*, edited by Lynn L. Larson and Dennis E. Lewarch, pp. 7-1 – 7-181. Submitted to CH2M Hill, Bellevue Washington. Prepared for King County Department of Metropolitan Services. Prepared by Larson Anthropological/Archaeological Services, Seattle.

Matson, R. G., and G. Coupland
1995 *The Prehistory of the Northwest Coast.* Academic Press, San Diego.

Mitchell, D. H.
1971 Archaeology of the Gulf of Georgia, a natural region and its cultural types. *Syesis* 4 (Suppl.1), Victoria, BC.

Stein, J. K.
1992 Interpreting Stratification of a Shell Midden. In *Deciphering a Shell Midden*, edited by J. K. Stein, pp. 71-93. Academic Press, New York.

Stewart, H.
1973 *Indian Artifacts of the Northwest Coast.* University of Washington Press, Seattle.

8

Bone and Antler Tools

Catherine Foster West

West describes the importance of bone and antler tools in Gulf of Georgia prehistory. She hypothesizes that if the shell ridge at OpD represents a house, this should be reflected by evidence for household activities at the site. She describes the tool types found at OpD and discusses the spatial distribution of tool types across the site. Based on the types of bone and antler tools found at OpD, West concludes that household activities did occur there, but refrains from making specific spatial interpretations of the data.

Investigations of prehistoric technology on the Northwest Coast often focus on stone artifacts, but studies of bone and antler tools broaden our understanding of the range of materials prehistoric people utilized and the kinds of activities they performed. Archaeological and ethnographic evidence demonstrate that people on the Northwest Coast made heavy use of bone and antler for woodworking, fishing, hunting, and domestic activities (Samuels 1989, 1991; Stewart 1977, 1996). Pacific Northwest Coast shell middens, like those excavated at English Camp, provide excellent conditions for the preservation of these organic materials.

BACKGROUND

The presence and abundance of bone and antler tool types have served as important criteria in defining cultural phases for the Gulf of Georgia culture area. In particular, an increase in the abundance of bone and antler tools found in archaeological sites marks the transition from the Marpole to the San Juan phase, when OpD was occupied (Ames and Maschner 1999; Carlson 1960; Matson and Coupland 1995). While the increase in bone and antler tools during the San Juan phase might be explained by better preservation, the shift from the Marpole to the San Juan phase is marked also by a relative decrease in the number of chipped stone tools (Matson and Coupland 1995). More specifically, frequencies of composite harpoon valves and bone points increase dramatically in the San Juan phase, and weaving technology also becomes more common (Ames and Maschner 1999; Matson and Coupland 1995). These changes may indicate an increasing emphasis on fishing and use of marine resources during the San Juan phase because bone points were used for fish hooks, spears, and herring rakes, woven nets were used for large fish harvests, and bone and antler harpoons were used to hunt sea mammals (Matson and Coupland 1995).

Like other Northwest Coast artifacts, bone and antler tools have been classified according to their form and use, and the assemblage recovered from OpD may indicate how this site was used. Stein (2000) has hypothesized that the shape and form of the shell midden at OpD is consistent with a house structure, so the bone and antler tool remains should reflect household activities. If the OpD shell midden is a house structure where people were making and discarding tools during the transition from the Marpole to the San Juan phase, the tool assemblage should fit predictions regarding household organization and activities. For instance, household activities will be rep-

Chapter opening photo: Bone point being recovered in the field.

Table 8.1 Bone and antler tools

SAJH Number	Tool Type	Condition	Material	Taxon
106426	Awl	Broken	Bone	Deer sized
106427	Awl		Bone	Deer sized
128649	Awl		Bone	Deer sized
128666	Awl		Bone	*Odocoileus hemionus*
128667	Awl		Bone	Mammal
106424	Awl	Broken	Bone	*Odocoileus hemionus*
107518	Awl		Bone	Deer sized
106425	Awl	Broken & gnawed	Bone	*Odocoileus hemionus*
106423	Awl/ulna tool?	Broken	Bone	Mammal
106432	Bead	Complete	Bone	Mammal
41067	Bead		Bone	Mammal
106438	Decorative		Bone	Sea mammal
128641	Decorative	Broken	Bone	Mammal
128638	End use tool	Complete	Antler	Artiodactyl
128665	End use tool	Broken	Bone	Mammal
139549	End use tool	Broken	Bone	Mammal
106429	End use tool	Burned	Antler	Artiodactyl
106444	Harpoon	Broken	Bone	Sea mammal?
106445	Harpoon	Broken	Bone	Sea mammal?
106446	Harpoon	Broken	Bone	Sea mammal?
128622	Harpoon	Broken	Bone	Mammal
128636	Harpoon		Bone	Mammal
128642	Harpoon	Broken	Bone	Mammal
128654	Harpoon	Broken	Bone	Mammal
139556	Harpoon	Broken	Bone	Mammal
106447	Harpoon	Broken & burned	Bone	Sea mammal?
139565	Harpoon	Broken & burned	Bone	Mammal
106437	Historic		Bone	Mammal
106443	Miscellaneous point	Broken	Bone	Mammal
128630	Miscellaneous point	Broken	Bone	Mammal
128643	Miscellaneous point		Bone	Mammal
128644	Miscellaneous point	Broken	Bone	Mammal
128651	Miscellaneous point	Broken	Bone	Mammal
128656	Miscellaneous point	Broken	Antler	Artiodactyl
128659	Miscellaneous point	Broken	Bone	Mammal
128660	Miscellaneous point	Broken	Bone	Mammal
128671	Miscellaneous point	Broken	Bone	Mammal
128672	Miscellaneous point	Broken	Bone	Mammal
139548	Miscellaneous point	Broken	Bone	Mammal
139551	Miscellaneous point	Broken	Bone	Mammal
139552	Miscellaneous point	Broken	Bone	Mammal

Table 8.1 Bone and antler tools (continued)

SAJH Number	Tool Type	Condition	Material	Taxon
139555	Miscellaneous point	Broken	Bone	Mammal
41065	Miscellaneous point	Broken	Bone	Mammal
41071	Miscellaneous point		Bone	Mammal
128648	Miscellaneous point	Broken & burned	Bone	Mammal
128650	Needle		Bone	Mammal
128652	Needle	Broken	Bone	Mammal
128668	Needle	Broken	Bone	Mammal
128618	Point	Broken	Bone	Mammal
128640	Point	Complete	Bone	Mammal
128645	Point		Bone	Mammal
128634	Point, shaft	Broken	Bone	Mammal
106431	Sectioned		Bone	Mammal
128646	Wedge		Antler	Artiodactyl
41066	Wedge		Antler	Artiodactyl
106442	Worked bone		Bone	Bird
128625	Worked bone		Bone	Bird
128627	Worked bone		Bone	Bird
128655	Worked bone	Broken	Bone	Mammal
128662	Worked bone		Bone	Mammal
139547	Worked bone	Broken	Bone	Mammal
139561	Worked bone		Bone	Bird
139563	Worked bone		Bone	Bird
41072	Worked bone		Antler	Artiodactyl

resented by tools related to weaving, woodworking, sewing, hunting, and fishing. If OpD is a house, the spatial distribution of these tools may be similar to other houses found in this region, such as those at Ozette and the Meier site.

This chapter describes the classification of 64 bone and antler tools found at OpD, discusses their spatial distribution, and addresses the hypothesis that the OpD shell midden is a house.

METHODOLOGY

Bone and antler tools were collected from different provenience contexts, and I categorized modified bone and antler according to widely used classifications of Northwest Coast bone and antler tools (Drucker 1943; McMurdo 1972; Mitchell 1971; Stewart 1996). These categories, described in detail below, are based on type of modification, location of wear, shape and cross-section of object, and proposed function. I assessed the completeness of each artifact (Table 8.1), tabulated frequencies of tool types (Figure 8.1), and identified location within the site (Figure 8.2) to assess patterning in spatial distribution of tools. Length, width, and thickness measures were recorded for each artifact, but the fragmentary condition and small sample size of artifacts prevent meaningful quantitative analyses of these measurements.

CLASSIFICATION & DESCRIPTIVE SUMMARY

Awls

Awls, often made from long bones, are pointed tools used for multiple functions. Two types of awl—ulna and splinter—were found at OpD. Ulna awls are made by grinding the thin distal end of a deer ulna to point, which often appears polished from use (Figure 8.3). While modified ulnae often belong to a category of their own and are described as both awls and knives (Mitchell 1971; Stewart 1996), different ulna tools are often difficult to differentiate and are called awls in this analysis (see Carlson 1960; Drucker 1943). A splinter awl is made from a section of splintered long bone, with one end of the splinter ground to a point and polished from use.

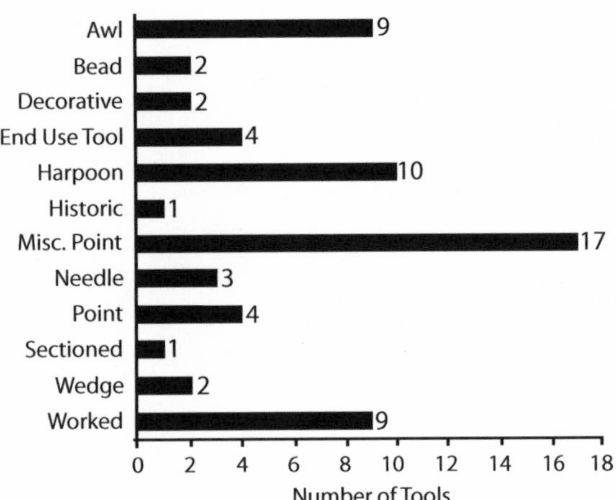

Figure 8.1 Frequencies of bone and antler tool types.

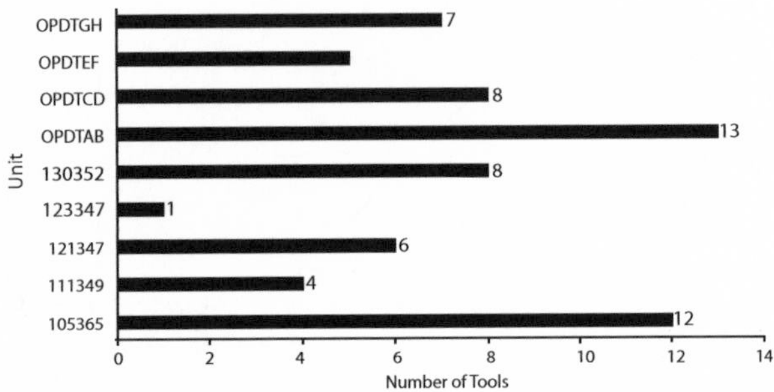

Figure 8.2 Frequencies of bone and antler tools in each excavation unit.

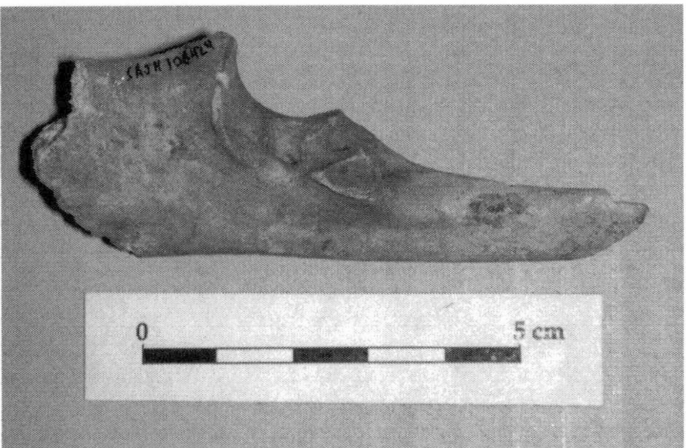

Figure 8.3 An ulna awl (SAJH 106424).

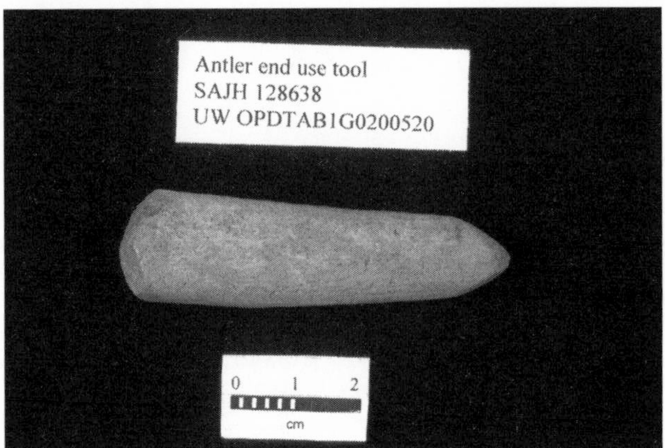

Figure 8.4 An antler end use tool from Trench AB (SAJH 128638).

End Use Tools

End use tools are not as pointed as awls; they are sections of long bone ground to a rounded shape at one end (Figure 8.4). Like awls, they often appear polished from use in a variety of tasks, including scraping, basketry, weaving, and food preparation (Stewart 1996).

Spear Points

Spears mounted with bone points were used to hunt a variety of animals in the Northwest. Harpoons were used primarily to kill sea mammals but were also used to harvest large fish. Other types of spears were used for smaller fish, birds, and smaller sea and terrestrial mammals (Stewart 1977, 1996). The bone spear points from OpD came in a variety of forms including detachable harpoon points, fixed points, barbed points, and toggling harpoons (Figure 8.5).

Detachable Harpoon Points

Detachable harpoon points are connected to the main shaft or foreshaft of the spear by a line, which was used to prevent sea mammals from escaping or breaking the spear after they were harpooned. A line guard is found at the base of the detachable harpoon point and holds the line from the shaft onto the harpoon. The base of the harpoon point is modified to secure the line; it could be unilaterally shouldered, bilaterally shouldered (Drucker 1943), or have horizontal projections to hold the line in place (Stewart 1996).

Fixed Points

Fixed points are permanently attached to the spear shaft and often have long, slender bases for attachment to the spear shaft. Sometimes, several points were clustered on a shaft for a more effective hunting tool, and were used to hunt smaller sea mammals, birds, or other small animals (Stewart 1996).

Barbed Points

A barbed point (Figure 8.6) prevents a point from slipping from an animal's flesh after spearing. These points are either unilaterally or bilaterally barbed (Stewart 1996).

Toggling Harpoons

A toggling harpoon is designed to enter an animal, detach from the shaft, and expand laterally to lodge in an animal's flesh (Stewart 1996). Composite toggling harpoons consist of valves and a point. The valves hold the point of the harpoon in place and provide barbs on either side of the point to secure the harpoon in an animal.

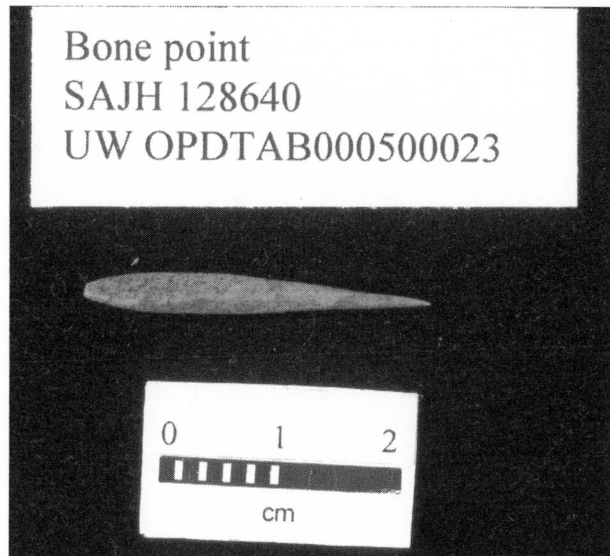

Figure 8.5 A bone point from Trench AB (SAJH 128640).

Wedges

Wedges were most often used for woodworking and are ground at an angle at one end to create a flat face and point for splitting (Stewart 1996). Wedges show polish and chipping at the convergent end, and chipping and battering at the squared end from use in wood splitting (Chatters 1988). The two wedges recovered at OpD (SAJH 41066 and 128646) are made from antler, which was a commonly used durable material for this tool, but wedges were also occasionally made from large limb bones (Stewart 1996).

Needles

Needles are useful for sewing hides, weaving, and a variety of other household purposes. They are recognized by a thin shaft, pointed and polished ends, and a drilled or incised eye. Drilling creates a circular eye, while incising creates an oval-shaped eye (Drucker 1943; Stewart 1996). Needles from OpD have oval-shaped eyes made by incising (Figure 8.7).

Decorative Items

Decorative items, such as beads, pendants, pins, and other decorated implements, are less common in the San Juan phase than they are in the Marpole phase (Matson and Coupland 1995). Two beads (SAJH 106432, 41067) from OpD were made by grinding or cutting bone into a round shape and then drilling a hole through the middle. Two other decorative items, a piece of drilled sea mammal bone (SAJH 106438; Figure 8.8), and a section of bone incised with lines (SAJH 128641), also were recovered at OpD.

Miscellaneous Points

Miscellaneous points refer to a broad array of slender, pointed bones that appear to be portions of larger, broken tools. Drucker (1943:56) describes them as "small slender pointed bone objects [that] may have

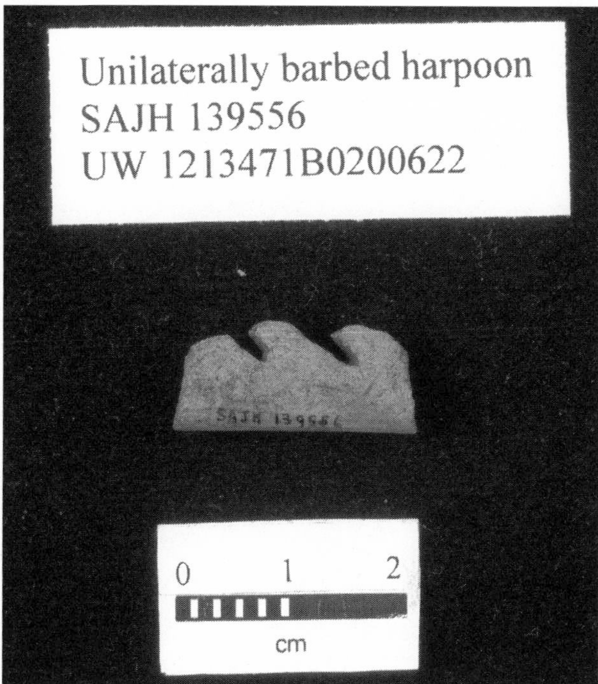

Figure 8.6 A unilaterally barbed harpoon point from OpD (SAJH 139556).

served various purposes." At OpD, these fragments appear to be broken points, awls, harpoon barbs or tips, needles, and broken end-use tools. Their abundance is consistent with an increase in small, pointed bone objects during the San Juan phase (Matson and Coupland 1995).

Worked Bones

Worked bone includes all bone and antler not identifiable as a tool or miscellaneous point, but exhibiting abrasion, grinding, or polish (Phillips 2002).

Historic Artifacts

OpD is part of San Juan Island's English Camp where British soldiers discarded objects during their occupation (Stein 2000). One historic bone artifact, a bone and iron handle of a utensil that was likely from the British occupation (SAJH 106437), was recovered from the prehistoric midden at OpD (Chapter 4, Figure 16, this volume).

RESULTS AND DISCUSSION

The bone and antler artifacts described above were found in both the ridge and depression of the OpD shell midden (Figure 8.2), and just 64 artifacts were recovered. In general, the tools are distributed evenly among excavation units with the highest number of tools found in Unit 105 365 (n =12) and OPDTAB (n = 13) on the ridge, and the lowest number from Unit 123 347 inside the ridge (n = 1). Overall, more tools were recovered from units in the shell ridge (n = 42 in Units 105 365; 111 349; OPDTAB; OPDTCD; OPDTEF)

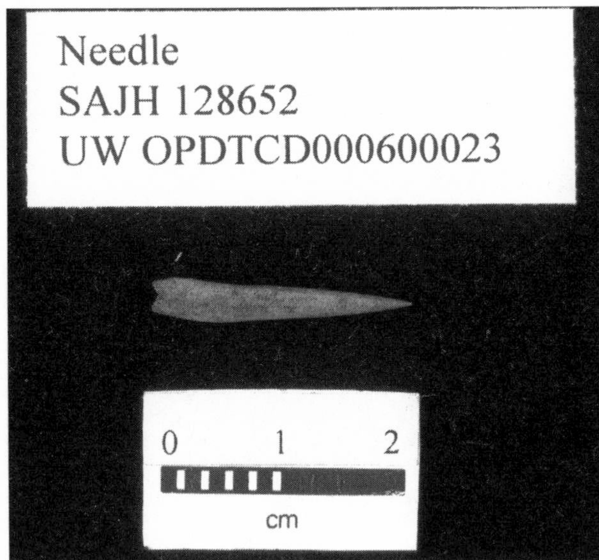

Figure 8.7 A bone needle from Trench CD (SAJH 128652).

than from units within and in front of the depression (n = 22 in Units 121; 123 347). This is likely because the excavation within and in front of the depression was less extensive than on the shell ridge.

Further, no spatial or temporal patterning is discernible within the units themselves. The few recovered tools are distributed widely among many facies from the top to the bottom of the excavation. This distribution may be due to the rapid accumulation of the midden (Stein et al. 2003), poor organic preservation, or that bone and antler tools were made and used less often than stone tools at OpD.

Burned bone tools (SAJH 106429, 139565, 106447, 128648) were found in both the ridge and the depression, and the majority of identifiable tools are broken (Table 8.1). The single historic bone artifact (SAJH 106437) was found in the upper layers of Unit 121/347, and may have been deposited during the British occupation or moved during previous excavation (see Chapter 2, this volume).

While the small number of bone and antler tools recovered from OpD makes behavioral interpretations difficult, the analysis of these artifacts may be useful for examining the hypothesis that the shell ridge and depression at OpD are the remains of a domestic structure. Recall the argument that if OpD is a house, it should fit predictions about household activity: the tools types and their distributions should be related to household activities and may be similar to other house sites in the region.

Bone and antler tools presumed to be associated with household activities such as weaving, woodworking, sewing, as well as hunting and fishing, have been recovered from archaeological houses throughout the Northwest (Ames et al. 1992; Chatters 1981; Larson 1995; Samuels 1989, 1991), and the artifacts at OpD are comparable to artifacts found in these houses. As described, the OpD bone artifact assemblage includes awls and end-use tools for weaving, needles for sewing, wedges for woodworking, and a variety of hunting and fishing tools. Based on the presence of these tools types, it is apparent that household activities occurred in the area around OpD, and the bone and antler tool types indirectly indicate activities associated with Northwest Coast houses.

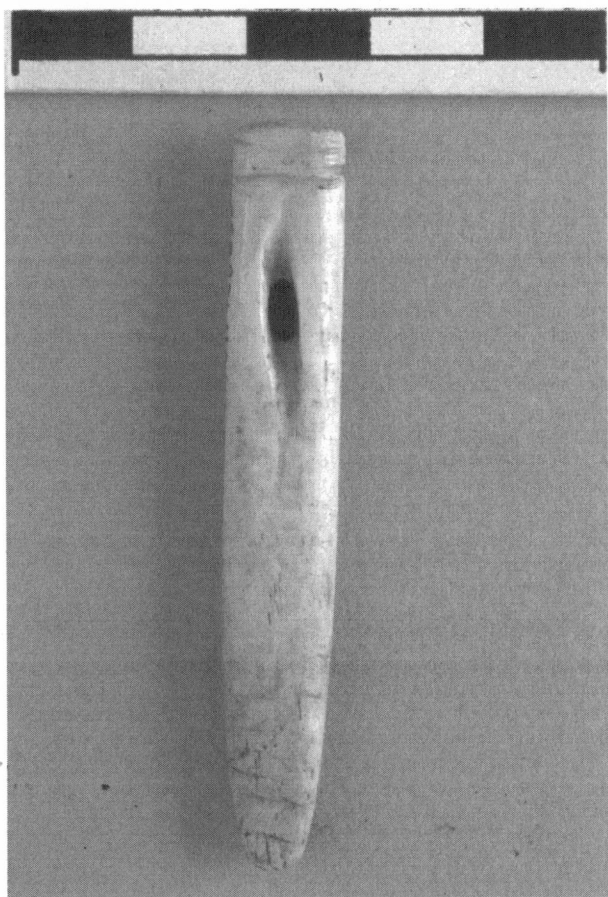

Figure 8.8 A possible decorative item artifact made from drilled sea mammal bone (SAJH 106438).

On the other hand, it is difficult to make any interpretations about where such activities occurred at OpD, given the broad distribution of artifacts throughout the site. Other Northwest Coast houses, such as the Ozette and Meier sites, produced bone and antler tools within well preserved house structures and middens (Ames et al. 1992, Samuels 1989, 1991). These excavations indicate that the bone and antler tools were used for household activities, until they were discarded outside the houses. Mauger (1991:162) notes that people at the Ozette site transported household debris, including bone and antler tools, outside the house and created "deep exterior house middens." At the Meier site, Ames et al. (1992) observe that household artifacts were found primarily in pits, postholes and under the plank floor, and argue that artifacts in the exterior midden likely represented house cleaning. While these descriptions indicate that Northwest Coast people were using bone and antler tools inside the houses, it is difficult to make a similar argument for patterning of bone and antler tools at OpD. Excavation units were small samples of the topographic ridge and depression, and the scattered distribution of bone and antler in those units provides little information about where the tools were used.

CONCLUSIONS

Stein (2000) has argued that OpD may represent a house structure, and the bone and antler tools have been used to assess this hypothesis. The tool types identified at OpD are consistent with the tool types identified for the Marpole and San Juan phases in the Gulf of Georgia, which were used for a variety of household activities. While the overall assemblage indicates that people at OpD were engaging in household activities, an analysis of the spatial distribution of the bone and antler tools is less revealing. The tools are distributed relatively evenly throughout the site, and there is no patterning that suggests areas of activity or a house structure. Despite this lack of patterning, it is clear that the bone and antler artifacts recovered at OpD were used for a variety of domestic tasks, and were associated with people engaged in weaving, sewing, woodworking, and other household activities.

REFERENCES

Ames, K. M., D. F. Raetz, S. Hamilton, and C. McAfee
1992 Household Archaeology of a Southern Northwest Coast Plank House. *Journal of Field Archaeology* 19(3): 275-290.

Ames, K. M., and H. D. G. Maschner
1999 *Peoples of the Northwest Coast: Their Archaeology and Prehistory.* Thames and Hudson, London.

Carlson, R. L.
1960 Chronology and Culture Change in the San Juan Islands. *American Antiquity* 25: 562-586.

Chatters, J. C.
1981 *Archaeology of the Sbabadid Site, 45KI51, King County, Washington.* Office of Public Archaeology, Institute for Environmental Studies, University of Washington, Seattle.
1988 *Tualdad Altu.* First City Equities, Seattle.

Drucker, P.
1943 *An Archaeological Survey on the Northern Northwest Coast.* Anthropology Paper No. 20 Bulletin 133. Bureau of American Ethnology, Washington DC.

Larson, L. L.
1995 Modified Bone and Antler. In *The Archaeology of West Point,* edited by L. L. Larson and D. E. Lewarch, pp. 10-1 – 10-25. Prepared by Larson Anthropological and Archaeological Services. Seattle.

Matson, R.G. and G. Coupland
1995 *The Prehistory of the Northwest Coast.* Academic Press, San Diego.

Mauger, J. E.
1991 Shed-Roof Houses at Ozette and in a Regional Perspective. In *Ozette Archaeological Project Research Reports, Vol. I, House Structure and Floor Midden.* Reports of Investigations 63, edited by S.R. Samuels, pp. 28-173. Department of Anthropology, Washington State University, Pullman, and National Park Service, Pacific Northwest Regional Office, Seattle.

McMurdo, A.
1972 *Barbed Harpoon Types.* Unpublished Master's Thesis, Department of Archaeology, Simon Fraser University, Burnaby, BC.

Mitchell, D. H.
1971 Archaeology of the Gulf of Georgia, a natural region and its cultural types. *Syesis* 4 (Suppl.1), Victoria, BC.

Phillips, L. S.
2002 Bone and Antler Tools. In *Vashon Island Archaeology: A View from Burton Acres Shell Midden, edited by J. K. Stein and L. S. Phillips. Burke Mu*seum of Natural History and Culture, Seattle.

Samuels, S. R.
1989 Spatial Patterns in Ozette Longhouse Floor Middens. In *Households and Communities,* edited by S. MacEachern, D. J.W. Archer, and R. D. Garvin, pp. 143-156. The University of Calgary Archaeological Association.
1991 (ed.) *Ozette Archaeological Project Research Reports, Vol. I, House Structure and Floor Midden.* Reports of Investigations 63. Department of Anthrpology, Washington State University, Pullman, and National Park Service, Pacific Northwest Regional Office, Seattle.

Stein, J. K.
2000 *Exploring Coast Salish Prehistory: The Archaeology of San Juan Island.* University of Washington Press, Seattle.

Stein, J. K., J. N. Deo, and L. S. Phillips
2003 Big Sites—Short Time: Accumulation Rates in Archaeological Sites. *Journal of Archaeological Science* 30:297-316.

Stewart, H.
1977 *Indian Fishing: Early Methods on the Northwest Coast.* J. J. Douglas, Vancouver.
1996 *Stone, and Shell.* University of Washington Press, Seattle, WA.

9

Faunal Analysis: Mammals

Cristie M. Boone

Boone presents an analysis of mammal bone found at OpD, listing the types of mammals represented at the site and presenting a quantitative analysis of the data. Her goal is to determine if variation in mammals represented in different areas of OpD can help to determine whether the horseshoe-shaped ridge at the site was once a domestic structure. Identifiable mammal bone is scarce at OpD, and some units have more identifiable taxa than others. Differences in proportions of taxa between units inside and outside the ridge may be the result of taphonomic processes rather than differences in use of space.

Over 12,000 mammal bones were collected from six units at English Camp, but only a small percentage of those were identifiable to element and taxon. A total of 1,220 specimens were identified, and proportions of elements and taxa were compared among units and facies. An appendix that includes these data is on file at the Burke Museum of Natural History and Culture. The goal of the analysis was to determine if variation in fauna found inside and outside of the shell ridge were consistent with differences in use of space inside and outside of a domestic structure. If the shell ridge resulted from midden built up around a house, there should be statistically significant differences between faunal assemblages found in ridge facies and elsewhere at OpD. Domestic refuse piles are associated with different behaviors and taphonomic histories than activity areas. If no significant differences are found throughout the site, this suggests that the shell ridge may be associated with non-domestic features or natural processes.

METHODOLOGY

Mammal bones were identified from six excavation units: 105 365, 107 341, 111 349, 121 347, 123 347, and 130 352. These units were chosen instead of the trench because they represented locations inside the ridge, on the ridge, and behind the ridge. Additionally, the trench comprised a greater number of bones, and rather than sample the trench data, 100% of the potentially identifiable bones from the units were analyzed. Mammal bones used for the analysis were presorted by Kristine Bovy. Ribs were not included in the general analysis due to the difficulty identifying them to species, but they were considered while looking for bone modifications. Specimens distinguishable to element were also identified to the most specific possible taxon. Unmodified bones that could not be identified to element were removed from faunal analyses for this chapter, but *modified* indeterminate mammal bones are included in the discussion of modifications below.

Identifications were based on comparative specimens from the Burke Museum and through consultation with Northwest Coast faunal specialists Michael Etnier (University of Washington, Applied Osteology), and Robert Kopperl (University of Washington, Northwest Archaeological Associates). Specimens were counted using Number of Identified Specimens (NISP), thus the total of identifiable bones represents the maximum possible number of individuals that could have created the assemblage. While this quantification method may inflate the numbers of individuals, using Minimum Number of Individuals (MNI) to

Chapter opening photo: A field school student lays on the ground in Unit 130 352 in order to draw a stratigraphic profile.

Table 9.1 Indentified mammal specimens (NISP)

Scientific Name	Common Name	Unit						Total
		105 365	107 341	111 349	121 347	123 347	130 352	
Mammalia	mammals	13	3	14	27	39	27	123
Artiodactyla	artiodactyls	31	21	11	58	68	32	221
Odocoileus c.f. *hemionus*	mule deer	100	9	17	100	73	76	375
Cervus elaphus	elk	-	-	-	1	2	3	6
Bovidae	cattle, sheep, goats	-	-	-	1	-	-	1
Oreamnos americanus	mountain goat	-	-	-	2	1	-	3
Sus sp.	pig	-	-	-	1	-	-	1
Carnivora	carnivores	2	-	-	5	2	1	10
Canidae	foxes, wolves, coyotes, dogs	7	-	4	7	4	5	27
Canis sp.	wolves, coyotes, dogs	1	1	3	7	10		22
Canis lupus familiaris	domestic dog	8	-	-	2	5	1	16
Canis latrans	coyote	-	-	-	1	-	-	1
Phocidae	earless seals	-	-	-	-	4	13	17
Phoca vitulina	harbor seal	2	-	5	13	19	13	52
Otariidae	eared seals, sea lions	5	-	1	-	-	-	6
Eumetopias jubatus	Stellar sea lion	-	-	-	-	-	13	13
Procyon lotor	raccoon	2	-	2	-	1	4	9
Mustelidae	weasels, minks, etc.	-	-	6	1	-	5	12
Mustela vison	mink	-	-	-	2	-	-	2
Lontra canadensis	river otter	-	-	-	1	3	-	4
Oryctolagus cuniculus	domestic rabbit	1	-	2	1	-	2	6
Odontoceti	toothed whales	-	-	-	-	-	6	6
Delphinidae	dolphins, porpoises, orcas	-	-	1	-	-	-	1
Rodentia	rodents	5	2	46	44	9	20	126
Castor canadensis	beaver	1	-	-	-	-	-	1
Sciuridae	squirrels	-	-	-	2	-	-	2
Muridae	mice, rats, voles, & relatives	2	-	35	10	16	28	91
Arvicolinae	arviconlinae rodents, voles, lemmings	2	1	6	3	7	34	53
Arvicolinae c.f. *Microtus* sp.	voles	-	-	-	1	-	-	1
Sigmodontinae	mice, woodrats	1	-	-	5	-	4	10
Peromyscus sp.	deer mice	-	-	-	-	2	-	2
Total		183	37	153	295	265	287	1220

count taxa may underestimate numbers of individuals, lead to aggregation errors, and tends to generate data redundant to NISP (Grayson 1984). Following Lyman (1994:100), the term *element* in this chapter means a "discrete, natural anatomical unit of a skeleton, such as a humerus, a tibia, or a tooth." A *specimen* refers to an archaeologically discrete unit that can be either a fragment or a complete element. A *fragment* is a specimen that is only a portion of an element.

DESCRIPTIVE SUMMARY

The following section lists the total number of specimens of each element for each taxon in all six units. Table 9.1 summarizes these taxonomic data by unit. Relevant information, such as a species' range or its behavior, is included for each taxon in the written text. A total of 38 specimens for which the taxonomic identifications were slightly more tentative have been treated as though they were certain. The tentative identifications include: 10 specimens of *Canis* c.f. *familiaris*, 1 *Canis* c.f. *latrans*, 2 c.f. *Procyon lotor*, 1 c.f. Mustelidae, 3 c.f. *Lontra canadensis*, 5 c.f. Otariidae, 1 c.f. *Phoca vitulina*, 8 c.f. Muridae, 2 c.f. *Peromyscus*, 2 c.f. Sciuridae, 1 c.f. *Castor canadensis*, and 2 c.f. *Oryctolagus cuniculus*. In general, the tentative identifications are those which looked similar to an available comparative skeleton, but for which comparative material of all related species were not available.

Class Mammalia (Mammals)

Mammalia, Unidentified

Material: 9 skull fragments (3 auditory bullae, 1 occipital, 1 parietal, 4 indeterminate), 1 mandible, 22 teeth (1 molar, 21 indeterminate), 2 manubria, 61 vertebrae (1 axis, 2 cervical, 2 thoracic, 2 lumbar, 2 caudal, 51 indeterminate, 1 modified), 2 innominates (1 acetabulum, 1 modified ilium, 1 fragment), 1 scapula (proximal), 1 radius (proximal), 3 tibiae (shaft), 1 patella, 2 carpals, 1 metacarpal (size of marten), 7 metapodia (1 is modified, 4 are size of marten/rabbit), 7 phalanges (3 2nd, 1 3rd, 3 indeterminate), 2 sesamoids.
Total: 123 specimens.
Remarks: These specimens were identified as mammal based on their robusticity and morphology.

Mammalia, Indeterminate Element

Material: 6 modified limb bone shafts, 2 indeterminate modified fragments.
Total: 8 specimens.
Remarks: Modified mammal specimens are listed because they are included below in a discussion of modifications. Unmodified mammal specimens that could not be identified to element are not included in this analysis.

Order Artiodactyla (even-toed hoofed mammals)

Artiodactyla, Unidentified

Material: 6 teeth (1 incisor, 1 lower incisor, 2 premolars, 1 upper 1st premolar, 1 molar), 43 antler pieces (36 fragments, 4 tines, 3 modified), 1 possible antler, 1 hyoid, 40 vertebrae (1 atlas, 6 axes, 3 cervical, 11 thoracic, 1 thoracic/lumbar neural spine, 7 lumbar, 4 sacral, 1 caudal, 6 indeterminate fragments), 4 innominates (1 acetabulum, 2 ilia, 1 ischium), 1 scapula, 2 humeri (1 distal, 1 shaft), 9 radii (1 proximal, 8 shaft), 2 ulnae (1 olecranon epiphysis, 1 styloid process), 8 femora (3 distal, 1 proximal, 4 shaft), 11 tibiae (1 distal, 10 shaft), 3 carpals (1 2nd/3rd, 1 4th, 1 ulnar), 17 tarsals (7 astragali, 2 calcanei, 2 lateral cuneiforms, 1 medial cuneiform, 5 naviculo-cuboids), 11 metacarpals (2 proximal, 9 shaft), 7 metatarsals (2 proximal, 5 shaft), 30 metapodials (9 distal, 1 proximal, 20 shaft), 20 phalanges (12 1st, 4 2nd, 2 3rd, 2 indeterminate), 4 vestigial phalanges (2 1st, 2 3rd), 1 proximal sesamoid.
Total: 221 specimens.
Remarks: There are four families of artiodactyls found in Washington: the Suidae (pigs), Cervidae (deer), Antilocapridae (pronghorns) and Bovidae (sheep, goats, bison). Most of the specimens identified to Order Artiodactyla are likely *Odocoileus* c.f. *hemionus*, but are too fragmentary to remove other ruminant artiodactyls from consideration. The bovids and suid are probably from disturbed deposits and will be discussed further below.

Figure 9.1 Tibia, radius, and astragalus bones from a mule deer.

Family Cervidae (Deer)

Odocoileus c.f. *hemionus* (mule deer) (Figure 9.1).

Material: 2 maxillae (1 with premolar fragment, one with premolars and molars except for 2nd premolar), 2 teeth (1 premolar, 1 upper 1st premolar), 2 antler (burr, fit together), 56 vertebrae (11 atlases, 6 axes, 3 C7, 17 cervical, 10 thoracic, 1 thoracic/lumbar, 6 lumbar, 2 sacral), 15 innominates (6 ilia, 5 ischia, 4 pubes), 10 scapulae, 13 humeri (2 proximal, 5 distal, 6 shaft), 14 radii (8 proximal, 4 distal, 2 shaft), 19 ulnae (10 proximal, 1 distal, 4 shaft, 4 modified), 18 femora (5 proximal, 9 distal, 4 shaft), 18 tibiae (4 proximal, 5 distal, 9 shaft), 6 fibulae, 4 patellae, 21 carpals (5 2nd/3rd, 4 4th, 1 accessory, 2 intermediate, 5 radial, 4 ulnar), 56 tarsals (11 astragali – 3 fit together, 26 calcanei, 2 lateral cuneiforms, 17 naviculo-cuboids), 10 metacarpals (4 proximal, 1 distal, 5 shaft), 23 metatarsals (8 proximal, 1 distal, 14 shaft), 16 metapodials (14 distal, 2 shaft), 57 phalanges (28 1st, 21 2nd, 7 3rd, 1 indeterminate), 5 vestigial phalanges (2 1st, 3 3rd), 8 proximal sesamoids.
Total: 375 specimens.
Remarks: Several sets of bone fragments of this species fit together. *Odocoileus hemionus* is nearly indistinguishable from *Odocoileus virginianus* (white-tailed deer) from the bones alone, so identification of this species

was based on the range of each species. In Washington, *O. hemionus* is found throughout the state including the San Juan Islands, but *O. virginianus* is located only in the northeastern corner and along the southern border (Ingles 1965). Since *O. virginianus* does not live in western Washington, specimens identified as genus *Odocoileus* are considered to be species *hemionus*. There are six subspecies of *O. hemionus* in the Pacific states (Ingles 1965), but no attempt was made to distinguish them.

Cervus elaphus (Elk)

Material:1 mandible, 1 radius (distal), 3 femora (shafts), 1 metapodial (distal).
Total: 6 specimens.
Remarks: All three femoral shaft fragments fit together. Here, *Cervus elaphus* refers to elk found in North America, though elk in this region are also occasionally called *Cervus canadensis*. Ingles (1965) describes *Cervus canadensis* as being found west of the Cascades in Washington.

Family Bovidae
(Cattle, Sheep, Goats, Old World Antelopes)

Material: 1 tibia (distal)
Total: 1 specimen.
Remarks: King (1950) found mountain sheep, mountain goat, and one cattle bone at the Cattle Point site. San Juan Island has been home to grazing cattle in more recent times, thus bones of *Bos* sp. could certainly appear in this assemblage. Additionally, both British and American settlers kept domestic sheep in historic times (Thompson 1972).

Oreamnos americanus (Mountain Goat)

Material: 1 tooth (upper molar), 1 humerus (distal), 1 phalanx (1st).
Total: 3 specimens.
Remarks: These were identified as *Oreamnos americanus* based on comparisons between this species and *Ovis canadensis* (mountain sheep). As mentioned above, King (1950) found mountain goat and sheep bones in the Cattle Point assemblage. It is possible that people traveled to the mainland to acquire either of these species, or traded with mainland groups for their meat.

Family Suidae (Pigs)
Sus scrofa

Material: 1 metatarsal (proximal with shaft).
Total: 1 specimen.
Remarks: *Sus scrofa* (wild boar) was introduced by the Europeans and is only currently found in California (Ingles 1965). This specimen may be from a historic period domestic pig, an intrusive specimen from a later occupation.

Order Carnivora (Carnivorous Mammals)
Carnivora, Unidentified

Material: 1 skull fragment (parietal), 2 teeth (1 canine, 1 indeterminate), 1 sternebra, 2 vertebrae (1 thoracic, 1 indeterminate), 1 scapula, 1 tibia (distal), 1 tarsal (calcaneus), 1 1st phalanx.
Total: 10 specimens.
Remarks: The sternebra and vertebrae are marine mammals. The tooth is possibly phocid.

Family Canidae
(Foxes, Wolves, Coyotes, Domestic Dogs)

Material: 2 skull fragments (1 basiocciput, 1 interparietal), 11 teeth (3 canines, 1 lower incisor, 1 lower 2nd premolar, 3 lower premolars, 1 lower 1st molar, 1 upper 1st premolar, 1 upper premolar), 2 vertebrae (1 atlas, 1 cervical), 2 humeri (shafts), 1 tibia (shaft), 2 carpals (1 2nd, 1 accessory), 3 tarsals (1 3rd, 1 astragalus, 1 navicular), 1 metacarpal (1st), 3 phalanges (1 2nd, 2 3rd).
Total: 27 specimens.
Remarks: The only wild species from the Family Canidae that occur in reasonable proximity to the San Juan Islands in modern times are the red fox (*Vulpes fulva*), gray wolf (*Canis lupus*), and coyote (*Canis latrans*) (Ingles 1965). Dalquest (1948) provides distribution maps of the coyote, wolf, and red fox indicating that none of these taxa inhabited the San Juan Islands; however, more recent studies show that wolves were present on the islands before the arrival of European-Americans (National Park Service 2004a). King (1950) found elements from both the Puget Sound wolf (*Canis gigas*) and gray wolf (*Canis nubilis*) at the Cattle Point site. Domestic dogs were raised by indigenous peoples before the arrival of Europeans (Dalquest 1948), and King (1950) identified domestic dog at Cattle Point. The red fox is mainly an alpine species (Dalquest 1948; Ingles 1965), but can be found occasionally at lower elevations in California (Ingles 1965). Red foxes have more recently been introduced to San Juan Island (National Park Service 2004b). Specimens from the OpD site were generally too large to fall within the size range for fox.

Canis spp. (Wolves, Coyotes, Domestic Dogs)

Material: 7 skull fragments (1 auditory bulla, 1 basiocciput, 1 edentulous maxilla), 1 occipital, 1 palatine, 2 temporals), 1 mandible (with 3rd and 4th premolar, 1st molar), 5 teeth (1 1st molar, 2 lower 2nd premolars, 1 lower 3rd molar, 1 upper 2nd molar), 3 vertebrae (1

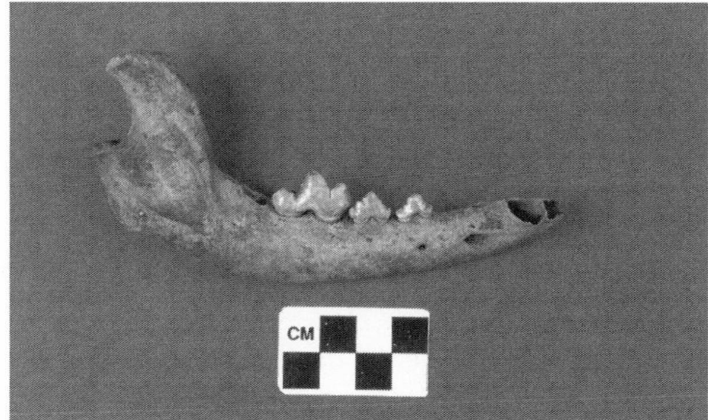

Figure 9.2 Mandible from a domestic dog.

atlas, 1 axis, 1 cervical), 1 radius (proximal), 1 tarsal (astragalus), 1 metapodial (proximal with shaft), 3 phalanges (2 1st, 1 2nd).
Total: 22 specimens.
Remarks: The identification *Canis* spp. includes gray wolf (*Canis lupus*), coyote (*Canis latrans*), and domestic dog (*Canis lupus familiaris*). Most specimens seemed too small to be wolf, but were too fragmented to confidently identify to species. Domestic dog probably comprised the only member of the *Canis* genus present on the San Juan Islands, though people could have acquired wolves from the mainland.

Canis lupus familiaris (Domestic Dog) (Figure 9.2)
Material: 6 skull fragments (2 auditory bullae, 2 temporals, 2 zygomatic arches), 1 mandible, 4 tibiae (1 distal, 3 shaft), 1 fibula (distal), 4 tarsals (1 4th, 2 astragali, 1 calcaneus).
Total: 16 specimens.
Remarks: In 1993, *Canis familiaris* was reinterpreted as being simply a subspecies of *Canis lupus*, rather than a species in its own right. All of the tibia fragments fit together.

Canis c.f. *latrans* (Coyote)
Material: 1 radius (shaft)
Total: 1 specimen.
Remarks: Coyotes are found throughout Washington State in every environment (Ingles 1965), though not specifically on the San Juan Islands (Dalquest 1948). This one specimen of *Canis* c.f. *latrans* was identified as such partly because it looked like coyote, and partly because it did not look like the domestic dog comparative specimen that was available. A more varied comparative collection of domestic dogs might cause this specimen to be re-identified as *Canis lupus familiaris*.

Family Phocidae (Earless Seals)
Phocidae, Unidentified
Material: 9 vertebrae (1 axis, 1 thoracic, 1 lumbar, 6 indeterminate), 1 femur (proximal), 1 ulna (shaft), 1

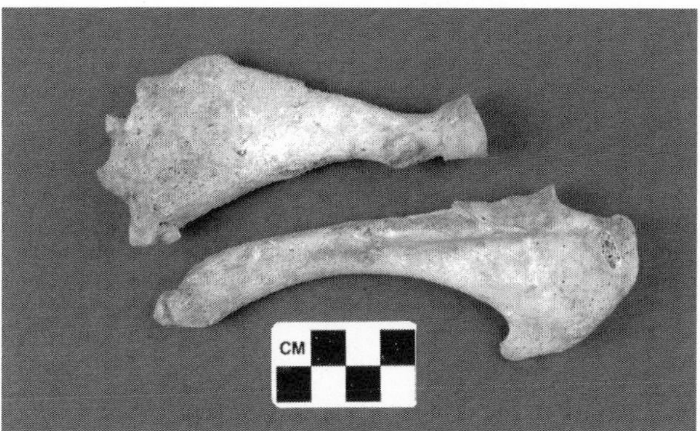

Figure 9.3 Radius and ulna from a harbor seal.

metacarpal (1 4th), 5 phalanges (1 1st, 3 2nd, 1 3rd).
Total: 17 specimens.
Remarks: Phocid species found in the north Pacific are the harbor seal (*Phoca vitulina*) and northern elephant seal (*Mirounga angustirostris*) (Ingles 1965; Osborne et al. 1988). Based on size, many of these specimens are probably harbor seal.

Phoca vitulina (Harbor Seal) (Figure 9.3)
Material: 14 vertebrae (2 C7, 3 cervical, 3 thoracic, 1 lumbar, 2 S1, 3 indeterminate) 5 sternebrae, 1 scapula, 1 humerus (shaft), 2 radii (1 proximal, 1 complete), 1 ulna (complete), 2 femora (2 shaft), 2 carpals (2 radial), 5 tarsals (2 1st, 1 cuboid, 2 naviculars), 3 metacarpals (1 2nd, 1 3rd, 1 indeterminate), 4 metatarsals (1 1st, 1 4th, 1 5th, 1 indeterminate), 1 metapodial (distal), 11 phalanges (4 1st, 3 2nd, 1 3rd, 3 indeterminate).
Total: 52 specimens.
Remarks: Harbor seals usually live in protected bays but are sometimes found on islands without protected water (Ingles 1965). English Camp would have provided a good habitat for harbor seals because it is located on the shore of a large protected bay. Harbor seals are the most common seal in the Strait of Juan de Fuca and Puget Sound (Dalquest 1948; Osborne et al. 1988), and in modern times they are especially concentrated in the San Juan Islands (Osborne et al. 1988). This may explain why they are the most abundant pinniped found in this archaeological assemblage.

Family Otariidae (Eared Seals, Sea Lions)
Otariidae, Unidentified
Material: 4 teeth (fragments), 1 vertebra (thoracic), 1 metacarpal (distal).
Total: 6 specimens.
Remarks: Otariid species found off the Washington coast include the Steller sea lion (*Eumetopias jubatus*), northern fur seal (*Callorhinus ursinus*) (Ingles 1965), Guadalupe fur seal (*Arctocephalus townsendi*) (Etnier 2002a), and California sea lion (*Zalophus californianus*) (Dalquest 1948). The Steller sea lion breeds and pups

on coastal islands along the Pacific Rim from California to Russia in late spring and early summer (Angell and Balcomb 1982), but they do not have any rookeries in Washington (Allen and Angliss 2009). In fall and winter, this species is abundant throughout Puget Sound, especially in the northern region (Angell and Balcomb 1982). The northern fur seal was aggressively hunted for its furs during historic times and nearly became extinct (Ingles 1965). In modern times, northern fur seals breed only at six sites, mostly in the northern Pacific and Bering Sea, but with one site on San Miguel Island off the California coast. Archaeological data, however, suggest that their breeding distribution was once much more extensive (e.g., Etnier 2002b; Gifford-Gonzalez et al. 2005; Hildebrandt and Jones 1992; Lyman 1995; Newsome et al. 2007). Guadalupe fur seal populations were historically thought to be limited to southern California and further south, but modern strandings and archaeological data indicate they range at least up to the Olympic Peninsula in Washington (Etnier 2002a). California sea lions, though common in Puget Sound today (NMFS 1997), were likely quite rare in the past, based on the near-absence of their bones at archaeological sites like Ozette, a site on the coast of northwest Washington (Etnier 2004). In the OpD assemblage, no otariid specimens were found that could be identified as northern fur seal, and only one element (in 13 fragments) could be identified to Steller sea lion (see below). Two of the tooth fragments fit together.

Eumetopias jubatus (Steller sea lion)

Material: 13 ulna fragments.
Total: 13 specimens.
Remarks: All of these fragments fit together, and therefore represent a single element from this species. Steller sea lions are most frequently found on rocky coasts but sometimes swim up rivers (Ingles 1965). They breed in a few places along the Washington coast in late May (Dalquest 1948).

Family Procyonidae (Raccoons)
Procyon lotor (Raccoon)

Material:1 edentulous mandible, 3 vertebrae (1 axis, 1 thoracic, 1 lumbar), 1 innominate (ischium), 1 scapula, 1 tarsal (navicular), 2 phalanges (1 2nd, 1 3rd).
Total: 9 specimens.
Remarks: Raccoons occur in Washington in all environments except for the deserts, most commonly near lakes, marshes, and streams (Ingles 1965). King (1950) did not note any raccoon remains at the Cattle Point site. Specimens identified as raccoon are found throughout OpD, and at varying depths.

Family Mustelidae (Weasels, Minks, Martens, Fishers, Wolverines, Badgers, and Otters)
Mustelidae, Unidentified

Material:1 tooth (incisor), 4 vertebrae (indeterminate centra), 1 humerus (distal), 1 tarsal (astragalus), 5 phalanges (1 1st, 3 2nd, 1 3rd).
Total: 12 specimens.
Remarks: Numerous species of the Mustelidae family are found in Washington. Around the San Juan Islands, minks (*Neovison vison*) and river otters (*Lontra canadensis*) are the only species present today. Historic period harvesting of sea otters (*Enhydra lutris*) for their pelts caused them to become locally extinct (Dalquest 1948), but they are once again found along the coast of Washington after being reintroduced in the mid-to-late 20th century.

Neovison vison (American Mink)

Material: 2 skull fragments (1 auditory bulla, 1 maxilla with 2nd premolar).
Total: 2 specimens.
Remarks: Until recently, all minks were found in the genus *Mustela*, but American minks are now considered their own genus: *Neovison* (Wilson and Reeder 2005). The mink is found throughout Washington near lakes, streams, and marshes that provide fish. On the San Juan Islands, minks are often found in upland habits (Dalquest 1948). They are considered valuable for their pelts and their predatory capabilities (Ingles 1965).

Lontra canadensis
(formerly *Lutra canadensis*, River Otter)

Material: 2 tibiae (1 distal, 1 shaft), 1 ulnar carpal, 1 1st phalanx.
Total: 4 specimens.
Remarks: The two tibia fragments from this species fit together. New World otters are now in the genus Lontra, separated from other otters (Wilson and Reeder 2005). River otters generally spend their lives in fresh water, although some live in the marine environment around the San Juan Islands (Dalquest 1948; Ingles 1965).

Order Lagomorpha (Hares, Rabbits, Pika)
Family Leporidae (Hares, Rabbits)
Oryctolagus cuniculus (Domestic Rabbit)

Material: 2 teeth, 2 vertebrae (lumbar), 1 metacarpal (proximal), 1 metatarsal (proximal).
Total: 6 specimens.
Remarks: No wild lagomorphs are found on the San Juan Islands (Dalquest 1948). The snowshoe hare (*Lepus americanus*) is found on the mainland throughout

western Washington (Ingles 1965). The European rabbit (*Oryctolagus cuniculus*) was introduced to the San Juan Islands, possibly during the time of the Hudson's Bay Company (Ingles 1965). Since the European rabbit is the only lagomorph on San Juan Island, the specimens from OpD are intrusive to the archaeological site. Two of the *Oryctolagus* specimens are found in facies 2D02 near the bottom of Unit 111 349.

Order Cetacea (Whales)
Suborder Odontoceti (Toothed Whales)

Material: 6 vertebrae (5 caudal, 1 indeterminate).
Total: 6 specimens.
Remarks: The 5 caudal vertebrae fragments all fit together, which means this taxon is represented by at most two elements. Numerous species of whale are found in the Pacific; Dall's porpoise, harbor porpoise, orca, and Pacific white-sided dolphins are common in the San Juan Islands. Short-finned pilot whales and false killer whales are rare, but appear occasionally. Several species strand occasionally in the inland waters (Osborne et al. 1988).

Family Delphinidae (Dolphins, Porpoises, Orcas)

Material: 1 tooth.
Total: 1 specimen.
Remarks: This specimen was identified as delphinid by Michael Etnier (University of Washington and Applied Osteology). Several delphinids are found frequently in the Puget Sound and San Juan Islands region, including Dall's porpoises, harbor porpoises (Osborne et al. 1988), orcas, Pacific white-sided dolphins, and short-finned pilot whales (Angell and Balcomb III 1982).

Order Rodentia (Rodents)
Rodentia, Unidentified

Material: 9 skull fragments (1 frontal, 3 maxillae, 1 occipital, 1 premaxilla, 3 temporals), 8 mandibles (1 with incisor, 1 with incisor and 2nd molar, 6 without teeth), 7 teeth (2 incisors, 5 upper incisors), 1 manubrium, 48 vertebrae (2 atlases, 6 axes, 1 C7, 2 cervical, 11 thoracic, 16 lumbar, 1 S1, 1 sacral, 6 caudal, 2 indeterminate), 3 innominates (3 acetabula), 4 scapulae, 13 humeri (3 distal, 5 distal with shaft, 5 shaft), 1 radius (complete), 3 ulnae (1 proximal, 2 proximal with shaft), 14 femora (5 proximal, 2 proximal with shaft, 3 distal, 4 shaft), 11 tibiae (1 proximal, 3 distal, 4 distal with shaft, 3 shaft), 1 fibula (shaft), 1 metatarsal (complete), 1 metapodial (complete), 1 phalanx.
Total: 126 specimens.
Remarks: Most of these specimens are so small and unmodified that they are probably intrusive in the archaeological site.

Family Castoridae (Beavers)
c.f. *Castor canadensis* (Beaver)

Material: 1 vertebra (thoracic).
Total: 1 specimen.
Remarks: The beaver is the largest rodent found in North America, and is valued for its pelt (Ingles 1965). This species depends on a stream habitat. Beavers were hunted to extinction on the San Juan Islands by Euroamericans but were later re-introduced (Dalquest 1948).

Family c.f. Sciuridae (Squirrels)

Material: 1 mandible (with incisor), 1 humerus (distal with shaft).
Total: 2 specimens.
Remarks: This family includes marmots, ground squirrels, chipmunks, and tree squirrels. Ground squirrels are not found near the west coast of Washington, although the other taxa are (Ingles 1965). According to Dalquest (1948), the only species found on the San Juan Islands is the Douglas squirrel (*Tamiasciurus douglasii*).

Family Muridae (Mice, Rats, Voles, and relatives)

Material: 25 skull fragments (4 frontals, 1 interparietal, 11 maxillae: 1 with 2nd and 3rd molars and 10 edentulous, 1 parietal, 3 premaxillae, 1 premaxilla/maxilla, 1 sphenoid, 3 temporals), 12 mandibles (2 with incisor and 3rd molar, 5 with incisor, 1 with incisor and 1st and 2nd molars, 1 with incisor and 1st molar, 3 edentulous), 2 teeth (upper incisors), 15 vertebrae (4 atlases, 1 axis, 1 cervical, 2 thoracic, 6 lumbar, 1 S1), 5 innominates (2 ilia, 1 acetabulum, 1 ischium, 1 nearly complete), 1 scapula, 14 humeri (1 proximal, 13 distal with shaft), 1 radius (proximal), 11 femora (8 proximal with shaft, 2 distal, 1 shaft), 5 tibiae (1 proximal, 2 shaft, 2 distal with shaft).
Total: 91 specimens.
Remarks: Several of these elements are probably from the same individual, based on size, morphology, and surface discoloration. Two of the frontals fit together. This Family is a broad category encompassing several familiar species of rodent, divided into Subfamilies.

Subfamily Arvicolinae
(Arvicolinae Rodents, Lemmings, Voles)

Material:1 anterior skull (maxilla, premaxilla, frontal), 17 skull fragments (2 auditory bullae, 8 maxillae, 1 nasal, 1 occipital, 1 orbitosphenoid, 1 premaxilla, 1 premaxilla/maxilla, 2 temporals: zygomatic arches), 6 vertebrae (1 atlas, 2 cervical, 1 thoracic, 2 lumbar), 13 mandibles (some with teeth), 5 teeth (1 lower incisor , 2 lower 1st molars, 2 molars), 4 humeri (2 proximal, 2 distal with shaft), 5 femora (3 proximal with shaft, 2

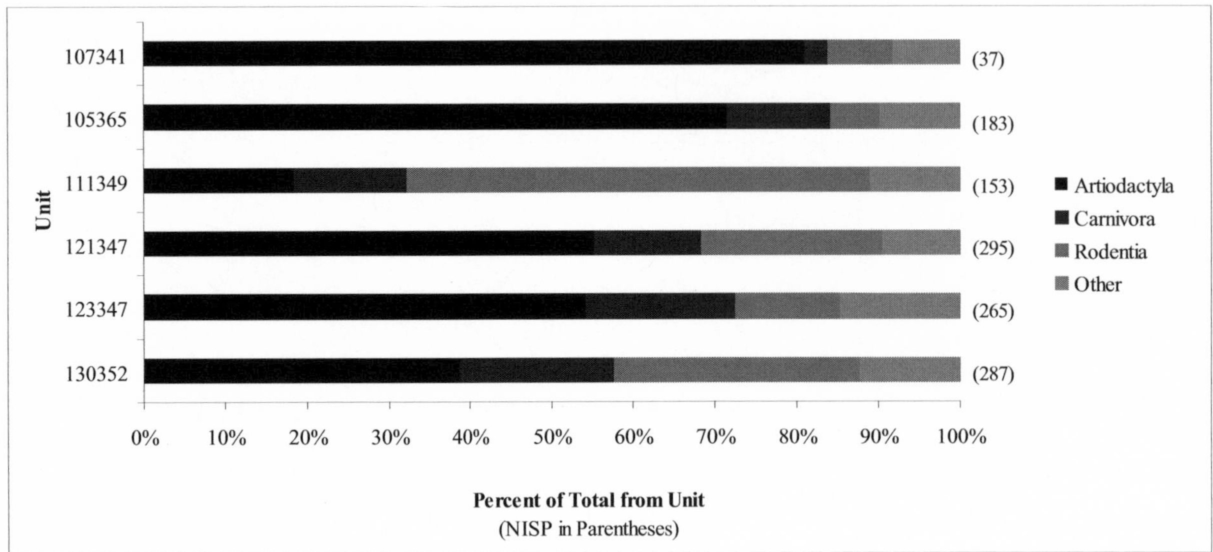

Figure 9.4 Percentages of Mammalian Families for each unit.

distal), 2 tibiae (shaft).
Total: 53 specimens.
Remarks: Members of this Subfamily are easy to tell apart using their teeth. Several of these specimens probably come from the same individual.

Arvicolinae c.f. *Microtus* (Voles)
Material: 1 mandible (body with incisor and 1st molar).
Total: 1 specimen.

Sigmodontinae (Mice, Woodrats)
Material: 3 maxillae (1 with molar, 2 edentulous), 6 mandibles (5 with incisor, 1 edentulous), 1 tibia (distal with shaft).
Total: 10 specimens.

c.f. *Peromyscus* spp. (Deer Mice)
Material: 1 humerus (distal with shaft), 1 femur (shaft).
Total: 2 specimens.
Remarks: One subspecies (*Peromyscus hollisteri*) is the only deer mouse to be found on the San Juan Islands. It is not found anywhere else in Washington (Dalquest 1948).

QUANTITATIVE SUMMARY AND ANALYSIS

The main goals of this analysis are to provide a quantitative summary of faunal remains, and to determine whether there are significant differences among the units inside the ridge, on top of the ridge, and behind the ridge. If the ridge indeed defines a midden deposited around a house, there should be different faunal remains "inside" the house and around it.

A total of 1,220 mammal bones identifiable to element and representing 31 taxa were excavated from six units at English Camp. Of these, 1,097 were identified to at least Order level. The main Families comprising the assemblage are Cervidae, Canidae, Phocidae, and Muridae. Based on numbers of identified specimens, artiodactyls are the most abundant Order in every unit except for 111 349, which is dominated by rodent bones (Table 9.1; Figure 9.4). The category of "Other" includes Cetacea, Leporidae, and specimens that could not be identified more specifically than Class Mammalia. It comprises 8-15% of each unit, and is mostly Mammalia.

The possibility was considered that the abundance of artiodactyl bones was due to greater fragmentation from being cracked open for marrow (e.g., Binford 1981). Figure 9.5 compares Artiodactyla specimens to Carnivora (including all taxa identified to more specific levels in these categories), separated out by element segment. "Fragment' in this case refers to pieces of all elements that are not long bones, and can therefore be compared with the categories from "Distal/shaft" to "Shaft," which represent the long bones. Given that all artiodactyl segments, not just those that contain marrow, are more abundant than all carnivore segments, it appears that fragmentation is not responsible for the prevalence of artiodactyl specimens.

In general, identifiable mammal bones were sparsely distributed throughout the site. Only in a few places do species have a higher count per volume than 0.1/liter (i.e., 1 specimen per 10 liters). For the most part these are artiodactyl and rodent taxa, with the one exception of *Eumetopias jubatus* in facies 1D01 in unit 130 352. The *E. jubatus* fragments are all part of the same ulna, and thus only represent one element. Even the total number of identified specimens in each facies is small

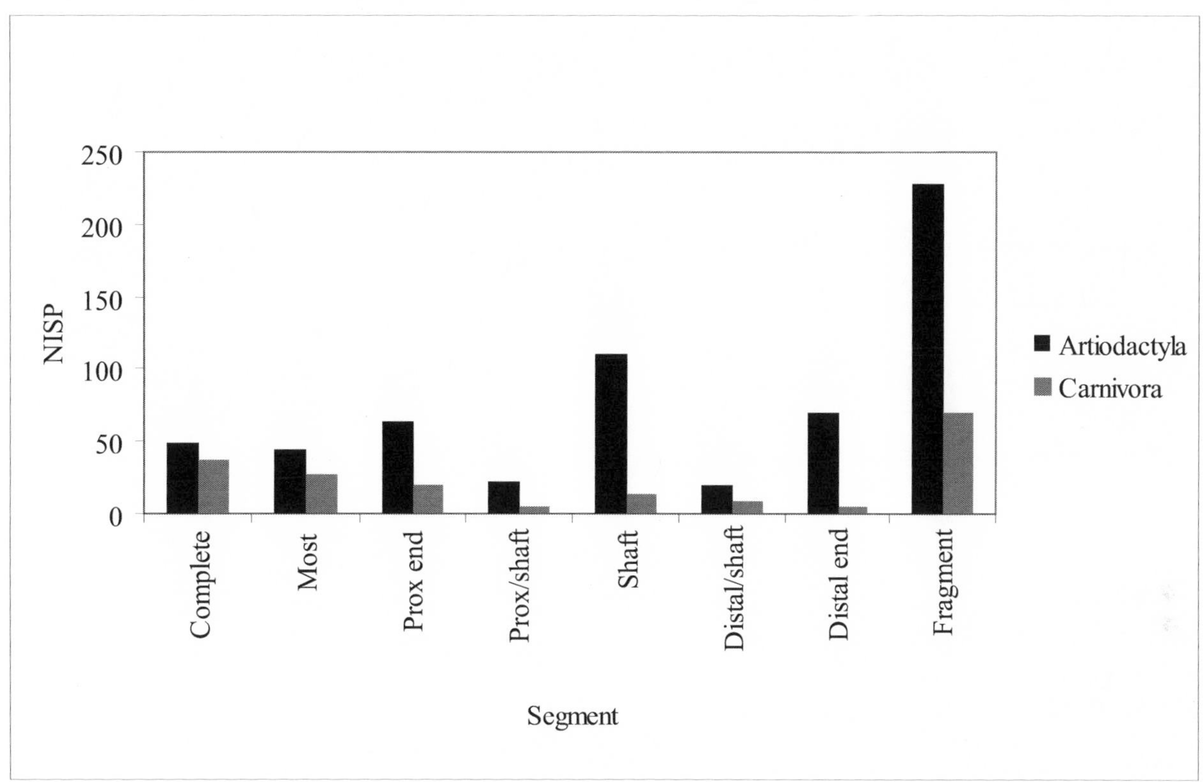

Figure 9.5 A comparison of bone fragmentation between Artiodactyla and Carnivora specimens.

enough to create a count/volume value of <0.1/liter in most units. The only two units with a higher count per volume were 121 347 and 123 347, both of which are inside the ridge. The values are still so low (0.2/liter) that they seem unlikely to represent a significant difference in use of space. The three units inside the ridge –121 347, 123 347, 130 352– are the ones with the largest sample sizes and the highest number of identified taxa. The first two units are the only places where bovid and suid bones are found, which is consistent with historic artifacts found in the upper 50 cm of units 121 347 and 123 347. The two units that have high numbers of identified taxa but lower sample sizes are 105 365 and 111 349, both of which are located on the ridge. One delphinid and one castorid bone are present on the ridge but not elsewhere.

Certain units have more identified taxa (higher richness) than others (Table 9.1). Sample size is known to affect richness levels (e.g., Grayson 1984; Grayson and Delpech 1998), thus linear regressions were performed on the data (Figure 9.6).

If identification at all taxonomic levels is considered, a linear regression indicates a significant correlation between number of identified taxa per unit and the total sample size for each unit. The high r^2 value (0.8762) indicates that a high percentage of the variability in numbers of identified taxa is explained by the sample size: more taxa are identified simply because there is a greater pool of specimens from which to identify them. Interestingly, the correlation is much less significant when the data are analyzed without looking at species, and using family, order, and class information only (Figure 9.7). Although the r^2 value drops to 0.65, there is still a weak correlation between sample size and number of taxa identified, suggesting that taxonomic richness is not a good indicator for differences among ridge locations.

BURNING

If the depression inside the ridge does represent a house, the highest percentage of burning should be found within or on top of the ridge near cooking areas. During analysis, bones were marked as burned, calcined, both, or neither. This determination was made based on visual cues, and must be considered subjective. Sometimes chemical processes during diagenesis can cause a bone to change color in a way that resembles burning (Shipman et al. 1984), which means that burning can be misidentified when color is the only criteria used for identification. Color is the most common criteria archaeologists use to identify burning (Lyman 1994), in part because other techniques are significantly more expensive. Since color was the only trait used to identify burning in the OpD assemblage, identification was made conservatively. Burned specimens not identifiable to element were excluded from this description

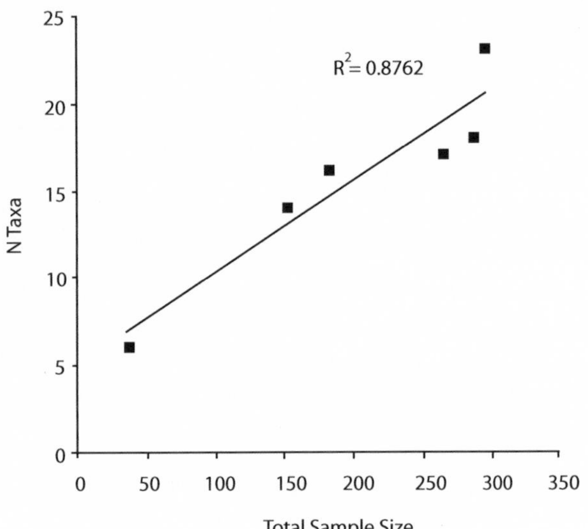

Figure 9.6 A linear regression showing the relationship between sample size and richness using identification of all taxonomic levels.

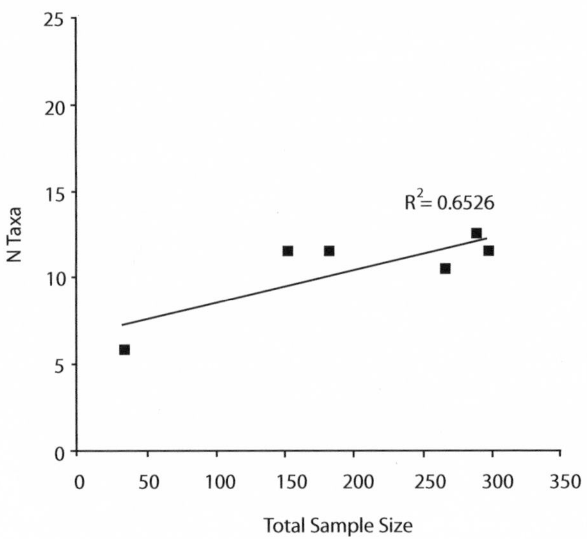

Figure 9.7 A linear regression showing the relationship between sample size and richness using only family, order, and class identifications.

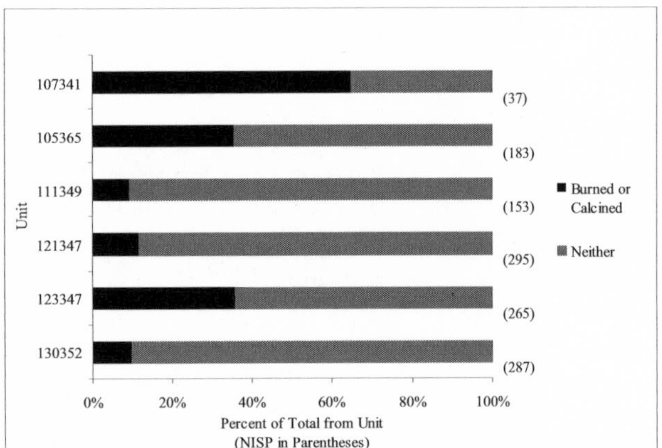

Figure 9.8 Percentages of bones burned or calcined for each unit.

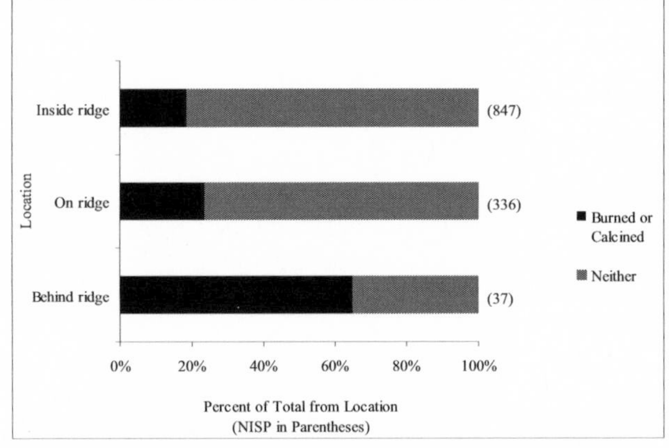

Figure 9.9 Percentages of bones burned or calcined at each area of the site.

to maintain consistency with other comparisons between units.

Contrary to the expected pattern if OpD was a domestic structure, the unit with the highest percentage of burned or calcined specimens was 107 341, behind the ridge (Figure 9.8, 9.9). This unit is also the one with the smallest total number of identifiable mammal bones, but since unidentifiable specimens were removed from analysis for this chapter, it is possible that the total sample size from this unit is artificially deflated. Unit 107 341 is the only unit where calcined bones are more common than bones that were only blackened, which means they were exposed to higher temperatures.

BODY PART REPRESENTATION

To investigate body part representation, elements were put into broader categories based on general region of the body. Binford (1981) reports that ethnographically, most groups that separate the forelimb into smaller parts do so by disarticulating between the carpals and the radio-cubitus. In this analysis, the forelimb includes the scapula, humerus, radius and ulna; the hindlimb comprises the femur, tibia, and fibula. The distal limbs (metapodials, podials) were separated out to see how these lower utility parts compared to the higher utility proximal limbs. The innominate is considered part of the axial category. A comparison of the distribution of body part segments among units (Figure 9.10) reveals that the unit behind the ridge (107 341) has a much larger proportion of podia, phalanges, and sesamoids than the other units. This may be explained by the small sample size.

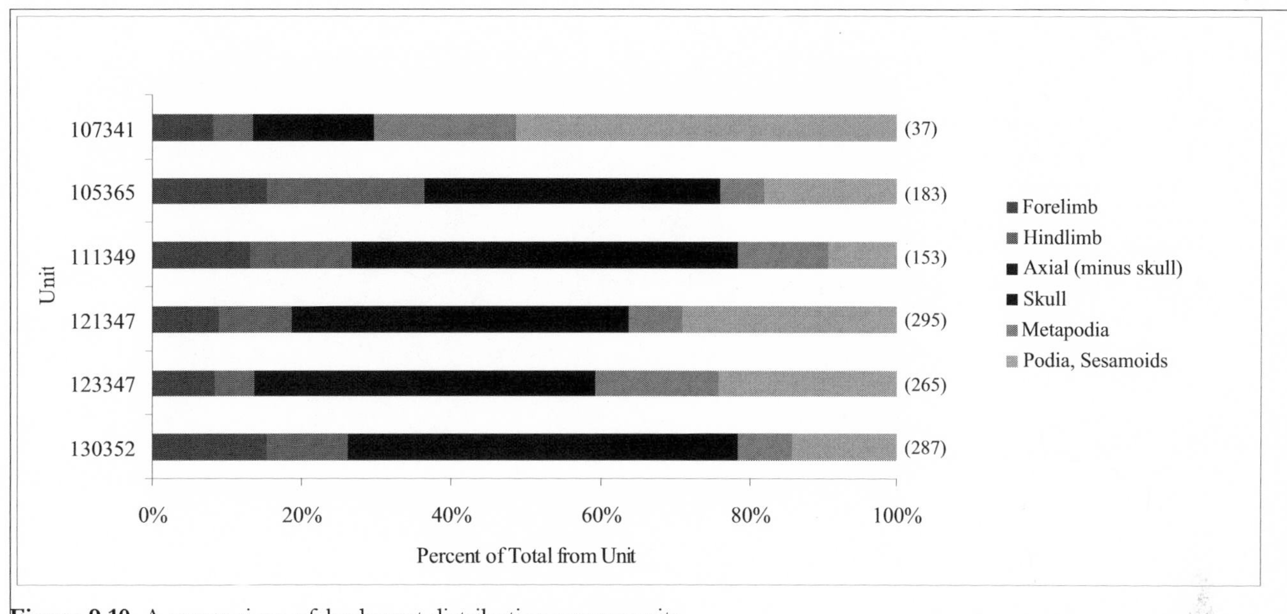

Figure 9.10 A comparison of body part distribution among units.

Table 9.2 NISP of bone modification by unit.

Unit	Modification										Total Modified
	None	Cut	Drilled	Ground/ Polished	Saw	Wedge	Scratched	Gnawed	Digested	Weathered	
107 341	36	1	-	-	-	-	-	-	-	-	1
105 365	172	2	-	4	-	-	3	2	-	-	11
111 349	146	2	-	1	1	-	-	1	2	-	7
121 347	268	3	1	1	-	1	1	-	-	20	27
123 347	258	5	-	-	2	-	-	-	-	-	7
130 352	278	6	-	-	-	-	-	3	-	-	9
Total	1158	19	1	6	3	1	4	6	2	20	62

OTHER MODIFICATIONS

Quantification of non-burning modifications includes mammal bones that could not be identified to element (Table 9.2). These modifications were only described generally, and without the use of a microscope. The high number of weathered specimens in unit 121 347 results from several antler fragments (some possibly from the same antler) found in facies 1D01-1D02. Of the saw marks, only one is definitive, and it comes from facies 1A03 of Unit 123 347, a level that may include historic or modern materials. In general, the level of modification of any form (aside from burning) is rather low, whether enacted by human, carnivore, or the environment. Only 5% of the assemblage is modified, with the highest percentage of modification by unit occurring with the weathered antler. No type of modification occurs in more than 2% of the assemblage.

CONCLUSIONS

With a total of 1,220 mammal bones identified at OpD, few significant differences were detected among the units inside the ridge, on the ridge, and behind the ridge. Identifiable mammal bone densities are extremely low throughout the site, typically less than 0.1 specimens per liter. Artiodactyls are the most common taxa in all units, except for Unit 111 349 where rodents dominate. A fairly strong correlation between taxonomic richness and sample size suggests that the greater number of taxa identified inside the ridge is due to sampling, and is insignificant. The most noticeably different unit assemblage comes from Unit 107 341, which has the smallest sample size, the highest rate of burning/calcining, and the largest proportion of elements with little nutritional value (podials, phalanges, and sesamoids). This unit is behind the ridge, so it is conceivable that these differences are attributable to a different use of space than inside the ridge. It is also possible that the unit was more heavily affected by density-mediated destruction, increasing the proportion of small, dense bones. While this analysis sheds little light on whether the ridge built up around a house, it does provide an in-depth summary of the mammal species people exploited during their occupation of this site, and which taxa may have been the most important during their daily lives.

REFERENCES

Allen, B. M., and R. P. Angliss
2009 *Steller Sea Lion (Eumetopias jubatus): Eastern U.S. Stock*. NOAA-TM-AFSC-206.

Angell, T., and K. C. Balcomb, III
1982 *Marine Birds and Mammals of Puget Sound.* Washington Sea Grant Publication: Distributed by the University of Washington Press, Seattle.

Binford, L. R.
1981 *Bones: Ancient Men and Modern Myths.* Academic Press, New York.

Cannon, K. J.
1997 Administrative History: San Juan Island National Historical Park. Prepared for the National Park Service, Seattle Support Office.

Dalquest, W. W.
1948 *Mammals of Washington.* University of Kansas Publications Museum of Natural History 2. University of Kansas, Lawrence.

Etnier, M. A.
2002a Occurrences of Guadalupe fur seals (Arctocephalus townsendi) on the Washington coast over the past 500 years. *Marine Mammal Science* 18(2):551-557.
2002b *The Effects of Human Hunting on Northern Fur Seal (Callorhinus ursinus) Migration and Breeding Distributions in the Late Holocene.* Ph.D. Dissertation, University of Washington, Seattle.
2004 The potential of zooarchaeological data to guide pinniped management decisions in the eastern North Pacific. In *Zooarchaeology and Conservation Biology*, edited by R. L. Lyman and K. P. Cannon, pp. 88-102. University of Utah Press, Salt Lake City.

Gifford-Gonzalez, D., S. D. Newsome, P. L. Koch, T. P. Guilderson, J. J. Snodgrass, and R. K. Burton
2005 Archaeofaunal insights on pinniped-human interactions in the northeastern Pacific. In *The Exploitation and Cultural Importance of Marine Mammals, 9th ICAZ Conference, Durham, 2002*, edited by G. Monks, pp. 19-38. Vol. 7. Oxbow Books, Oxford.

Grayson, D.K.
1984 *Quantitative Zooarchaeology: Topics in the Analysis of Archaeological Faunas.* Studies in Archaeological Science. Academic Press, Inc., Orlando.

Grayson, D. K., and F. Delpeche
1998 Changing Diet Breadth in the Early Upper Paleolithic of Southwestern France. *Journal of Archaeological Science* 25:1119-1130.

Hildebrandt, W. R., and T. L. Jones
1992 Evolution of Marine Mammal Hunting: A View from the California and Oregon Coasts. *Journal of Anthropological Archaeology* 11(4):360-401.

Ingles, L. G.
1965 *Mammals of the Pacific States: California, Oregon, and Washington.* Stanford University Press, Stanford.

King, A. R.
1950 Cattle Point: A Stratified Site in the Southern Northwest Coast Region. *Memoirs of the Society for American Archaeology* 7:1-94.

Lyman, R. L.
1994 *Vertebrate Taphonomy.* Cambridge Manuals in Archaeology. Cambridge University Press, Cambridge.
1995 On the evolution of marine mammal hunting on the west coast of North America. *Journal of Anthropological Archaeology* 14(1):45-77.

NMFS (National Marine Fisheries Service)
1997 Investigation of Scientific Information on the Impacts of California Sea Lions and Pacific Harbor Seals on Salmonids and on the Coastal Ecosystems of Washington, Oregon, and California. U.S. Dep. Commer., NOAA Tech. Memo. NMFS-NWFSC-28, 172 p.

National Park Service
2004a San Juan Islands National Historical Park: Nature and Science. http://www.nps.gov/sajh/pphtml/subanimals6.html.
2004b San Juan Islands National Historical Park: Nature and Science. http://www.nps.gov/sajh/pphtml/animals.html.

Newsome, S. D., M. A. Etnier, D. Gifford-Gonzalez, D. L. Phillips, M. van Tuinen, E. A. Hadly, D. P. Costa, D. J. Kennett, T. P. Guilderson, and P. L. Koch
2007 The shifting baseline of northern fur seal ecology in the northeast Pacific Ocean. *PNAS* 104:9709-9714.

Osborne, R., J. Calambokidis, and E. M. Dorsey
1988 *A Guide to Marine Mammals of Greater Puget Sound.* Island Publishers, Anacortes, WA.

Shipman, P., G. Foster, and M. Schoeninger
1984 Burnt Bones and Teeth: An Experimental Study of Color, Morphology, Crystal Structure and Shrinkage. *Journal of Archaeological Science* 11:307-325.

Wilson, D. E., and D. M. Reeder (editors)
2005 *Mammal Species of the World: A Taxonomic and Geographic Reference*. 3rd ed. Johns Hopkins University Press, Baltimore.

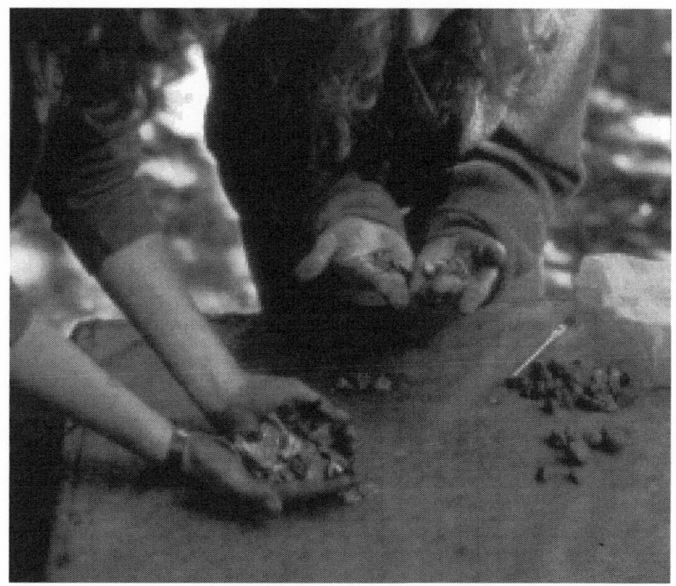

10

Faunal Analysis: Birds

Kristine M. Bovy

This chapter provides both a descriptive summary of the types of birds represented at OpD and a quantitative analysis of those remains. The descriptive summary presents information regarding types of birds found both prehistorically and in modern times at the OpD location. An unexpectedly high percentage of distal wing bones were found at the site. Bird bone fragmentation and the importance of screen size are also discussed.

Bird bones are relatively scarce at the OpD locality of the British Camp site, comprising less than 1% of all vertebrate remains. Despite these small numbers, however, the assemblage is interesting for a number of reasons. First, at least 34 different taxa were identified, including both aquatic (e.g., ducks, gulls, alcids, loons, etc.) and terrestrial species (passerines, owls, eagles, grouse, etc.). Second, only certain parts of the aquatic birds, primarily distal wing bones, were deposited in the midden. Finally, the systematic use of ⅛" screens at the British Camp site decreases the magnitude of recovery bias. Therefore, although the assemblage is small, it provides a hint of what species and elements may be missing when only ¼" screens are used.

METHODOLOGY

The bird remains discussed here were recovered from the six excavation units that were selected using a stratified random sample: behind the shell ridge (107 341), on the ridge (105 365, 111349), and inside the ridge (121 347, 123 347, 130 357). I conducted the initial sort of the approximately 48,860 fragments of fish, mammal, bird and unidentifiable bone from these units. Of these fragments, less than 1% (309) were identified as bird bone. Given the small number of bird bones, I will report 100% of the bird bones recovered.

All taxonomic identifications were made using the substantial comparative skeletal collections at the Burke Museum of Natural History and Culture. However, I made no attempt to identify small passerine specimens or phalanges, vertebrae, and ribs beyond the class level. In addition to taxonomic designations, I also recorded the presence of burning and other taphonomic modifications. This analysis was originally reported in my Master of Arts research competency paper (Bovy 1998). However, in preparation for this manuscript, I revised some of the initial identifications and added a few additional bird bones, which I had not been able to identify earlier. Also, unlike earlier analyses (Bovy 1998, 2002a) I have made no distinction here between potentially pre- and post- contact levels.

I have quantified the assemblage using both NISP (Number of Identified Specimens) and MNE (Minimum Number of Elements). NISP is used for the general descriptive summary, and in the screen-size analysis. During the identification process, I attempted to refit any possible fragments of the same taxon and element. Refitted fragments were counted as one specimen (unless otherwise noted; see Table 10.3). MNE values were calculated in order to analyze the skeletal part percentages. This analytical unit takes fragmentation into account by considering non-overlapping frag-

Chapter opening photo: Students sorting bone and shell in the field lab.

Table 10.1 Total number of avian specimens identified by unit, scientific, and common name (listed in taxonomic order)

Scientific Name	Common Name	Unit					Total
		105365	111349	121347	123347	130352	
cf. Anatidae	Goose, Swan, Duck			1			1
Anserini, unidentified	Goose	2		1			3
Branta bernicla	Brant				1		1
Branta canadensis	Canada Goose					1	1
Anatinae, unidentified	Duck	16	10	8	4	9	47
Anas sp.	Dabbling Duck			1			1
Aythya sp.- medium	Greater Scaup or Redhead			1			1
Mergini, unidentified	Sea Duck		1		1	2	4
Melanitta sp. (small)	Surf or Black Scoter				1		1
Melanitta perspicillata	Surf Scoter	5					5
Melanitta fusca	White-winged Scoter	1					1
cf. *Melanitta fusca*	White-winged Scoter		1				1
Clangula hyemalis	Long-tailed Duck	2			1	2	5
Bucephala albeola	Bufflehead	1			1	2	4
Bucephala sp. (large)	Common or Barrow's Goldeneye					2	2
cf. *Lophodytes cucullatus*	Hooded Merganser		1				1
Mergus merganser	Common Merganser	1					1
Odontophoridae	Quail	1		1			2
Callipepla californica	California Quail	2					2
Gallus gallus	Domestic Chicken			3	1		4
Tetraoninae, unidentified	Grouse			1		1	2
Dendragapus fuliginosus (=*obscurus*)	Blue Grouse	1	1				2
Meleagris gallopavo	Wild Turkey			1			1
Gavia sp.	Loon					1	1
Gavia pacifica	Pacific Loon		2				2
Podilymbus podiceps	Pie-billed Grebe	1					1
Podiceps sp.	Grebe		1				1
Phoebastria cf. *albatrus*	Short-tailed Albatross				2		2
Phalacrocorax auritus	Double-crested Cormorant					1	1
Accipitrinae- large	Bald or Golden Eagle					2	2
Haliaeetus leucocephalus	Bald Eagle			2	1	3	6
Charadriinae, unidentified	Plover	1					1
Laridae (small), unidentified	Gull, Tern	1					1
Larinae (small), unidentified	Gull		2			1	3
Larus sp. (small)	Gull (small)		1		1	1	3
cf. *Larus* sp. (small)	Gull (small)					1	1
Larus sp. (large)	Gull (large)	8	2	2	1	3	16
Uria cf. *aalge*	Common Murre		1	1	1	3	6
Brachyramphus marmoratus	Marbled Murrelet				1	4	5
Columbidae, unidentified	Pigeon, Dove					1	1
cf. *Patagioenas fasciata*	Band-tailed Pigeon				1		1
Megascops kennicottii	Western Screech-Owl		6				6
cf. *Megascops kennicottii*	Western Screech-Owl		1				1
Glaucidium gnoma	Northern Pygmy-Owl					2	2
Megaceryle (=Ceryle) alcyon	Belted Kingfisher			1			1
Picoides sp.	Woodpecker	1	1				2
Passeriformes (small), unidentified	Perching Bird (small)	9	3			2	14
Passeriformes (large), unidentified	Perching Bird (large)		1				1
Corvus cf. *caurinus*	Northwestern Crow	1	1	6			8
Corvus corax	Common Raven					6	6
Unidentified Bird	Bird	18	18	27	23	35	121
Total		72	54	57	41	85	309

ments of the same element and taxon as potentially representing the same element. Therefore, if certain bones (e.g., ulna shafts) are highly fragmented, the NISP value would be inflated relative to the MNE value, with the latter potentially providing a more accurate estimate of the relative skeletal part proportions.

RESULTS & DISCUSSION

The results of the bird bone analysis are presented in three different ways. The descriptive summary lists all of the specimens by taxa and identified elements. The quantitative section describes the relative abundance of different taxa at the site. Finally, the taphonomic summary includes information about burning, bone modification, bird skeletal part representation, and screen-size data. An appendix showing all results is available on file at the Burke Museum of Natural History and Culture.

Descriptive Summary

This section provides descriptive information on all of the identifiable birds in this assemblage. Where necessary, the criteria used to distinguish closely related species are provided. The modern range distributions of the birds are also discussed, using information primarily from Lewis and Sharpe (1987) and Angell and Balcomb (1982), but also Bakus (1965), Miller et al. (1935), National Geographic Society (1987), National Park Service (1995), and Vernon (1996). The taxonomic names used here follow the Seventh Edition of the American Ornithologists' Union check-list (1998), as well as recent changes to this check-list (AOU 2000; Banks et al. 2003, 2004, 2006, 2007, 2008; Chesser et al. 2009). For example, there has been a recent change of sequence in the check-list, with the Anseriformes and Galliformes now being listed prior to Gaviiformes (Banks et al. 2003:923). The avian osteological terms used follow Howard (1929). Table 10.1 lists the total number of avian specimens identified by unit, scientific, and common name (listed in taxonomic order).

Class Aves (Birds)
Aves, unidentified

Material: 3 skull fragments (2 basipterygoids, 1 parietal/frontal), 3 trachial rings, 24 vertebrae (2 atlases, 15 cervicals, 3 thoracics, 2 caudal, 1 centrum, 1 indeterminate), 10 ribs (1 proximal, 2 sternal, 7 shafts), 1 sternum fragment, 4 ulnae shafts, 2 carpals (1 cuneiform, 1 scapholunar), 4 carpometacarpi (2 proximal, 1 distal, 1 shaft), 1 proximal femur, 2 distal tibiotarsi, 3 tarsometatarsi (1 proximal, 2 distal), 34 phalanges (23 complete, 4 proximal, 7 distal), 22 limb bone (indeterminate shafts), 8 indeterminate fragments.

Total: 121 specimens.

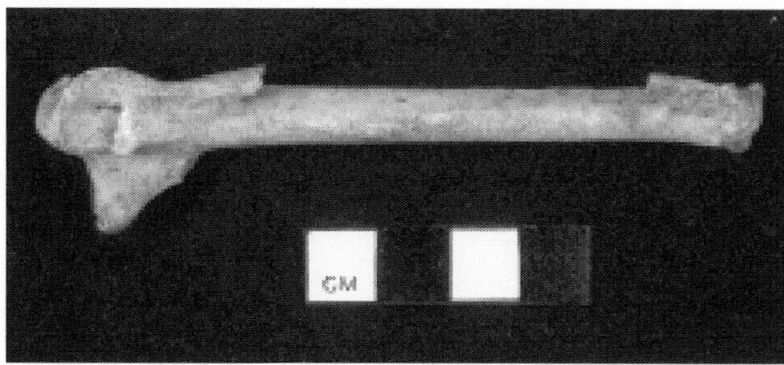

Figure 10.1 Carpometacarpus (right), Canada Goose (*Branta canadensis*); SAJH 106117.

Remarks: The majority of the unidentified bird bone from the assemblage is comprised of phalanges, vertebrae, and ribs. No attempt was made to identify these elements to the ordinal level. The remaining unidentified bird elements were generally too fragmented to be identified below the class level.

Order Anseriformes (Swans, Geese, Ducks)
Family Anatidae (Swans, Geese, Ducks)
cf. Anatidae (Swans, Geese, Ducks)

Material: 1 sternum fragment.

Total: 1 specimen.

Remarks: This small sternum fragment, the carinal apex, is most similar in shape to either a small goose or large duck.

Subfamily Anserinae (Swans, Geese)
Tribe Anserini (Geese)

Material: 1 carpal (cuneiform), 1 proximal carpometacarpus, 1 third wing digit.

Total: 3 specimens.

Remarks: Five species of geese are relatively common in the region: the Greater White-fronted Goose (*Anser albifrons*), Snow Goose (*Chen caerulescens*), Brant (*Branta bernicla*), Cackling Goose (*Branta hutchinsii* (=*canadensis*) and Canada Goose (*Branta canadensis*). Formerly considered a sub-species of the Canada Goose, the smaller-bodied Cackling Goose, has just recently been designated a separate species by the American Ornithologists' Union on the basis of mitochondrial DNA evidence (Banks et al. 2004). Although migrating geese are most often seen flying, they stop occasionally to feed in wetlands and grasslands on the San Juan Islands. Geese were used by Coast Salish peoples as a source of food and down, and were processed and hunted in similar ways to other dabbling waterfowl.

Branta bernicla (Brant)

Material: 1 skull fragment (pterygoid).

Total: 1 specimen.

Remarks: The smallest of the geese in the region, Brants occasionally stop on islands in the Gulf of Georgia during winter and spring months to obtain gravel necessary for their food processing. The pterygoid specimen was identified as a Brant on the basis of its small size.

Branta canadensis (Canada Goose)

Material: 1 carpometacarpus (Figure 10.1)
Total: 1 specimen.
Remarks: Canada Geese are the most widely distributed and best known of all American geese (Todd 1996:124). Although more frequently seen while migrating, some Canada Geese reside all year round in the San Juan Islands. This specimen was distinguished from smaller geese on the basis of its very large size.

Subfamily Anatinae (Ducks)
Anatinae, Unidentified

Material: 1 sternum fragment, 1 coracoid fragment, 1 distal radius, 12 carpals (8 cuneiform, 4 scapholunar), 4 distal carpometacarpi, 12 pollices, 2 third wing digits, 13 second wing digits (6 first phalanges, 7 second phalanges), 1 fibula.
Total: 47 specimens.
Remarks: At least twenty-six species of ducks are found in the Gulf of Georgia. These ducks are divided into 4 tribes: Anatini (Dabbling Ducks- 10 species), Aythyini (Bay Ducks/ Pochards- 4 species), Mergini (Sea Ducks- 11 species), and Oxyurini (Ruddy Duck- 1 species). Ethnographic accounts suggest that ducks were hunted during the spring and fall as a supplement to other food resources, and for their down, which was woven with goat or dog wool or nettle fiber to make blankets and clothing. The hunting and processing techniques and uses of waterfowl are discussed in detail in numerous Coast Salish ethnographies (e.g., Barnett 1955; Batdorf 1990; Eells 1985; Gunther 1927; Jenness n.d.; Stern 1934; Suttles 1951).

In addition to the direct comparison with modern zoological specimens, I used the criteria discussed by Woolfenden (1961) to distinguish between the different Anatid tribes. No attempt was made to identify the carpals, pollices, and second and third wing digits beyond the subfamily level.

Tribe Anatini (Dabbling Ducks)
Anas sp. (Dabbling Duck)

Material: 1 sternum fragment.
Total: 1 specimen.
Remarks: There are ten species of dabbling ducks found in the region: the Green-winged Teal (*Anas crecca*), Mallard (*A. platyrhynchos*), Northern Pintail (*A. acuta*), Blue-winged Teal (*A. discors*), Cinnamon Teal (*A. cyanoptera*), Northern Shoveler (*A. clypeata*), Gadwall (*A. strepera*), Eurasian Wigeon (*A. penelope*), American Wigeon (*A. americana*), and the Wood Duck (*Aix sponsa*). These ducks are of varying sizes and have different migratory behaviors, but all feed on seeds and other vegetal resources near the surface of shallow wetlands and grassy fields.

According to Suttles (1951), dabbling and diving ducks were hunted in different ways because of their different habitat preferences. While dabbling ducks were occasionally hunted with arrows, slings, and snares, they were most commonly caught by Coast Salish peoples using nettle twine nets (raised nets or hand nets). Raised nets were attached to high poles, and placed at narrow waterways to catch birds on their way to their feeding grounds or on their migration route (e.g., Curtis 1913; Eells 1985; Jenness n.d.). Early European explorers in the Northwest, including members of Vancouver's crew, observed the duck poles and speculated about their purpose (Meany 1942; Menzies 1923; Wagner 1933). Although good locations for raised duck nets were limited, one such location was Mosquito Pass, located between San Juan and Henry Island, quite close to the British Camp site (Suttles 1951). Another was Pole Pass, between Orcas and Crane Islands (Burn 1983 [1946]; Suttles 1951).

Tribe Aythyini (Bay Ducks, Pochards)
Aythya sp. (medium) (Greater Scaup or Redhead)

Material: 1 carpometacarpus.
Total: 1 specimen.
Remarks: There are five species of pochards which inhabit the open water and protected bays of the San Juan Islands. The Canvasback (*Aythya valisineria*), Greater Scaup (*A. marila*) and Lesser Scaup (*A. affinis*) are relatively common winter residents in the islands, while the Ring-necked Duck (*A. collaris*) is present year round. In addition, the Redhead (*A. americana*) is a rare visitor in fresh-water habitats during the winter months (Lewis and Sharpe 1987). These diving ducks generally forage in shallow water, but are adept swimmers capable of diving deep beneath the surface.

I have measured a series of modern comparative specimens at the Burke Museum in an attempt to distinguish between these species (Bovy 2005). The ranges of the greatest length (GL) measurement (see von den Driesch 1976) of the carpometacarpi were as follows: *A. valisineria*= 51.0- 53.0mm (n=5), *A. americana*= 47.7- 51.7mm (n=9), *A. marila*= 45.7- 50.1mm (n=27), *A. affinis*= 41.6- 44.3mm (n=6), and *A. collaris*= 38.7- 42.8mm (n=19). The greatest length of the element in the OpD assemblage (SAJH 104343) is 46.7mm. It is therefore very likely a Greater Scaup, or possibly a small Redhead.

Tribe Mergini (Sea Ducks)

Mergini, Unidentified

Material: 1 sternum fragment, 1 coracoid fragment, 1 scapula fragment, 1 proximal radius.
Total: 4 specimens.
Remarks: The 11 species of the tribe Mergini that are present in the Gulf of Georgia are divided into sea ducks (*Histrionicus, Clangula, Melanitta, Bucephala*) and mergansers (*Lophodytes, Mergus*). The sea ducks are primarily found in open bodies of water, while the mergansers inhabit both fresh- and salt- water. All are well-adapted to searching underwater for aquatic prey. The Lummi and other Coast Salish peoples in the region hunted these diving ducks (e.g., scoters) at night from canoes using pronged duck spears (Barnett 1955; Stern 1934; Suttles 1951). Also, submerged horizontal duck nets were placed in herring spawning grounds, trapping and drowning the ducks that dove to eat the spawn (see Stern 1934 and Suttles 1951 for detailed descriptions of this hunting method).

Melanitta sp. (small) (Surf or Black Scoter)

Material: 1 proximal carpometacarpus.
Total: 1 specimen.
Remarks: There are two species of scoters that have smaller, more gracile wing elements: *Melanitta nigra* (Black Scoter) and *M. perspicillata* (Surf Scoter). Both are migrants and primarily winter residents, although small non-breeding populations are present during the summer months. The Black Scoter is the least common species of scoter in the Gulf of Georgia.

Melanitta perspicillata (Surf Scoter)

Material: 5 carpometacarpi.
Total: 5 specimens.
Remarks: These complete carpometacarpi can be distinguished from *M. nigra* based on the greatest length (GL) of the element, and the width of the proximal shaft (WS) measured just distal to the pollical facet (Bovy 2005). Black Scoters have relatively longer and narrower shafts (GL= 51.2- 56.0mm, WS= 4.0- 4.6mm, n=13), while those of Surf Scoters are relatively shorter and wider (GL= 46.6- 52.4mm, WS= 4.1- 4.6mm, n= 20). In addition to size, there are slight morphological differences. The lobe on the proximal rim of the trochlea (internal surface) is much larger in *M. perspicillata*, than *M. nigra*. Also, the extensor attachment extends farther down the sloping edge of the process of metacarpal I in *M. perspicillata*.

Melanitta fusca (White-winged Scoter)

Material: 1 proximal carpometacarpus.
Total: 1 specimen.
Remarks: The White-winged Scoter is the "chunkiest of the scoters, and one of the largest of northern ducks" (Todd 1996:403). They are common migrants and winter residents of the San Juan Islands, often congregating on the water in huge rafts. This carpometacarpus was identified as *Melanitta fusca* due to its large size and robustness.

cf. *Melanitta fusca* (White-winged Scoter)

Material: 1 distal carpometacarpus.
Total: 1 specimen.
Remarks: This specimen is similar to *Melanitta fusca* in size (and morphology), but cannot be securely distinguished from other large sea ducks (e.g., *Mergus merganser*).

Clangula hyemalis (Long-tailed Duck)

Material: 1 radius, 4 carpometacarpi.
Total: 5 specimens.
Remarks: These winter residents of the San Juan Islands are commonly found among the huge rafts of scoters in the San Juans. They are the deepest-diving of all waterfowl, having been taken in fish nets at depths of up to 70 meters (Todd 1996).

Bucephala albeola (Bufflehead)

Material: 2 distal radii, 1 distal ulna, 1 distal carpometacarpus.
Total: 4 specimens.
Remarks: These tiny diving ducks are common migrants and winter residents of the shallow bays, lakes and estuaries of the region.

Bucephala sp. (large)
(Common or Barrow's Goldeneye)

Material: 1 coracoid, 1 proximal ulna.
Total: 2 specimens.
Remarks: Of the three species of the genus *Bucephala* in the region, the goldeneyes are distinguished by their significantly large size compared to the Bufflehead (*B. albeola*). The Common Goldeneye (*B. clangula*) and Barrow's Goldeneye (*B. islandica*) are common migrants and winter residents.

cf. *Lophodytes* (= *Mergus*) *cucullatus* (Hooded Merganser)

Material: 1 proximal carpometacarpus.
Specimen: 1 specimen.
Remarks: The Hooded Merganser is a common breeding resident, inhabiting the secluded ponds and lakes of the San Juan Islands. This fragmented proximal carpometacarpus is difficult to distinguish from *Aythya collaris*.

Mergus merganser (Common Merganser)
Material: 1 proximal carpometacarpus.
Specimen: 1 specimen.
Remarks: There are two species of large mergansers in the archipelago. Common Mergansers are breeding residents, while Red-breasted Mergansers (*M. serrator*) are migrants and winter residents. This specimen was identified as a Common Merganser, likely a male, due its wide and robust shaft (the width of the shaft just distal to the pollical facet was 5.0mm). Preliminary measurements suggest that the carpometacarpi of male Common Mergansers are significantly larger than both female Common Mergansers and male Red-breasted Mergansers (Bovy 2005).

Order Galliformes (Pheasants, Grouse, Quail)
Family Odontophoridae (Quail)
Odontophoridae, Unidentified
Material: 1 coracoid fragment, 1 scapula fragment.
Total: 2 specimens.
Remarks: All three species of quail that currently inhabit the islands were introduced by Euro-Americans near the turn of the century (Lewis and Sharpe 1987). Unlike the Northern Bobwhite (*Colinus virginianus*) and Mountain Quail (*Oreortyx pictus*), which are now quite rare (if present at all), the California Quail (*Callipepla californica*) is common here. These specimens were recovered from upper facies of 105 365 and 121 347.

Callipepla californica (California Quail)
Material: 1 sternum, 1 coracoid.
Total: 2 specimens.
Remarks: Abundant in the San Juan Islands since the 1930s, the California Quail favors habitats with shrubby thickets. These specimens were found in upper facies of 105 365.

Family Phasianidae (Pheasants, Grouse, Turkeys, Quail)
Subfamily Phasianinae (Partridges, Pheasants)
Gallus gallus (Domestic Chicken)
Material: 2 skull fragments (1 premaxilla, 1 quadrate), 1 coracoid fragment, 1 proximal humerus.
Total: 4 specimens.
Remarks: These domestic chicken bones were found in the upper facies of units 121 347 and 123 347 and were presumably deposited by British soldiers or subsequent American settlers.

Subfamily Tetraoninae (Grouse)
Tetraoninae, Unidentified
Material: 1 furcula fragment, 1 proximal tarsometatarsus.
Total: 2 specimens.
Remarks: According to Vernon (1996), the Sooty Grouse (*Dendragapus fuliginosus* (=*obscurus*)), formerly known as the Blue Grouse (Banks et al. 2006), is the only grouse occupying the San Juan Islands today. However, the Ruffed Grouse (*Bonasa umbellus*) was also native to the islands, but is no longer extant due to changes in vegetation (Lewis and Sharpe 1987). Coast Salish peoples hunted grouse with bows and arrows, slings, and snares (Curtis 1913; Suttles 1990); their eggs were eaten as well (Barnett 1955).

Dendragapus fuliginosus (=*obscurus*) (Sooty (=Blue) Grouse)
Material: 1 carpal (cuneiform), 1 carpometacarpus.
Total: 2 specimens.
Remarks: Although not particularly abundant today, Sooty Grouse, which inhabit open coniferous woodlands, are one of the two fowl-like birds native to the San Juan Islands. These elements were distinguished from Ruffed Grouse (*Bonasa umbellus*) on the basis of their larger size.

Subfamily Meleagridinae (Turkeys)
Meleagris gallopavo (Wild Turkey)
Material: 1 skull fragment (quadrate).
Total: 1 specimen.
Remarks: Wild Turkeys were introduced into the San Juans during the 20th century (perhaps in the 1960s; see Lewis and Sharpe 1987). This archaeological specimen was found near the top of 121 347 and may be either domestic or Wild Turkey.

Order Gaviiformes (Loons)
Family Gaviidae (Loons)
Gavia sp. (Loons)
Material: 1 pollex.
Total: 1 specimen.
Remarks: Four species of loons have been observed in the open water and quiet bays of the San Juan Islands during the winter months. The Pacific Loon (*Gavia pacifica*) and the Common Loon (*G. immer*) are common migrants, while the Red-throated Loon (*G. stellata*) and Yellow-billed Loon (*G. adamsii*) are less frequently observed. Loons dive for prey in both shallow and deep waters. Native peoples hunted loons with bows and arrows (Stern 1934), and also harvested their eggs (Barnett 1955). This specimen is most similar in size to *Gavia immer*.

Gavia pacifica (Pacific Loon)
Material: 1 proximal radius, 1 proximal carpometacarpus.
Total: 2 specimens.
Remarks: Ornithologists have long debated the clas-

sification of the Pacific and Arctic (*G. arctica*) Loons. Once considered to be a variant of the Arctic Loon (e.g., AOU 1983; Bakus 1965), they are now considered to be two distinct species (AOU 1998; Lewis and Sharpe 1987). Both specimens can be distinguished from *G. immer* and *G. adamsii* on the basis of their smaller size. The curve of the proximal radius shaft is distinct from *G. stellata*, in that the shaft of *G. pacifica* is straighter in dorsal view. The carpometacarpi of *G. pacifica* and *G. stellata* vary in both size (Fitzgerald 1980) and morphology (Howard 1929). The San Juan Archipelago and Gulf Islands are home to the largest wintering population of Pacific Loons in North America (Lewis and Sharpe 1987).

Order Podicipediformes (Grebes)
Family Podicipedidae (Grebes)
Podilymbus podiceps (Pied-billed Grebe)

Material: 1 proximal carpometacarpus.
Total: 1 specimen.
Remarks: The Pied-billed Grebe is the only member of the genus in North America. Unlike the other grebe species, the Pied-billed Grebe is a year round resident in the Gulf of Georgia region.

Podiceps sp. (Grebes)

Material: 1 pollex.
Total: 1 specimen.
Remarks: Podiceps is one of three genera of grebes that inhabit the open water and protected bays of the San Juan Islands during the winter months. The species of Podiceps present in the region are the large Red-necked Grebe (*Podiceps grisegena*), and the smaller Horned (*P. auritus*) and Eared Grebe (*P. nigricollis*). This specimen is similar in size to either *P. auritus* or *P. grisegena.*

Order Procellariiformes (Albatrosses, Shearwaters, Petrels)
Family Diomedeidae (Albatrosses)
Phoebastria (= *Diomedea*) cf. *albatrus* (Short-tailed Albatross)

Material: 1 distal ulna, 1 proximal carpometacarpus.
Total: 2 specimens.
Remarks: True pelagic birds, albatross are only rare or accidental visitors to the San Juan Islands. The Short-tailed Albatross is a federally endangered species today (USFWS 2010), but was once much more common. A specimen was collected near the turn of the century from Sinclair Island on the east edge of the San Juan Archipelago (Miller et al. 1935). They are also common in some archaeological assemblages from the Northwest Coast, such as the Maple Bank site in Victoria, British Columbia (Crockford et al. 1997) and the Yuquot site (McAllister 1980) on the outer coast of Vancouver Island. Short-tailed Albatross can be distinguished from the Black-footed (*P. nigripes*) and Laysan Albatross (*P. immutabilis*) on the basis of their large size (see Porcasi 1999).

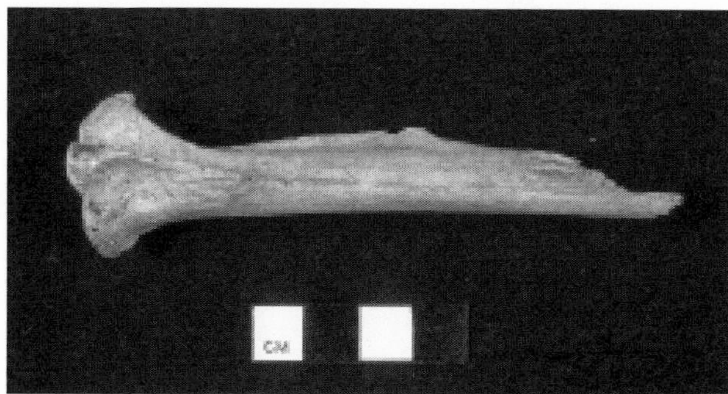

Figure 10.2 Proximal tibiotarsus (left); Bald Eagle (*Haliaeetus leucocephalus*); SAJH 127634.

Order Pelecaniformes (Pelicans, Cormorants)
Family Phalacrocoracidae (Cormorants)
Phalacrocorax auritus (Double-crested Cormorant)

Material: 1 second wing digit (second phalanx).
Total: 1 specimen.
Remarks: Inhabiting rocky shorelines, the Double-crested Cormorant is a permanent resident of the San Juan Islands. Cormorants are weak fliers, but strong divers, feeding on fish in deep and shallow water. Coast Salish peoples used the feathers of cormorants to fletch arrows (Curtis 1913; Elmendorf 1960; Suttles 1951). The second digit recovered from OpD is larger than comparative specimens of the Pelagic Cormorant (*Phalacrocorax pelagicus*) and Brandt's Cormorant (*P. penicillatus*), which are also present in the region.

Order Falconiformes (Hawks, Eagles, Falcons)
Family Accipitridae (Ospreys, Kites, Hawks, Eagles)
Accipitrinae (large) (Bald or Golden Eagle)

Material: 1 radius, 1 ulna.
Total: 2 specimens.
Remarks: The largest members of the Accipitrinae family are the Bald Eagle (*Haliaeetus leucocephalus*; Figure 10.2) and the Golden Eagle (*Aquila chrysaetos*), both of which are year-round residents in the Gulf of Georgia. Ethnographic accounts suggest that eagles were not eaten (Haeberlin and Gunther 1930), but their feathers were used on arrows to hunt waterfowl and to decorate ceremonial attire (Barnett 1955; Stern 1934; Suttles 1951). The radius and ulna found in this assemblage are juvenile, and could not be identified to the species level.

Haliaeetus leucocephalus (Bald Eagle)

Material: 1 skull fragment (quadrate), 1 second wing digit (first phalanx), 1 pelvis fragment (acetabulum/

ischium), 1 proximal femur, 2 tibiotarsi (1 complete, 1 distal).
Total: 6 specimens.
Remarks: Bald Eagles remain a "sensitive species" in Washington State (WDFW 2010), but are common breeders on San Juan Island due to the large population of introduced European Hares (*Oryctolagus cuniculus*). The Bald Eagle bones from OpD were found scattered throughout multiple units and depths, so probably reflect more than one individual. The distal tibiotarsus and the second wing digit, both of which were recovered from 121 347 Facies 1D01, appear to be from a subadult individual.

Order Charadriiformes (Shorebirds, Gulls, Alcids)
Family Charadriidae (Plovers, Lapwings)
Subfamily Charadriinae (Plovers)
Material: 1 distal tibiotarsus.
Total: 1 specimen.
Remarks: There are four species of plovers inhabiting the tidal flats and grasslands in the Gulf of Georgia: the Black-bellied Plover (*Pluvialis squatarola*), American Golden Plover (*P. dominica*), Semipalmated Plover (*Charadrius semipalmatus*), and Killdeer (*C. vociferus*). Although not intentionally hunted by native peoples, Underhill (1944) notes that small shore birds such as plovers may have been caught in the hanging nets used to catch flying ducks.

Family Laridae (small) (Gulls, Terns)
Material: 1 second wing digit fragment (first phalanx).
Total: 1 specimen.
Remarks: The family Laridae includes gulls (Larinae) and terns (Sterninae), of which there are 11 relatively common species in the region and 10 rare or accidental visitors (Lewis and Sharpe 1987). All other identified Laridae specimens from this assemblage are gulls (see below).

Subfamily Larinae (small) (Gulls)
Material: 1 distal ulna, 2 carpals (cuneiforms), 3 second wing digits (2 first phalanges, 1 second phalanx).
Total: 6 specimens.
Remarks: Small-bodied gulls in the Gulf of Georgia include the relatively abundant Franklin's Gull (*Leucophaeus pipixcan*), Bonaparte's Gull (*Chroicocephalus philadelphia*), Heermann's Gull (*Larus heermanni*), and the Mew Gull (*Larus canus*). Rare visitors include the Little Gull (*Hydrocoloeus minutus*), Black-legged Kittiwake (*Rissa tridactyla*) and Sabine's Gull (*Xema sabini*). In addition, the Black-headed Gull (*Chroicocephalus ribidundus*), a casual Eurasian straggler, has also been observed on nearby Vancouver Island, and there is one possible observation of the Red-legged Kittiwake (*Rissa brevirostris*) in the archipelago (Lewis and Sharpe 1987). Gulls have diversified feeding strategies, including scavenging dead animals and human garbage, searching for invertebrates, raiding seabird colonies for eggs, and stealing catches from other birds (Lewis and Sharpe 1987). Gulls are discussed in much less detail than ducks in the ethnographic literature. However, Curtis (1913) notes that gulls, which were used principally for down in weaving, were killed in great numbers by children using slings and snares. The eggs of gulls were also eaten by Coast Salish peoples (Barnett 1955; Gunther 1927).

cf. Larinae (small) (Gulls)
Material: 1 carpal fragment (cuneiform).
Total: 1 specimen.
Remarks: This fragmented cuneiform is very similar in morphology to that of the small gulls of the genus *Larus*.

Larus sp. (large) (Gulls)
Material: 1 sternum fragment, 1 distal radius, 1 distal ulna, 6 carpals (5 cuneiforms, 1 scapholunar), 2 carpometacarpi (1 complete, 1 proximal), 3 pollices, 2 second wing digits (second phalanges).
Total: 16 specimens.
Remarks: The seven larger species of gulls found in the region include the Ring-billed Gull (*Larus delawarensis*), California Gull (*L. californicus*), Herring Gull (*L. argentatus*), Thayer's Gull (*L. thayeri*), Western Gull (*L. occidentalis*), Glaucous-winged Gull (*L. glaucescens*), and the rare Glaucous Gull (*L. hyperboreus*). These gulls are primarily winter residents in the region, with the exception of the Glaucous-winged Gull, a common year-round resident.

Family Alcidae (Auks, Murres, Puffins)
Uria cf. *aalge* (Common Murre)
Material: 1 skull fragment (quadrate), 1 sternum fragment, 2 radii (1 complete, 1 proximal), 1 distal ulna, 1 carpal (scapholunar).
Total: 6 specimens.
Remarks: Common Murres (*Uria aalge*) are very abundant in the San Juan Islands from late summer to early spring, at which time they migrate to their breeding colonies on the outer coast. The bones of the Common Murre cannot be easily distinguished from those of the more northerly- distributed Thick-billed Murre (*Uria lomvia*), which is a rare accidental visitor to the Gulf of Georgia (Lewis and Sharpe 1987).

Brachyramphus marmoratus (Marbled Murrelet)
Material: 2 mandible fragments (articular), 1 coracoid,

1 carpometacarpus, 1 femur.
Total: 5 specimens.
Remarks: The tiny Marbled Murrelet (*Brachyramphus marmoratus*) is a migrant and winter resident in the San Juans, feeding on small school fish in open water habitats. The Marbled Murrelet, which nests in trees in old growth forests, has been classified as a "threatened species" in Washington (WDFW 2010) and the United States (USFWS 2010). Marbled Murrelet bones have been identified from a small number of archaeological sites in the region (Hobson and Driver 1989).

Columbiformes (Pigeons, Doves)
Columbidae, Unidentified (Pigeons, Doves)
Material: 1 second wing digit (second phalanx).
Total: 1 specimen.
Remarks: The San Juans are home to two native species of columbids: the Band-tailed Pigeon (*Patagioenas fasciata*) and the Mourning Dove (*Zenaida macroura*). In addition, the Rock Pigeon (*Columba livia*), commonly seen in urban habitats, was introduced near the turn of the 20th century. This second digit was too fragmented to identify to genus.

cf. *Patagioenas* (=*Columba*) *fasciata* (Band-tailed Pigeon)
Material: 1 carpometacarpus.
Total: 1 specimen.
Remarks: Given its context in a deeper facies (123 347 1I01), this nearly complete carpometacarpus is most likely the Band-tailed Pigeon. It could not be distinguished morphologically from the introduced Rock Pigeon (*Columba livia*), however.

Order Strigiformes (Owls)
Family Strigidae (Typical Owls)
Megascops (=*Otus*) *kennicottii* (Western Screech-Owl)
Material: 1 distal femur, 3 tibiotarsi (1 complete, 1 proximal, 1 distal), 1 fibula, 1 proximal tarsometatarsus.
Total: 6 specimens.
Remarks: A common breeding resident in the region, the Western Screech-Owl inhabits low elevation open woodlands. Ethnographic accounts suggest owls were never killed or eaten because of their mythological associations with the dead (e.g., Stern 1934). All of these skeletal specimens were found quite near each other during excavation, and are likely the remains of a single individual.

cf. *Megascops* (=*Otus*) *kennicottii* (Western Screech-Owl)
Material: 1 distal tarsometatarsus.
Total: 1 specimen.
Remarks: This medial trochlea fragment is likely a Western Screech-Owl (*Megascops kennicottii*) given its close proximity to the other similarly-sized owl fragments recovered at the site. However, it is too fragmented to be identified on the basis of morphology.

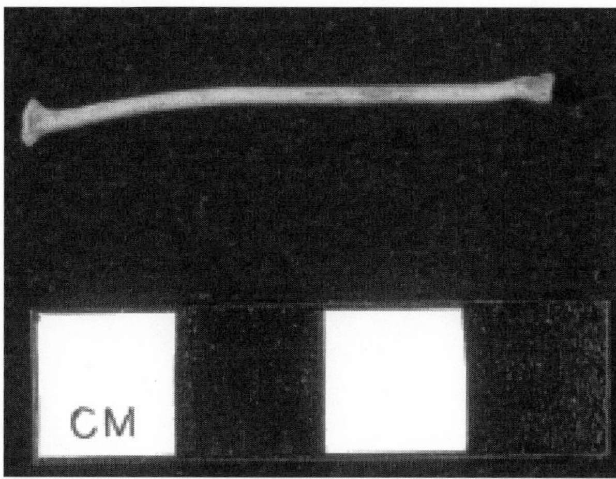

Figure 10.3 Left radius of Pygmy Owl (*Glaucidium gnoma*); SAJH 105931.

Glaucidium gnoma
(Northern Pygmy-Owl; Figure 10.3)
Material: 1 radius, 1 ulna.
Total: 2 specimens.
Remarks: Inhabiting clearings in coniferous forests, this small owl is a fierce hunter, sometimes catching prey larger than itself. These elements were easily identified on the basis of their small size.

Order Coraciiformes (Kingfishers)
Family Alcedinidae (Kingfishers)
Megaceryle (=*Ceryle*) *alcyon* (Belted Kingfisher)
Material: 1 proximal carpometacarpus.
Total: 1 specimen.
Remarks: Belted Kingfishers, which hunt for fish in quiet bays and lakes, are the only representative of the family Alcedinidae in the Northwest. According to Eells (1985), the Coast Salish Indians of Puget Sound believed a piece of Kingfisher skin placed on their fishing lines would attract fish.

Order Piciformes (Woodpeckers)
Family Picidae (Woodpeckers)
Picoides sp. (Woodpeckers)
Material: 1 scapula fragment, 1 proximal ulna.
Total: 2 specimens.
Remarks: There are two common species of woodpeckers of the genus Picoides residing in the San Juan Islands: the Hairy Woodpecker (*Picoides villosus*) and the smaller Downy Woodpecker (*P. pubescens*). Woodpeckers were used by Coast Salish people for their feathers (Underhill 1944).

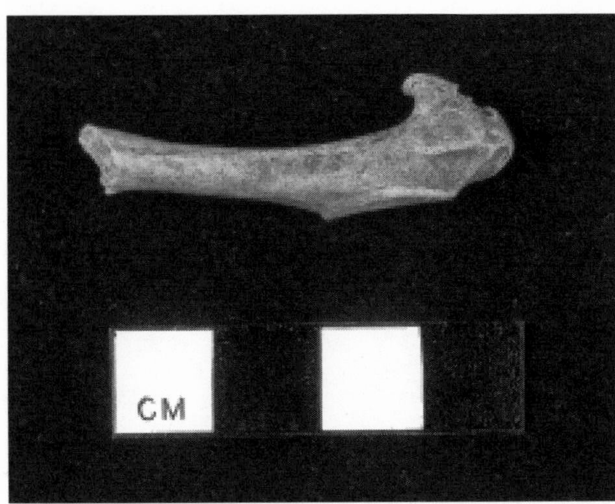

Figure 10.4 Coracoid (left), Raven (*Corvus corax*); SAJH 106060.

Order Passeriformes (Perching Birds)

Passeriformes (Small), Unidentified

Material: 1 sternum fragment, 1 coracoid, 1 proximal ulna, 1 carpometacarpus, 2 femora (1 complete, 1 distal), 6 tibiotarsi (1 proximal, 5 distal), 2 tarsometatarsi (1 complete, 1 distal).
Total: 14 specimens.
Remarks: Lewis and Sharpe (1987) list 110 species of perching birds which can be found in the San Juan Islands. Given this large number, no attempt was made to identify the smaller passerine specimens to species. These 14 specimens were all significantly smaller than crows.

Passeriformes (Large), Unidentified

Material: 1 sternum fragment.
Total: 1 specimen.
Remarks: This specimen is a crow-sized costal facet fragment.

Corvus cf. *caurinus* (Northwestern Crow)

Material: 1 proximal humerus, 3 carpometacarpi, 2 third wing digits, 2 distal tarsometatarsi.
Total: 8 specimens.
Remarks: Ornithologists have debated whether the Northwestern Crow is conspecific with, or a subspecies of, the American Crow (*C. brachyrhynchos*) (AOU 1983, Lewis and Sharpe 1987). The Northwestern Crow is distinguished only by its coastal distribution and slightly smaller size. Since Lewis and Sharpe (1987) indicate that the larger mainland species does not occur in the San Juan Islands, I have identified these specimens as *Corvus* cf. *caurinus*. Crows are common scavengers on the shorelines and urban areas.

Corvus corax (Common Raven; Figure 10.4)

Material: 1 coracoid, 1 distal radius, 1 proximal ulna, 1 carpal (cuneiform), 1 pollex, 1 tarsometatarsus.
Total: 6 specimens.
Remarks: The largest of the passerines, the Common Raven is a permanent resident in rural areas of western Washington. Ravens are powerful predators and scavengers. Barnett (1955) indicates that ravens and crows were never eaten by the Coast Salish because of mythological associations.

Quantitative Summary

There were a total of 309 bird bone specimens recovered from the six randomly selected excavation units at OpD. Of these, 279 (90%) were identified to element, and 188 (61%) were identified beneath the class level. Table 10.1 lists the taxa recovered by excavation unit. Unit 107 341 is not shown because it did not contain any bird bone. The most abundant taxa in the assemblage are ducks and geese (n=80; 43%), perching birds (29; 15%), gulls (24; 13%), alcids (11; 6%), owls (9; 5%), and eagles (8; 4%). The remaining taxa (chickens, grouse, quail, loons, grebes, albatrosses, pigeons, woodpeckers, kingfishers, plovers, turkeys and cormorants) are minor components of the assemblage (with 5 or fewer specimens present).

While there is a large variety of dabbling and diving ducks (over 25 species) inhabiting the Gulf of Georgia, 96% of the identified duck specimens (n=27) from the OpD assemblage are diving sea ducks, such as scoters, Long-tailed Ducks, Bufflehead, goldeneyes, and mergansers. In this, the OpD avian assemblage is similar to other Strait of Georgia sites (Hanson 1991). Pegg (1999) analyzed a small sample (7% by volume) of the vertebrates from OpA at British Camp as part of his study on the taphonomic history of the faunal assemblage. Like at OpD, Pegg found birds to be a very small percentage of the identified specimens (0.5%; n=101), and ducks were the most common taxa (50%). However, of the ducks he could identify to genera (n=24), more than half were dabbling ducks (58%, n=14). Despite the small sample sizes, this difference is statistically significant ($\chi 2=18.26$, $P<0.001$): the OpA portion of the site has more dabblers relative to divers than at OpD. A more in-depth analysis of the OpA bird assemblage would be necessary to explore this apparent difference further.

Some researchers have argued that the dominance of diving ducks in Gulf of Georgia assemblages is indicative of the use of submerged nets. For example, Monks (1987) identified Greater Scaup (*Aythya marila*) bones, bone points that may have been used as leisters or herring rakes, and a rock-wall tidal trap at the Deep Bay site on Vancouver Island, and argued that these ducks were caught with submerged nets while feed-

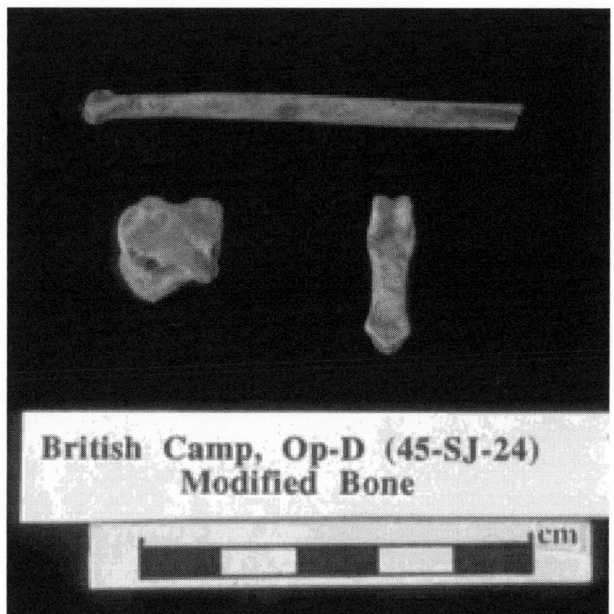

Figure 10.5 Three bird bones with cut marks. Top: Common Murre (*Uria* cf. *aalge*) proximal radius (SAJH 105844); Left: Pacific Loon (*Gavia pacifica*) (SAJH 104100); Right: Bird phalanx (likely owl or eagle) (SAJH 104269).

ing on herring and roe caught in the trap. Also, Stiefel (1985) suggested that the presence of diving ducks and significant amounts of herring in Locarno Beach-aged (3.5-2.4 kya) sites in the Gulf of Georgia was an indication of the development of submerged netting technology. Herring is also quite abundant at the OpD assemblage (see Chapter 12, this volume), and it is possible this hunting technique was used here in the past.

Taphonomic Summary

Cultural Modification

Approximately 8% of the bones in the prehistoric assemblage are heat-modified. Of these 5% (n=16) are blackened or charred, and 3% (n=8) are calcined (whitish in color). The burning is more prevalent on the bones of aquatic birds than terrestrial birds (only 1 terrestrial bird bone was burnt). Four specimens in the assemblage show evidence of butchery: a Common Murre radius (SAJH 105844) has multiple parallel cut marks distal to the head on the external edge of the shaft; a phalanx of a raptor (SAJH 104269) has multiple parallel cut marks on the plantar surface; a distal ulna of a large gull (SAJH 103697) has two parallel cut marks on the distal surface of the trochlea, and finally, a proximal Pacific Loon carpometacarpus (SAJH 104100) appears to have been cut and broken at the shaft (Figure 10.5). Only three bones show evidence of significant grinding or cultural modification; these are all indeterminate limb bone shafts recovered from Unit 130 352 (see Chapter 8, this volume for more details).

Other Modification

Two specimens have surface modifications indicative of having been digested: a duck cuneiform is very pitted and irregular (SAJH 40694), and a spine of thoracic vertebra (possibly a loon) is pitted and polished (SAJH 104269). In addition, a small percentage of bones (3%, n=10) in the assemblage have pitted or polished surfaces, which are sometimes accompanied by abrasion scratches. They do not appear to be as pitted and irregular as the digested bone, however. It is not clear what processes may have caused this surface modification. Two indeterminate limb bone shaft fragments have numerous parallel scratches which are likely the result of rodent gnawing (SAJH 128625 and 128627). Also, one specimen, a juvenile eagle proximal ulna fragment (SAJH 105967), has a puncture mark that could have inflicted by carnivores. Finally, three of the bone fragments (SAJH 103649, 103700 and 104378) have "root etching" marks, possibly caused by acids in decaying roots or the fungi associated with this decay (Lyman 1994).

Skeletal Part Distribution

An unusual pattern of avian skeletal part distribution has been observed in numerous archaeological sites in many different parts of the world (Bovy 2002a). In these sites, bird wings far outnumber both axial and leg elements. This pattern occurs in a great many of the analyzed bird assemblages in the Northwest Coast: Yuqout (McAllister 1980), Shoemaker Bay (Calvert and Crockford 1982), Departure Bay (Wilson and Crockford 1994), Locarno Beach (Stiefel 1985), Musqueam NE (Stiefel 1985), St. Mungo (Ham et al. 1984), Tsawwassen (Kusmer 1994), Beach Grove (Matson et al. 1980), Whalen Farm (Seymour 1976; Stiefel 1985), Crescent Beach (Ham 1982), Cowichan Bay (Yip 1982), Pender Canal (Hanson 1991), Maple Bank (Crockford et al. 1997), Esquimalt Lagoon (Blacklaws 1979), Watmough Bay (Bovy 2005, 2007), Ozette (DePuydt 1994), Hoko River Rockshelter (Wigen and Stucki 1988), West Point (Lyman 1995), and Tualdad Altu (Chatters et al. 1990). While most of these sites are younger than 3,000 years, analyses of the birds from Ferndale, a mid-Holocene site (Nokes 2004), and Dalles Roadcut (Hansel-Kuehn 2003), an early Holocene site, also show this pattern. The bird assemblage from Burton Acres site on Vashon Island had greater numbers of wings compared to legs, but also had large numbers of axial elements, especially vertebrae and ribs (Bovy 2002b).

In order to compare the different proportions of skeletal parts in the OpD assemblage, I calculated relative percentages of skull/axial, pectoral girdle, wing and leg elements. These are then compared to the per-

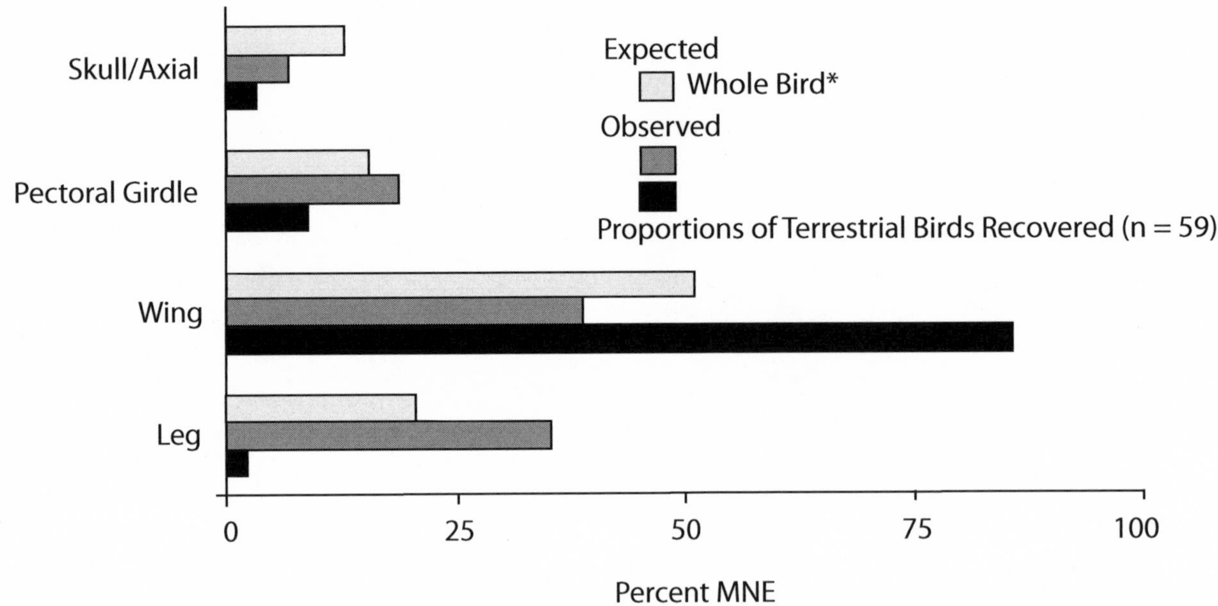

Figure 10.6 The skeletal part percentages (% MNE) of terrestrial and aquatic birds recovered from of Op-D, British Camp. * The values for the whole bird are weighted for the skeletal elements identified the analysis: Skull/Axial= skull (1), hemi-mandible (2), hemi-pelvis (2); Pectoral Girdle= furcula (1), scapula (2), coracoid (2), sternum (1); Wing= humerus (2), radius (2), ulna (2), scapholunar (2), cuneiform (2), carpometacarpus (2), digit 2 phalanx 1 (2), digit 2 phalanx 2 (2), pollex (2), third digit (2); Leg= femur (2), tibiotarsus (2), fibula (2), tarsometatarsus (2).

centages expected in a complete bird (see Figure 10.6). The expected percentages are weighted to account for the differing number of elements that I attempted to identify in each skeletal part. For example, six of the 39 bones that I attempted to identify are in the pectoral girdle (sternum, furcula, scapulae, coracoids), and therefore account for 15% of the skeletal elements in an intact bird. The expected percentage for wing elements (51%) is much greater than leg elements (21%) because I did not attempt to identify phalanges of the foot.

The MNE values are listed in Table 10.2 by skeletal part (e.g., leg), element and taxonomic order. In addition, the skeletal part proportions of the terrestrial (e.g., crows, ravens, eagles, grouse, quail, pigeons, owls, woodpeckers) and aquatic birds (e.g., ducks/geese, gulls, alcids, loons, albatross, cormorant, grebes) from the OpD assemblage are depicted graphically in Figure 10.6. It is obvious that wing elements of aquatic birds are over-represented, comprising 86% of the assemblage. A goodness-of-fit test indicates that the observed frequency of wing elements for aquatic birds compared to all other elements differs significantly from the expected value (χ^2=58.92, P<0.001). Indeed, an individual comparison of wing with leg (χ^2=36.00, P<0.001), axial (χ^2=24.06, P<0.001) and pectoral (χ^2=12.58, P<0.001) elements reveals significant differences; in each case wing elements are significantly more abundant than the other skeletal parts. In contrast, there are more leg bones than expected for terrestrial birds (χ^2=8.23, P=0.004). Similarly, Hansel-Kuehn (2003) noted that the gulls and cormorants at the Dalles Roadcut site had significantly more wings than expected, while the raptors (California Condors, Bald Eagles) had skeletal part proportions similar to those expected in a complete bird.

Further investigation reveals that the wing elements of the ducks, gulls, and other aquatic birds from the OpD assemblage are clearly dominated by distal wing bones (Figure 10.7). A complete bird has two of each of the elements listed. The most abundant element in the aquatic bird assemblage is the carpometacarpus (n=29), while no humeri were recovered. This overabundance of carpometcarpi has been observed elsewhere in the region (e.g., Crockford et al. 1997; Matson et al. 1980; Seymour 1976). For example, the large diving duck assemblage from Watmough Bay (45SJ280) on Lopez Island is comprised of 98% carpometacarpi and distal wing digits (Bovy 2005, 2007).

A number of hypotheses have been suggested for the abundance of wings in archaeological assemblages, including curation of wings for tool use, processing and consumption practices, differential transport, scavenging of beached bird carcasses (Schalk 1993), scavenger damage, and differential preservation. Elsewhere (Bovy 2002a), I have summarized these hypotheses and conducted a preliminary test of the differential preservation hypothesis, which suggests that wing

Table 10.2 Avian skeletal element distribution (MNE) by taxonomic order

	Aves	Aquatic Birds[1]							Terrestrial Birds[2]						Total
	(unid.)	ANSER	GAVII	PODIC	PROCE	PELEC	CHARA	CORAC	GALLI	FALCO	COLUM	STRIG	PICIF	PASSE	
Axial Skeleton															
skull	3	1	-	-	-	-	1	-	2	1	-	-	-	-	8
mandible	-	-	-	-	-	-	2	-	-	-	-	-	-	-	2
trachial ring	3	-	-	-	-	-	-	-	-	-	-	-	-	-	3
vertebra	24	-	-	-	-	-	-	-	-	-	-	-	-	-	24
rib	10	-	-	-	-	-	-	-	-	-	-	-	-	-	10
pelvis	-	-	-	-	-	-	-	-	-	1	-	-	-	-	1
Total Axial	40	1	-	-	-	-	3	-	2	2	-	-	-	-	48
Pectoral Girdle															
sternum	1	4	-	-	-	-	2	-	1	-	-	-	-	1	9
furcula	-	-	-	-	-	-	-	-	1	-	-	-	-	-	1
coracoid	-	3	-	-	-	-	1	-	3	-	-	-	-	2	9
scapula	-	1	-	-	-	-	-	-	1	-	-	-	1	1	4
Total Pectoral	1	8	-	-	-	-	3	-	6	-	-	-	1	4	23
Proximal Wing															
humerus	-	-	-	-	-	-	-	-	1	-	-	-	-	1	2
radius	-	5	1	-	-	-	3	-	-	1	-	1	-	1	12
ulna	4	2	-	-	1	-	3	-	-	1	-	1	1	2	15
Total Prox. Wing	4	7	1	-	1	-	6	-	1	2	-	2	1	4	29
Distal Wing															
cuneiform	1	9	-	-	-	-	8	-	1	-	-	-	-	1	20
scapholunar	1	4	-	-	-	-	2	-	-	-	-	-	-		7
carpometacarpus	4	22	1	1	1	-	3	1	1	-	1	-	-	4	39
pollex	-	3	-	-	-	-	-	-	-	-	-	-	-	2	5
digit 3	-	7	-	-	-	-	3	-	-	-	1	-	-		11
digit 2 phalanx 1	-	12	1	1	-	-	3	-	-	-	-	-	-	1	18
digit 2 phalanx 2	-	6	-	-	-	1	3	-	-	1	-	-	-		11
Total Dist. Wing	6	63	2	2	1	1	22	1	2	1	2	-	-	8	111
Leg															
femur	1	-	-	-	-	-	1	-	-	1	-	1	-	2	6
tibiotarsus	2	-	-	-	-	-	1	-	-	2	-	2	-	5	12
fibula	-	1	-	-	-	-	-	-	-	-	-	1	-	-	2
tarsometatarsus	3	-	-	-	-	-	-	-	1	-	-	1	-	5	10
phalanx	31	-	-	-	-	-	-	-	-	-	-	-	-	-	31
Total Leg	37	1	-	-	-	-	2	-	1	3	-	5	-	12	61
Grand Total	88	80	3	2	2	1	36	1	12	8	2	7	2	28	272

[1]ANSER= Anseriformes; GAVII= Gaviiformes; PODIC= Podicipediformes; PROCE= Procellariformes; PELEC= Pelecaniformes; CHARA= Charadriiformes; CORAC= Coraciiformes
[2]GALLI= Galliformes; FALCO= Falconiformes; COLUM= Columbiformes; STRIG= Strigiformes; PICIF= Piciformes; PASSE= Passeriformes

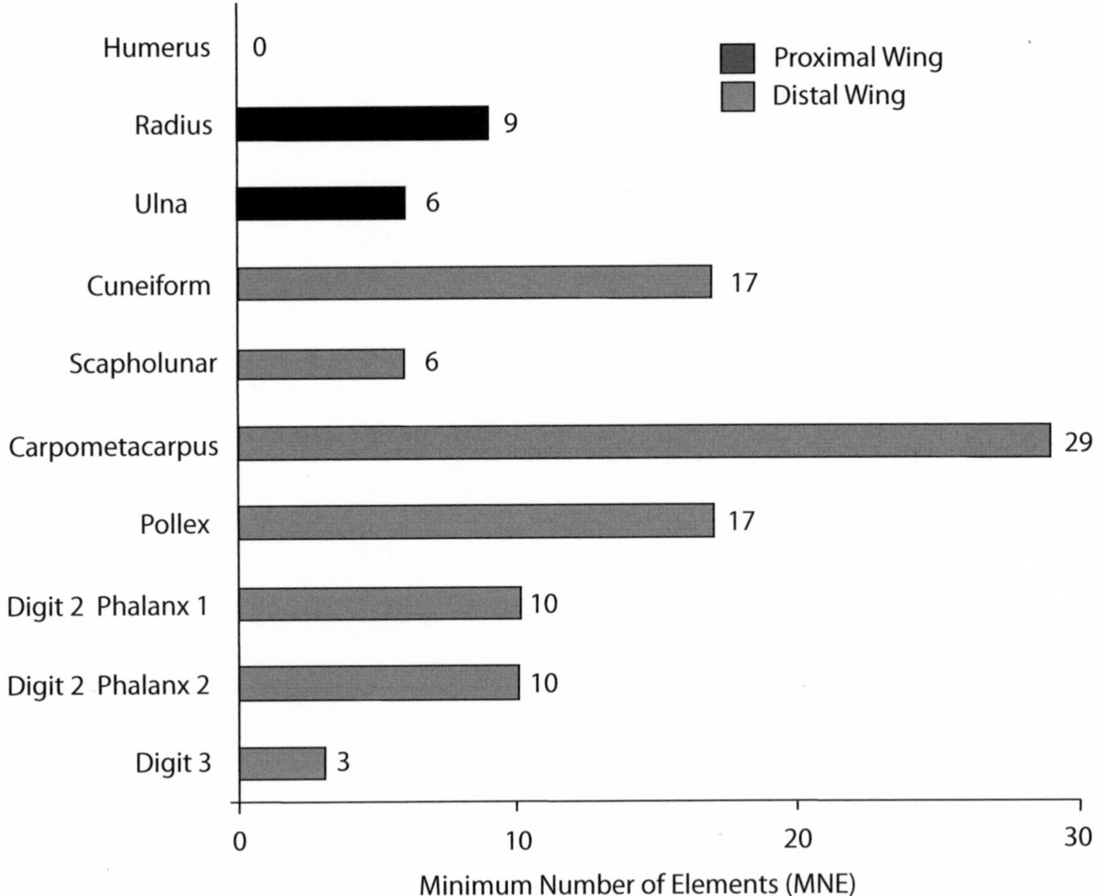

Figure 10.7 Frequency of wing elements for aquatic birds recovered from Op-D, British Camp.

bones survive better than leg bones because they are denser. I conclude that this density hypothesis is not well supported by the available data. Furthermore, I would argue that the prevalence and extreme dominance of distal wings in many of the Gulf of Georgia middens is the result of some human hunting, processing, or consumption behavior unique to this region.

Screen-size/ Fragmentation

As discussed in Chapter 4, all of the excavated material from OpD was screened through nested 1", ½", ¼" and ⅛" screens. Therefore, by comparing the material recovered in the ⅛" to that recovered from the larger screens, we can get an idea of what may be missing from other sites in the region that were screened using larger mesh (e.g., Watmough Bay). Table 10.3 lists all of the OpD bird material that was identified to element by screen-size. Both complete and fragmented specimens, and large and small taxa, are included. The table also lists the percentage of each element that was recovered for each screen size (e.g., 83% of the phalanges were recovered in the ⅛" screen). In this table, refit specimens are counted separately if they were recovered in different levels, facies or screen-size. In total, 50% of those bird bones identified to element were recovered from the ⅛" screens (n=147). Of these, 50% were complete or nearly complete (n=74) and 50% were fragmented (n=73). The complete specimens recovered in the ⅛" were primarily small elements of the distal wing (e.g., carpals, third wing digits, pollices), phalanges and vertebrae.

If we look at the bones of the distal wing, for which there is the largest sample size, it is evident that the elements vary in terms of their ¼" recovery rate. For example, 80% of the carpometacarpi and 73% of the second wing digits (digit 2 phalanx 1) were recovered using ¼" or larger screens. In contrast, all other distal wing elements (carpals, pollices, digit 3, digit 2 phalanx 2) were recovered in lower frequencies (20-40%) in the larger mesh screens.

In addition to the kinds of elements recovered with different screen-sizes, the OpD assemblage is also informative in terms of which taxa may be lost without the use of ⅛" screens. The following are the taxa with ≥75% of specimens recovered in the ⅛" screens: Brant (n=1), Bufflehead (n=4), small grebes (n=2), plover (n=1), small gulls (n=8), Marbled Murrelet (n=5), Northern Pygmy-owl (n=2), woodpecker

Table 10.3 OpD bird material identified to element by screen-size

	1"		1/2"		1/4"		1/8"		Total
	NISP	%	NISP	%	NISP	%	NISP	%	NISP
Axial Skeleton									
skull	-	-	-	-	5	55.6	4	44.4	9
mandible	-	-	-	-	1	50.0	1	50.0	2
trachial ring	-	-	-	-	-	-	3	100.0	3
vertebra	-	-	7	29.2	6	25.0	11	45.8	24
rib	-	-	-	-	2	20.0	8	80.0	10
pelvis	-	-	1	100.0	-	-	-	-	1
Total Axial	-	-	8	16.3	14	28.6	27	55.1	49
Pectoral Girdle									
sternum	-	-	4	36.4	3	27.3	4	36.4	11
furcula	-	-	-	-	1	100.0	-	-	1
coracoid	-	-	2	20.0	5	50.0	3	30.0	10
scapula	-	-	-	-	-	-	4	100.0	4
Total Pectoral	-	-	6	23.1	9	34.6	11	42.3	26
Proximal Wing									
humerus	-	-	2	100.0	-	-	-	-	2
radius	1	7.1	4	28.6	4	28.6	5	35.7	14
ulna	1	5.6	4	22.2	9	50.0	4	22.2	18
Total Prox. Wing	2	5.9	10	29.4	13	38.2	9	26.5	34
Distal Wing									
cuneiform	-	-	-	-	8	40.0	12	60.0	20
scapholunar	-	-	-	-	1	14.3	6	85.7	7
carpometacarpus	1	2.4	13	31.7	19	46.3	8	19.5	41
pollex	-	-	-	-	6	33.3	12	66.7	18
digit 3	-	-	-	-	1	20.0	4	80.0	5
digit 2 phalanx 1	-	-	1	9.1	7	63.6	3	27.3	11
digit 2 phalanx 2	-	-	-	-	3	27.3	8	72.7	11
Total Dist. Wing	1	0.9	14	12.4	45	39.8	53	46.9	113
Leg									
femur	-	-	1	16.7	2	33.3	3	50.0	6
tibiotarsus	2	11.8	1	5.9	6	35.3	8	47.1	17
fibula	-	-	-	-	-	-	2	100.0	2
tarsometatarsus	-	-	-	-	7	58.3	5	41.7	12
phalanx	-	-	-	-	6	17.1	29	82.9	35
Total Leg	2	2.8	2	2.8	21	29.2	47	65.3	72
Grand Total	5	1.7	40	13.6	102	34.7	147	50.0	294

**refit specimens were counted separately if they were from a separate level, facies or screen-size.*

(n=2), and small passerines (n=14). With the exception of the Brant, all of these taxa are relatively small-bodied birds, weighing less than 450 kg (1 pound) (Sibley 2000). The Brant specimen (SAJH 40824) was a fragment of a small skull bone (pterygoid).

CONCLUSION

Birds are minor components of many archaeological assemblages in the Gulf of Georgia (Butler and Campbell 2004; Hanson 1991). This is true at OpD, where birds comprise approximately 0.6% of the vertebrate assemblage. Given the small sample size, it is therefore impossible to draw meaningful conclusions about change through time or differences across space (e.g., inside the ridge versus the ridge itself). The small assemblage does, however, provide a glimpse into the varied bird species that were hunted by native people.

Diving ducks, such as scoters and long-tailed ducks, are relatively common in the assemblage, and may possibly have been caught using submerged nets. A variety of other kinds of waterbirds (e.g., gulls, alcids, loons, grebes, albatross) and more terrestrially-oriented birds were also recovered from the site (e.g., crows, raven, small passerines, owls, eagles, grouse, pigeons, woodpeckers). The upper facies of the site contained a few domestic chicken, Wild or Domestic Turkey, and California Quail bones, all of which are non-native species. This isn't surprising given the presence of historic artifacts (metal, glass), probable cow bones with metal saw marks, and bones from the introduced European Hare (*Oryctolagus cuniculus*) in these facies.

Diving ducks, as well as some of the other species recovered (e.g., Marbled Murrelets, Pacific loons, grebes) are present in the Gulf of Georgia primarily in the winter months, suggesting the site was occupied at that time. However the presence of a juvenile eagle radius and ulna in the assemblage, along with an unidentified juvenile bird phalanx, indicates that the site may also have been occupied in spring or summer months.

An interesting aspect of the bird assemblage is the skeletal part distribution. At OpD, like many other archaeological sites in the region and worldwide, wing bones are more abundant than either axial or leg elements. In particular, there are significantly more distal wing elements of aquatic birds than expected in this assemblage. On the basis of my previous research on this question (2002a), I believe this pattern is due to a cultural explanation (e.g., hunting or butchering practices) rather than a post-depositional explanation (e.g., differential preservation). Interestingly, an opposite pattern occurs for terrestrial birds at this site, with leg bones significantly outnumbering wing bones. It would appear that whatever human behavior is creating the abundance of bird wings, terrestrial birds were treated differently; this is also true at the Watmough Bay site (Bovy 2005). This is not surprising, perhaps, given that many of the terrestrial species recovered from the site are not typically considered to be food items (e.g., small passerines, ravens, owls, eagles, woodpeckers).

Finally, the well-excavated OpD bird assemblage was analyzed in terms of screen-size recovery. Certain elements of the distal wing (e.g., carpals, pollices, digit 3, digit 2 phalanx 2) were recovered more frequently in the ⅛" than the ¼" screens. Likewise, certain taxa, such as small passerines and small waterbirds (Bufflehead, Marbled Murrelet, grebes, gulls) were recovered more frequently in the ⅛" screens. These findings demonstrate that when analyzing birds from assemblages that were screened using ¼" mesh, researchers should use caution in making interpretations about the relative abundance of these smaller taxa and elements.

REFERENCES

Angell, T. and K. Balcomb
1982 *Marine Birds and Mammals of Puget Sound.* Puget Sound Books, University of Washington, Seattle.

American Ornithologists' Union (AOU)
1983 *Check-list of North American Birds.* 6th ed. American Ornithologists' Union, Committee on Classification and Nomenclature, Allen Press, Lawrence, Kansas.
1998 *Check-list of North American Birds.* 7th ed. American Ornithologists' Union. Washington, D.C.
2000 Forty-second Supplement to the American Ornithologists' Union Check-list of North American Birds. *The Auk* 117:847-858.

Bakus, G. J.
1965 *Avifauna of San Juan Island and Archipelago, Washington.* Allen Hancock Foundation, University of Southern California, Los Angeles. Manuscript on file at the University of Washington Library Special Collections.

Banks, R. C., C. Cicero, J. L. Dunn, A. W. Kratter, P. C. Rasmussen, J. V. Remsen, Jr., J. D. Rising, and D. F. Stotz
2003 Forty-fourth Supplement to the American Ornithologists' Union Check-list of North American Birds. *The Auk* 120:923-931.
2004 Forty-fifth Supplement to the American Ornithologists' Union Check-list of North American Birds. *The Auk* 121:985-995.
2006 Forty-seventh Supplement to the American Ornithologist's Union Check-list of North American Birds. *The Auk* 123:926-936.

Banks, R. C., R. T. Chesser, C. Cicero, J. L. Dunn, A. W. Kratter, I. J. Lovette, P. C. Rasmussen, J. V. Remsen, Jr., J. D. Rising, and D. F. Stotz
2007 Forty-eighth Supplement to the American Ornithologist's Union Check-list of North American Birds. *The Auk* 124:1109-1115.

Banks, Richard C., R. T. Chesser, C. Cicero, J. L. Dunn, A. W. Kratter, I. J. Lovette, P. C. Rasmussen, J. V. Remsen, Jr., J. D. Rising, D. F. Stotz, and K. Winker
2008 Forty-ninth Supplement to the American Ornithologist's Union Check-list of North American Birds. *The Auk* 125:758-768.

Barnett, H. G.
1955 *The Coast Salish of British Columbia.* University of Oregon Press, Eugene, Oregon.
Batdorf, C.
1990 *Northwest Native Harvest.* Hancock House Publishers, Blaine, Washington.
Blacklaws, R. W.
1976 *Excavations at Esquimalt Lagoon: a Contribution to Straits Salish Prehistory.* Unpublished M.A. thesis, Department of Archaeology, Simon Fraser University, Burnaby.
Bovy, K. M.
1998 *Avian Skeletal Part Distribution in the Northwest Coast: Evidence from the British Camp Site, OpD (45-SJ-24).* Unpublished M.A. thesis, Department of Anthropology, University of Washington, Seattle.
2002a Differential Avian Skeletal Part Distribution: Explaining the Abundance of Wings. *Journal of Archaeological Science* 29:965-978.
2002b Faunal Analysis: Mammal and Bird Remains. In *Vashon Island Archaeology: A View from Burton Acres Shell Midden*, edited by J. K. Stein and L. S. Phillips, pp. 91-104. Burke Museum of Natural History and Culture Research Report No. 8, Burke Museum, Seattle.
2005 *Effects of Human Hunting, Climate Change, and Tectonic Events on Waterbirds along the Pacific Northwest Coast during the Late Holocene.* Unpublished PhD thesis, Department of Anthropology, University of Washington.
2007 Prehistoric Human Impacts on Waterbirds at Watmough Bay, Washington, USA. *Journal of Island and Coastal Archaeology* 2:210-230.
Burn, J.
1983 [1946] *100 Days in the San Juans: a 1946 Voyage Through the San Juan Islands*, edited by T. Morrow and N. Prindle. Long House Printcrafters and Publishers, Friday Harbor, Washington.
Butler, V. L., and S. K. Campbell
2004 Resource Intensification and Resource Depression in the Pacific Northwest of North America: A Zooarchaeological Review. *Journal of World Prehistory* 18:327-405.
Calvert, G., and S. Crockford
1982 Appendix IV: Analysis of Faunal Remains from the Shoemaker Bay Site (DhSe 2). In *Alberni Prehistory: Archaeological and Ethnographic Investigations on Western Vancouver Island*, edited by A. D. McMillan and D. E. St. Claire, pp. 174-219. Theytus Books, Penticton and Port Alberni, British Columbia.
Chatters, J. C., D. E. Rhode, and K. A. Hoover
1990 Tualdad Altu (45KI59): a Prehistoric Riverine Village in Southern Puget Sound. *Archaeology in Washington* II:23-48.
Chesser, R. T., R. C. Banks, F. K. Barker, C. Cicero, J. L. Dunn, A. W. Kratter, I. J. Lovette, P. C. Rasmussen, J. V. Remsen, Jr., J. D. Rising, D. F. Stotz, and K. Winker
2009 Fiftieth Supplement to the American Ornithologist's Union Check-list of North American Birds. *The Auk* 126:705-714.
Crockford, S., G. Frederick, and R. Wigen
1997 A Humerus Story: Albatross Element Distribution from Two Northwest Coast Sites, North America. *International Journal of Osteoarchaeology* 7:287-291.
Curtis, E.
1913 *The North American Indian: Being a Series of Volumes Picturing and Describing the Indians of the United States, the Dominion of Canada, and Alaska, Volume 9*, edited by F. W. Hodge, pp. 3-139. Plimpton Press, Norwood, Massachusetts.
DePuydt, R. T.
1994 Cultural Implications of Avifaunal Remains Recovered from the Ozette site. In *Ozette Archaeological Project Research Reports, Vol. II: Fauna, edit*ed by S. R, Samuels, pp. 197-263. Washington State University, Department of Anthropology, Reports of Investigations No. 66, Pullman.
Eells, M.
1985 *The Indians of Puget Sound: The Notebooks of Myron Eells*, edited by G. P. Castile. University of Washington Press, Seattle.
Elmendorf, W. W.
1960 *The Structure of Twana Culture.* Research Studies: A Quarterly Publication of Washington State University (Monograph Supplement No. 2) 28(3):1-576.
Fitzgerald, G. R.
1980 Pleistocene Loons of the Old Crow Basin, Yukon Territory, Canada. *Canadian Journal of Earth Science* 17:1593-1598.
Gunther, E.
1927 Klallam Ethnography. *University of Washington Publications in Anthropology* 1:171-314.
Haeberlin, H., and E. Gunther
1930 The Indians of Puget Sound. *University of Washington Publications in Anthropology* 4(1):1-84.
Ham, L. C.
1982 *Seasonality, Shell Midden Layers, and Coast Salish Subsistence Activities at the Crescent Beach Site, DgRr 1.* Unpublished Ph.D. dissertation, Department of Anthropology, University of British Columbia, Vancouver.
Ham, L. C., A. J. Yip, and L. V. Kullar
1984 *The 1982/83 Archaeological Excavations at the*

St. Mungo Site (DgRr 2), North Delta, British Columbia, Vol. 1. Report on file at the Ministry of Small Business, Tourism and Culture, Victoria, British Columbia.

Hanson, D. K.
1991 *Late Prehistoric Subsistence in the Strait of Georgia Region of the Northwest Coast*. Unpublished Ph.D. dissertation, Department of Archaeology, Simon Fraser University, Burnaby.

Hansel-Kuehn, V. J.
2003 *The Dalles Roadcut (Fivemile Rapids) Avifauna: Evidence for a Cultural Origin*. Unpublished M.A. thesis, Department of Anthropology, Washington State University, Pullman.

Hobson, K. A., and J. C. Driver
1989 Archaeological Evidence for Use of the Strait of Georgia by Marine Birds. In *The Ecology and Status of Marine and Shoreline Birds in the Strait of Georgia, British Columbia*, edited by K. Vermeer and R. W. Butler, pp. 168-173. Canadian Wildlife Service, Ottawa.

Howard, H.
1929 *The Avifauna of Emeryville Shellmound*. University of California Publications in Zoology 32.

Jenness, D.
n.d. *The Saanich Indians of Vancouver Island*. Manuscript submitted to B.C. Provincial Archives.

Kusmer, K.
1994 Faunal Remains. In *Archaeological Investigations at Tsawwassen, B.C., Vol. II: Archaeology*. Report by Arcas Consulting Archaeologists Ltd, on file at Archaeology Branch, Port Moody, British Columbia.

Lewis, M. G., and F. A. Sharpe
1987 *Birding in the San Juan Islands*. The Mountaineers, Seattle.

Lyman, R. L.
1994 *Vertebrate Taphonomy*. Cambridge Manuals in Archaeology. Cambridge University Press, Cambridge.
1995 Mammalian and Avian Zooarchaeology of the West Point, Washington, Archaeological Sites (45KI428 and 45KI429). In *The Archaeology of West Point, Seattle, Washington: 4,000 Years of Hunter-Fisher-Gatherer Land Use in Southern Puget Sound, Vol. 1, Part 2*, edited by L. L. Larson and D. E. Lewarch. Report by Larson Anthropological/Archaeological Services, Seattle.

McAllister, N. M.
1980 Avian Fauna from the Yuquot Excavation. In *The Yuquot Project, Vol. 2*, edited by W. J. Folan and J. Dewhirst, pp. 103-174. National Historic Parks and Sites Branch, History and Archaeology No. 43, Ottawa.

McCutcheon, P. T.
1992 Burned Archaeological Bone. In *Deciphering a Shell Midden*, edited by J. K. Stein, pp. 347-370. Academic Press, San Diego.

Matson, R. G., D. Ludowicz, and W. Boyd
1980 *Excavations at Beach Grove in 1980*. Report on File, Heritage Conservation Branch, Victoria.

Meany, E.
1942 *Vancouver's Discovery of Puget Sound: Portraits and Biographies of the Men Honored in the Naming of Geographic Features of Northwestern America*. Binfords and Mort., Portland, Oregon.

Menzies, A.
1923 Menzies' Journal of Vancouver's Voyage, April to October, 1792. In *Archives of British Columbia Memoirs 5*, edited by C. F. Newcombe, Victoria, British Columbia.

Miller, R. C., E. D. Lumley, and F. S. Hall
1935 Birds of the San Juan Islands, Washington. *The Murrelet: A Journal of Northwestern Ornithology and Mammalogy* XVI(3):51-65.

Monks, G.
1987 Prey as Bait: the Deep Bay Example. *Canadian Journal of Archaeology* 11:119-142.

National Geographic Society (NGS)
1987 *Field Guide to the Birds of North America*. 2nd ed. National Geographic Society, Washington D.C.

National Park Service (NPS)
1995 *Birds of American Camp, San Juan Island, National Historic Park (check-list)*. Archipelago Press, Friday Harbor, Washington.

Nokes, R. D.
2004 *Mid-Holocene Terrestrial Animal Use in the Gulf of Georgia Region: A Case Study from the Ferndale Site, Lower Nooksack River, Washington*. Unpublished M.A. thesis, Department of Anthropology, Western Washington University, Bellingham.

Pegg, B. P.
1999 *The Taphonomic History of the Vertebrate Faunal Assemblage from British Camp, San Juan Islands, Washington*. Unpublished Ph.D. dissertation, Department of Archaeology, Simon Fraser University, Burnaby.

Porcasi, J. F.
1999 A Statistical Method for Identification of Albatross (*Phoebastria*) Species. *Pacific Coast Achaeological Society Quarterly* 35(2/3):60-68.

Schalk, R.
1993 *Birds Without Legs? Avian Skeletal Part Frequencies on the Northwest Coast*. Paper presented at the Northwest Anthropological Conference, Bellingham, Washington.

Seymour, B.
1976 1972 Salvage Excavations at DfRs 3, the Whalen Farm Site. In *Current Research Reports*, edited by R. Carlson, pp. 83-98. Simon Fraser University, Department of Archaeology, Publication No. 3, Burnaby, British Columbia.

Sibley, D. A.
2000 *National Audubon Society: The Sibley Guide to Birds.* Alfred A. Knopf, New York.

Stern, B. J.
1934 *The Lummi Indians of Northwest Washington.* Columbia University Press, New York.

Stiefel, S. K.
1985 *The Subsistence Economy of the Locarno Beach Culture (3300- 2400 B.P.).* Unpublished M.A. thesis, Department of Anthropology, University of British Columbia, Vancouver.

Suttles, W. P.
1951 *Economic Life of the Coast Salish of Haro and Rosario Straits.* Unpublished Ph.D. dissertation, Department of Anthropology, University of Washington.

Todd, F. S.
1996 *Natural History of the Waterfowl.* Ibis Publishing Company, Vista, California.

Underhill, R.
1944 *Indians of the Pacific Northwest.* Education Division of the U.S. Office of Indian Affairs, Washington.

U.S. Fish and Wildlife Service (USFWS)
2004 Species Information: Threatened and Endangered Animals and Plants. Electronic document. http://www.fws.gov/endangered/wildlife.html, accessed February 2, 2010.

Vernon, S.
1996 *Wildlife of the San Juan Islands.* Archipelago Press, Friday Harbor, Washington. [pamphlet]

von den Driesch, A.
1976 *A Guide to the Measurement of Animal Bones from Archaeological Sites.* Peabody Museum of Archaeology and Ethnology Bulletin 1, Harvard University, Cambridge.

Wagner, H. R.
1933 *Spanish Explorations in the Strait of Juan de Fuca.* AMS Press, New York.

Washington Department of Fish and Wildlife (WDFW)
2004 Species of Concern. Electronic document. http://wdfw.wa.gov/wildlife/management/endangered.html, accessed February 2, 2010.

Wigen, R. J., and B. R. Stucki
1988 Taphonomy and Stratigraphy in the Interpretation of Economic Patterns at Hoko River Rockshelter. In *Research in Economic Anthropology, Supplement 3: Prehistoric Economies of the Pacific Northwest Coast*, edited by B. Isaac, pp. 87-146. JAI Press, Greenwich, Connecticut.

Wilson, I. R., and S. Crockford
1994 *Public Archaeological Excavations at the Departure Bay Midden, DhRx 16; Permit 1992-29.* Report prepared for Nanaimo District Museum, Nanaimo, British Columbia.

Woolfenden, G. E.
1961 Postcranial Osteology of the Waterfowl. *Bulletin of the Florida State Museum: Biological Sciences* 6:1-129.

Yip, A. J.
1982 *Archaeological Investigations at the Cowichan Bay Site, DeRv 107, Duncan, British Columbia.* Report to the Heritage Conservation Branch, Victoria, British Columbia.

11

Faunal Analysis: Shellfish

Phoebe S. Daniels

Daniels details the sampling strategy at OpD as it relates to the collection of shell and describes shellfish taxa present at the site. She presents a quantitative analysis that focuses on spatial patterns in relative abundance of shellfish at OpD and shell fragmentation as an indicator of post-depositional processes. Her results indicate that OpD could have been a house, but other interpretations of the data are possible. Following this discussion, Daniels also provides a brief comparison the OpD assemblage with shell data from archaeological sites on the Northwest Coast.

Typical of shell middens on the Northwest Coast, the archaeological deposits at OpD, English Camp contain an abundance of shell remains. Northwest Coast ethnographers describe historic shellfish gathering in great detail (e.g., Ellis and Swan 1981; Ellis and Wilson 1981; Gunther 1927; Sepez 2001; Suttles 1951, 1974). Shellfish were collected predominantly by women, who scraped epifaunal species off rocks and dug infaunal species using digging sticks. As they were collected, shellfish were carried in open weave baskets that allowed water to drain out the bottom. They were processed in the field and also carried home whole for processing. Most shellfish were cooked on beds of heated beach cobbles, steamed, and smoked or dried for winter storage. Clams and cockles were the taxa most often mentioned in the context of drying and winter storage (Suttles 1951:66; Nugent 1985:51).

Analysis of over 100,000 shell remains (43,000 grams of shell) from Unit 105 365 and Unit 123 347 at OpD provides new insights into shellfish collection, processing, and consumption on the San Juan Islands. An appendix showing all results is available on file at the Burke Museum of Natural History and Culture. The shell remains at this site are dominated by bent-nose clam (*Macoma nasuta*), common littleneck clam (*Protothaca staminea*), and the heart cockle (*Clinocardium nuttallii*). Since all three prefer protected habitats, their dominance in the midden indicates that the most commonly exploited intertidal area was the mixed sand and gravel beach on Garrison Bay immediately adjacent to OpD. Garrison Bay is a protected bay with calm, shallow waters and a sandy substrate. A majority of the other shellfish taxa identified at OpD could have been collected from the shore in front of the site. Other taxa identified in the site that would not have been found in Garrison Bay are those species that prefer slightly more active waters and rocky substrates, the most abundant of which were *M. edulis* and *Balanus* spp. Suitable environments for these taxa are easily found on San Juan Island. The nearest rocky beach is less than half a mile from the site and would have been easily accessible by foot or canoe.

The shells at OpD were deposited such that a U-shaped ridge developed on the landscape. Taxonomic relative abundance and taphonomic analyses were performed to test the hypothesis that the U-shaped midden developed around a house structure. While taxonomic results do not support the hypothesis, taphonomic analysis indicates more fragmentation in Unit 123 347 inside the ridge than in Unit 105 365 on the ridge. The data presented in this chapter indicate that shellfish analyses result in conflicting implications

---

Chapter opening photo: Abundant shell exposed during exacavation.

for the house hypothesis and as a result are insufficient for evaluating the hypothesis.

SAMPLING

To obtain samples appropriate for analyzing site matrix materials, including shellfish, bulk samples were collected in the field. These samples were floated to separate the light and heavy fractions which were then bagged and returned to the lab for analysis. The heavy fractions of two units, 105 365 and 123 347 were selected for shell analysis. These units were selected because of the completeness of their samples and their spatial locations, on the ridge and within the ridge respectively. A Jones Splitter was used to remove a representative two-liter sample from the heavy fraction. Test analyses indicated that two-liter samples were sufficient to reach redundancy at the ¼" size fraction. In other words, additional amounts did not significantly change the relative abundance of identified species. Samples of less than two liters were analyzed in their entirety.

IDENTIFICATION

All of the shell recovered from the 1", ½" and ¼" size fractions from Unit 105 365 and Unit 123 347 were identified to the finest taxonomic level possible using the comparative collection of the Burke Museum, Archaeology Department and dichotomous keys for the Pacific Northwest Coast (Kozloff 1996; Foster 1991). The ⅛" fraction was identified to redundancy, but since no new taxa were identified in the ⅛" fraction it is not included here. Tiny *Stronglyocentrotus droebachiensis* (green sea urchin) spines are more abundant in the ⅛" fraction and may be somewhat underrepresented in the larger screen meshes.

MEASURING

Once grouped by taxa, provenience, and screen size, the shell material was weighed and counted for NISP (number of individual specimens) and MNI (minimum number of individuals). MNI was calculated as follows: snail gastropods by the total counts of all collumella, limpets by the total count of identified specimen, bivalves by the total hinges divided by two, sea urchin by total mouth parts divided by 10, and chiton by total plates divided by 6. To avoid counting the same individual more than once, elements used for MNI were only counted if they were at least 50% complete.

BURNING TAPHONOMY

A taphonomic analysis of burning was initiated however it quickly became apparent that almost all shell was significantly burned. Burning was evident by gray discoloration and chalkiness of shell remains. From this it was decided that a qualitative note of heavy burning on the majority of shell remains was sufficient and no significant additional information would be gained by recording specific incidences of burning.

DESCRIPTIVE SUMMARY

Three different phyla are represented by the identified invertebrate remains: mollusca, arthropoda, and echinodermata. The methods used to identify each taxon are presented below along with their total weight and count. Additionally, the habitat, modern abundance, and representation in Northwest Coast archaeological sites are briefly described for each taxa. Habitat descriptions and modern abundances are based on Kozloff (1993) and Rudy and Rudy (1983) unless otherwise noted.

Phylum Mollusca (Molluscs)

Material: calcium carbonate shell fragments
Total Weight: 6893.43 g
Count: 11,436
Remarks: These specimens could be identified as mollusks because the hard calcium carbonate shell that surrounds and protects the soft body of most invertebrates. No distinguishing features, structures or shapes could be identified.

Class Bivalvia (Bivalves)

Material: Indistinct calcium carbonate valve and hinge fragments
Total Weight: 6622.68 g
Count: 8,333
Remarks: Bivalves are mollusks with two shell valves joined by a hinge. The specimens in this category include all indistinct bivalve fragments and were identified by their calcium carbonate material and general morphological characteristics including relatively flat shape, interior muscle attachment scars and pallial line. The majority of these specimens are *Saxidomous giganteus*, *Tresus* spp., and *Macoma nasuta*, none of which have distinguishing valve patterning.

Order Veneroida
Family Cardiidae
Clinocardium nuttallii (Heart or Basket Cockle)

Material: Whole valves, valve and hinge fragments
Total Weight: 15605.96 g
Count: 21,729
Remarks: *Clinocardium nuttalii* is common today and in archaeological sites throughout the Gulf of Georgia.

Figure 11.1 Specimens identified as *Clinocardium nuttallii.*

Figure 11.2 A specimen identified as *Mytilus edulis.*

It exploits from the high intertidal to the subtidal in soft sand, gravel or mud substrates. *C. nuttallii* is found a few centimeters below the surface. It is identified by its hinge and by coarse radial ribs with crescent-shaped nodes or riblets traversing the ribs (Foster 1991:75). Other species exist in the Northwest Coast with radial ribs making the hinge necessary to be completely confident that a specimen is *C. nuttallii.* However, since none of these species were identified in the site, all non-hinge fragments are identified as *Clinocardium* cf. *nuttallii*, and subsequently lumped with *C. nuttallii* during analysis (Figure 11.1).

Family Mactridae
Tresus spp. (Horse and Gaper Clams)

Material: Whole valve, hinge
Total Weight: 228.70 g
Count: 40
Remarks: There are two species of *Tresus* spp. in the Gulf of Georgia, *T. capax* and *T. gapperi. Tresus* spp. is common in the Gulf of Georgia and present in low abundances in archaeological sites. It exploits sandy to muddy substrates in protected bays at depths ranging from 30 cm to 50 cm below the surface depending on the substrate. Of the two, *T. capax* is more common, however, distinguishing between these species is difficult because their valves are unmodified and their hinges very similar. For this analysis, all *T. capax* hinges are defined as *Tresus* spp.

Order Mytiloida
Family Mytilidae
Mytilus spp. (Blue Mussel)
Mytilus edulis (Bay Mussel)

Material: Hinges, cross-section of valve fragments
Total Weight: 373.43 g
Count: 2,812
Remarks: There are four species within the Mytilidae family that are common to the Pacific Northwest Coast: *Mytilus edulis*, *Mytilus californianus*, *Moliolus rectus*, and *Moliolus flabellatus* (sometimes described as a subspecies of *Moliolus rectus*). Mussel valve fragments are identified by their blue/purple hue and, when color has been leached, by plated shell layers visible in cross-section. *Mytilus* spp. exploits the high to low intertidal rocky nearshore, while *Moliolus* spp. is restricted to the subtidal rocky nearshore. On the basis of habitat preference and absence of *Moliolus* spp. hinges, all mussel fragments are assumed to be *Mytilus* spp. Within *Mytilus* spp., *M. edulis* prefers relatively low-action waters and is common in the protected waters of the Gulf of Georgia. Alternatively, *Mytilus californianus* prefers the high-action waters and is common on the unprotected, outer coast (Kozloff 1993:204-205; Rudy and Rudy 1983:1641). *M. edulis* can be identified by its hinge and thin, delicate shell. Based on the location of English Camp in the Gulf of Georgia and the delicacy of the specimens, all hinges were identified as *M. edulis.* All other fragments were identified as *Mytilus* cf. *edulis*, and subsequently lumped with *M. edulis* during analysis (Figure 11.2).

Order Ostreoida
Family Ostreidae
Ostrea lurida (Native Oyster)

Material: Valve fragments with hinge.
Total Weight: 3 g
Count: 5
Material: *Ostrea lurida* is the only oyster native to the Gulf of Georgia. Today, it is widespread but low in abundance. It is often found on the underside of rocks, although in muddy substrates it prefers the tops of rocks. Other oysters found in the region, *Crassostrea gigas* (Japanese oyster) and *Crassostrea virginica* (Atlantic

Figure 11.3 A specimen identified as *Protothaca staminea.*

Figure 11.4 Specimens identified as *Saxidomus giganteus.*

oyster), were introduced historically. The native oyster is distinguishable by its relatively small size, absence of fluting, and hinge.

Family Tellindae
Macoma spp.
Macoma nasuta (Bent-Nose Clam)

Material: Hinge fragments
Total Weight: 599.31 g
Count: 8,612
Remarks: There are several species of *Macoma* spp. common in the Northwest Coast, including *Macoma nasuta*, *M. bahlica*, *M. inquirnata*, and *M. secta*. *Macoma* spp. prefers muddy sand substrates with the exception of *M. secta*, which prefer protected bays. *Macoma* spp. are commonly found 10-15 cm below the surface. The hinges of these species are similar and do not preserve well, making it difficult to distinguish them by hinge alone. Valves of *M. nasuta* are identifiable by a sharp bent in the valve near the posterior end. All valve fragments with the distinguishing bent are identified as *M. nasuta*. The abundance of identified *M. nasuta* valve fragments suggests that *Macoma* spp. hinges are most likely all from *M. nasuta*, and so are recorded as *Macoma* cf. *nasuta* and lumped with *M. nasuta* in analyses.

Family Veneridae (Venus Clam)
Protothaca staminea (Native Littleneck Clam)

Material: Whole valves, valve and hinge fragments
Total Weight: 8571.03 g
Count: 4,868
Remarks: *Protothaca staminea* is common today and in archaeological sites throughout the Gulf of Georgia. It exploits the mid to low intertidal zones between 3-8 cm below the surface and prefers coarse gravel and sandy substrates. It is identified by its hinge and also its radial and concentric sculpture (Foster 1991:107). The Japanese littleneck (*Tapas japonica*) has similar sculpture, but the two are distinguishable by the length of their pallial sinus, which extend more than halfway to the anterior adductor muscle in the native littleneck (Chew and Ma 1987). Additionally, since the Japanese littleneck was introduced historically, it can be assumed that all valves with radial and concentric sculpture recovered from the site, excluding the uppermost layers, are *P. staminea*. Additional species exist in the Northwest Coast with radial ribs and concentric sculpture making the hinge necessary to be confident that a specimen is *P. staminea*. However, since none of these species were identified at OpD, all non-hinge fragments are identified as *Protothaca* cf. *staminea*, and are subsequently lumped with *P. staminea* during analysis (Figure11.3).

Saxidomus giganteus (Butter Clam)

Material: Whole valves, hinge fragments
Total Weight: 1661 g
Count: 340
Remarks: *Saxidomus giganteus* is common today and in archaeological sites in the Gulf of Georgia. *S. giganteus* exploits gravel, sand, and muddy substrates of the lower intertidal zone. It can be found as deep as 30 cm below the surface. The two species of *Saxidomus* spp. present on the Northwest Coast are *S. nuttallii* and *S. giganteus*. *S. nuttallii* is quite rare this far north. Although the hinges of *Saxidomus* spp. are similar, they are not identical. *S. nuttallii* is distinguishable by prominent concentric ridges that are lacking in *S. giganteus*. Due to the absence of any distinguishing features, *S. giganteus* can only be identified by its hinge. It is likely underrepresented relative to other bivalves that can be identified by valve fragments alone (Figure 11.4).

Class Gastropoda (Snails and Slugs)

Material: Columellae fragments
Total Weight: 2.12 g
Count: 3
Remarks: These univalve specimens could not be identified to a finer taxonomic level due to the absence of distinguishing features on the columellae. The most common gastropods in Northwest Coast archaeological sites are limpets, periwinkles, whelks and moon snails. Due to their morphologies and fragmentation rates, most gastropods are either identifiable to the genus or species level or to the mollusk level.

Order Mesogastropoda
Family Littorinidae
Littorina sitkana (Sitka Periwinkle)

Material: Whole or mostly whole shells
Total Weight: 2.71 g
Count: 18
Remarks: In the Gulf of Georgia there are two *Littorina* species in the spray zone and high intertidal: *L. sitkana* and *L. scutulata.* The Sitka periwinkle is distinguishable by its relatively fatter or rounder shape and stronger spiral sculpturing. Due to their relatively small size (less than 1.5 cm), identified periwinkles from OpD were whole or mostly whole. All specimens were identified as *L. sitkana.*

Order Patellogastropoda
Family Acmaeidae
Family Lottidae
Collisella pelta (Shield Limpet)

Material: Whole or mostly whole shells
Total Weight: 3.30 g
Count: 33
Remarks: *Collisella pelta* exploits the mid to high intertidal of rocky substrate in estuarine environments. It is abundant today in the Gulf of Georgia, but rare in archaeological sites. It is distinguished from other limpets by its elevated height, ribbed shell and sub-center apex. Post-depositional processes may erode the ribs, creating the potential for confusing *C. pelta* with other limpet species.

Order Neogastropoda
Family Nucellidae
Nucella spp. (Dogwinkle)

Material: Whole shell, body whorl, columellae, aperture
Total Weight: 2.14 g
Count: 3
Remarks: *Nucella* spp. is a common intertidal predator in the Gulf of Georgia, feeding predominantly on barnacles and mussels. It is present in low abundances in archaeological sites. *Nucella* spp. is easily identified by its thick shell, body whorl, columellae, and aperture morphology. There are three common *Nucella* species: *N. emarginata*, *N. canaliculata*, and *N. lamellosa.* Differences in body whorl sculpturing distinguish the three species, but species level identification is limited by post-depositional weathering of ribs and frills.

Nucella emaginata (Rock and Dogwinkle)

Material: Whole shell, body whorl
Total Weight: 4.74 g
Count: 4
Remarks: *Nucella emarginata* has alternating thick and thin spiral ribs.

Nucella canaliculata (Channeled/Purple Dogwinkle)

Material: Whole shell, body whorl
Total Weight: 3.63 g
Count: 4
Remarks: *Nucella canaliculata* has uniform ribs.

Nucella lamellose (Frilled Dogwinkle)

Material: whole shell, body whorl
Total Weight: 37.59 g
Count: 19
Remarks: *Nucella lamellosa* is typically larger and more abundant than the other two *Nucella* species. It is identified by its axial frills which are often eroded in archaeological context but sometimes remain visible.

Class Polyplacophora (Chiton)

Material: Calcareous plate
Total Weight: 6.23 g
Count: 15
Remarks: There are several species of chiton in the Gulf of Georgia. The most common species identified archaeologically are *Mopalia* spp., *Katharina tunacada*, and *Cryptochiton stelleri.* Chiton shells are composed of eight calcareous plates. Chitons cling to rocks and other hard substrate from the high intertidal to the subtidal zones. *C. stelleri* is significantly larger than either *Mopalia* spp. or *K tunacada* and easily distinguished. No specimen identified as Polyplacophora were large enough to be *C. stelleri.* Additionally, no genus level identification was made of *Mopalia* spp., which suggests that all Polyplacophora at OpD are *K tunacada.*

Katharina tunacada (Black Katy, Black Chiton)

Material: calcareous plate
Total Weight 12.4 g
Count: 13
Remarks: *Katharina tunacada* is the most common chi-

ton in Pacific Northwest archaeological sites. It clings to rocks in the high and low intertidal zone. It is an herbivore grazer, feeding mostly on diatoms and other algae. *K. tunacada* is distinguished by its heart-shaped plates. All chiton remains identified to species/genus level at OpD are *K. tunacada.*

Order Caenogastropoda
Family Cerithiidae
Bittium eschrichtii (Estricht's Bittium)

Material: Whole shell
Total Weight: 0.79 g
Count: 4
Remarks: *Bittium eschrichttii* is the only common slender, drill shaped snail in the spray zone on the Northwest Coast. It prefers rocky substrates and is commonly found under rocks. Its shell is often utilized by very young hermit crabs. *B eschritchttii* is rare in archaeological sites.

Phylum Arthropoda
Class Cirripedia
Order Throacica
Balanus spp. (Acorn Barnacle)

Material: Basal, opercular, and interlocking plates
Total Weight: 1595.4 g
Count: 7,489
Remarks: Several acorn barnacle specimens inhabit the rocky substrates of the Gulf of Georgia from the high intertidal to the subtidal. *Balanus cariosus* and *Balanus glandula* are commonly identified in archaeological sites. The larger *B. cariosus* is distinguished in this analysis, but due to an abundance of variously shaped smaller specimens that may represent multiple species, *B. glandula* is not identifiable. Due to the identification of *B. cariosus*, *Balanus* spp. is mostly composed of *B. glandula* and other small barnacles. Many of the smaller barnacles were incidentally collected with the mussels; however, ethnographic data indicates that some barnacles were occasionally eaten (Suttles 1974:122). Their abundance relative to mussels at OpD supports an interpretation of intentional collection.

Balanus cariosus (Thatched Barnacle)

Material: Interlocking plates
Total Weight: 8.14.90 g
Count: 1,095
Remarks: *Balanus cariosus* is common on rocky substrates in the high intertidal. It can grow to a maximum diameter of 5 cm, however, when densely packed will grow in a thin, columnar shape. *B. cariosus* is identifiable by the round, sponge-like textured parietal tubes of its interlocking plates (Fournier and Dewhirst 1980). Based on its relatively large size, *B. cariosus* was likely intentionally collected and eaten.

Class Malacostraca
Order Decopoda
Family Cancridae
Cancer spp. (Crab)

Material: Claw exoskeleton fragments
Total Weight: 2.87 g
Count: 9
Remarks: The crab chitin exoskeleton is fragile and it preserves poorly in archaeological sites. Historic and ethnographic accounts suggest that crabs were a valued intertidal resource (Suttles 1974:121; Sepez 2001:154), indicating that their low abundances in archaeological sites is a product of preservation bias. Crabs can live in a variety of substrates ranging from muddy to rocky. They spend most of their time in the subtidal zone but forage in the high and low intertidal. The only *Cancer* spp. fragments that preserved at OpD came from claws and were too small to determine species.

Phylum Echinodermata
Class Echinodea
Stronglyocentrous droebachiensis (green sea urchins)

Material: exoskeleton test and spines
Total Weight: 17.40 g
Count: 494
Remarks: Sea urchin exoskeleton is easy to identify but fragile. A significant amount of sea urchin material was likely destroyed by post-depositional processes. Additionally, spines of *Stronglyocentrous droebachiensis* may have been removed from the sample during the flotation process. Microartifact analysis of sediment samples from Operation A at English Camp resulted in a high percentage of sea urchin spines. Results from OpD (¼" and ⅛" fraction) indicates a smaller percentage of sea urchin spine. *S. droebachiensis* prefers relatively calm waters like those around the San Juan Islands. It can be distinguished from *S. franciscanus* (red sea urchin), and *S. purpuratus* (purple sea urchin) by its size and color. *S. franciscanus* spines can reach lengths of 8 cm and *S. purpuratus* spines reach lengths of 4-5 cm, while *S. drobachiensis* spines are much smaller at around 1-2 cm in length.

Phylum Echinodermata
Class Echinodea
Stronglyocentrous purpuratus (purple sea urchins)

Material: Spines
Remarks: Of the local three sea urchins, *S. pupuratus* is the medium sized one. It can be distinguished from

Table 11.1 Shellfish analysis results at OpD

Taxon	NISP			Relative Abundance (NISP)		Weight (g)		
	Unit 105 365 (39 levels)	Unit 123 347 (14 levels)	Total	Unit 105 365	Unit 123 347	Unit 105 365	Unit 123 347	Total
Katharina tunacata	10	3	3	0.0	0.0	10	2	12
Polyoplacaphora cf. *K tunacata*	5	14	30	0.0	0.1	4	4	8
Gastropoda	0	1	3	0.0	0.0	0	1	1
Collisella pelta	0	1	3	0.0	0.0		<1	1
Collisella digitalis	1	0	1	0.0	0.0	1.3	<1	1
Littorina sitkana	17	4	21	0.0	0.0	1.9	<1	2
Bittium eschrichtii	3	1	4	0.0	0.0	<1	<1	1
Notacmaea scutum	31	1	32	0.0	0.0	6.2	<1	6
Nucella canaliculata	2	1	3	0.0	0.0	2	2	4
Nucella lamellosa	16	5	21	0.0	0.0	25	16	41
Nucella spp.	6	1	7	0.0	0.0	4	<1	4
Bivalvia	1603	471	2074	1.9	2.5	783	182	965
Large Bivalve	941	511	1452	1.1	2.7	2192	808	3000
Small Bivalve	4307	938	5245	5.2	5.0	1740	261	2001
Mollusca	28407	5925	34332	34.0	31.8	4887	1212	6099
Chlamys spp.	4	0	4	0.0	0.0	5	0	5
Mytilus edulis	2851	147	2998	3.4	0.8	379	23	402
Ostrea lurida	0	5	5	0.0	0.0	0	3	3
Clinocardium nuttalli	16855	5622	22483	20.2	30.1	11085	2117	13202
Tresus spp.	27	13	40	0.0	0.1	143	57	200
Macoma nasuta	7682	830	8512	9.2	4.4	5325	356	5681
Protothaca staminea	12067	2505	13908	14.4	13.4	6114	1019	7133
Saxidomus giganteus	282	79	361	0.3	0.4	1581	167	1748
Balanus cariousus	394	733	1127	0.5	3.9	237	591	828
Balanus spp.	7514	827	8341	9.0	4.4	1252	160	1412
Cancer spp.	8	0	0	0.0	0.0	3	0	3
Stronglyocentrotus cf. *droebachiensis*	506	15	521	0.6	0.1	5	1	6
Stronglyocentrotus cf. *purpuratus*	3	0	3	0.0	0.0	<1	0	1
Total	8468	18653	101533	100.0	100.0	1543	6982	8525

the other two by its size, as well as its purple color. *Stronglyocentrotus purpuratus* is dependent on high wave action and is rare in the San Juan Islands. Few specimens of *S. purpuratus* were identified from the OpD shellfish assemblage.

RESULTS

Analysis of shell remains from OpD, indicates that people subsisted on a variety of shellfish species. Of the 101,533 identified shell remains, approximately 65% were identified to either genus or species (Table 11.1). The three most common taxa identified, by weight and NISP, are *Clinocardium nuttallii* (22483 NISP, 13201g), *Macoma nasuta*/small bivalve (13757 NISP, 7682g), and *Protothaca staminea* (13908 NISP, 7569g). Together they account for approximately half of all shell by NISP and about 65% of all shell by weight.

Table 11.2 NISP and relative abundance shown for each facies of Unit 105 365

Facies/level	Mollusca	Bivalivia	Large Bivalve	Small Bivalve	*Clinocardium nuttallii*	*Tresus* spp.	*Mytilus eduils*	*Chlamys* spp.	*Macoma nasuta*	*Protothaca staminea*	*Saxidomous giganteus*	*Littorina sitkana*	*Notacmaea scutum*	*Collisella digitalis*	*Nucella* spp.	*Nucella canaliculata*	*Nucella lamellosa*	*Bittium eschrichtii*	Polyoplacaphora cf. *K. tunacata*	*Katharina tunacata*	*Balanus* spp.	*Balanus cariousus*	*Cancer* spp.	*Strongylocentrotus* cf. *droebachiensis*	*Strongylocentrotus* cf. *purpuratus*	Total
1A01	13	29	8	7	92	2	3		8	41					1						5	5				214
1A02	545	23	52	28	406		70		42	78	4										65	11				1324
1B01	1142	163	28	11	493	4	22		114	370	11	1									298	18				2675
1B02	1046	14	37	76	208		214	2	140	209	16		2			1		1			254	12				2232
1B03	1418	10	24	292	446		113		438	431	12		4								172	8		27		3395
1B04	416	6	15	166	172		8		240	157	3										22	3				1208
1B05	588	7	14	124	207	1	12		249	281	2										35	1		1		1522
1B06	418		5	208	368				222	110	3										16			15		1365
1B07	639	5	12	167	448		7		219	454							2				71	3		11		2038
1B08	886		10	121	461		3		254	531	2						4				31	4				2307
1B09	572	6	16	122	323		4		221	351	6						7				22					1650
1B10	996	157	23	52	352		7		366	626	6	1						1			24	1				2612
1C01	2153	48	103	150	657	2	203	1	185	431	20	1			4		1		1		241	42		202		4445
1D01	1095	87	19	29	551		377	1	182	214	9										412	8		25		3009
1D02	1070		34	142	413		78		163	218	7										200	13				2338
1D03	937	34	84	72	597		23		78	113	10		1								273	16		13		2251
1D04	793	119	12	18	574	3	180		97	261	10	1				1			1		386	9		4		2469
1D05	526	38	28	76	750	2	38		187	909	9								1		57	3				2624
1E01	789	1	7	150	160		10		294	178	2	1									50	2		8		1652
1G01	478	73	12	72	554	1			230	248	2						1				3					1674
1H01	454	4	18	108	154		55		148	773	3	1								3	178	15		22		1936
1H02	272	98	7	13	185		15		110	387	3								2		72	9		2		1175
1I01	1188		20	216	424	3	19		425	975	6									3	182	6		8		3475
1J01	586	46	16	30	654		99		224	218	9										286	3		2		2173
1K01	159		15	49	182		123		56	93	7	1	5								459	6		2		1157
1K02	272		9	127	569		7		182	24	2		2								28					1222
1L01	533		35	118	421	1	30		177	237	14	1									53	2	1			1623
1M01	550		69	161	158	1	13		84	256	12	1									33	1				1339
1N01	287		11	78	207	1	40		134	243	5										174	5		9		1194
1O01	958		59	234	453		14		262	382	15	1								1	83	7				2469
1O02	415		26	125	167		33		217	176	8		2				1				264	15		4		1453
1P01	374	198			348	3	10		176	205	24		2								49	3				1392
1Q01	328		15	61	435		57		135	185	6	1									92	2				1317
1R01	283		21	70	306	1	341		121	131	6	1	2	1				1			165	12		61		1523
1S01	6	173	5	23	394				130	28	2	1									659	43	3			1467
1T01	268	22	26	157	735	2	201		186	175	8		6		1						675	45	3	11		2521
1U02	2811	71	8	352	1333		33		382	612	8	1									222	9		26		5868
1U03	1219	8	6	140	1023		288		273	185	3		1								371	14		3		3534
1V01	128	107	9	9	177		38		68	186	3	1	3							2	187	7	1	1		927
1W01	796	56	23	153	298		63		263	385	4	2	1							1	645	31		49	3	2773
Total	28407	1603	941	4307	16855	27	2851	4	7682	12067	282	17	31	1	6	2	16	3	5	10	7514	394	8	506	3	83542

Table 11.3 NISP and relative abundance shown for each facies of Unit 123 347

Facies/level	Mollusca	Bivalivia	Large Bivalve	Small Bivalve	*Clinocardium nuttallii*	*Tresus* spp.	*Mytilus edulis*	*Chlamys* spp.	*Macoma nasuta*	*Protothaca staminea*	*Saxidomous giganteus*	*Littorina sitkana*	*Notacmaea scutum*	*Collisella digitalis*	*Nucella* spp.	*Nucella canaliculata*	*Nucella lamellosa*	*Bittium eschrichtii*	Polyoplacaphora cf. *K. tunacata*	*Katharina tunacata*	*Balanus* spp.	*Balanus cariousus*	*Cancer* spp.	*Strongylocentrotus* cf. *droebachiensis*	*Strongylocentrotus* cf. *purpuratus*	Total
1A01	284	42	37	101	236	3	8	1	59	215	5						1				2	47	18	18	1	1078
1A02	408	8	58	144	274		2		93	248	6											14	16	16		1287
1A03	778	66	48	125	403		3		127	113	14									3		37	24		2	1743
1A04	1068	45	55	139	958		11	2	104	425	10									2		37	24		3	2883
1A05	662	15	31	59	417	3	12		87	316	14							3			1	43	36			1699
1B01	654	57	58	104	673	2	2	2	39	175	4					1				1		14	20		2	1808
1B02	448	34	75	41	842	1	15		45	166	9	1										27	108		4	1816
1C01	287	9	26	6	156	1	6		5	91	7											9	44			647
1D01	476	78	69	54	1081	1			85	253	2											74	361		3	2537
1F01	355	26	21	68	293	1	1		66	301	5							1		2		40	36			1216
1G01	99	18	8	18	104		3		22	45	1									2		21	10			351
1G02	57	52			63				4	28	1											2				207
1H01		4			1					1										2		4				12
1H02													2													2
1I01	236	10	21	44	115		49		39	78	1		2	1	1			1	1	2		320	28			949
1I02	113	7	4	35	6	1	35		55	50												138	8			452
Total	5925	471	511	938	5622	13	147	5	830	2505	79	1	4	1	1	1	1	5	1	14	3	827	733	34	15	18687

Taxonomic Distribution

In previous shellfish analyses MNI, NISP and weight measurements have all been used to interpret the dietary contribution of shellfish (Claassen 1998; Glassow 2000; Mason et al. 2000). For this analysis all three quantification methods were used to ensure that these shellfish data are comparable with data from as many previous shellfish analyses as possible. Relative abundance analysis is limited to NISP measurements because it has been shown that NISP and MNI are strongly correlated (Grayson and Frey 2004), making using multiple measures redundant. More importantly, the non-repeating elements for barnacles and sea urchins were rarely identified in the samples thus MNI relative abundances would fail to include these taxa. NISP counts may under represent abundances of taxa that are more difficult to identify and over represent taxa with easily fractured shells, but these problems can be overcome by comparing percentages rather than counts.

Temporal relative abundance analysis is used here to identify patterns in relative abundances over time. This will provide general information about how the diet changed over time as a result of shellfish availability and/or shellfish selection. In addition, an abrupt change or loss of pattern from Unit 105 365 to Unit 123 347 would support a house hypothesis. If Unit 123 347 was created as the result of slumping of the uppermost levels of Unit 105 365 then any taxonomic relative abundance pattern should be obscured by that process. If the house hypothesis is correct, Unit 105 365 should exhibit a relative abundance pattern that shows some form of human selection or preference while Unit 123 347 should deviate from this pattern.

The relative abundance of identified taxa for Unit 105 365 indicates that all of the common taxa fluctuate through time (Table 11.2). Throughout the unit, epifaunal species are significantly less abundant that infaunal ones, indicating that the local beach was the primary shellfishing area. Within the infaunal taxa, the most abundant across all levels are *Clinocardium nuttalii*, *Macoma nasuta*, and *Protothaca staminea*. The relative abundances measures show an inverse relationship between *C. nuttallii* and the other dominant taxa, *P. staminea* and *M. nasuta* (Figure 11.5). However, there is no direction to this relationship; rather they seem

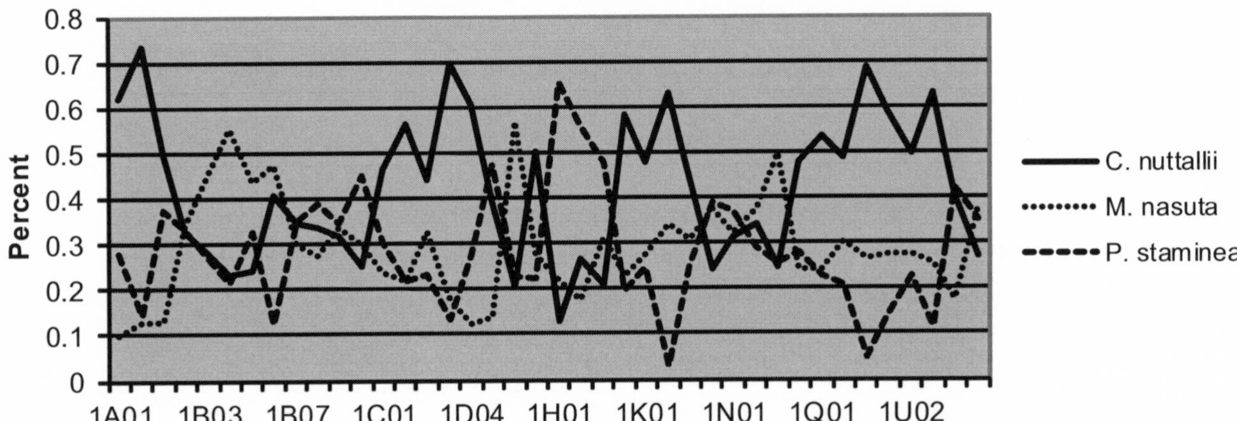

Figure 11.5 Change over time in relative abundance of *Clinocardium nuttalii*, *Macoma nasuta*, and *Protothaca staminea* in Unit 105 365.

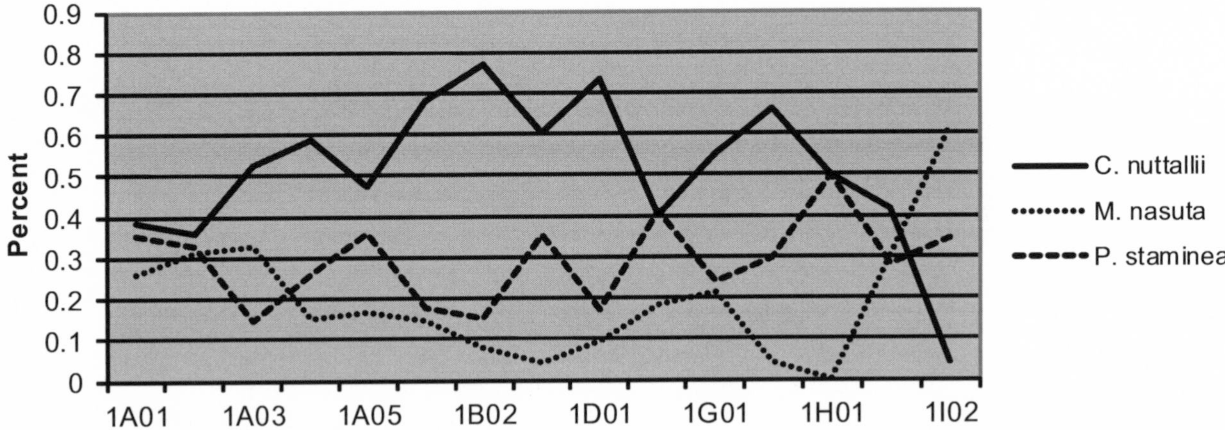

Figure 11.6 Change over time in relative abundance of *Clinocardium nuttalii*, *Macoma nasuta*, and *Protothaca staminea* in Unit 123 347.

to oscillate relative to each other throughout the unit. The cyclical oscillation is more suggestive of environmental change and species availability than changing shellfishing preferences.

The relative abundance results for Unit 123 347 bear a striking resemblance to results Unit 105 365. All commonly identified taxa fluctuate across all levels and infaunal taxa are more abundant than the epifaunal taxa (Table 11.3). As with Unit 105 365, the most abundant species were *C. nuttallii*, *P. staminea*, and *M. nasuta*. Again, *C. nuttallii* appear to be inversely correlated with the other two species (Figure 11.6). This relationship would be even stronger if small bivalves, which are likely *M. nasuta*, are grouped with *M. nasuta*. As in Unit105 365, the oscillation is most readily explained by environmental changes rather than human preference.

The taxa identified in Units 105 365 and 123 347 are similar, with differences in taxonomic richness limited to rare taxa. A high degree of relative abundance fluctuation in both units makes assessing the potential that Unit 123 347 originated from the uppermost portion of Unit 105 365 difficult. However, since the inverse relationship between *C. nuttalli* and *P. staminea* and *M. nasuta* holds across both units it seems unlikely that Unit 123 347 was created by a slumping event. If Unit 123 347 was formed during slumping, levels would have mixed and this relationship would have disappeared. Taxonomic relative abundance in both units may instead reflect human shellfishing choices. The expression of these choices in the archaeological record is similar in both Unit 105 365 and Unit 123 347. Thus, taxonomic relative abundance of shell provides some evidences to refute the house hypothesis.

Taphonomy

A comparison of total weights and NISP counts indicates that shell accumulated unequally in Units 105 365 and 123 347. Differences in excavated volume were controlled for by dividing total volume of shellfish excavated by the number of levels per unit to determine average level NISP and weight for each unit. The average Unit 105 365 level has more shell by NISP and significantly more shell by weight than Unit 123 347. This suggests that more shell was deposited

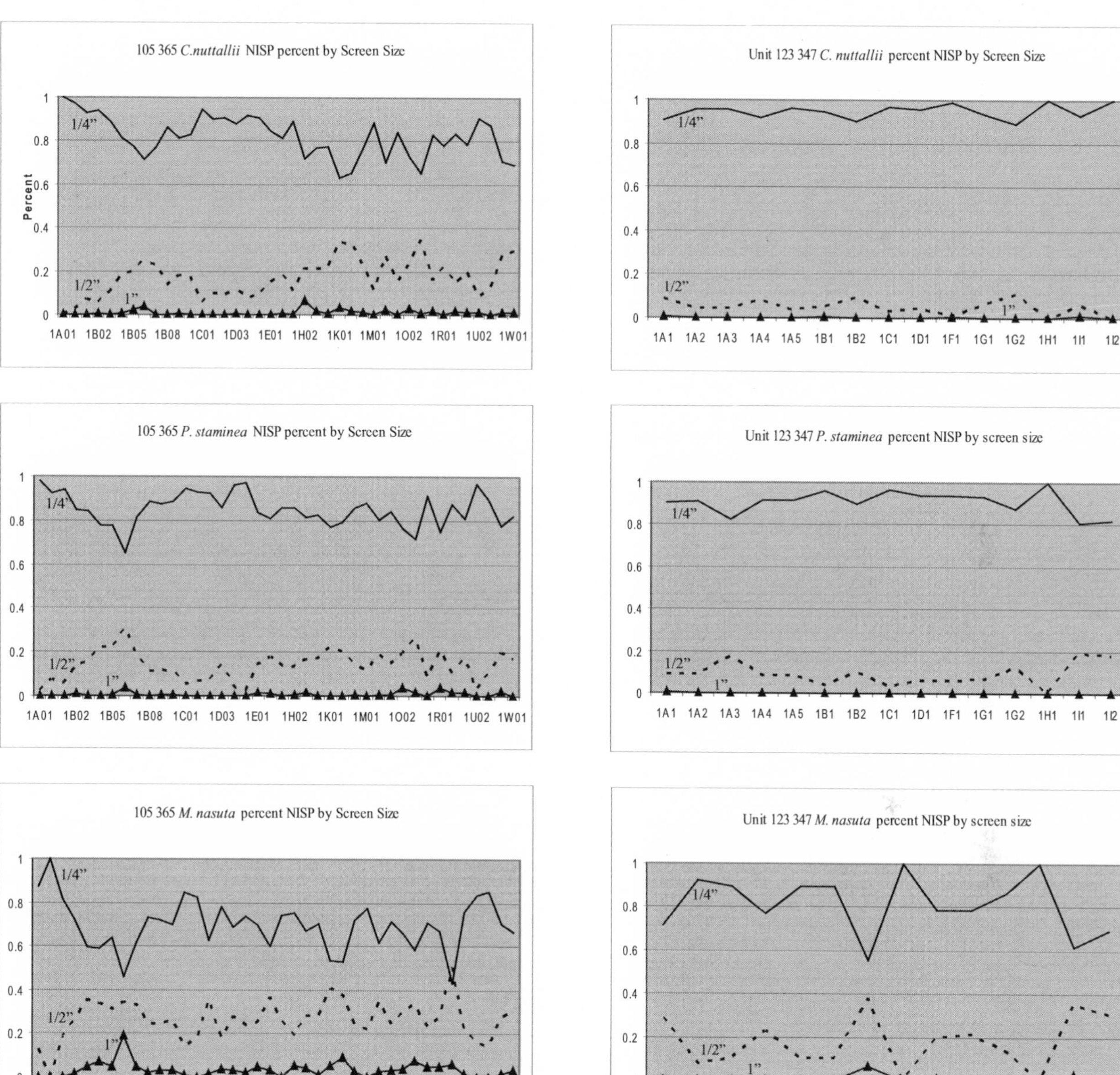

Figure 11.7 Change over time in relative fragmentation of *Clinocardium nuttalii*, *Macoma nasuta*, and *Protothaca staminea* in Unit 105 365 and Unit 123 347.

in Unit 105 365 overall, but Unit 123 346 was subject to more intensive post-depositional breakage.

The degree to which shell remains are fragmented can inform on the intensity of post-depositional processes that occurred at a site. Assuming that shellfish were processed and discarded similarly across time and space, differences in fragmentation can be interpreted as differences in the intensity of post-depositional forces across time or space. Such information is critical in identifying the presence of a house lacking more traditional house features.

Screening shell samples through nested screens divides the shell into four size categories: 1", ½ ", ¼" and ⅛". The relative abundance of shell within each screen size category can be used to infer intensity of post-depositional processes. Morphological differences across shellfish species result in variability in their sensitivity to agents of fragmentation (Claassen 1998), thus size analyses are conducted for individual species. *Clinocardium nuttallii*, *Macoma nasuta* and *Protothaca staminea* are used here because they are the most commonly indentified species in the site and therefore provide the most robust sample sizes. By comparing relative abundances of screen size categories for these taxa both horizontally and vertically across the site, it is possible to determine how post-depositional processes varied across time and space at OpD.

Due to its relatively thick shell, *Clinocardium nuttallii* is fairly resistant to fragmentation. It is most sensitive to fragmentation where it is the thinnest, between the radial ridges. Additionally, *C. nuttallii* can grow to a fairly large size and fragmentation may increase with size once maximum thickness is reached. In Unit 105 365, the ¼" size fraction fluctuated between 60% and 100% of all *C. nuttallii* NISP (Figure 11.7). There is a gradual positive relationship between depth and percent of shell in the ¼" fraction. In other words, shell becomes increasingly fragmented at greater depths. In comparison, in Unit 123 347 the percentage of ¼" *C. nuttallii* shell was consistently over 80%. This indicates that fragmentation in Unit 123 347 was more intense and more consistent at different depths than in Unit 105 365. In both units, the ½" fraction accounts for the majority of the remaining shell.

Macoma nasuta should be the most sensitive to fragmentation of the three species used to measure fragmentation. Although its shell is relatively flat, protecting it from fragmentation in some cases, its thinness increases its fragility. In Unit 105 365, the fragmentation of *M. nasuta* was more variable than that of *C. nuttallii* (Figure 11.7). The ¼" fraction accounts for anywhere from 40%-100% of all *M. nasuta* shell, but averages around 70%. In Unit 123 347, the ¼" size fraction accounts for 60-100% of *M. nasuta* shell, with an average around 80%. Again, the ½" fraction accounts for the majority of the remaining shell in both units. In both units, there are significant fluctuations in the percent of shell across the ½" and ¼" screen sizes. In Unit 105 365, the ½" and 1" fractions spike in the earliest and latest levels. In Unit 123 347, the percentage of shell in the ½" fraction spikes in levels 1A01, 1B02, and 1I01 and 2 fluctuated significantly over time, although the ¼" screen size always accounts for more of the shell than the ½" screen. In these levels, decreases in fragmentation intensity may be affecting taxonomic relative abundance measures. Overall, size fraction analysis of *M. nasuta* shell indicates that the ¼" fraction accounts for a majority of the NISP, which is consistent with the other fragmentation analyses. Together these analyses suggest that with a few exceptions, fragmentation was relatively high, especially in Unit 123 347, and fairly consistent over time.

The general morphology of *P. staminea* suggests that it should be fairly resistant to fragmentation. Its shell is relatively thick and it rarely grows to significantly large sizes. Therefore, it is unlikely to exhibit the same intensity of fragmentation as *C. nuttallii* and *M. nasuta.* Despite its seeming durability, *P. staminea* is also highly fragmented. In Unit 105 365 (Figure 11.7), the ¼" fraction accounted for 80-85% of *P. staminea* shell and in Unit 123 347 it accounted for 90% of the shell. In both units, the percent of shell in the different screen sizes remained fairly constant through time.

The screen size fragmentation analysis of *Clinocardium nuttallii*, *Macoma nasuta*, and *Protothaca staminea* suggest that the shell remains in Unit 123 347 were subject to greater post-depositional activity than Unit 105 365. For all three species, the ¼" fraction accounted for a higher percentage of the NISP in Unit 123 347 than in Unit 105 365. These data support the hypothesis that OpD was used as a domestic structure. If shell from ridge Unit 105 365 was piled up around house walls, it should be less fragmented than shell from depression Unit 123 347 where shell slumping would lead to more fragmentation. It is difficult, however, to rule out alternative explanations for greater fragmentation in Unit 123 347. Analysis of shell fragmentation alone cannot be used to confidently evaluate the house hypothesis.

COMPARISON WITH OTHER NORTHWEST COAST SITES

Shellfish are abundant in Northwest Coast archaeological sites beginning approximately 4500 BP (Ames and Maschner 1990). Typical Northwest Coast shellfish analyses focus on reconstructing diet, but have also addressed a variety of other issues including season of site occupation (Ham 1976), post-depositional processes (Ford 1995), site formation processes (Blukis Onat 1985), and social stratification (Wessen 1988).

One common shellfish pattern identified in Northwest Coast shell middens is a replacement of mussel with clam species (Ford 1990; Ham 1976; Hanson 1996; Mason et al. 1991; Wessen 1988). This transition has been attributed to a variety of factors including substrate environment change (Ham 1976; Hanson 1995; Larson 1990), over-exploitation (Rankin 1991), and the transition to a storage economy (Croes and Hackenberger 1988). Although these studies all propose different causes for this replacement they all explicitly or implicitly argue that mussels were preferred for some reason over clams and that only when their availability declines, for whatever reason, did people begin intensively harvesting clams.

The pattern of clams replacing mussels is not found at OpD at English Camp. Abundance of epifaunal species increases in the lowest levels of Unit 123 347, but even in those levels they are significantly less abundant than clams and cockles. This is mostly explained by the substrate of Garrison Bay. Garrison

Bay is dominated by a muddy substrate, excellent for clams and cockles but poorly suited for mussel and barnacles. People living at Garrison Bay could have collected clams and cockles without any additional costs or delays associated with traveling to rocky substrates and carrying mussels and barnacles back to a habitation site.

If clams and cockles were preferred prehistorically because of species distribution on the island, then it should follow that clams and cockles are more abundant in the lowest levels and mussels and barnacles more abundant in upper levels if shellfishing intensified or clams decreased in availability. The data do not support this prediction; clams and cockles do not steadily decline in importance, nor do mussels and barnacles increase. Instead, all species fluctuate randomly throughout the facies, with the exception of a relative decrease in mussels and barnacles after the deposition of the first two levels of Unit 123 347. There is no clear explanation at this time for the fluctuating relative abundances. One possible explanation is that the mirror a natural change in species abundance through time. If true, this would further suggest that people were not collecting shellfish intensely enough to deplete shellfish beds.

CONCLUSIONS

Shellfish remains from OpD of the English Camp site indicate that shellfish were a consistent component of the diet. The identified taxa are consistent with the taxa that inhabit Garrison Bay and its surrounding areas today. Therefore, it is likely that people were collecting and processing shellfish locally. This does not necessarily lead to the conclusion that people were living there. The shellfish could have been cooked, shells discarded, and meat returned to a base camp located elsewhere.

The taxonomic relative abundance analysis neither supports nor refutes the proposed house hypothesis. Both units have similar relative abundance patterns and high degrees of fluctuation across all taxa. This suggests that the shell from Unit 123 347 could have originated from Unit 105 365; however, without a clear connection between the top of Unit 105 365 and the bottom of Unit 123 347 any such conclusion would be highly speculative. Fractionation analysis provides tentative support for the idea that Unit 123 347 represents the wall of a house and Unit 105 365 represents a depression associated with the inside of a house. Analysis of breakage across three size classes for three different species all indicate that the shell recovered from Unit 123 347 was more highly fragmented than the shell from Unit 105 365. The increased fragmentation of Unit 123 347 could be explained by secondary, post-depositional fragmentation resulting from slumping following the removal or decomposition of a house structure. However, these data only tentatively support the house hypothesis; numerous alternative hypotheses could also explain the data.

REFERENCES

Blukis Onat, A.
1985 Multifunctional Use of Shellfish Remains: From Garbage to Community Engineering. *Northwest Anthropological Research Notes* 19(2):201-207.

Chew, K. K., and A. P. Ma
1987 Species profiles: Life histories and environmental requirements of coastal fishes and invertebrates (Pacific Nrothwest)-common littleneck clam. U.S. Fish and Wildlife Service Biological Report 82 (11.78). U.S. Army Corps of Engineers, TR-EL-82-4:1-22.

Claassen, C.
1998 *Shells*. Cambridge Manuals in Archaeology. Cambridge University Press, Cambridge.

Croes, D. R., and S. Hackenberger
1988 Hoko River Archaeological Complex: Modeling Prehistoric Northwest Coast Economic Evolution. In *Prehistoric Economies of the Pacific Northwest Coast*, edited by B.L. Isaac, pp. 19-85. Research in Economic Anthropology, Supplement 3, JAI Press, Greenwich.

Ellis, D. W., and S. Wilson
1981 *The Knowledge and Usage of Marine Invertebrates by the Skidegate Haida People of the Queen Charlotte Islands*. Queen Charlotte Islands Museum Society, Vancouver.

Ellis, D. W., and L. Swan
1981 *Teachings of the Tides: Uses of Marine Invertebrates by the Manhousat Peoples*. Theytus Books, Nanaimo, BC.

Ford, P.
1995 Appendix 6: Invertebrate Fauna. In *The Archaeology of West Point, Seattle, Washington: 4,000 Years of Hunter-Fisher-Gatherer Land Use in Southern Puget Sound*, edited by L.L. Larson and D.E. Lewarch, pp.1-44. Larson Anthropological/ Archaeological Services, Seattle.

Foster, N. R.
1991 *Intertidal Bivalves: A Guide to the Common Marine Bivalves of Alaska*. University of Alaska Press, Anchorage.

Fournier, J. A., and J. Dewhirst
1980 Zooarchaeological Analysis of Barnacle Remains from Yuquot, British Columbia. In *The Yuquot Project Volume 2*, edited by W.J. Folan and

J. Dewhirst. National Historic Parks and Sites Branch, Parks Canada, Ottawa.

Glassow, M. A.

2000 Weighing vs. Counting Shellfish Remains: A comment on Mason, Peterson, and Tiffany. *American Antiquity* 65(2): 407-414.

Grayson, D. K.

1984 *Quantitative Zooarchaeology.* Academic Press, New York.

Grayson, D. K., and C. J. Frey

2004 Measuring Skeletal Part Representation in Archaeological Faunas. *Journal of Taphonomy* 2(1): 27-42.

Gunther, E.

1927 Klallam Ethnography. *Publications in Anthropology* 1(5): 171-314. University of Washington, Seattle.

Ham, L. C.

1976 Analysis of Shell Samples from Glenrose. In *The Glenrose Cannery Site*, edited by R.G. Matson, pp. 42-78. Archaeological Survey of Canada Mercury Series No. 52, National Museum of Man, Ottawa.

Hanson, D. K.

1995 Subsistence During the Late Prehistoric Occupation of Pender Canal, British Columbia (DeRt-1). *Canadian Journal of Archaeology* 19:29-48.

Kozloff, E. N.

1993 *Seashore Life on the Northern Pacific Coast: An Illustrated Guide to Northern California, Oregon, Washington and British Columbia.* University of Washington Press, Seattle.

1996 *Marine Invertebrates of the Pacific Northwest.* University of Washington Press, Seattle.

Larson, L.

1995 Subsistence Organization. In *The Archaeology of West Point, Seattle, Washington: 4,000 years of Hunter-Fisher-Gatherer Land Use in Southern Puget Sound*, edited by L. Larson and D.E. Lewarch. Larson Anthropological/Archaeological Services, Seattle.

Matson, R. D., M. L. Peterson, and J. A. Tiffany

1991 Weighing vs. Counting: Measuring Reliability and the California School of Midden Analysis. *American Antiquity* 63(2):303-324.

Matson, R. D., and G. Coupland

1995 *The Prehistory of the Northwest Coast.* Academic Press, New York.

Mitchell, D. H.

1971 Archaeology of the Gulf of Georgia, a natural region and its cultural types. *Syesis* 4 (Suppl.1), Victoria, BC.

Nugent, A.

1985 *Lummi Elders Speak.* Lummi Indian Business Council and Tribune, Lynden, WA.

Rankin, L.

1991 *Shellfish in 1989 and 1990 Crescent Beach Excavations, Final Report*, edited by R.G. Matson, H. Pratt, L. Rankin. University of British Columbia, Vancouver.

Rudy, P., and L. H. Rudy

1983 *Oregon Estuarine Invertebrates: An Illustrated Guide to the Common and Important Invertebrate Animals.* U.S. Fish and Wildlife Service Biological Service Program. FWS/OBS-83/16.

Suttles, W. P.

1951 *Economic Life of the Coast Salish of Haro and Rosario Straits.* Unpublished Ph.D. Dissertation, Department of Anthropology, University of Washington, Seattle.

1974 The Economic Life of the Coast Salish of Haro and Rosario Straits. In *Coast Salish and Western Washington Indians I*, edited by D.A. Horr, pp. 41-570. Garland Publishing Company, New York.

Sepez, J.

2001 *Political and Social Ecology of Contemporary Makah Subsistence Hunting Fishing, and Shellfish Collecting Practices.* Unpublished Ph.D. Dissertation, Department of Anthropology, University of Washington, Seattle.

Wessen, G.

1988 The Use of Shellfish Resources on the Northwest Coast: The View from Ozette. In *Prehistoric Economies of the Northwest Coast*, edited by B.L. Isaac, pp. 179-207. Research in Economic Anthropology, Supplement 3, JAI Press, Greenwich.

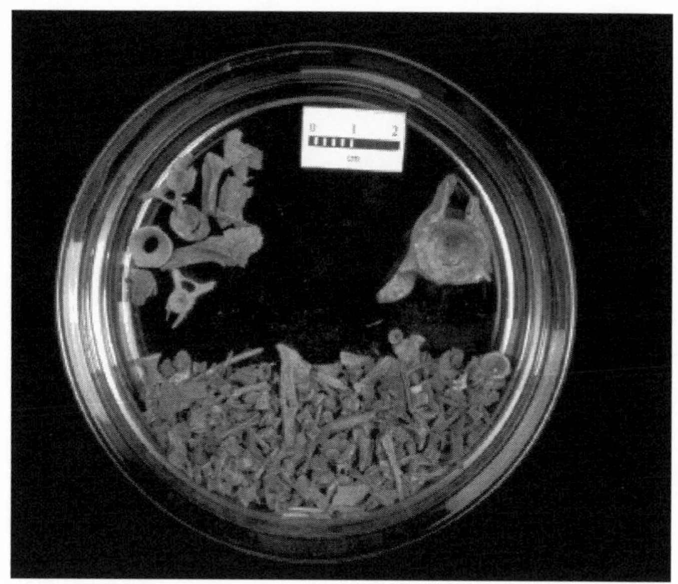

12

Faunal Analysis: Fish

Robert E. Kopperl

Kopperl presents a descriptive summary of the types of fish bones present at OpD and the results of quantitative analyses of those remains. The fish assemblage is dominated by salmonid and herring and is remarkably well preserved. Kopperl suggests that the fish remains from OpD are not sufficient to determine if the shell ridge was a domestic area per s; however, they can be used to investigate the activities associated with topographical features in the shell midden. He notes that differential representation of the major fish taxa across the site may indicate differential disposal of food remains across space.

Fish remains are a major component of the OpD shell midden assemblage, providing a large volume of information on Native American fishing, fish habitat, and midden formation processes. A sample of approximately 25% of the fish bones was analyzed from the six 1 x 2 meter OpD excavation units placed in three distinctive topographic zones in front of, within, and behind a large depression. Of this sample of 15,168 specimens, 9,124 or about 60% were identified to at least the taxonomic level of Order. Of the identified specimens, salmon, herring, and dogfish dominated the assemblage, with smaller numbers of greenling, sculpin, flatfish, and other fish remains also found. The fish bone assemblages recovered from different parts of the OpD midden contain different proportions of salmon, herring, and other identifiable fish taxa, suggesting differential use or disposal patterns occurred across a relatively small area. An appendix showing all results is available on file at the Burke Museum of Natural History and Culture (and see Table 12.1).

METHODS

Sorting and Sampling

Given time and budgetary constraints, the entire fish bone assemblage from OpD could not be analyzed. The assemblage was sampled in a manner that provided even spatial coverage, addressed the general research interests of the project and yielded adequate samples to make statistically valid inferences about Native American fish utilization at British Camp. Fish bones from the first and every fourth bucket from each excavation level and screen size were separated from the rest of the assemblage for analysis.

Analysis Protocol

Fish remains from the OpD assemblage were identified to the finest taxonomic level possible using personal comparative material of over 150 complete fish skeletons representing all economically important fish taxa found in the Puget Sound and Strait of Georgia region, and numerous skeletons of other species as well. That comparative collection is now housed with the Fish Collection at the School of Aquatic and Fishery Sciences/Burke Museum of Natural and Cultural History. Each bag of fish bones was separated by finest taxonomic identification, skeletal element and element portion, side (if the specimen is from a sided element), presence of diagnostic landmark, and whether the specimen was burned.

Analysis was conducted at the Department of Anthropology at the University of Washington, and at the home laboratory of the author. Each bag of fish bones

Chapter opening photo: Fish bone specimens from the site.

Table 12.1 NISP of major fish taxa by unit and facies

Layer	Volume (liters)	Taxa														NISP/ Density per liter
		Dogfish	Skate	Ratfish	Herring	Salmonid	Smelt	Cod	Surf perch	Mackerel	Rockfish	Greenling	Sculpin	Flatfish	Unid.	
Unit 105 365																
1A	32	1			1	3									7	12 / 0.4
1B	136	25		2	37	44	3					12	3	2	106	234 / 1.7
1C	8	2				6						1			18	27 / 3.4
1D	96	18	1		9	30						7		1	48	114 / 1.2
1G	8														4	4 / 0.5
1H	40	37	1		43	79	1					9		2	139	311 / 7.8
1J	48	55			38	42	1		5		1	8	2		125	277 / 5.8
1K	72	25			33	120	3		2			5			182	370 / 5.1
1L	40	19			25	161	3		2			6	1	1	212	430 / 10.8
1M	24	10			8	23						4	1		68	114 / 4.8
1N	8					8						1				9 / 1.1
1O	80	10			147	68	2				1	15	8	1	259	511 / 6.4
1P	16	2			18	13									9	42 / 2.6
1Q	16	1			83	11						2	1	1	74	173 / 10.8
1R	8	1			21	3						3			17	45 / 5.6
1S	48	13	1		224	100			1			73	6	2	322	742 / 15.5
1T	32	2			80	36	1						4	1	81	205 / 6.4
1U	64	7			11	24						8	2		28	80 / 1.3
1V	32	5			36	9	1					2	19		101	173 / 5.4
1W	32	4			51	17						1	12		77	162 / 5.1
00	80	41		1	453	226	2					10	61	1	794	1589 / 19.9
Unit 107 341																
1A	16	1				1										2 / 0.1
1B	8	10				9			1			1			3	24 / 3.0
1C	40	12				8						1			5	26 / 0.7
1D	8	5			4	6						4	1		12	32 / 4.0
Unit 111 349																
1A	16	1			125	6			2			1	1		50	186 / 11.6
1B	72	11	2		48	20					1	13	3		55	153 / 2.1
1D	8	1			11	1							1		8	22 / 2.8
1E	8				2							1	2		1	6 / 0.8
1G	80	7		1	64	30	1					6	10		110	229 / 2.9
1H	16	3			14	2						3	1		12	35 / 2.2
1I	8	6				3									3	12 / 1.5
1J	24	1			2	8						2			8	21 / 0.9
1K	24	1			6	3						9	5		14	38 / 1.6
1L	24	2			21	14						7	2	1	16	63 / 2.6
1M	32	1			39	19						3	5	1	29	97 / 3.0
1O	8				1	3						10	6		11	31 / 3.9
1P	8	1			3	3						12	6		25	50 / 6.3
1R	8				4	48	1						5		39	97 / 12.1
1S	16	4			17	22						2	5		40	90 / 5.6
1U	16	3			1	15							1		35	55 / 3.4
1W	16	29			3	16						8	6		36	98 / 6.1
1X	8				2	6						1	3		19	31 / 3.9

Table 12.1 NISP of major fish taxa by unit and facies (continued)

Layer	Volume (liters)	Taxa														NISP/ Density per liter
		Dogfish	Skate	Ratfish	Herring	Salmonid	Smelt	Cod	Surf perch	Mackerel	Rockfish	Greenling	Sculpin	Flatfish	Unid.	
Unit 111 349 (continued)																
1Y	8												3		10	13 / 1.6
1Z	8	2			4	26			3			1	33	1	47	117 / 14.6
2A	24	3		1	31	74					1	9	19		125	263 / 11.0
2B	8					7						1	1		7	16 / 2.0
2C	8	5			5	15			2				3		14	44 / 5.5
2D	32	11			52	58						15	16	1	107	260 / 8.1
2E	72	26	6		158	132	1				1	21	24	1	322	692 / 9.6
2F	8	4		1	14	5						2			12	38 / 4.8
00	136	45		2	348	196				1	1	38	68	2	494	1195 / 8.8
Unit 121 347																
1A	24	4										1	1		1	7 / 0.3
1B	168	24		2	31	88			11			14	15	4	85	274 / 1.6
1C	32	12			10	38						3	5		29	97 / 3.0
1D	96	51	1	1	79	116					3	18	15	3	162	449 / 4.7
1F	8	1			2	3			1			2		3		12 / 1.5
1G	8				2	4						2	1			9 / 1.1
1H	16	1			13	8					3		2	1	26	54 / 3.4
1I	24	2				6			1					1		10 / 0.4
00	24	1				8									2	11 / 0.5
Unit 123 347																
1A	216	80		1	79	402		3	7		5	50	29	3	228	887 / 4.1
1B	8	2				10						1		3		16 / 2.0
1C	8	6		1	2	8							1	1	5	24 / 3.0
1D	8	2			1	2									1	6 / 0.8
1G	64	12			24	49						12	6		47	150 / 2.3
1H	40	8		2	7	35						8	5	1	68	134 / 3.4
1I	24	5			12	36						10			25	88 / 3.7
Unit 130 352																
1A	136	141			246	266					2	33	13	2	232	935 / 6.9
1B	120	171	2		130	354			3		4	45	34	2	415	1160 / 9.7
1C	40	122			15	103			1		1	12	14		141	409 / 10.2
1D	24	18			18	37						3	2		16	94 / 3.9
1E	16	12			4	9									1	26 / 1.6
1G	40	24			49	82						1	3	1	91	251 / 6.3
1H	8	2			4	8						1	3			18 / 2.3
1I	8	7			2	20									23	52 / 6.5
1K	8					38								4		42 / 5.3
1L	8										1					1 / 0.1
00	24	3			5	40					1	1			55	105 / 4.4

Table 12.2 Number of Identified Fish Specimens (NISP)

Scientific Name	Common Name	Unit						Total
		105 365	107 341	111 349	121 347	123 347	130 352	
Chondrichthys	Cartilaginous Fish	1						1
Squalus acanthias, c.f.	Spiny Dogfish	278	28	167	96	115	512	1196
Raja sp.	Skate	2		8			2	12
Raja rhina, c.f.	Lognose Skate	1			1			2
Hydrolagus colliei	Spotted Ratfish	5		5	3	4		17
Clupea harangus pallasi	Pacific Herring	1318	4	976	137	125	493	3053
Oncorhynchus sp.	Salmon and Trout	1020	24	740	271	542	1027	3624
Salvelinus malma, c.f.	Dolly Varden	3						3
Osmeridae	Smelt	17		3				20
Gadidae	Codfish					3		3
Embiotocidae	Surfperch	9	1	7	10	5	5	37
Cymatogaster aggregata, c.f.	Shiner Perch						1	1
Embiotoca lateralis, c.f.	Striped Seaperch				2			2
Rhacochilus vacca, c.f.	Pile Perch	1			1	2		4
Scomber japonicus, c.f.	Chub Mackerel			1				1
Scorpaeniformes	Rockfish, Greenlings, Sculpins	6						6
Scorpaenidae	Rockfish	2		4	6	5	9	26
Hexagrammidae	Greenlings	145	4	154	36	76	96	511
Hexagrammos lagocephalus, c.f.	Rock Greenling	3		4	1			8
Hexagrammos stelleri, c.f.	Whitespotted Greenling	15	2	1	1		1	20
Ophiodon elongatus, c.f.	Lingcod	4		6	2	6	5	23
Cottidae	Sculpins	99		201	31	34	60	425
Enophrys bison, c.f.	Buffalo Sculpin	3		6		2	2	13
Hemilepidotus sp., c.f.	Irish Lord	6		1				7
Leptocottus armatus	Pacific Staghorn Sculpin	1		4		1	4	10
Leptocottus armatus, c.f.	Pacific Staghorn Sculpin	20	1	9	8	3	9	50
Scorpaenichthys marmoratus, c.f.	Cabezon			11		1		12
Pleuronectiformes	Flatfish	8		7	8	4	4	31
Hippoglossus stenolepis	Pacific Halibut				1			1
Platichthys stellatus, c.f.	Starry Flounder	4					1	5
Unidentified Fish	Unidentified Fish	2671	20	1655	308	377	1013	6044
Total		5642	84	3970	923	1305	3244	15168

within the sample had an individual catalog number comprised of the unit, stratum, level, bucket, material, and screen-size. After fish bones from each bag were sorted by the characteristics listed above, each group was entered into an Excel spreadsheet, and weighed by quantity.

Fish remains were quantified using NISP, or Number of Identified Specimens, which is the quantity of all remains identified for each taxon. Each specimen is treated as a single NISP. Other methods of quantification were not used, such as Minimum Number of Individuals (MNI), which is the minimum number of individuals of a particular taxon represented by an aggregate of specimens. Numerous studies have shown that NISP and MNI are highly correlated (e.g., Butler 1987; Grayson 1984). Given the aggregation problems associated with MNI, NISP was used to quantify taxonomic abundance for this analysis. MNI can be calculated, however, from the information provided in the analysis.

DESCRIPTIVE SUMMARY

This section provides descriptions of each fish taxon identified in the analyzed OpD assemblage, in standard phylogenetic order following Hart (1973). Of the 15,168 specimens analyzed, 9,124 (60.1%) were identified to a finer taxonomic level. Scientific and common names for each taxon followed by a list of the data described in this section are also shown in Table 12.2.

Class Chondrichthyes (cartilaginous fish)

Material: 1 undiff. vertebra.
Total: 1 specimen.
Remarks: This taxonomic Class includes cartilaginous fishes, such as lampreys, sharks, skates, rays, and ratfish. All of these groups are represented on the Northwest Coast, and the remains of some, most notably dogfish and skates, are common in many shell middens in the Straits and Puget Sound region. Miller and Borton (1980) note ten species of shark from seven Families, one species from the electric ray Family, four species from the skate Family, and one species from the chimaerid Family observed in the Straits and Puget Sound region. Of these, only the dogfish, skate, and ratfish are commonly encountered.

Besides teeth and spines, vertebrae of some kinds of cartilaginous fish ossify and therefore may be preserved in archaeological sites. Although almost all specimens identified from the OpD assemblage are identified to a finer taxon than Class, one vertebral specimen is morphologically different from the available dogfish (*S. acanthias*), skate (*Raja* sp.), and ratfish (*H. colliei*) comparative material.

Subclass Elasmobranchii (sharks, rays)
Order Squaliformes
Family Squalidae
c.f. *Squalus acanthias* (Spiny Dogfish)

Material: 1171 undiff. vertebrae, 15 spines, 9 teeth.
Total: 1196 specimens.
Remarks: Dogfish (Figure 12.1) are the most abundant of the seven shark Families and ten shark species found in Puget Sound (Miller and Borton 1980). Interestingly, their modern distribution in the waters surrounding San Juan Island is concentrated in San Juan Channel east of the Island opposite the location of British Camp (Miller and Borton 1980:7.2). Dogfish inhabit both shallow and deep water, feeding on small fish such as herring and smelt. Historically, they were harvested on a commercial scale for their oil, first used for lamps and as an industrial lubricant and later as a vitamin supplement (Hart 1973:44-46). Spiny dogfish vertebrae have a very distinctive spool-shape, and their teeth and the cross-sections of their spines are distinctive as well, often allowing for species-level identification when encountered.

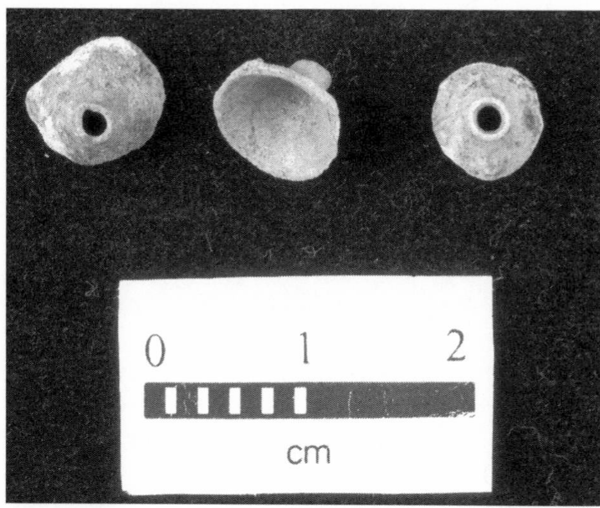

Figure 12.1 Dogfish vertebrae (SAJH 127237).

Order Rajiformes (skates and rays)
Family Rajidae
Raja sp. (Skate)

Material: 1 vertebra, 7 dermal denticles, 4 teeth.
Total: 12 specimens.
Remarks: There are four species of skate found in Puget Sound today, all being shallow bottom-feeders. *Raja binoculata* (big skate) and *Raja rhina* (longnose skate) are by far the most common skate species in the area and have been observed on the eastern shore of San Juan Island near Friday Harbor (Miller and Borton 1980). Ethnographically, skates were caught with spears near-shore by the Lummi (Stern 1934:51). Skate vertebrae and dermal denticles have distinctive morphology that allows them to be identified to the Genus level.

c.f. *Raja rhina* (Longnose Skate)

Material: 2 dermal denticles.
Total: 2 specimens.
Remarks: Dermal denticles are the element from skates that are the most distinctive to species. Several denticle specimens were found in the OpD assemblage that were intact and most closely resembled those of the *Raja rhina* in the comparative collection, which had a well-defined star-shaped base.

Order Chimaeriformes
Family Chimaeridae (Chimeras)

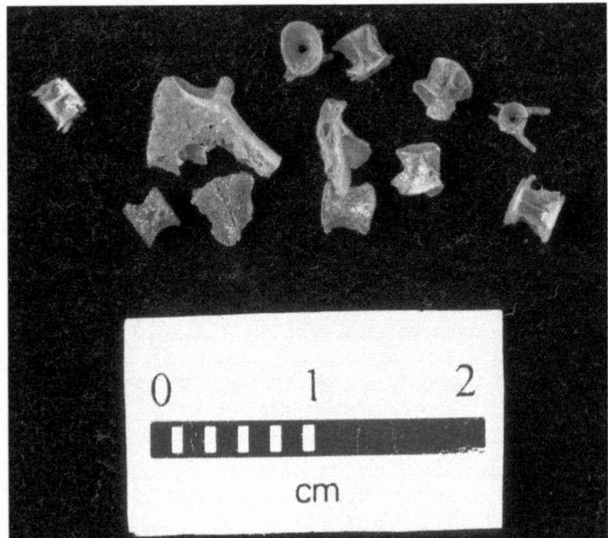

Figure 12.2 Herring specimens (SAJH 127445).

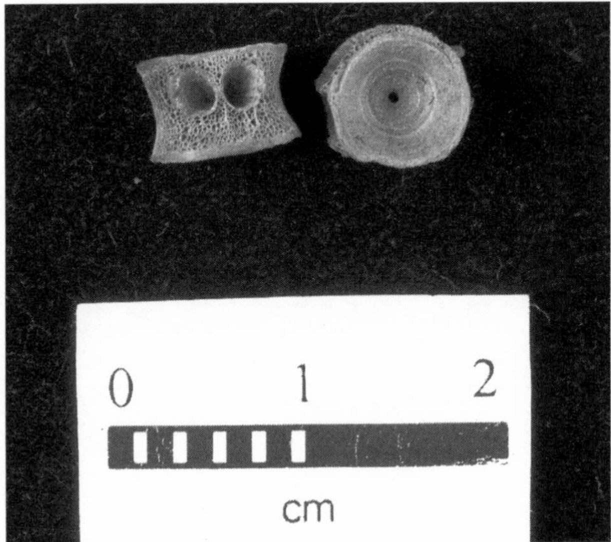

Figure 12.3 Salmon vertebrae (SAJH 127194).

Hydrolagus colliei (Spotted Ratfish)

Material: 10 undiff. teeth, 2 lower teeth, 5 upper medial teeth.

Total: 17 specimens.

Remarks: The spotted ratfish is the only member of the order Chimaeriformes found along the Northwest Coast (Hart 1973:65). Identification is therefore made at the species level. The fish often inhabits deep waters but has been known to exhibit seasonal variation in its depth in Puget Sound. This occurs mainly in the spring when the spotted ratfish shows greater abundance in shallower water (Quinn et al. 1980). They have been observed historically off the western shore of San Juan Island, but are more common on the eastern shore (Miller and Borton 1980:11.1). Despite their unpopularity in the modern fishing and culinary community, their remains are sometimes found in abundance in archaeological shell middens and speculated by some archaeologists to be consumed during lean subsistence times (e.g., Cannon 1995). The teeth of the spotted ratfish are distinctive wavy bony plates with vertical ridges perpendicular to the cutting edge.

Class Osteichthys (Bony Fishes)
Order Clupeiformes
Family Clupeidae
Clupea harengus pallasi (Pacific Herring)

Materials: 46 1st vertebrae, 665 thoracic vertebrae, 1895 caudal vertebrae, 15 ultimate vertebrae, 22 angulars, 13 basioccipitals, 14 ceratohyals, 4 cleithra, 16 dentaries, 5 epihyals, 19 exoccipitals, 11 frontals, 10 hyomandibulars, 1 hypohyal, 3 hypurals, 13 maxillae, 1 mesopterygoid, 19 opercles, 2 orbitosphenoids, 2 parietals, 2 postcleithra, 10 posttemporals, 8 prefrontals, 1 premaxilla, 3 preopercles, 161 prootics, 57 pterotics, 7 quadrates, 13 sphenotics, 6 subopercles, 1 supracleithra, 1 supramaxilla, 6 supraoccipitals, 1 vomer.

Total: 3053 specimens.

Remarks: Herring (Figure 12.2) is one of the most abundant fish taxa in the OpD fish bone assemblage. Two native species from this Family are found in the northeast Pacific: *C. harengus pallasi* (Pacific herring) and *Sardinops sagax* (Pacific sardine) (Hart 1973:94). Herring migrate to shallow water in the late winter to spawn, remaining in protected bays and coves until the early spring (e.g., Hart 1973:96-99). Today the sardine is very rare in Puget Sound and the Straits region, whereas herring are abundant. Miller and Borton (1980:14.2) and Kerwin (2002:60) have reported herring spawning areas clustered around Westcott Bay. The remains found at British Camp OpD are considered Pacific herring.

The Lummi traditionally collected herring eggs by anchoring the top boughs of young cedar trees to ropes submerged in shallow marine water, removing them after sufficient eggs have accumulated and are ready to be dried. Herring attracted other prey as well; during the herring spawn, other animal such as ducks could be netted as they fed on the eggs (Stern 1934:41,50; see also Monks 1987). The presence of herring bones in many archaeological sites in the region attests to the consumption of large quantities of mature herring as well (e.g., Kopperl 2001a).

Order Salmoniformes
Family Salmonidae
Oncorhynchus sp. (Pacific salmon and trout)

Materials: 4 1st vertebrae, 388 thoracic vertebrae, 32 precaudal vertebrae, 357 caudal vertebrae, 2 penultimate vertebrae, 1 ultimate vertebra, 2704 undiff. vertebra

fragments, 23 basipterygia, 5 branchials, 4 branchiostegal rays, 4 ceratobranchials, 2 coracoids, 2 undiff. cranial fragments, 1 dentary, 2 epibranchials, 1 epihyals, 2 epiotics, 17 epurals, 4 exoccipitals, 1 hyomandibular, 2 hypobranchials, 12 hypurals, 1 interopercle, 1 lingual plate, 3 maxillae, 2 mesocoracoids, 1 middle postcleithrum, 2 postcleithra, 3 posttemporals, 1 prootic, 1 pterotic, 1 quadrate, 16 scapulae, 1 supracleithrum, 18 teeth, 1 toothed bone, 1 undiff. fragment, 1 urohyal.
Total: 3624 specimens.
Remarks: The waters of the Straits and Puget Sound region are home to seven species in the genus *Oncorhynchus* (Figure 12.3), two species of *Salvelinus* (*S. malma* – dolly varden; *S. confluentus* – bull trout), and one species of whitefish (*Prosopium williamsoni*) (Miller and Borton 1980). Any of these species might be represented in the OpD assemblage, although the size of the specimens strongly suggests they are the remains of salmon, *Oncorhynchus*. Around San Juan Island, pink (*O. gorbuscha*) and chum (*O. keta*) salmon are found most frequently near Friday Harbor, while sockeye (*O. nerka*) salmon are found off the south shore near Cattle Point. Coho (*O. kisutch*) and chinook (*O. tshawytscha*) are the salmon species that have historically been observed near Westcott Bay (Miller and Borton 1980:16.1-16.7). Aside from anecdotal reports of pink and coho salmon spawning in streams on the larger San Juan Islands, however, most salmonids caught in the archipelago are on their way to spawning areas in larger mainland rivers such as the Fraser and Skagit Rivers (Kerwin 2002).

The vertebrae and many other skeletal elements of salmon and trout are easy to identify because of their morphology (Cannon 1987). Abdominal, precaudal, and caudal vertebrae can be distinguished on the basis of caudal and haemel processes (Butler 1993). Taxonomic discrimination beyond genus level, however, is very difficult to accomplish. Butler (1987) developed a discriminant function analysis that uses a combination of measurements on the 1st vertebrae of salmon to assign a specimen to a particular species group. Only four salmonid 1st vertebrae were found in this assemblage, and identification of all salmonid specimens were limited to the genus level.

Family Salmonidae

c.f. *Salvelinus malma* (Dolly Varden)

Materials: 2 thoracic vertebrae, 1 caudal vertebra.
Total: 3 specimens.
Remarks: Dolly varden have been historically observed along the mainland, as close to San Juan Island as the Skagit River delta (Miller and Borton 1980:16.8). Three salmonid specimens are tentatively identified as *S. malma*. The basis of the identification is the morphological similarity to comparative dolly varden skeletons, and substantial difference in size between the archaeological specimens and whole vertebrae of all other species within the Salmonid family that are found in the region today.

Family Osmeridae (smelt, eulachon)

Materials: 1 thoracic vertebra, 1 caudal vertebra, 17 dentaries, 1 premaxilla.
Total: 20 specimens.
Remarks: Five species of smelt are found in the Straits and Puget Sound region today. Three of them, surf smelt (*H. pretiosus*), longfin smelt (*S. thaleichthys*), and eulachon (*T. pacificus*) are common to the San Juan archipelago (Miller and Borton 1980:17.1-17.5). Surf smelt may spawn at any time of the year along beaches without heavy surf action (Hart 1973:140). This species of smelt are known to spawn along the more steeply-backed shore of Westoctt Bay southwest of OpD (Kerwin 2002). Identification of smelt specimens was made to the Family level, as most of their elements, including vertebrae and jaws, are morphologically similar.

Order Gadiformes

Family Gadidae (codfish)

Material: 3 caudal vertebrae.
Total: 3 specimens.
Remarks: Three species from the Gadid family are found in the Straits and Puget Sound area: Pacific cod (*Gadus macrocephalus*), Pacific tomcod (*Microgadus proximus*), and walleye pollock (*Theragra chalcogramma*). None are commonly found along the west shore of San Juan Island; Pacific cod and Pacific tomcod are more commonly observed in waters off Orcas Island, while walleye pollock are frequently observed as close as Friday Harbor (Miller and Borton 1980:24.1-24.4). The Strait of Georgia is spawning ground for both Pacific cod and walleye pollock, offering a seasonally congregated fish resource in mid-spring (Hart 1973:222-229). Because there is little morphological difference in most elements between species, the Gadid vertebrae specimens in the OpD assemblage were not given a finer taxonomic identification.

Order Perciformes

Family Embiotocidae (surfperch)

Material: 2 1st vertebrae, 11 thoracic vertebrae, 8 precaudal vertebrae, 9 caudal vertebrae, 1 basioccipital, 1 ceratohyal, 1 lower pharyngeal plate, 1 undiff. pharyngeal plate fragment, 2 pharyngeal teeth, 1 upper pharyngeal plate.
Total: 37 specimens.

Figure 12.4 Perch specimens (SAJH 40753).

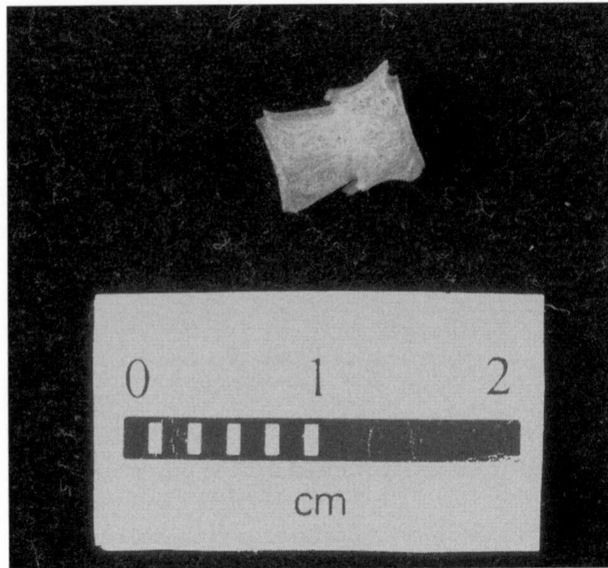

Figure 12.5 Mackerel vertebra (SAJH 127461).

Remarks: There are six species of surfperch that inhabit the Straits and Puget Sound region today. Four species, *B. frenatus* (kelp perch), *C. aggregata* (shiner perch), *E. lateralis* (striped seaperch), and *R. vacca* (pile perch) have been observed in the vicinity of Westcott Bay and the western shore of San Juan Island (Miller and Borton 1980:36.1-36.6). These relatively small fish can be found year-round in a variety of near-shore marine habitats, including sandy beaches, eelgrass and kelp beds, and rocky reefs (Lamb and Edgell 1986:59). Although many of their elements are quite distinct to taxonomic Family, especially their toothed pharyngeal plates, most of their vertebrae and individual pharyngeal teeth are morphologically similar. These elements and fragments of others were therefore identified to Family level (Figure 12.4).

c.f. *Cymatogaster aggregata* (Shiner Perch)

Material: 1 lower pharyngeal plate.

Total: 1 specimen.

Remarks: Shiner perch are the smallest species of surfperch in the region, rarely reaching 6 inches in length. Mature shiner perch inhabit deeper water in the winter months, and move closer to shore during the summer, where they are often found feeding near mussel and barnacle clusters on reefs and wharves (Hart 1973:305). The archaeological specimen was identified as shiner perch based on morphology and size.

c.f. *Embiotoca lateralis* (Striped Seaperch)

Material: 1 1st vertebra, 1 angular.

Total: 2 specimens.

Remarks: Striped seaperch congregate in the summer along shallow, rocky shores (Lamb and Edgell 1986:60). These archaeological specimens were identified as striped seaperch based on morphology.

c.f. *Rhacochilus vacca* (Pile Perch)

Material: 1 frontal, 3 lower pharyngeal plates.

Total: 4 specimens.

Remarks: Pile perch are found most commonly during the summer months in shallow water such as that of Westcott Bay (Lamb and Edgell 1986:61; Miller and Borton 1980:36.6). Their toothed pharyngeal plates are larger relative to other species of surfperch, reflecting a dietary focus on mussels as opposed to smaller invertebrates (Hart 1973:313). The OpD specimens were identified tentatively as pile perch given their fragmentary condition.

Family Scombridae (Mackerels and Tuna)

c.f. *Scomber japonicus* (Pacific Chub Mackerel)

Material: 1 undiff. vertebra.

Total: 1 specimen.

Remarks: Specimens from the Scombrid family are unusual in archaeological assemblages in the Straits and Puget Sound. Isolated specimens of bluefin tuna (*T. thynnus*) have been found occasionally in sites in more open coastal settings (e.g., Cannon 1991; McMillan 1979; Samuels 1994:79). Two species have been recorded live in modern waters of the region: the Pacific bonito (*Sarda chiliensis*) has been observed several in times in central Puget Sound, and the Pacific chub mackerel (*Scomber japonicus*) which has been observed once in Possession Sound near Everett (Miller and Borton 1980:49.1-49.2). The bonito is the larger of the two species. Both species spawn off the coast of California well to the south. Mackerel (Figure 12.5) are known to be highly migratory and range across much of the Pacific. Although uncommon in the area today in any age category, large numbers of immature mackerel were reported in the Strait of Georgia in 1940 (Hart 1973:373-376). Their presence in the Pacific Northwest in recent years is associated with El Niño years (Lamb and Edgell 1986). Based on size of the specimen, it was tentatively identified as chub mackerel.

Order Scorpaeniformes (Rockfish, Greenlings, Sculpins)
Material: 2 thoracic vertebrae, 2 caudal vertebrae, 1 epibranchial, 1 exoccipital.
Total: 6 specimens.
Remarks: Species of Scorpaeniformes are diverse, and comprise the greatest number of fish species of any Order within the Straits and Puget Sound region (Miller and Borton 1980). The constituent Families, including rockfish, greenling, and sculpins, are characterized by large heads and mouths relative to the remainder of their bodies. Most elements are distinctive to at least family, if not a finer taxon. Smaller or more highly fragment specimens that exhibit typical morphological characteristics of Scorpaeniformes, however, sometimes could not be identified to a particular family, and therefore placed in this general category.

Family Scorpaenidae (Rockfish)
Material: 1 thoracic vertebra, 7 precaudal vertebrae, 5 caudal vertebrae, 1 undiff. vertebra, 1 interopercle, 1 parasphenoid, 1 posttemporal, 3 premaxillae, 1 prootic, 2 pterygiophores, 1 radial, 1 retroarticular, 1 spine.
Total: 26 specimens.
Remarks: Numerous species of rockfish (Figure 12.6) inhabit the waters of the Straits and Puget Sound region, and include two taxonomic genera: *Sebastes* and *Sebastolobus*. Rockfish are highly adaptable and inhabit a variety of marine habitats, including rocky shorelines and deep open water (Hart 1973:388-454; Love et al. 2002). Rockfish inhabit both near-shore and open water at a variety of depths, feeding on crustaceans and smaller fish. Of the 27 species that have been observed in the modern waters of the Straits and Puget Sound region, six have been recorded along the northwest shore of San Juan Island near Westcott Bay: the copper rockfish (*S. caurinus*), rosethorn rockfish (*S. helvomaculatus*), quillback rockfish (*S. maliger*), black rockfish (*S. melanops*), china rockfish (*S. nebulosus*), and the canary rockfish (*S. pinniger*). Despite the great diversity of rockfish in the region, their skeletal elements have yet to be systematically differentiated by zooarchaeologists, and specimens in this assemblage were identified to Family level.

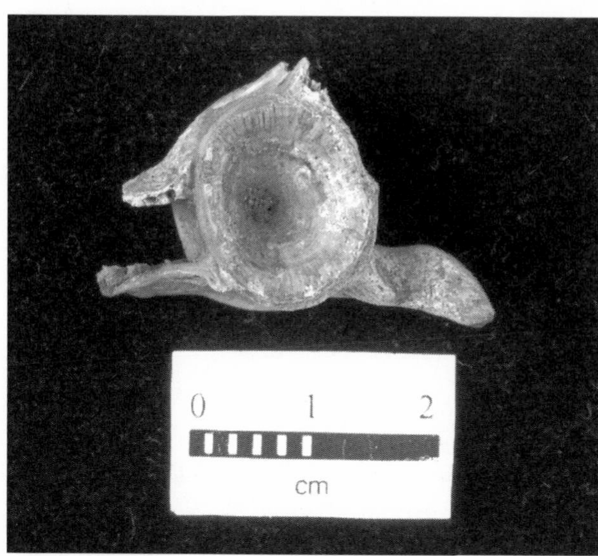

Figure 12.6 Rockfish vertebra (SAJH 127494).

Family Hexagrammidae (Greenlings)
Material: 7 1st vertebrae, 82 thoracic vertebrae, 35 precaudal vertebrae, 258 caudal vertebrae, 2 penultimate vertebrae, 4 ultimate vertebrae, 2 angulars, 1 basibranchial, 1 basipterygium, 1 branchial, 1 ceratohyal, 1 cleithrum, 7 dentaries, 2 ectopterygoids, 2 epibranchials, 12 epihyals, 3 epiotics, 1 ethmoid, 3 exoccipitals, 1 frontal, 2 hyomandibulars, 2 undiff. hypohyals, 3 lower hypohyal, 2 upper hypohyals, 1 interopercle, 1 lachrymal, 6 maxillae, 1 mesopterygoid, 5 opercles, 5 palatines, 2 parashpenoids, 1 parietal, 6 posttemporals, 2 prefrontals, 7 premaxillae, 1 preopercle, 2 prootics, 5 pterotics, 10 quadrates, 9 radials, 1 retroarticular, 1 sphenotic, 2 suborbitals, 3 supracleithra, 1 symplectic, 1 urohyal, 3 vomers.
Total: 511 specimens.
Remarks: The greenling Family is represented in the Straits and Puget Sound region by six species (Miller and Borton 1980:54.1-54.6). Like other Families within the Order Scorpaeniformes, they inhabit a variety of near-shore and open water marine settings and can be caught near land throughout the year (Lamb and Edgell 1986:125). One exception is the lingcod (*O. elongatus*), which voraciously feeds on forage fish such as herring and sand lance and often follows its prey into deeper waters (Hart 1973:468-469). Because comparative skeletal material used for this analysis included four of the six greenling species, most specimens were identified only to Family level.

c.f. *Hexagrammos lagocephalus* (Rock Greenling)
Material: 1 basioccipital, 1 hyomandibular, 3 posttemporals, 1 prefrontal, 1 quadrate, 1 supracleithrum.
Total: 8 specimens.
Remarks: The rock greenling has been observed occa-

sionally throughout the region, including Friday Harbor and False Bay (Miller and Borton 1980:54.2). They are known to be solitary and elusive to catch (Lamb and Edgell 1986:128). Specimens identified as c.f. *H. lagocephalus* were identical to the comparative skeletal material of this species, but those identifications remain tentative.

c.f. *Hexagrammos stelleri* (Whitespotted Greenling)

Material: 2 1st vertebrae, 1 angular, 2 dentaries, 4 hyomandibulars, 1 maxilla, 1 opercle, 2 palatines, 4 premaxillae, 2 quadrates, 1 vomer.

Total: 20 specimens.

Remarks: The white-spotted greenling, unlike the other smaller members of the same genus, is abundant throughout the San Juan archipelago (Miller and Borton 1980:54.3). This species favors shallow sandy subtidal areas with eelgrass or other plants adjacent to rocky outcroppings, where they congregate and are relatively easily caught (Lamb and Edgell 1986:127). Specimens identified as c.f. *H. stelleri* were identical to the comparative skeletal material of this species, but those identifications remain tentative.

c.f. *Ophiodon elongatus* (Lingcod)

Material: 1 thoracic vertebra, 4 precaudal vertebrae, 12 caudal vertebrae, 1 undiff. vertebra, 1 basioccipital, 1 certatohyal, 1 ectopterygoid, 1 epihyal, 1 premaxilla.

Total: 23 specimens.

Remarks: Lingcod are the largest members of the greenling family, and is abundant throughout the San Juan archipelago (Miller and Borton 1980:54.4). Although this species can be found in deeper waters in pursuit of forage fish, it may also be caught in shallows, where spawning occurs from December to March. Hart (1973:468) notes that individual lingcod exhibit two patterns of behavior: some are almost completely sedentary once matured, while others migrate to different depths and habitats throughout their lives. Although identifications of lingcod specimens are tentative, their larger size than other greenling specimens make their identifications somewhat more secure.

Family Cottidae (Sculpins)

Material: 12 1st vertebrae, 87 thoracic vertebrae, 6 precaudal vertebrae, 183 caudal vertebrae, 1 penultimate vertebrae, 6 ultimate vertebrae, 8 angulars, 8 basioccipitals, 1 basipterygium, 1 ceratobranchial, 8 ceratohyals, 1 cleithrum, 5 misc. cranium fragments, 14 dentaries, 1 ectopterygoid, 1 epihyal, 5 exoccipital, 1 frontal, 6 hyomandibulars, 1 hypural, 2 lachrymals, 4 maxillae, 6 opercles, 3 palatines, 1 parasphenoid, 5 parietals, 5 pharyngeal plates, 6 pharyngobranchials, 5 posttemporals, 8 premaxillae, 4 preopercles, 12 quadrates, 1 scapula, 3 toothed bone fragments, 1 urohyal, 3 vomers.

Total: 425 specimens.

Remarks: A total of 36 sculpin species have been observed in the Puget Sound and Straits region in modern times (Miller and Borton 1980). These species are highly variable in size, salinity tolerance, habitat preference, and behavior (Hart 1973:472-546). Although most sculpin elements are not identifiable beyond the family level, some are distinctive to genus and others are identifiable to species based on texture, size, or unique landmarks in the case of some cranial bones such as the preopercle.

c.f. *Enophrys bison* (Buffalo Sculpin)

Material: 8 misc. cranium fragments, 1 dentary, 1 palatine, 1 premaxilla, 2 preopercles.

Total: 13 specimens.

Remarks: The buffalo sculpin is a medium-sized sculpin that does not grow longer than about 14 inches. Abundant along most of the shore of San Juan Island (Miller and Borton 1980:55.13), this species tends to be solitary and inhabits shallow water year-round amongst plant growth that aids in camouflage (Hart 1973:499-500; Lamb and Edgell 1986:165). Tentative identification was made on specimens based upon the distinctive morphology of toothed bones and the preopercle, and the surface texture of cranial bones.

c.f. *Hemilepidotus* sp. (Irish Lord)

Material: 1 epihyal, 1 ethmoid, 1 mesopterygoid, 1 parashpenoid, 1 premaxilla, 1 quadrate, 1 symplectic.

Total: 7 specimens.

Remarks: Two species of the medium-sized Irish Lord genus inhabit the Puget Sound and Straits region, the red Irish Lord (*H. hemilepidotus*), and the brown Irish Lord (*H. spinosus*), although the brown Irish Lord is has been observed only rarely (Miller and Borton 1980:55.15-55.16). Irish Lord are voracious eaters and prefer a variety of shallow habitats to feed while being relatively sedentary (Hart 1973:502-505; Lamb and Edgell 1986:166-167). Tentative identification was made based upon the distinctive morphology of cranial bones.

Leptocottus armatus (Pacific Staghorn Sculpin)

Material: 10 preopercle spines.

Total: 10 specimens.

Remarks: The Pacific staghorn sculpin is a common species of medium-sized sculpin that can be found from shallow to moderate depths across the Pacific Northwest. They prefer silt- or mud-bottomed nearshore subtidal areas, however, as well as estuaries and lower portions of coastal streams (Hart 1973:518-519;

Lamb and Edgell 1986:168). They have been observed in abundance in Garrison Bay, Friday Harbor, Griffin Bay, and False Bay (Miller and Borton 1980:55.22). Identification of specimens to this species was based upon their distinctive antler-shaped preopercle spine.

c.f. *Leptocottus armatus* (Pacific Staghorn Sculpin)

Material: 2 1st vertebrae, 4 angulars, 2 basioccipitals, 7 certaohyals, 1 cleithrum, 3 dentaries, 2 frontals, 4 hyomandibulars, 1 interopercle, 7 opercles, 1 parietal, 4 posttemporals, 3 premaxillae, 4 preopercles, 3 quadrates, 1 scapula, 1 vomer.
Total: 50 specimens.
Remarks: Aside from the spine of the preopercle, other elements and portions of elements are distinct enough to make tentative identifications to the species-level, including the 1st vertebrae which exhibit morphology and texture different from other taxa of sculpin.

c.f. *Scorpaenichthys marmoratus* (Cabezon)

Material: 11 caudal vertebrae, 1 frontal.
Total: 12 specimens.
Remarks: The cabezon is largest sculpin species inhabiting Puget Sound and the Straits. Although they are most commonly found at moderate depths, adult cabezon often swim into very shallow water in pursuit of prey or to spawn, which occurs January through March (Hart 1973:540-541). They have been observed in shallow bays throughout the San Juan archipelago, including Garrison Bay (Miller and Borton 1980:55.33). Tentative identification of this species was based upon size and morphology of vertebrae, and size and texture of the one frontal specimen found in the assemblage.

Order Pleuronectiformes (Flatfish)

Material: 2 thoracic vertebrae, 2 precaudal vertebrae, 20 caudal vertebrae, 1 basipterygium, 1 hyomandibular, 1 interhaemel spine, 1 premaxilla, 1 pterotic, 1 quadrate, 1 vomer.
Total: 31 specimens.
Remarks: Two taxonomic Families of the Order Pleuronectiformes are found in the Puget Sound and Straits region: 13 species of right-eyed flounders (Pleuronectidae) and two species of left-eyed flounders (Bothidae) (Miller and Borton 1980). Flatfish are distinguished by their flattened bodies and asymmetrical crania in which their eyes migrate as juveniles to either their left or right side. Adult flatfish species vary greatly in size and depth preference, but all are normally bottom-dwellers (Hart 1973:595). Despite morphological characteristics that distinguish flatfish skeletal specimens from other taxonomic orders of fish — most notably lateral projections of the vertebral centrum — many specimens in this assemblage could not be identified to a finer taxonomic level.

Family Pleuronectidae (Right-Eyed Flounders)
Hippoglossus stenolepis (Pacific Halibut)

Material: 1 thoracic vertebra.
Total: 1 specimen.
Remarks: The halibut is the largest species of flatfish in the Pacific Ocean, often attaining lengths exceeding 6 feet. Although halibut live and spawn in deep to moderate depths (>275 meters), juveniles mature in shallower water (Hart 1973:614-615). Halibut are rarely observed in the San Juan archipelago and Strait of Georgia, instead being seen and caught in deeper waters of the Strait of Juan de Fuca and the Puget Sound (Miller and Borton 1980:59.5). Identification of the one vertebra specimen in the assemblage was based upon centrum morphology and size.

c.f. *Platichthys stellatus* (Starry Flounder)

Material: 3 caudal vertebrae, 1 dermal denticle, 1 premaxilla.
Total: 5 specimens.
Remarks: The starry flounder is a medium-sized (less than 36 inches in length) flatfish that inhabits a variety of depths and habitats, including estuaries and lower courses of freshwater streams, and despite belonging to the family of right-eyed flounders may become right- or left-eyed upon maturity. They spawn between February and April, but may be found in shallow water during the rest of the year as well (Hart 1973:631-632; Lamb and Edgell 1986:204). Starry flounder are abundant throughout the San Juan archipelago, and have been observed in Garrison Bay (Miller and Borton 1980:59.11). Identification of the vertebrae and premaxilla specimens were based upon morphology, and the star-shaped dermal denticle is distinctive to the starry flounder (Hart 1973:632).

Unidentified Fish

Material: 2 thoracic vertebrae, 5 caudal vertebrae, 30 undiff. vertebrae, 1 cleithrum, 1 epibranchial, 1 exoccipital, 1 hypural, 6 toothed bone fragments, 2779 misc. ray or spine fragments, 3218 unidentified fragments.
Total: 6044 specimens.
Remarks: In most cases, specimens of a known element could be further identified, but for some specimens, most notably vertebra fragments, this was not possible. The majority of unidentified fish specimens, however, were very small fragments from undetermined elements or ray or spine fragments that would not likely be identified to a finer taxonomic level even if the ray or spine were intact.

RESULTS AND DISCUSSION

In terms of overall relative taxonomic abundance, the identified OpD fish bone assemblage is dominated by salmonids (40%) and herring (33%), with lesser quantities of dogfish (13%), greenlings (6%), sculpins (5%), and eight other major taxonomic kinds of fish (3%). Elements from the entire fish skeleton are represented at the site by most taxa of bony fishes with a sample size greater than a few specimens. For example, salmonid remains are predominantly vertebrae and vertebral fragments; however cranial fragments, teeth, and bones of the pelvic and pectoral girdle are also represented. This indicates both salmon heads and bodies were discarded of at OpD. The herring, greenling, and sculpin bones are represented by most cranial elements as well as vertebrae and post-cranial elements. This analysis has also shed light on taphonomic processes affecting the OpD fish bones, variability of those remains within the OpD deposits, and similarities and differences between this assemblage and others across the region

Taphonomy

The OpD fish bone assemblage is well preserved, which is expected of faunal remains in alkaline shell midden deposits such as this (Stein 1992). Fish bones of varying density are represented, from vertebrae and teeth of larger fish to very delicate cranial elements of smaller fish. Factors such as bone density, degree of burning, and ground-water saturated depositional environments are known to structure the survivorship of fish remains (Butler and Chatters 1994; Lubinski 1996; Pegg 1999).

Burned fish bones are present in small numbers in the assemblage, and were recorded during analysis as being either charred or calcined. Color is the most commonly used characteristic for identifying thermal alteration of bone, although numerous chemical processes unrelated to burning can have a similar effect on the structure of bone (Lyman 1994; Shipman et al. 1984). The most effective means of identification of burned bone and the temperature range in which a specimen has been burned is by scanning-electron microscopic examination of the specimen's crystalline structure (e.g., McCutcheon 1992). Because the procedure was not practical for this analysis, it was assumed that specimens exhibiting blackening, whitening, or a combination of the two underwent some form of thermal alteration. Blackened specimens were identified as "charred", and are assumed to have been carbonized at a relatively low temperature. Whitened specimens that also exhibited a brittle, chalky texture were identified as "calcined", and are assumed to have been heated to higher temperatures in which much of the organic material within the mineral structure of the bone has been removed.

A total of 299 specimens, or about 2%, of the entire analyzed assemblage of 15,168 fish specimens were either charred or calcined. Of these burned bones, 202 were charred and 97 were calcined. The specimens are distributed randomly across the excavation units and facies in proportion to the total numbers of fish bones in each aggregation. By taxon, the specimens are also distributed in proportion to the total assemblage with the greatest number of burned specimens from salmonids, herring, dogfish, and greenling. Burned fish bones within the OpD assemblage suggest either cooking, heat smoking or drying, or disposal of fish in fire at British Camp, although their small numbers and random distribution throughout the assemblage preclude more detailed inferences.

Differential survivorship of bone fragments may also be attributed to the bone density of particular elements of fish taxa deposited at British Camp. Butler and Chatters (1994) measured bone densities of salmon elements, noting that in general post-cranial elements such as vertebrae are much denser than cranial elements. Therefore, inferences about salmon processing based on presence or absence of cranial elements in an assemblage may be inaccurate. The salmonid remains in the OpD assemblage are dominated by vertebrae, however less dense elements such as the coracoid, basipterygium, and exoccipital are also represented. Also, vertebrae are the element most easily identifiable to taxon in highly fragmented assemblages such as that of OpD. The presence throughout the units and facies of salmonid cranial elements, as well as abundant cranial specimens of herring, suggests that bone density has not played a substantial role in survivorship.

The OpD fish bones are highly fragmented, despite the apparently minor role of differential bone density and burning in structuring the assemblage. The screen-size distribution of the fish bone assemblage reflects degree of fragmentation as well as abundance of small-bodied fish. The mesh sizes of screens used during excavation of OpD were as fine as ⅛". Although very small fragments of fish bone pass through mesh of this size (e.g., Cannon 2000), the screens used at OpD were small enough to retain the bones of fish such as smelt, herring, and shiner perch that were ethnohistorically some of the smallest economically important fish taxa used in the Straits region. Of the four screen-size fractions (1", ½", ¼", and ⅛"), the majority of specimens were from the 1/8-inch fraction. In all six units analyzed, abundance within screen-size fractions

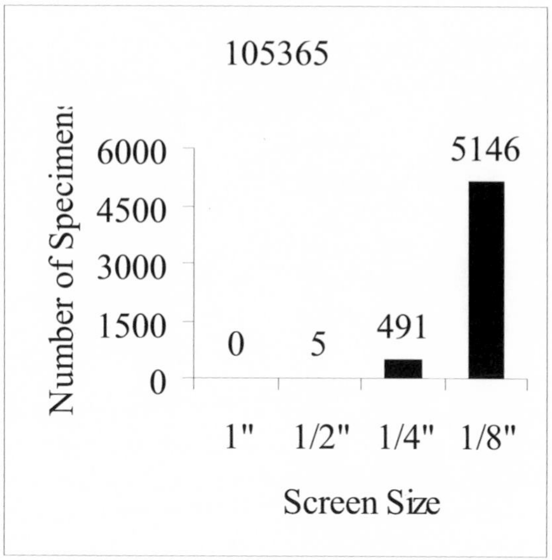

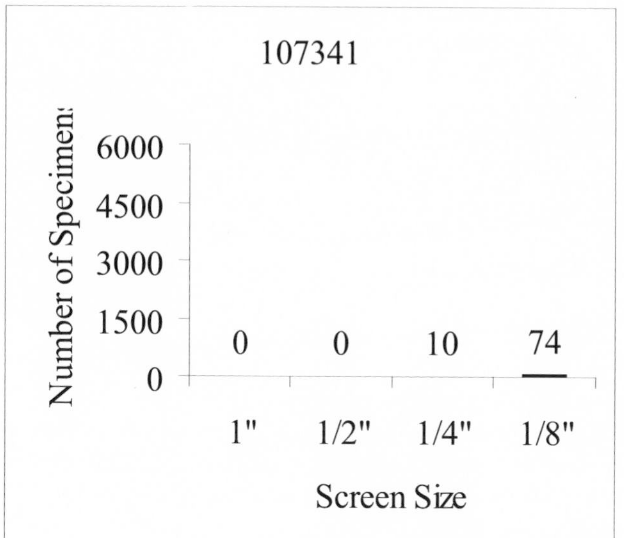

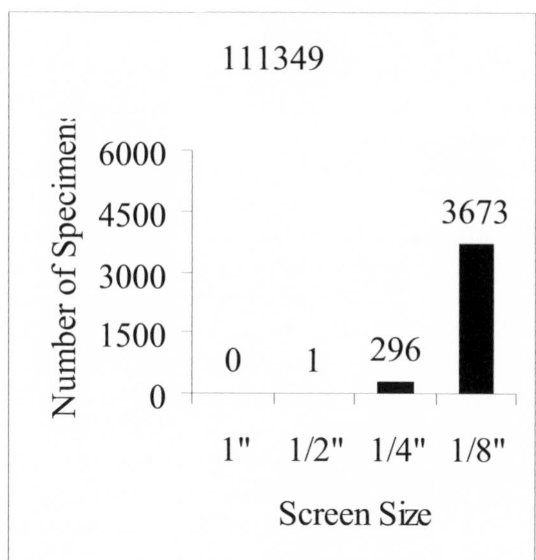

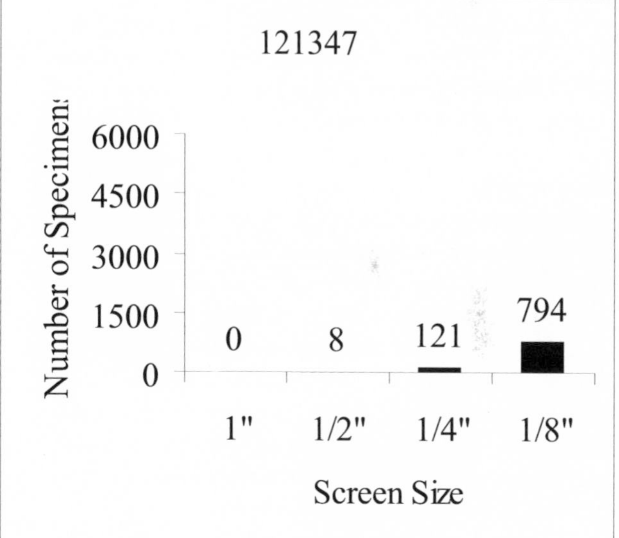

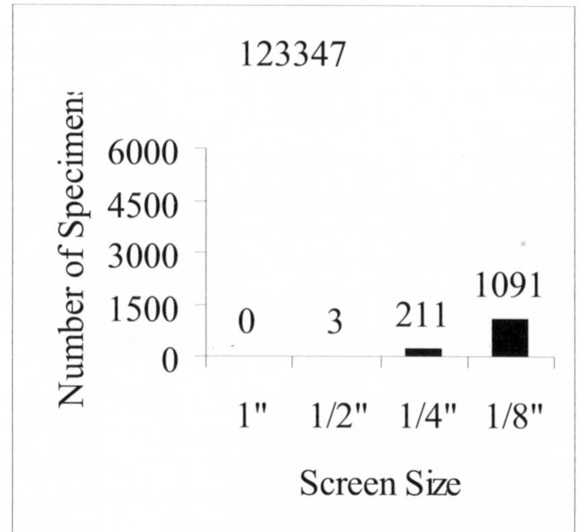

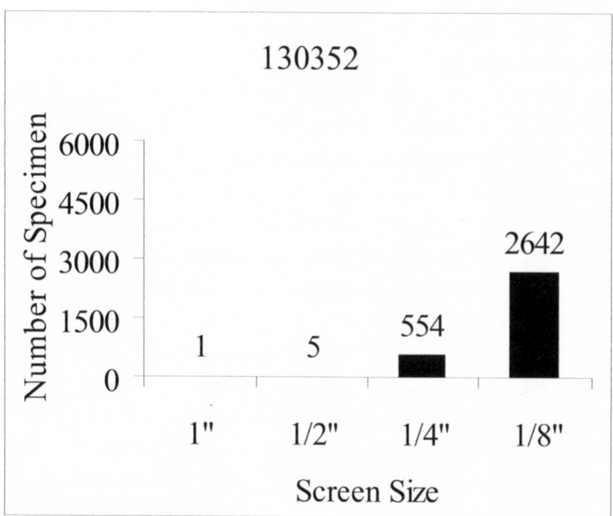

Figure 12.7 Screen-size distribution of fish remains in six Op D excavation units.

Table 12.3 Number of Identified Fish Specimens (NISP) observed/expected/residuals in different areas of OpD

Unit	Salmonid	Herring	Other Identified Fish
Ridge Units (107-/105-/111-)	1787 / 2129.3 / -342.3	2298 / 1792.3 / +505.7	1265 / 1428.4 / -163.4
Depression Units (121-/123-)	813 / 614.1 / +198.9	262 / 516.9 / -254.9	468 / 412.0 / +56.0
Ridge-Front Unit (130-)	1027 / 887.9 / +139.1	493 / 747.4 / -254.4	711 / 595.7 / +115.3

χ^2=544.837 p(df=4)<0.001 * Shaded boxes indicate fewer NISP than expected; unshaded boxes indicate greater NISP than expected.

increases geometrically as screen size decreases (Figure 12.7). The one 1" specimen is a rockfish precaudal vertebra, and the ½" specimens are from various elements of large-bodied fish: salmon, lingcod, rockfish, halibut, and cabezon.

Because OpD represents deposition of a large amount of material over relatively brief time span between about 1,000 and 2,000 radiocarbon years BP, comparison of fish remains across space by excavation unit may more informative than comparison through time by facies. One of the most distinctive aspects of OpD is its topography forming a ridge of shell midden around a square depression open towards Garrison Bay. Unit 107 341, 105 365 and 111 349 were placed behind and near the crest of the topographic ridge, units 121 347 and 123 347 were placed within the square depression, and unit 130 352 was placed slightly in front of the depression between its breach and Garrison Bay.

Relative taxonomic abundances of certain fish taxa are expected to differ between excavation units if the distinct topographic divisions of OpD were functionally different. Do the three major taxonomic groups represented at the site (salmonids, herring, and other identifiable fish) have the same distribution across space? A chi-squared analysis of their abundances within the three spatial zones (Units 107-/105-/111-; Units 121-/123-; and Unit 130-) is shown as a contingency table (Table 12.3). The chi-squared value is highly significant, reflecting a substantial difference in fish taxonomic composition between the three zones. Based on the residuals, also given in Table 12.3, the fish bone assemblage from the ridge of shell midden surrounding the depression consisted of a greater abundance of herring than expected. The assemblage from the units within the depression contained a greater abundance of salmonid and other identified fish remains and fewer herring than expected. Likewise, the unit placed in front of the depression opening contained more salmonid and other fish and fewer herring than expected. Although other hypotheses may explain the differences in relative taxonomic abundance across the site, such as differential preservation conditions, this gives some support to other lines of evidence that may be present for differential disposal of food remains across space.

Fish remains from the OpA portion of the British Camp site were analyzed by Brian Pegg (1999) and provide data from another part of the site. Unlike OpD, which is set back several meters from the wave-cut bank of Garrison Bay, OpA is adjacent to the high-tide line and wave-cut bank. The effects of ground-water saturation of the shell midden deposits of OpA were the focus of geoarchaeological research by Stein (1992) and later examined specific to the vertebrate faunal remains by Pegg (1999). His research supported the hypothesis that the fish bone assemblage at OpA was structured in part by ground-water saturation, which isn't apparent in the OpD deposits. Of 20,293 analyzed specimens, almost 20,000 were fish bones and 70% of those were identified to a finer taxonomic level. By far the majority of identified fish specimens were of herring, followed distantly by salmonids, dogfish, surfperch, sculpins, rockfish, flatfish, and other fish taxa. Although the two most abundant taxa in the OpA and OpD assemblages are the same, herring and salmonids, the majority of the OpA assemblage is herring and the OpD assemblage is much more even between these two taxa. Aside from a lack of greenlings in the OpA assemblage, the assemblages are very similar in terms of taxonomic presence and relative abundance. Unlike OpD, change over time of the abundance of particular OpA taxa was examined by facies corresponding with depth, although no particular diachronic patterns in the fish remains were noted (Pegg 1999:66-67). Rather, changes in fragmentation of salmonid vertebrae and bone density of fish specimens with depth suggest differential post-depositional weathering.

Inter-Site Variability

Comparison of the OpD fish bone assemblage with others in the Puget Sound and Strait of Georgia region is difficult because of differential excavation and analytical methods between archaeological sites. Basic comparisons, however, do show some variability that may reflect similarities and differences in fishing behav-

Table 12.4 Selected Strait of Georgia and Puget Sound shell midden sites with analyzed fish bone assemblages

Site and Site Type	Finest Screen Size	NISP	# Taxa Identified	Dominant Taxa	Reference
British Camp, Op D (45-SJ-24) Large Residential, Coastal	1/8"	15168	31	Salmonid, Herring	This Report
British Camp, Op A (45-SJ-24) Large Residential, Coastal	1/8"	19582	16	Herring, Salmonid	Pegg 1999
Deep Bay (DiSe-7) Large Residential, Coastal	1/8"	?	4	Herring, Dogfish, Salmonid	Monks 1977, 1987
Pender Canal (DeRt-1) Large Residential, Coastal	1 mm	6822	37	Surfperch, Herring, Rockfish	Hanson 1991, 1995
Tsawwassen (DgRs-2) Large Residential, Coastal	2 mm	1326	11	Flatfish, Salmonid, Herring	Kusmer 1994
Cama Beach (45-IS-2) Large Residential, Coastal	1/8"	77528	41	Flatfish, Sculpin, Salmonid, Surfperch	Kopperl 2001b, Wigen 2002, Schalk and Nelson 2010
West Point (45-KI-428/429) Large Residential, Coastal	1/8"	27025	39	Salmonid, Flatfish, Sculpin	Wigen 1995
Old Man House (45-KP-2) Large Residential, Coastal	?	1239	13	Herring, Salmonid, Flatfish	Schalk and Rhode 1985
Burton Acres (45-KI-437) Camp/Processing, Coastal	1/8"	8826	21	Herring	Kopperl 2001a
Harbour Pointe (45-SN-93) Camp/Processing, Bluff-top	1/8"	11	1	Flatfish	Kopperl 2005
Fort Rodd Hill (DcRu-78) Camp/Processing, Coastal	1/8"	1286	21	Salmonid, Herring	Mitchell 1981

ior and availability of particular kinds of fish in local habitats.

Table 12.4 lists shell midden sites in the region from which the fish bones have been analyzed and reported, and whose data were available for this analysis. The sample size in most cases is the result of project constraints, although a few of the assemblages come from fine-screen samples of large volumes of midden and yet contained very few fish remains (e.g., Harbour Pointe). Likewise, the overall taxonomic richness of each assemblage in many cases is a product of comparative collection availability. Some patterns do emerge, however, that highlight fishing patterns at these midden sites. Fish remains from sites interpreted to be large residential occupations, when sampled using fine-mesh screens, consistently show large abundances of herring and salmon relative to other taxa. In addition to herring and salmon, some assemblages reflect intensive use of other kinds of fish, such as surfperch at Pender Canal (DeRt-1), flatfish at Tsawwassen (DgRs-2), and sculpin at Cama Beach (45-IS-2).

Shell midden sites interpreted as more specialized resource procurement and processing camps are more variable in terms of taxonomic richness and dominant taxa. The Fort Rodd Hill (DcRu-78) and Burton Acres (45-KI-437) sites are inferred as seasonal or specialized-use camps, yet contain fish bone assemblages with taxonomic richness well within the range found at larger sites interpreted as more permanent settlement sites. The Harbour Pointe site (45-SN-93), on the other hand, is a spatially extensive bluff-top site with abundant shellfish yet very sparse vertebrate faunal remains, including only 11 flatfish bones in 32 one square-meter excavation units.

CONCLUSIONS

Analysis of the OpD fish bones provides a means of quantifying fish use and disposal of fish remains at the British Camp site. Fish remains are quite abundant in the OpD shell midden deposits. A roughly 25% sample of all fish bones collected from six one-meter by two-meter excavation units yielded 15,168 specimens, of which 9,124 or 60.1% were identified to one of 31 taxonomic categories of fish. Most of the identified remains are from salmonids and herring, with dogfish, greenling, and sculpin also abundant. The screen-size distribution of the remains reflects both a high degree of fragmentation and the presence of small-bodied fish. Although much of the assemblage, including most of the salmonid bones, was highly fragmented, most of the specimens were not burned.

The OpD assemblage shows variability in the distribution of fish taxa within the site and shows similarities and differences to other shell middens in the region. Within the OpD portion of British Camp, herring comprised a greater proportion of the fish taxa than expected in the shell midden ridge surrounding the large square depression, while within and front of the depression a greater proportion of salmonid remains than expected were found. Although taphonomic or post-depositional process may account for this variability, differential disposal of fish taxa across this portion of the site may also be an explanation. A previously completed analysis of fish remains from OpA, to the south of OpD within British Camp, generally shows a similar taxonomic dominance by herring and salmonids, although relative abundance of fish at OpA is much more heavily skewed towards herring. These two taxa dominant most other coastal shell middens in the Puget Sound and Strait of Georgia region, although both larger occupation sites and those inferred to be more specialized processing camps often contain one or more other taxa such as flatfish or sculpin that were apparently targeted in large numbers as well.

REFERENCES

Butler, V. L.

1987 Distinguishing Natural from Cultural Salmonid Deposits in the Pacific Northwest of North America. In *Natural Formation Processes and the Archaeological Record*, edited by D. T. Nash and M. D. Petraglia, pp. 131-149. BAR International Series 352, Oxford.

1993 Natural Versus Cultural Salmonid Remains: Origin of the Dalles Roadcut Bones,Columbia River, Oregon, U.S.A. *Journal of Archaeological Science* 20:1-24.

Butler, V. L., and J. C. Chatters

1994 The Role of Bone Density in Structuring Prehistoric Salmon Bone Assemblages. *Journal of Archaeological Science* 21:413-424.

Cannon, A.

1991 *Economic Prehistory of Namu*. Publication Number 19. Department of Archaeology, Simon Fraser University, Burnaby, British Columbia.

1995 The Ratfish and Marine Resource Deficiencies on the Northwest Coast. *Canadian Journal of Archaeology* 19:49-60.

2000 Assessing Variability in Northwest Coast Salmon and Herring Fisheries: Bucket-Auger Sampling of Shell Midden Sites on the Central Coast of British Columbia. *Journal of Archaeological Science* 27:725-737.

Cannon, D. Y.

1987 *Marine Fish Osteology, A Manual for Archaeologists*. Publication Number 18. Department of Archaeology, Simon Fraser University, Burnaby, British Columbia.

Grayson, D. K.

1984 *Quantitative Zooarchaeology*. Academic Press, New York.

Hanson, D. K.

1991 *Late Prehistoric Subsistence in the Strait of Georgia Region of the Northwest Coast*. Unpublished Ph.D. dissertation, Simon Fraser University, Burnaby, British Columbia.

1995 Subsistence During the Late Prehistoric Occupation of Pender Canal, British Columbia (DeRt-1). *Canadian Journal of Archaeology* 19:29-48.

Hart, J. L.

1973 *Pacific Fishes of Canada*. Fisheries Research Board of Canada, Bulletin 180. Ottawa.

Kerwin, J.

2002 *Salmon and Steelhead Habitat Limiting Factors Report for the San Juan Islands (Water Resources Inventory Area 2)*. Washington Conservation Commission, Olympia.

Kopperl, R. E.

2001a Herring Use in Southern Puget Sound: Analysis of Fish Remains at 45-KI-437. *Northwest Anthropological Research Notes* 35(1):1-20.

2001b Fish Remains. In *Archaeological Testing at Cama Beach State Park*, edited by R. Schalk, pp. 7.1-7.11. Report produced by Cascadia Archaeology, Seattle, Washington.

2005 *Data Recovery Excavations at Harbour Pointe, Site 45-SN-93*. Report prepared for the Burnstead Company, Bellevue, Washington.

Kusmer, K. D.

1994 Changes in Subsistence Strategies at the Tsawwassen Site, a Southwestern British Columbia Sell Midden. *Northwest Anthropological Research Notes* 28(2):189-210.

Lamb, A., and P. Edgell

1986 *Coastal Fishes of the Pacific Northwest*. Harbour Publishing, Madeira Park, British Columbia.

Love, M. S., M. Yaklvich, and L. Thorsteinson
2002 *The Rockfishes of the Northeast Pacific*. University of California Press, Berkeley.

Lubinski, P.
1996 Fish Heads, Fish Heads: An Experiment on Differential Bone Preservation in a Salmonid Fish. *Journal of Archaeological Science* 23(2):175-181.

Lyman, R. L.
1994 *Vertebrate Taphonomy*. Cambridge University Press, Cambridge.

McCutcheon, P. T.
1992 Burned Archaeological Bone. In *Deciphering a Shell Midden*, edited by J. K. Stein, pp. 347-370. Academic Press, San Diego.

McMillan, A. D.
1979 Archaeological Evidence for Aboriginal Tuna Fishing on Western Vancouver Island. *Syesis* 12:117-119.

Miller, B. S., and S. F. Borton
1980 *Geographical Distribution of Puget Sound Fishes, Maps and Data Source Sheets*. Fisheries Research Institute, University of Washington, Seattle.

Mitchell, D. H.
1981 DcRu 78: A Prehistoric Occupation of Fort Rodd Hill National Historic Park. *Syesis* 14:131-150.

Monks, G. G.
1977 Archaeological Salvage Excavations at the Deep bay Site (DiSe 7), Vancouver Island: Preliminary Report. In *Annual Report for the Year 1975: Activities of the Archaeological Sites Advisory Board of British Columbia and Selected Research Reports*, edited by B. Simonsen, pp. 123-153. Government of British Columbia, Ministry of Recreation and Conservation, Victoria, British Columbia.
1987 Prey as Bait: The Deep Bay Example. *Canadian Journal of Archaeology* 11:119-142.

Pegg, B. P.
1999 *The Taphonomic History of the Vertebrate Faunal Assemblage from British Camp, San Juan Islands, Washington*. Unpublished M.A. thesis, Department of Archaeology, Simon Fraser University, Burnaby, British Columbia.

Quinn, T. P., B. S. Miller, and R. C. Wingert
1980 Depth Distribution and Seasonal and Diet Movements of Ratfish, *Hydrolagus colliei*, in Puget Sound, Washington. *Fisheries Bulletin* 78:816-821.

Samuels, S. R.
1994 *Ozette Archaeological Project Research Reports: Volume II, Fauna*. Reports of Investigations 66. Washington State University Department of Anthropology, Pullman.

Schalk, R. F., and M. A. Nelson (editors)
2010 *The Archaeology of the Cama Beach Shell Midden (45IS2), Camano Island, Washington*. Cascadia Archaeology, Seattle.

Schalk, R. F., and D. Rhode
1985 *Archaeological Investigations on the Shoreline of Port Madison Indian Reservation, Kitsap County, Washington*. Office of Public Archaeology, University of Washington, Seattle.

Shipman, P., G. Foster, and M. Schoeninger
1984 Burnt Bones and Teeth: An Experimental Study of Color, Morphology, Crystal Structure and Shrinkage. *Journal of Archaeological Science* 11:307-325.

Stein, J. K. (editor)
1992 *Deciphering a Shell Midden*. Academic Press, San Diego.

Stern, B. J.
1934 *The Lummi Indians of Northwest Washington*. Columbia University Press, New York.

Wigen, R.
1995 Fish, 45KI428 and 45KI429. In *The Archaeology of West Point, Seattle, Washington: 4,000 Years of Hunter-Fisher-Gatherer Land Use in Southern Puget Sound*, edited by L. Larson and D. Lewarch, Volume 2, Appendix 5. Report prepared for King County Department of Metropolitan Services, Seattle, Washington.
2002 Vertebrate Faunal Remains. In *Supplemental Testing at 45IS2, Cama Beach State Park, Camano Island, Washington*, edited by R. Schalk, pp. 5.1-5.7. Report produced by Cascadia Archaeology, Seattle, Washington.

13

Conclusion

Amanda K. Taylor

This concluding summary considers results from each chapter in this volume and addresses the central question, "Is OpD a House?" While several of the contributing researchers indicated that their data were insufficient to address this question, juxtaposing all available lines of evidence supports a tentative hypothesis that OpD, if not a house, was at least used as a domestic structure.

When I began working with Julie Stein on the OpD edited volume we were also conducting research in the San Juan Islands at a landscape scale—a dating project that centered on reconstructing prehistoric settlement patterns in the Salish Sea. We often discussed the limitations of interpreting prehistory using a single site. Reading, editing, and communicating with researchers for the OpD manuscript reminded me that thorough excavations at single sites hold great potential to answer specific questions about the relationship between material culture and human activities. In Chapter 3, Parr, Phillips, and Stein provide a wealth of information on methods for the recovery of archaeological material and spatial associations between strata and topographic features at OpD. Detailed information on provenience and context at OpD allowed each researcher to examine whether material remains from the site exhibited spatial patterns consistent a "house" and "outside of house" distinction.

The contributors to this volume employed a variety of approaches to determine whether OpD was a house. Some inductively described the archaeological material, weighed the evidence, and determined that the dataset was insufficient to address the question. In Chapter 7, Chao's review of ground stone artifacts at the site indicates that if volume of excavated material is considered, spatial differences in amount of ground stone in different areas of the site may not be meaningful. West's analysis of bone and antler tools in Chapter 8 contends with a sample size that is too small to reach definitive conclusions, although she notes that the bone and antler tools at OpD are associated with activities that would occur at a habitation site. In Chapter 10, Bovy describes the avian assemblage and notes that the sample size is too small to examine change over time and space in a meaningful way.

Other chapters point to intriguing spatial differences in faunal remains across the site. In Chapter 2, Faith suggests that based on his analysis of faunal remains from the Treganza assemblage, harbor seals are abundant within the ridge, and elk remains are abundant on or outside the ridge. In Chapter 9, Boone notes a high rate of burning or calcining and a large number of low-nutritional value elements behind the ridge. In Chapter 11, Daniels shows that while relative abundances of taxa are similar both inside and outside the ridge, there is more breakage inside the depression. This could be caused by slumping of the house walls after abandonment. In Chapter 12, Kopperl notes more herring on and outside the ridge than in the depression and more salmon and other fish in the depression and in front of the depression than elsewhere at the site.

Chapter opening photo: Sailboats around San Juan Island.

Chapters on sediment and artifacts also emphasize differences in ridge and depression deposits. In Chapter 4, Stein, Taylor, and Daniels find that excavators and stratigraphers at OpD observed more shell in ridge deposits on and in front of the ridge than in the depression. In Chapter 5, Stein, Green, and Sherwood note significant variation in sediment across the site. Based on microartifact analysis, ridge deposits have a higher percentage of shell than elsewhere in the site, consistent with deliberate discard and placement of shell around the depression. The smaller-sized charcoal inside the depression than elsewhere at the site may indicate a poorly preserved floor. Micromorphological analysis also suggests more fine-grained particles in the depression than elsewhere at the site. In Chapter 6, Close reveals spatial patterns in stone artifact types and associated debris at OpD. She notes a relatively higher frequency of scaled pieces and naturally backed flakes inside the ridge and more triangles on the ridge.

Researchers who analyzed material remains from OpD were able to compare presence, abundance, and patterning in remains "inside" and "outside" the hypothetical house. None of the individual contributors to this volume definitively stated that his or her analysis led to an explicit conclusion that the U-shaped structure at OpD was absolutely a house. A synthesis of all of the chapters reinforces the impression that different topographic areas of the site were significantly different from one another in terms of faunal material, artifacts, stratigraphy, and sediment. The absence of features typically associated with Northwest Coast houses such as distinctive floor deposits, hearths, structured living areas, and post holes may be attributable to the small percentage of the site excavated or to post-depositional disturbance. Was it a house? What else could OpD have been?

Additional possibilities for non-domestic structures constructed from shell include defensive sites (e.g., Schaepe 2006), storage, or water storage (e.g., Marquardt 2010). A defensive structure seems unlikely because the opening of the U-shaped ridge points towards the water, the direction from which unwelcome visitors would likely have approached. Use of OpD for food storage seems unlikely because the depression did not contain a markedly higher frequency of faunal remains or artifacts than the ridge. Water storage is a possibility given the presence of nearby wetland areas and pits dug into the glacial marine drift. The porosity of the underlying glacial drift makes this unlikely. Water could have been collected from a year-round creek that flows to Garrison Bay from Mt. Cady, a high precipitation area on northern San Juan Island (Dietrich 1975; Wixom and Snow 2004). The OpD site was occupied during the Fraser Valley Fire Period, a drier period when freshwater would have been quite limited on the San Juan Islands (Lepofsky et al. 2005; Sugimura et al. 2008). If water storage was the main goal and activity of the people who created OpD, the abundance of household activity-related objects and food items in the depression and ridge warrants further explanation. Research on water storage structures has not yet been undertaken in the Gulf of Georgia region but presents a productive avenue for future research.

At present, the principle of Occam's Razor supports the hypothesis that OpD was a domestic structure — one where the top layers have been disturbed by previous excavations, historic activities, slumping, and root action. Distinctions in artifact and faunal remains at different parts of the site are consistent with structuring of domestic space and differences in activities associated with discard, food, and tool production. We hope these data allow readers to reach their own conclusions or ask and answer entirely new questions.

REFERENCES

Dietrich, W.
1975 Surface Water Resources of San Juan County. In *Geology and Water Resources of the San Juan Islands, San Juan County, Washington* , edited by R.H. Russell, pp. 59-126. Washington State Department of Ecology, Olympia.

Lepofsky, D., K. P. Lertzman, D. J. Hallett, and R. W. Mathewes
2005 Climate Change and Culture Change on the Southern Coast of British Columbia 2400-1200 Cal. B.P.: An Hypothesis. *American Antiquity* 70:267-293.

Marquardt, W. H.
2010 Shell Mounds in the Southeast: Middens, Monuments, Temple Mounds, Rings, or Work? *American Antiquity* 75:551-570.

Schaepe, D. M.
2006 Rock Fortifications: Archaeological Insights into Precontact Warfare and Sociopolitical Organization among the Stó:Lō of the Lower Fraser River Canyon, B.C. *American Antiquity* 71:671-706.

Sugimura, W. Y., D. G. Sprugel, L. B. Brubaker, and P. E. Higuera.
2008. Millenial-scale changes in local vegetation and fire regimes on Mount Constitution, Orcas Island, Washington, USA, using small hollow sediments. *Canadian Journal of Forest Research* 38:539-552.

Wixom, T., and B. Snow
2004 *San Juan County Water Resources Management Plan WRIA 2.* San Juan County Board of County Commissioners, Friday Harbor, WA.